SRA Imagine It!

Unit 10 · Windy Days

Level K

Program Authors

Carl Bereiter
Andrew Biemiller
Joe Campione
Iva Carruthers
Doug Fuchs

Lynn Fuchs
Steve Graham
Karen Harris
Jan Hirshberg
Anne McKeough
Peter Pannell

Marsha Roit
Marlene Scardamalia
Marcy Stein
Gerald H. Treadway Jr.
Michael Pressley

McGraw Hill **SRA**

Columbus, OH

ACKNOWLEDGMENTS

Grateful acknowledgment is given to the following publishers and copyright owners for permissions granted to reprint selections from their publications. All possible care has been taken to trace ownership and secure permission for each selection included. In case of any errors or omissions, the Publisher will be pleased to make suitable acknowledgments in future editions.

READ ALOUD

"CAN YOU SEE THE WIND?" from Rookie Reader series by Allan Fowler, copyright 1999 by Children's Press. All rights reserved. Recorded by permission of Children's Press an imprint of Scholastic Library Publishing, Inc.

BIG BOOK

From GILBERTO AND THE WIND by Marie Hall Ets, copyright © 1963 by Marie Hall Ets, renewed © 1991 by Marjorie M. Johnson. All rights reserved including the right of reproduction in whole or in part in any form. This edition published by arrangement with Viking Children's Books, a member of Penguin Young Readers Group, a division of Penguin Group (USA) Inc.

"Go Wind" From I FEEL THE SAME WAY by Lilian Moore. Copyright © 1967 Lilian Moore. All rights reserved. Used by permission of Marian Reiner.

From What Happens When Wind Blows? by Daphne Butler. Copyright © 1996 by Raintree/Steck-Vaughn. Reproduced by permission of Hodder and Stoughton Limited.

"Crick! Crack!" From BLACKBERRY INK by Eve Merriam. Copyright © 1985 Eve Merriam. Used by permission of Marian Reiner.

STORY TIME COLLECTION

WIND SAYS GOODNIGHT by Katy Rydell, illustrated by David Jorgensen. Text copyright © 1994 by Katy Rydell. Illustrations copyright © 1994 by David Jorgensen. Reprinted by permission of Houghton Mifflin Company. All rights reserved.

PICKLED PEPPERS

From ONE HUNGRY MONSTER by Susan Heyboer O'Keefe. Copyright © 1989 by Susan Heyboer O'Keefe (text); copyright © 1989 by Lynn Munsinger (illustrations). By permission of Little, Brown and Company (Inc.).

"Rope Rhyme" from HONEY, I LOVE by Eloise Greenfield. Used by permission of HarperCollins Publishers.

From WHO SAID RED? By Mary Serfozo, illustrated by Keiko Narahashi. Text copyright © 1988 by Mary Serfozo, Illustrations Copyright © 1988 by Keiko Narahashi. Reprinted by arrangement with Margaret K. McElderry Books, an Imprint of Simon & Schuster Children's Publishing Division. All rights reserved.

"Rhyme," by Elizabeth Coatsworth. Reprinted with permission of Elizabeth Gartner. All rights reserved.

"Tent" from BALLOONS AND OTHER POEMS by Deborah Chandra. Reprinted by permission of Farrar, Straus & Giroux, LLC.

"Little Pine" from MAPLES IN THE MIST, Text copyright © 1996 by Minfong Ho. Reprinted with permission of McIntosh & Otis. "Little Pine" illustration: Jean & Mou-sien Tseng. Used by permission.

"Houses/Casitas" text, from MY MEXICO/MEXICO MIO by Tony Johnston, copyright © 1996 by Roger D. Johnson and Susan T. Johnson as Trustees of the Johnson Family Trust, text. Used by permission of G.P. Putnam's Sons, A Division of Penguin Young Readers Group, A Member of Penguin Group (USA) Inc., 345 Hudson Street, New York, NY 10014. All rights reserved. "Houses/Casitas," illustrations by F. John Sierra, from MY MEXICO/MEXICO MIO by Tony Johnston, Illustrated by F. John Sierra, copyright © 1996 by F. John Sierra, illustrations. Used by permission of G.P. Putnam's Sons, A Division of Penguin Young Readers Group, A Member of Penguin Group (USA) Inc., 345 Hudson Street, New York, NY 10014. All rights reserved.

"Keep a Poem in Your Pocket" From SOMETHING SPECIAL by Beatrice Schenk de Regniers. Copyright © 1958 Beatrice Schenk de Regniers. © Renewed 1986. All rights reserved. Reprinted by permission of Marian Reiner.

Send all inquiries to this address:
SRA/McGraw-Hill
4400 Easton Commons
Columbus, OH 43219

ISBN: 978-0-07-616461-5
MHID: 0-07-616461-6

3 4 5 6 7 8 9 WEB 15 14 13 12 11 10 09 08

National Advisory Board

Patricia Appell
Instructional
Interventionist
Annapolis, MD

Christine P. Collins
Former Assistant Superintendent
for Instruction and Curriculum
Weymouth, MA

Betsy Degen
Curriculum Director
Shawnee Mission, KS

Bryan Ertsgaard
Teacher
Dayton, OH

James T. Garvin
Assistant Principal
Charlotte, NC

Patsy M. Hall
Title I Professional Development
Coordinator
Indianapolis, IN

Michelle L. King
Reading Enhancement Coach
Indianapolis, IN

Deb Owen
Assistant Superintendent for
Curriculum and Instruction
Effingham, IL

Patricia Schmella
Curriculum Director
Toppenish, WA

JoAnn Schweda
Teacher
Worley, ID

Sylvia Teahan
Teacher
Medford Lakes, NJ

Joseph Turner
Assistant Principal
Indianapolis, IN

Sue Wennerberg
Teacher
Oak Park, IL

Contributing Author

Michael Milone
Assessment Specialist
Placitas, NM

Literature Consultant

Dr. Laura Apol
Professor, Michigan State University
East Lansing, MI

Program Reviewers

Noemi Arteaga-Gonzales
Teacher
San Antonio, TX

Susan Beede
Consulting Teacher
Nampa, ID

Lisa Beringer
Teacher
Bonita Springs, FL

Paula Bleakley
Teacher
Leesburg, FL

Lisa Bohanan
Instructional Specialist
Pflugerville, TX

Judi Braxton
Reading Coach
Marianna, FL

Benjamin Broadwater
Teacher
Fort Worth, TX

Jodie Broussard
Reading Coach
Pensacola, FL

Jennifer Brown-Mendoza
Reading First Coach
Hominy, OK

Kristine Cain
Teacher
Pensacola, FL

Kellie Campbell
Teacher
Cocoa, FL

Caroline Carithers
Reading Resource Teacher
Pensacola, FL

Jenny Cronan
Literacy Coach
Pittsburg, CA

Margo DiBasio
Reading Specialist
Chelsea, MA

Jennie Eddy
Title I Literacy Coach
Moore, OK

Bryan Ertsgaard
Teacher
Dayton, OH

Tami Ethridge
Instructional Coach
Lancaster, SC

Pamela C. Fendrick
Reading Coach
Tallahassee, FL

Melanie Flores
Teacher
Austin, TX

Tim Francisco
Teacher
Colorado Springs, CO

Kari Franklin
Reading Coach
Pensacola, FL

Rosa Elia Garcia
Reading Specialist
San Antonio, TX

Ashley Garrett
Teacher
Austin, TX

James T. Garvin
Assistant Principal
Charlotte, NC

Dr. Marsha R. Glover
Elementary Reading and
Language Arts Developer
Tallahassee, FL

Elaine M. Grohol
Elementary Instructional
Specialist
Kissimmee, FL

Patricia Ingles
Teacher
Laguna Niguel, CA

Sarah Jordan
Literacy Specialist
Longview, WA

Cindy Kearney
Teacher
Tulsa, OK

Kim Kempa
Teacher
Santa Ana, CA

Kathy Kindelan
Reading Specialist
Winter Haven, FL

Michelle L. King
Reading Enhancement
Coach
Indianapolis, IN

Linda Ann Kosinski
Reading First Coordinator
La Quinta, CA

Sheryl Kurtin
Elementary Specialist,
Curriculum and Instruction
Sarasota, FL

Teresa Lopez
Supervisor, Academic
Achievement and
Accountability
Bakersfield, CA

Jan Maglione
Teacher
Upton, MA

Barbara Maspero
Teacher
San Antonio, TX

Chaitra S. McGrew
Teacher
Austin, TX

Kathy McGuire
Instructional Coach
Roseburg, OR

Becky McPherson
Literacy Coach
Cuthbert, GA

Sheila Menning
Teacher
Largo, FL

Tamarah Michalek
Teacher
Roseburg, OR

Michele Mower
Director of Professional
Development
Fontana, CA

Pamela W. Patterson
Instructional Specialist
East Point, GA

Susan Patterson
Reading Coach
Charlotte, NC

Angela Pilcher
Teacher
Stockton, CA

Dr. Jan Rauth
Educational Consultant
Longview, WA

Carlotta Ruiz
Reading Coach
Elk Grove, CA

Dr. Lynda Samons
Curriculum Director
Magnet Cove, AR

Jake Schweikhard
Teacher
Tulsa, OK

Nancy Snyder
Reading Coach
Spring Hill, FL

Dyan Wagner
District Reading Specialist
and Intervention
Coordinator
Milwaukee, WI

Darlene Watson
Instructional Lead Teacher
Valdosta, GA

Linda Webb
LA Program Specialist
Stockton, CA

Sue Wennerberg
Teacher
Oak Park, IL

Gayle Wilson
Preprimary Department
Head
Jacksonville, FL

Linda Wiltz
Instructional Support
Teacher
Orlando, FL

Meet the Imagine It! Authors

Carl Bereiter, Ph.D.

A professor emeritus and special advisor on learning technology at the Ontario Institute for Studies in Education, University of Toronto, Dr. Bereiter also invented Computer Supported Intentional Learning Environments, the first networked system for collaborative learning, with Dr. Marlene Scardamalia.

Andrew Biemiller, Ph.D.

A coordinator of elementary teacher education programs at the University of Toronto for thirty-six years, Dr. Biemiller's research on vocabulary development and instruction has had a significant effect on the shape of vocabulary instruction for elementary education in the twenty-first century.

Joe Campione, Ph.D.

A leading researcher on cognitive development, individual differences, assessment, and the design of innovative learning environments, Dr. Campione is a professor emeritus in the School of Education at University of California, Berkeley.

Iva Carruthers, Ph.D.

Equipped with both hands-on and academic experience, Dr. Carruthers serves as a consultant and lecturer in educational technology and matters of multicultural inclusion.

Doug Fuchs Ph.D.

Dr. Fuchs, the Nicholas Hobbs Professor of Special Education and Human Development at Vanderbilt University, has conducted programmatic research on response-to-intervention as a method for preventing and identifying children with learning disabilities and on reading instructional methods for improving outcomes for students with learning disabilities.

Lynn Fuchs, Ph.D.

A co-director of the Kennedy Center Reading clinic at Vanderbilt University, Dr. Fuchs also conducted research on assessment methods for enhancing instructional planning and instructional methods for improving reading and math outcomes for students with learning disabilities.

Steve Graham, Ph.D.

A professor of literacy at Vanderbilt University, Dr. Graham's research focuses on identifying the factors that contribute to writing development and writing difficulties.

Karen Harris, Ph.D.

The Currey-Ingram Professor of Special Education and Literacy at Vanderbilt University, Dr. Harris's research focuses on theoretical and intervention issues in the development of academic and self-regulation strategies among students who are at risk.

Jan Hirshberg, Ed.D.

Focusing on how children learn to read and write and the logistics of teaching reading and writing in the early grades, Dr. Hirshberg works as a language arts resource coordinator and consultant in Alexandria, Virginia.

Anne McKeough, Ph.D.

A professor in the Division of Applied Psychology at the University of Calgary, Dr. McKeough teaches graduate courses in cognitive development and educational assessment, as well as teacher preparation courses to undergraduates.

Peter Pannell, MA

Principal of Longfellow Elementary School in Pasadena, California, Mr. Pannell has worked to develop the literacy of countless students. To help accomplish this goal, he wrote and implemented a writing project that allowed his students to make great strides in their writing performance.

Marsha Roit, Ed.D.

The Director of Professional Development for SRA/McGraw-Hill, Dr. Roit spends considerable time in classrooms developing reading curricula and working with teachers and administrators in effective instructional practices.

Marlene Scardamalia, Ph.D.

Dr. Scardamalia is the Presidents' Chair in Education and Knowledge Technologies at the University of Toronto and is also the Director of the Institute for Knowledge Innovation and Technology. She received the 2006 World Award of Education from the World Cultural Council for outstanding work in education.

Marcy Stein, Ph.D.

Professor and founding faculty member of the education program at the University of Washington, Tacoma, Dr. Stein teaches At-Risk and Special Education graduate and teacher certification programs.

Gerald H. Treadway Jr, Ph.D.

Chair of the Literacy Education Program and professor of education at San Diego State University, Dr. Treadway teaches classes on reading methods, English Language Learner methods, balanced reading programs, assessment, and reading comprehension. He is also a consultant for the California Reading and Literature Project.

In memoriam

Michael Pressley, Ph.D.
1951–2006

Dr. Pressley was a tireless supporter of education. He championed the rights of all children to a quality education, made seminal contributions in research and practice, and nurtured the development of a host of beginning teachers, young scholars, and editors. While his work and spirit lives on in those he influenced and inspired, there is no substitute for the real thing. We will all miss his wisdom and friendship every day.

Unit 10

Windy Days

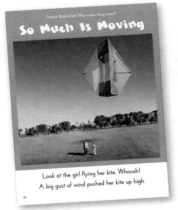

Note: You should preview any trade books and videos for appropriateness before recommending them to students.

Windy Days

OVERVIEW

Can you feel the wind? Is it soft and gentle or cold and biting? Does it whisper or howl? Where does the wind come from? What makes it change? Maybe you have questions about the wind too.

Theme Connection

Fine Art

Look at the painting *Breezing Up (A Fair Wind)* by Winslow Homer. What is this family doing? Why is their sailboat tipping to one side? How do you think this painting relates to Windy Days? What would happen if the wind stopped blowing?

Winslow Homer. *Breezing Up (A Fair Wind)*. 1873–1876. 24 ⅛ × 38 ⅛ in. National Gallery of Art, Washington, D.C.

BIG Idea

Why do we have wind?

T3

Launching the Theme

Setting Up the Theme

In this unit children will begin to notice the wind and ask questions about it. Their curiosity will come alive as they listen to selections that tell how the wind is created, how it changes, and how it can make our lives easier and more difficult. Through their own investigations, children will observe and experiment with the wind as they try to determine how it works.

To get students excited about Windy Days, try one or more of the following ideas:

- Fill your classroom with kites, pinwheels, paper fans and sailboats.
- Use the Unit 10 *eBackground Builder* video.

 **Inquiry** Students will decide on a unit investigation about the wind and will determine together how to share the results of their research. Students will use the **Concept/Question Board** as a tool to ask questions and share ideas about the wind.

Concept/Question Board

Using the **Concept/Question Board** as a tool, students will explore concepts and develop inquiry questions. Resources from the classroom as well as from home can be posted on the **Concept/Question Board.** Referring to the **Concept/Question Board** daily as part of your routine is a good way to emphasize to students the importance of this learning tool.

The following materials will encourage students to post their ideas and questions on the **Concept/Question Board:**

- Books and poems about the wind
- Cut-out shapes of kites, balloons, pinwheels, sailboats, and so on
- Construction paper and markers
- Old magazines for students to cut

Using the Inquiry Planner

Students will research the theme Windy Days using the steps below.

BIG Idea

Why do we have wind?

Read the Big Idea question to students. Then discuss how wind can help us. Students might point out that wind keeps us cool.

	Steps	Models
Week 1	**STEP 1** Begin discussing and sharing ideas.	**MODEL 1** *How can wind help us?* *What do you see that shows wind is blowing?* *Why is the wind sometimes strong and other times gentle?*
	STEP 2 Think about a question for the Concept/Question Board.	**MODEL 2** *What causes wind?*
Week 2	**STEP 3** Begin investigating and collecting information.	**MODEL 3** *Create wind instruments such as pinwheels or weather vanes to conduct experiments about the wind.*
	STEP 4 Generate a question or idea for the Concept/Question Board.	**MODEL 4** *Why is there wind?*
Week 3	**STEP 5** Share your findings with others.	**MODEL 5** *I will show my chart with drawings of the weather and say how fast the wind made my pinwheel move on each of those days.*
	STEP 6 Do you have more questions?	**MODEL 6** *How can wind be harmful?*

About the Authors and Illustrators

Author of *Can You See the Wind?*

Allan Fowler

Fowler likes to teach children about the world around them. His books cover many topics, but he always uses bright photographs and selects simple words so children of all ages can understand and enjoy his books.

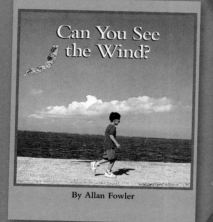

Read Aloud Collection

Author of *Gilberto and the Wind*

Marie Hall Ets

Ets was a social worker in Chicago before she started writing and illustrating children's books. Often her stories reflected on her past experiences. When she met an interesting boy in California, she drew pictures of the boy and was inspired to write *Gilberto and the Wind*.

Illustrator of *Gilberto and the Wind*

Loretta Krupinski

Krupinski paints ocean scenes with old lighthouses and boats because she grew up by the ocean and wants to preserve a piece of history in her paintings. She switched from pen and ink to using colors after a trip to Maine because she wanted to capture the vibrant colors of Maine's countryside.

Big Book

Author of *What Happens When Wind Blows?*

Daphne Butler

Butler has written many books that explain how things work. She wants to make science fun and interesting to children. She thinks of questions children might have about the world and then turns the answers into books.

Author of *Wind Says Good Night*

Katy Rydell

Rydell is a professional storyteller. She travels to schools, libraries, and festivals and uses puppets to make stories come alive. Rydell also teaches others to tell stories. She loves to read children's books. *Wind Says Good Night* is her first children's book.

Story Time Collection

Illustrator of *Wind Says Good Night*

David Jorgensen

Jorgensen has illustrated many children's books. His artwork has been exhibited in galleries and museums. When he is not creating new illustrations and artwork, Jorgensen teaches college students painting and drawing.

Unit Skills

★ Phonemic Awareness ★ Phonics
★ Fluency ★ Vocabulary ★ Comprehension

Week 1

Sounds and Letters

Phonics ★
- Initial, Medial Vowels, and Final Phoneme Replacement
- High-Frequency Words *be, she*

Alphabetic Knowledge ★
Long *Ee*

Reading and Responding

Comprehension ★
Strategies
- Clarifying
- Predicting
Skills
- ✓ Cause and Effect

Print and Book Awareness
✓ Selection Vocabulary ★

Inquiry

Language Arts

Writing
- Creating a Web
- Brainstorming Goals and Generating Questions

Grammar
Sentences

Week 2

Sounds and Letters

Phonics ★
- Initial, Internal, and Final Phoneme Deletion
- Blending
- Oral Language and Sentence Extension

Alphabetic Knowledge ★
- Short *Aa, Ii, Oo, Uu*
- Long *Aa, Ii, Oo, Uu*

Reading and Responding

Comprehension ★
Strategies
- Visualizing
- Asking Questions
- Clarifying
- Predicting
Skills
- ✓ Classify and Categorize

Print and Book Awareness

Selection Vocabulary ★

Inquiry

Language Arts

Writing
- Brainstorming Ideas and Forming Hypotheses
- Finding Information and Answering Questions
- Summarizing and Sequencing
- Collaborating to Report

Grammar
Sentences

Week 3

Sounds and Letters

B ✓ Phonics ★
- Blending and Sentence Extension

B ✓ Alphabetic Knowledge ★
- Short *Aa, Ee, Ii, Oo, Uu*
- Long *Aa, Ee, Ii, Oo, Uu*

Reading and Responding

Comprehension ★
Strategies
- Asking Questions
- Making Connections
- Clarifying
Skills
- B ✓ Reality and Fantasy

B Print and Book Awareness

B ✓ Selection Vocabulary ★

Inquiry

Language Arts

Writing
- Collaborating to Write Report
- Revising
- Drawing and Illustrating Findings
- Reflecting

Grammar
- B Position and Order Words
- B Pronouns

Key: ★ = five components of Reading   ✓ = Lesson Assessment   B = Benchmark Assessment

Assessment Plan for Making AYP

 is an ongoing cycle.

1 Screen

Administer the initial **Benchmark Assessment** as a screener to target students who are at risk for failing end of year measures.

Diagnose students' strengths and weaknesses, and **differentiate** instruction according to their abilities.

2 Diagnose and Differentiate

Diagnosing, differentiating instruction, and monitoring progress is an ongoing cycle.

3 Monitor Progress

Monitor progress weekly, monthly, or anytime as needed with both formal and informal assessments.

4 Measure Outcomes

Administer summative assessments, such as Lesson, Benchmark, or state assessments, to measure student outcomes.

Screen

At the beginning of the year or for students entering class after the school year has begun, administer the initial *Benchmark Assessment,* Benchmark 1, to target students at risk for reading failure.

Diagnose and Differentiate

Use the results from the *Lesson Assessments, Benchmark Assessments,* and informal observation measures to diagnose students' strengths and weaknesses and to differentiate instructions individually and in small groups.

	Approaching Level	On Level	English Learner	Above Level

Leveled Practice	• *Reteach*
	• Workshop Kit
	  - Activities
	  - Games
	• *Intervention Guide*
		• *Skills Practice 2*
		• Workshop Kit
		  - Activities
		  - Games
		• *Intervention Guide*
			• *English Learner Support Activities*
			• Workshop Kit
			  - Activities
			  - Games
				• *Challenge Activities*
				• Workshop Kit
				  - Activities
				  - Games

Technology	• *eSkills & eGames* • *eDecodables*	• *eSkills & eGames* • *eDecodables* • *eGames*	• *eSkills & eGames* • *eDecodables*	*eSkills & eGames*

Monitor Progress

Between *Benchmark Assessments,* use the following to monitor student progress. Regroup students daily or as needed, based on these formative assessment results.

Formal Assessment

- *Lesson Assessments*
- *Online Assessments*
- Comprehension Observation Log
- *Skills Practice 2*

Measure Outcomes

Assess student understanding and mastery of skills by using the *Lesson Assessments.*

Unit 10

Resources to **Monitor Progress**

Week 1

Skills Practice 2

Letter and Sound Identification, pp. 95–97, 99–100
Word Spacing, p. 98
Sentences, p. 101
Penmanship, p. 102

Reteach

Letter and Sound Identification, pp. 178, 184
Penmanship, pp. 179, 181–182, 185
Word Spacing, p. 180
Sentences, p. 183

Challenge Activities

Letter and Sound Identification, pp. 136, 138
Word Spacing, p. 137
Sentences, p. 139
Penmanship, p. 140

Decodables

***Decodable** 20: We Did It!*

Lesson Assessments

Lessons 3–4, pp. 89–90

Benchmark Assessments

Technology e-Suite

e Skills

Unit 10 Phonics

e Decodables

***Decodable** 20: We Did It!*

e Games

e Assess

Lesson Assessment, Unit 10, Lessons 3–4

Key: ✓ = Formal Assessment

Week 2

Letter and Sound Review, p. 103
Blending, pp. 104, 107–108
Punctuation, pp. 105–106

Blending, pp. 186–187, 190
Penmanship, p. 188
Punctuation, p. 189

Letter and Sound Review, p. 141
Punctuation, p. 142
Blending, p. 143

Lesson 8, p. 91

Unit 10 Phonics

Skill: Long- and Short-Vowel Review

Lesson Assessment, Unit 10, Lesson 8

Week 3

Blending, pp. 109, 111–112, 115–116
Position Words, p. 110
Pronouns, pp. 113–114

Penmanship, p. 191
Position Words, p. 192
Blending, pp. 193, 195
Pronouns, p. 194
Action Words, p. 196

Position Words, p. 144
Blending, pp. 145, 147
Pronouns, p. 146

Lessons 13–15, pp. 92–96

Benchmark 6

Unit 10 Phonics

Skill: Long- and Short-Vowel Review

Lesson Assessment, Unit 10, Lessons 13–15
Benchmark 6

Lesson Planner

Day 1

Day 2

Sounds and Letters

MATERIALS

- ◆ *Alphabet Letter Card: Ee*
- ◆ Routines 1, 2, 4
- ◆ *Skills Practice 2,* pp. 95–96, 99–100, 102
- ◆ *Pickled Peppers Big Book,* pp. 10, 16–27, 43
- ◆ *Pocket Chart Picture Cards*
- ◆ *Pocket Chart Letter Cards*
- ◆ *Decodable* 20

Day 1

Warming Up, pp. T24–T25
Phonemic Awareness
Phoneme Replacement: Initial Sounds, p. T25
Alphabetic Principle
- Reviewing Long-Vowel Sounds, p. T26
- Introducing the Sound of Long *Ee,* p. T26
- Listening for Initial /ē/, p. T26
- Penmanship, p. T27

Day 2

Warming Up, p. T32
Phonemic Awareness
Phoneme Replacement: Initial Sounds, p. T33
Alphabetic Principle
- Reviewing the Sound of Long *Ee,* p. T34
- Listening for Initial /ē/, p. T34
- Listening for Medial /ē/, p. T34
- *Pickled Peppers Big Book,* p. T35

Reading and Responding

MATERIALS

- ◆ *Windy Days Big Book,* pp. 4–23
- ◆ *Home Connection,* pp. 75–78
- ◆ *Read Aloud Collection: Can You See the Wind?*
- ◆ Routines 5–7

Day 1

Preview
- Browsing the Unit, p. T28
- Setting Reading Goals, p. T28
Inquiry, p. T29

Day 2

Read Aloud Collection: *Can You See the Wind?*
- Activate Prior Knowledge, p. T36
- Preview the Selection, p. T36
Vocabulary, p. T36
Discuss the Read Aloud, p. T39
Vocabulary Review, p. T39

Language Arts

MATERIALS

- ◆ *Language Arts Big Book,* pp. 7, 37, 56–57
- ◆ *Transparency* 46
- ◆ *Windy Days Big Book,* p. 48
- ◆ *Willy the Wisher,* p. 91
- ◆ *Story Lines Big Book,* p. 32
- ◆ *Skills Practice 2,* pp. 98, 101
- ◆ *Race Track Game Mats*
- ◆ *Alphabet Letter Cards*

Day 1

Writing Process
Prewrite: Choosing a Topic, p. T30
Fine Art
Discussing Fine Art, p. T31

Day 2

Writing Process
Model: Creating a Web, p. T40
Grammar, Usage, and Mechanics,
pp. T40–T41
Willy the Wisher, p. T41

Monitor Progress

- ✔ = **Formal Assessment**
- Ⓑ = **Benchmark Assessment**

Day 1

- ✔ Letter and Sound Identification, p. T26
- ✔ Penmanship, p. T27

Day 2

- ✔ Letter and Sound Identification, p. T34
- ✔ Word Spacing, p. T41

Literature Overview

Read Aloud **Can You See the Wind?**
by Allan Fowler

Big Book

Gilberto and the Wind
by Marie Hall Ets
illustrated by Loretta Krupinski

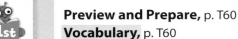
★ Phonemic Awareness ★ Phonics ★ Fluency ★ Vocabulary ★ Comprehension

Day 3

Warming Up, pp. T42–T43
Phonemic Awareness
Phoneme Replacement: Final Sounds, p. T43
Alphabetic Principle
• Reviewing the Sound of Long *Ee,* p. T44
• Listening for Medial /ē/, p. T44
• Linking the Sound to the Letter, p. T44
• Penmanship, p. T45

Preview and Prepare, p. T46
Vocabulary, p. T47
Read the Selection, p. T47
Comprehension Strategies, pp. T48, T50, T52
Print and Book Awareness, pp. T49, T51, T53
Discussing the Selection, p. T53
Vocabulary Review, p. T53

Writing Process
Prewrite: Creating a Web, p. T54
Story Crafting
Story Lines Big Book, p. T55

✓ Letter and Sound Identification, p. T44
✓ Penmanship, p. T45
✓ Vocabulary, p. T47

Day 4

Warming Up, p. T56
Phonemic Awareness
Phoneme Replacement: Final Sounds, p. T57
Alphabetic Principle
• Reviewing the Sound of Long *Ee,* p. T58
• Listening for Medial /ē/, p. T58
• Linking the Sound to the Letter, p. T58
• ***Pickled Peppers Big Book,*** p. T59

Preview and Prepare, p. T60
Vocabulary, p. T60
Read the Selection, p. T61
Comprehension Strategies, pp. T62, T64, T66
Comprehension Skills, pp. T63, T65
Reading with a Writer's Eye, pp. T63, T65, T67
Discussing the Selection, p. T67
Vocabulary Review, p. T67

Writing Process
Model: Brainstorming Goals and Generating Questions, p. T68
Grammar, Usage, and Mechanics, pp. T68–T69
Story Crafting
Story Lines Big Book, p. T69

✓ *Lesson Assessment Book,* p. 89
✓ Letter and Sound Identification, p. T58
✓ Sentences, p. T69

Day 5

Warming Up, pp. T70–T71
Phonemic Awareness
Phoneme Replacement: Medial Vowels, p. T71
Alphabetic Principle
• Reviewing the Sound of Long *Ee,* p. T72
• Listening for Medial /ē/, p. T72
• Blending with the Sound of Long *Ee,* p. T72
• Penmanship, p. T73
Reading a *Decodable*
***Decodable* 20:** *We Did It!,* pp. T74–T75

Inquiry
• Whole-Group Time, p. T76
• Small-Group Time, p. T77
• Concept Vocabulary, p. T77

Writing Process
Model: Brainstorming Goals and Generating Questions, p. T78
Grammar, Usage, and Mechanics, p. T78
Game Day
Race Track Game, p. T79

✓ *Lesson Assessment Book,* pp. 89–90
  • Comprehension Observation Log
✓ Letter and Sound Identification, p. T72
✓ Penmanship, p. T73

Student Resources

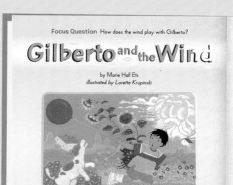

Focus Question How does the wind play with Gilberto?

Gilberto and the Wind
by Marie Hall Ets
illustrated by Loretta Krupinski

I hear Wind whispering at the door.
"You-ou-ou," he whispers. "You-ou-ou-ou!"
So I get my balloon, and I run out to play.

At first Wind is gentle and just floats my balloon around in the air. But then, with a jerk, he grabs it away and carries it up to the top of a tree. "Wind! Oh, Wind!" I say. "Blow it back to me! Please!" But he won't. He just laughs and whispers, "You-ou-ou-ou!"

4   5

Big Books

Audio CD

Big Book Selection

Windy Days Big Book

Gilberto and the Wind by Marie Hall Ets, pp. 4–23

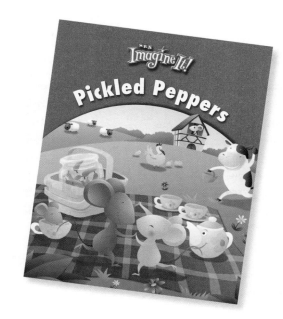

Pickled Peppers

Imagine It!

Decodable 20: *We Did It!*

We Did It!
by Tristan Harrom   illustrated by Laura Logan

Teacher Support

Language Arts Big Book

Language Arts Big Book
Imagine It!

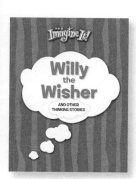

Willy the Wisher

Willy the Wisher
AND OTHER THINKING STORIES

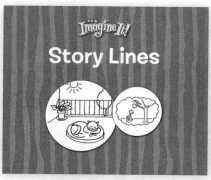

Story Lines Big Book

Story Lines

Curriculum Connections

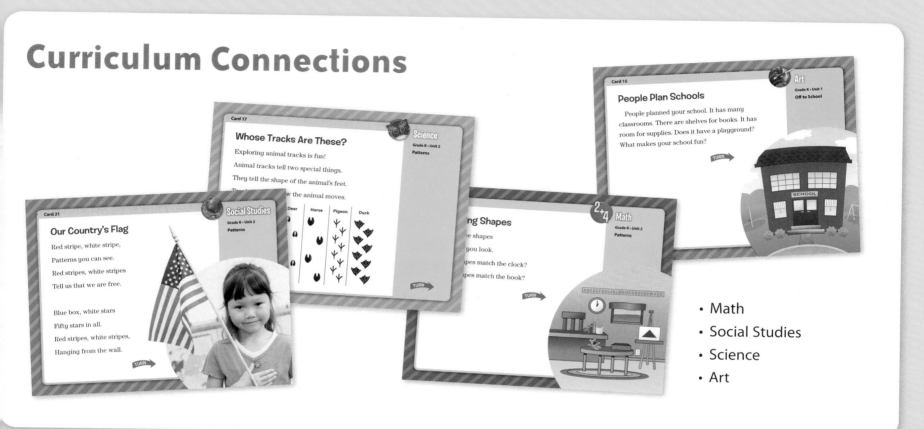

Card 17

Science
Grade K · Unit 2
Patterns

Whose Tracks Are These?

Exploring animal tracks is fun!

Animal tracks tell two special things.

They tell the shape of the animal's feet.

The____ ____ the animal moves.

Deer Horse Pigeon Duck

TURN

Card 21

Social Studies
Grade K · Unit 2
Patterns

Our Country's Flag

Red stripe, white stripe,

Patterns you can see.

Red stripes, white stripes

Tell us that we are free.

Blue box, white stars

Fifty stars in all.

Red stripes, white stripes,

Hanging from the wall.

TURN

2+4 Math
Grade K · Unit 2
Patterns

___ng Shapes

___e shapes

___ you look.

___pes match the clock?

___pes match the book?

TURN

Card 15

Art
Grade K · Unit 1
Off to School

People Plan Schools

People planned your school. It has many classrooms. There are shelves for books. It has room for supplies. Does it have a playground? What makes your school fun?

TURN

- Math
- Social Studies
- Science
- Art

Additional Skills Practice

Approaching Level	On Level	English Learner	Above Level
Reteach	**Skills Practice 2**	**English Learner Support Activities**	**Challenge Activities**
Letter and Sound Identification, pp. 178, 184	Letter and Sound Identification, pp. 95–97, 99–100	Lessons 1–5	Letter and Sound Identification, pp. 136, 138
Penmanship, pp. 179, 181–182, 185	Penmanship, p. 102		Penmanship, p. 140
Sentences, p. 183	Sentences, p. 101		Sentences, p. 139
Word Spacing, p. 180	Word Spacing, p. 98		Word Spacing, p. 137

Differentiating Instruction
for Workshop

Lessons 1-5 Overview

AYP

Day 1

Approaching Level	On Level	English Learner	Above Level
Sounds and Letters			
Alphabetic Principle: Guide students in completing the activities on *Reteach* page 178.	**Alphabetic Principle:** Students listen to "Apples and Bananas" on the *Listening Library CD.*	**Alphabetic Principle:** Refer to Unit 10 Lesson 1 of *English Learner Support Guide.*	**Alphabetic Principle:** Students work independently to complete *Challenge Activities* page 136.
Reading and Responding			
Preview: Browse the *Windy Days Big Book,* and let students point out anything that interests them.	**Preview:** Students browse the *Windy Days Big Book,* and ask questions about each selection.	**Preview:** Students listen to the *Read Aloud Collection: Can You See the Wind?* on the *Listening Library CD.*	**Preview:** Students draw pictures of objects the wind can move and share their drawings with you.
Language Arts			
Writing: Discuss idea webs with students.	**Writing:** Students assist you in filling in an idea web about colors.	**Writing:** Discuss idea verbs with students.	**Writing:** Students discuss what they know about idea webs.

Day 2

Approaching Level	On Level	English Learner	Above Level

Sounds and Letters

Alphabetic Principle: Use an activity from Unit 10 Lesson 2 of the **Intervention Guide** for additional help with the /ē/ sound.

Alphabetic Principle: Students use the **Listening Library CD** to listen to "Little Boy Blue" and identify the /ē/ sound.

Alphabetic Principle: Refer to Unit 10 Lesson 2 of the **English Learner Support Guide.**

Alphabetic Principle: Have students work independently with **eSkills** to review the /ē/ sound.

Reading and Responding

Vocabulary: Say the selection vocabulary words *leaned, rough, lane,* and *hitched.* Have students repeat the words.

Vocabulary: Students use the selection vocabulary words in complete sentences with partners.

Vocabulary: Refer to Unit 10 Lesson 2 of the **English Learner Support Guide.**

Vocabulary: Have students draw pictures, using words from the selection vocabulary.

Language Arts

Writing: Tell students they will help you fill in an idea web about colors.

Grammar: With your help, students complete **Reteach** page 180.

Writing: Students vote for their favorite colors from the web.

Grammar: Review with students spacing between words in sentences.

Writing: Students help you create a list of words about colors.

Grammar: Refer to Unit 10 Lesson 2 of the **English Learner Support Guide.**

Writing: Students create idea webs about colors.

Grammar: Have students complete **Challenge Activities** page 137.

Differentiating Instruction
for Workshop

Day 3

Approaching Level	On Level	English Learner	Above Level
Sounds and Letters			
Alphabetic Principle: Have students draw pictures of an eel after modeling one on the board or chart paper. Have them say the /ē/ sound and point to the eels when they are finished.	**Alphabetic Principle:** Have students use *eSkills* to review the /ē/ sound.	**Alphabetic Principle:** Refer to Unit 10 Lesson 3 of the ***English Learner Support Guide.***	**Alphabetic Principle:** Have students look through the ***Windy Days Little Big Book*** for words with the letter *Ee* and the /ē/ sound.
Reading and Responding			
Comprehension: Students browse the selection *"Gilberto and the Wind,"* and ask anything they may be puzzled about or wonder.	**Comprehension:** Invite students to share their thoughts about the story and how it relates to the unit theme.	**Comprehension:** Refer to Unit 10 Lesson 3 of the ***English Learner Support Guide.***	**Comprehension:** Invite students to think of places where they have seen the effects of wind.
Language Arts			
Writing: With your help, students brainstorm lists of colors while you fill in the idea web.	**Writing:** Discuss line graphs with students.	**Writing:** Students help you situate color words on an idea web.	**Writing:** Each student looks at the idea web and chooses their favorite colors.

Day 4

Approaching Level	On Level	English Learner	Above Level

Sounds and Letters

Phonemic Awareness: Refer to Unit 10 Lesson 4 of the *Intervention Guide* for additional support activities.

Phonemic Awareness: Students draw pictures of a cub and a cup and identify the sounds that are the same and different in each word. (/p/ replaces /b/)

Phonemic Awareness: Refer to Unit 10 Lesson 4 of the *English Learner Support Guide.*

Phonemic Awareness: Using words from the supplemental word list in the Appendix, continue the phoneme-replacement activity from the lesson.

Reading and Responding

Comprehension: Students retell the story of *"Gilberto and the Wind"* to partners.

Comprehension: Have students draw pictures of how the wind can be gentle.

Comprehension: Refer to Unit 10 Lesson 4 of the *English Learner Support Guide.*

Comprehension: Students use the Internet to find pictures of wind and post them on the **Concept/Question Board.**

Language Arts

Writing: Students look at the idea web and vote for their favorite colors.

Grammar: With your help, students complete *Reteach* page 183.

Writing: With your help, students create simple line graphs that represent their most to least favorite colors.

Grammar: Look at *"Gilberto and the Wind"* in the **Windy Days Big Book,** and have students count the spaces in the first sentence of the story.

Writing: Students vote for their favorite colors after you review the colors with them.

Grammar: Refer to Unit 10 Lesson 4 of the *English Learner Support Guide.*

Writing: Discuss line graphs with students, and help them make simple line graphs about their idea webs.

Grammar: Have students work independently to complete *Challenge Activities* page 139.

Differentiating Instruction
for Workshop

Day 5

Approaching Level	On Level	English Learner	Above Level
Sounds and Letters			
Reading a Decodable: Reread *Decodable* 20 with students, reviewing what is happening in the illustrations and the high-frequency words *be* and *she*.	**Reading a Decodable:** Students reread *Decodable* 20 with partners.	**Reading a Decodable:** Review *Decodable* 20 with students, pointing to the high-frequency words *be* and *she* as you read aloud to them.	**Reading a Decodable:** Have students reread using *eDecodable We Did It!*
Reading and Responding			
Inquiry: Students use magazines and newspapers to find pictures of where people experience wind and post them on the **Concept/Question Board.**	**Inquiry:** Students use the Internet to find pictures of the effects of wind and add them to the **Concept/Question Board.**	**Inquiry:** Students use magazines and newspapers to find pictures of where people experience wind and post the pictures to the **Concept/ Question Board.**	**Inquiry:** Students research the good and bad effects of wind and post them on the **Concept/Question Board.**
Language Arts			
Writing: With your help, students complete a graph showing the class's favorite colors from most to least favorite. **Grammar:** Refer to Unit 10 Lesson 5 of the ***Intervention Guide*** for additional support for this grammar activity.	**Writing:** Students sign their names to the graph showing the class's favorite colors. **Grammar:** Students each get a copy of the story "Gilberto and the Wind" and draw a slash mark where they see a space between words.	**Writing:** With your help, students complete a graph showing the class's favorite colors from the most favorite to the least favorite. **Grammar:** Refer to Unit 10 Lesson 5 of the ***English Learner Support Guide.***	**Writing:** Students create a line graph depicting their groups' color preference. **Grammar:** Students challenge partners to rewrite sentences they have created with no spaces.

Resources for
Differentiating Instruction

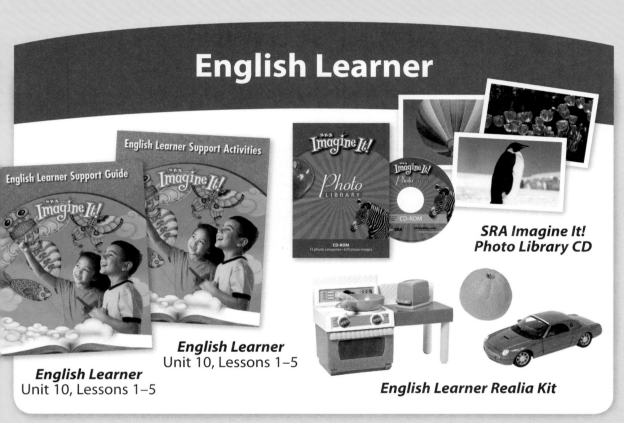

English Learner

English Learner Support Guide

English Learner Support Activities

SRA Imagine It! Photo Library CD

English Learner
Unit 10, Lessons 1–5

English Learner
Unit 10, Lessons 1–5

English Learner Realia Kit

Approaching Level

Intervention

Intervention Guide

Intervention

Intervention Guide

Intervention Workbook

Workshop Kits

- High-Frequency Words
- Letter Recognition
- Phonemic Awareness
- Phonics
- Print and Book Awareness
- Sequencing

Technology

eDecodable We Did It!

eSkills & eGames

Listening Library CD

Listening Library Unit 10

Lesson Assessment

Monitor Progress to Differentiate Instruction

Use these summative assessments along with your informal observations to assess student mastery.

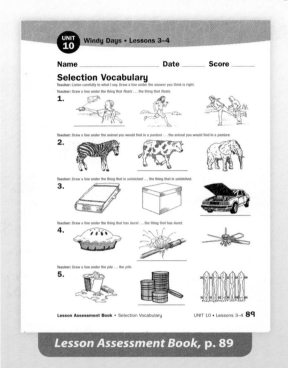

Lesson Assessment Book, p. 89

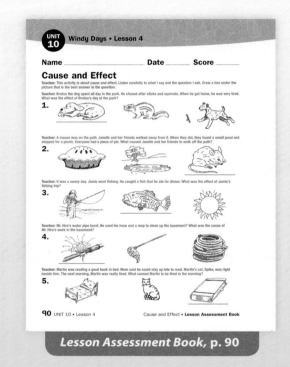

Lesson Assessment Book, p. 90

Lesson Assessment Book

Comprehension Observation Log

Student _____ Date _____

Unit _____ Lesson _____ Selection Title _____

General Comprehension
Concepts discussed: _____

Behavior Within a Group
Articulates, expresses ideas: _____

Joins discussions: _____

Collaborates (such as works well with other students, works alone): _____

Role in Group
Role (such as leader, summarizer, questioner, critic, observer, non-participant): _____

Flexibility (changes roles when necessary): _____

Use of Reading Strategies
Uses strategies when needed (either those taught or student's choice of strategy)/Describes strategies used:
_____
_____

Changes strategies when appropriate: _____

Changes Since Last Observation

110   Comprehension Observation Log • Lesson Assessment Book

Lesson Assessment Annotated Teacher's Edition, p. 110

The Comprehension Observation Log, found in the ***Lesson Assessment Annotated Teacher's Edition,*** is a vehicle for recording anecdotal information about individual student performance on an ongoing basis. Information such as students' strengths and weaknesses can be recorded at any time the occasion warrants. It is recommended that you maintain a folder for each student where you can store the logs for purposes of comparison and analysis as the school year progresses. You will gradually build up a comprehensive file that reveals which students are progressing smoothly and which students need additional help.

Sounds and Letters

OBJECTIVES

Students will
- ✦ replace initial phonemes.
- ✦ attach the /ē/ sound to the letter *Ee*.
- ✦ review writing the letters *Ss, Mm, Dd, Pp,* and *Aa*.
- ✦ practice writing words they have blended.

MATERIALS

- ✦ *Alphabet Letter Card Ee* for each student
- ✦ Routines 1, 2
- ✦ *Skills Practice 2,* pp. 95–96
- ✦ Supply Icons

Calendar

Su	M	T	W	Th	F	S
		1	2	3	4	5
6	7	8	9	10	11	12
13	14	15	16	17	18	19
20	21	22	23	24	25	26
27	28	29	30	31		

Point to the box that represents today. Take this opportunity to identify any important events that will happen during the coming weeks, such as students' birthdays, school functions, and national holidays, and discuss each one.

Warming Up

MORNING MESSAGE

Today's date is _____ .

We will practice _____ .

Can you find the _____ ?

M D J L P A T

P E S M C Q H

N R A D S B P

Kindergarten News

- ✦ Copy the text above on the board or on chart paper. Turn over responsibility to students for filling the blanks. For example, invite a student to write today's date in the blank.

- ✦ Ask a student to write *S, M, D, P,* or *A* in the blank in the third sentence. Then invite another student to come to the board and to circle the letter in the puzzle.

Oral Language

- ✦ Say several sentences with rhyming words, emphasizing the words that rhyme.

  Everyone had to wait *because we were* late.

  The child buried her hand *in the* sand.

  I ate a ripe peach *as I sat on the* beach.

✦ Tell students you will say a line and you want them to finish it by saying a word that makes a rhyme and then repeating its beginning sound. Begin with the following:

We wanted to scream *to cheer for our favorite* _____ . *team /t/*

After school *we swam in the* _____ . *pool /p/*

We sang a summertime tune *in the month of* _____ . *June /j/*

✦ Have students say their own incomplete sentences for their classmates to finish with rhyming words.

Phonemic Awareness

Phoneme Replacement: Initial Sounds

✦ Tell students the **Lion Puppet** wants to teach them something new.

✦ Say the word *hill*. Have students repeat the word. Then say */m/*, and ask students what word they make when they replace the first sound in *hill* with */m/. mill* Continue changing the initial phonemes, using /s/ and /p/.

✦ Then tell students that the puppet will say a word and a new beginning sound and that he wants them to use the sound to make a new word from the old one.

✦ Use the following procedure:

Puppet:	*The word is* sit. *The beginning sound is /l/. What is the new word?*
Students:	*lit*
Puppet:	*The word is* tap. *The beginning sound is /m/. What is the new word?*
Students:	*map*
Puppet:	*The word is* hat. *The beginning sound is /p/. What is the new word?*
Students:	*pat*

 Teacher Tip

LETTER FLUENCY Review the letters of the alphabet by having students play the Before and After game. Have individual students choose a letter card from a stack, look at the letter, and name the letters that come before and after that letter in the alphabet.

Differentiating Instruction **English Learners**

IF ... students have difficulty with the Phonemic Awareness activity, **THEN ...** refer to Unit 10 Lesson 1 of the **English Learner Support Guide.**

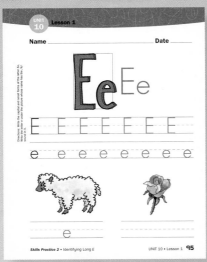

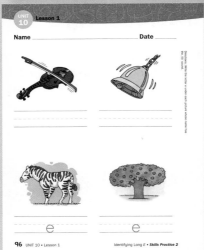

Skills Practice 2, pp. 95–96

Monitor Progress ✓

to Differentiate Instruction
Formal Assessment

Letter and Sound Identification Note how quickly students identify the /ē/ sound.

APPROACHING LEVEL

IF ... students are having difficulty,

THEN ... guide them in completing **Reteach** page 178.

ON LEVEL

IF ... students need more practice,

THEN ... have them continue the activity using **Skills Practice 2** page 96.

ABOVE LEVEL

IF ... students are comfortable,

THEN ... have them work independently to complete page 136 in **Challenge Activities.**

Alphabetic Principle

Reviewing Long-Vowel Sounds

✦ Have students tell what they know about vowels and how they are special. *Every word or syllable has to have a vowel sound; the letters are red on the cards; they can be long or short.* Ask volunteers to say the names of the vowels they remember learning about. *a, e, i, o, u* Then review the short-vowel sounds students have learned to attach to the vowels.

✦ Lead students in singing "Apples and Bananas." (See the Appendix and use the **Listening Library CD** if you wish.) Sing four verses—one each for long *a*, long *i*, long *o*, and long *u*.

Introducing the Sound of Long *Ee*

✦ Point to **Alphabet Sound Wall Card** Long *Ee*, and say a few words in which the letter *Ee* says its name, such as *even, eagle,* and *easy*. Remind students when *Ee* says its name, /ē/, it is called long *e,* and that is why the red *e* on the card is tall, or "long." Point to it on the card.

✦ Share with students the following rhyme to help them remember the sounds of *Ee:*

E's *my name.*

Two sounds for me:

Short e *in* hen,

Long e *in* he.

✦ Repeat the rhyme several times until students can easily recite it with you.

Listening for Initial /ē/

✦ Give each student an **Alphabet Letter Card** *Ee*. Ask students to raise the cards and say the sound when they hear a word with the /ē/ sound. Try the following words:

equal	*April*	*hole*	**eel**
open	**either**	**ecology**	**even**
ever	**evil**	*energy*	*use*

✦ Finish by having students open their **Skills Practice 2** to page 95. After students have completed the activity, make sure to review their work.

Alphabet Sound Wall Card 5

Penmanship

✦ Distribute a sheet of writing paper to each student, or have each student use a **White Board.**

✦ Place the Supply Icon for *pencil* on the board or in the **Pocket Chart.**

✦ Use the procedure established for writing letters to review how to form capital letter *S.* Also review how to form small *s.*

✦ Ask students to practice writing capital *S*s and small *s*'s, alternating across the top row of the papers or boards from left to right: *S s S s S s.*

✦ Repeat the procedure for the letters *Mm, Dd, Pp,* and *Aa.*

Guided Practice ROUTINE **2**

✦ Distribute another sheet of writing paper or a **White Board** to each student.

✦ Blend the word *sad* using the sound-by-sound blending routine.

✦ Guide students in blending the word sound by sound. */s/ /a/ /d/*

✦ After students have blended the word *sad,* have them read it again naturally, the way they would speak it. Then have students write the word *sad.* After students have written the word, have them read the word again.

✦ Repeat the procedure with the words *mad, dad,* and *pad.*

Monitor Progress

to Differentiate Instruction

Formal Assessment

Penmanship Note how easily students review penmanship.

APPROACHING LEVEL

IF ... students are having difficulty,   THEN ... help them complete **Reteach** page 179.

ON LEVEL

IF ... students need more practice,   THEN ... have them practice the strokes in watercolors on chart paper.

ABOVE LEVEL

IF ... students would enjoy a challenging activity,   THEN ... have them make a collage using cut-out letters.

Teacher Tip

LETTER-FORMATION PROCEDURES Consult the Appendix for specific instructions on the formation of each letter of the alphabet.

OBJECTIVES

Students will

✦ locate the Table of Contents and title of the **Big Book.**

✦ discuss the concept of the wind.

✦ set goals for reading each selection.

✦ generate questions and statements about the unit theme.

MATERIALS

✦ **Windy Days Big Book**

✦ **Home Connection,** pp. 75–76

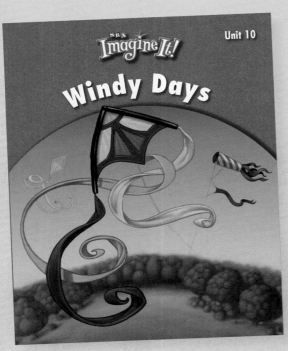

Windy Days Big Book

Give each student a copy of **Home Connection** page 75. This same information is also available in Spanish on **Home Connection** page 76. Encourage students to discuss the unit with their families and complete the activity provided.

Preview

Browsing the Unit

✦ Windy Days is the final unit in kindergarten. Learning about the wind provides an ideal opportunity for students to apply their growing knowledge of inquiry. Like scientists, they will continue to ask questions, develop conjectures, collect information, and share their new knowledge. Students will work in small groups to investigate wind and chart information and will consolidate the new information learned from each group.

✦ Display the **Windy Days Big Book,** and have a volunteer identify the front and back covers. Focus attention on the front cover illustration, and invite students to talk about what they see. Introduce the **Big Book** title and the Table of Contents. Point out to students that one of the selections tells about a little boy's good and bad experiences with the wind. Add that another selection shares information about different kinds of wind and two are poems about windy days. Explain that at the end of the unit, you will also read a make-believe story to them about how the night wind helps a child fall asleep. Browse the **Big Book** selections with students, and encourage them to make predictions about what each selection might say.

Setting Reading Goals

✦ Tell students in this unit they will be reading selections about the wind. Explain that the goals for reading these selections may include listening for enjoyment, listening for information, listening for ideas for answering their questions about the wind, and learning more about print and reading. Ask students to think of reasons for reading the selection "Gilberto and the Wind."

✦ Remind students readers are always thinking when they read. Tell them readers should get into the habit of setting reading goals for themselves.

Inquiry

✦ Students should be comfortable talking about being scientists—asking questions, developing conjectures (or possible answers), observing, investigating, collecting information, presenting their new information, and even evaluating their work. If you have posted the cards with the inquiry words, point them out. In this unit the class will be reading stories and poems about the wind.

✦ Create a three-column table to use in this unit. Write the title Wind. The headings should include the following: What We Know about Wind, Our Questions about Wind, and What We Discovered about Wind. Ask the class what they know about the wind, and write down the responses. Then ask them what questions they have about the wind, such as *What causes wind? Where does wind come from? How can wind help us?* Take time after reading and inquiry to add new questions and information to the chart.

✦ During the next few days, take a "wind walk." Have the class walk around outside, and discuss how they know there is wind. For example, ask *What does wind feel like? What do you see that shows wind is blowing? When the wind is blowing, do all things move?*

Concept/Question Board

Review with students the ways to use the **Concept/Question Board.** Remind students their questions about the wind will appear on the Question side. Questions about the wind might include the following:

- Why is there wind?
- Why is the wind sometimes strong and other times gentle?
- Where does the wind go when it is not blowing?

As students find answers to their questions, they should shift their questions/answers to the Concept side of the Board. Remind them they can also post on the Concept side any photos or drawings of the effects of wind. Refer to the Board every day so students understand and use it throughout the week. The more you talk about the Board, the more students will refer to and use it to share items from home.

 ## Teacher Tips

WORKSHOP During Workshop have books about the wind available for students to use. As they look through these books, tell them to think about what they are learning and what questions they have. At the end of Workshop, take time to write on the Wind Chart any new information and questions.

MATERIALS Begin collecting materials for students to use in wind experiments. In order for different groups of students to make wind direction indicators, pinwheels, anemometers, and wind vanes, you will need cardboard, plastic drink bottles, straws, small paper cups, and construction paper. These materials will be used in upcoming lessons.

Language Arts

Students will
+ choose a topic for a class report.
+ view, appreciate, and react to fine art.

+ *Language Arts Big Book,* p. 7
+ *Transparency* 46
+ *Windy Days Big Book,* p. 48

Language Arts Big Book, p. 7

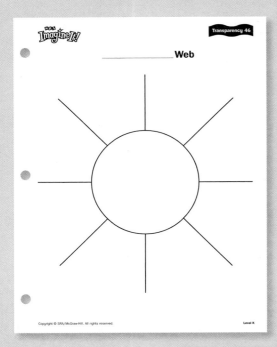

Transparency 46

Teacher Tip

PLAN AHEAD This writing activity will span three weeks throughout the unit. Be prepared to collect, assess, store, and reuse students' drawings and writing as you go.

Writing Process ⏱

Prewrite: Choosing a Topic

Teach

+ Display the **Language Arts Big Book** page 7, and read aloud the title *What Will I Write?* as you point to each word. Remind students that writers have to choose a topic, or something to write about, before they begin writing.

+ Tell students for their next writing assignment, as a class, they are going to write a report. This report will have something to do with the unit theme Windy Days.

+ Explain that they will also draw pictures to illustrate some of the information they want to share in their report. Have them keep this in mind as they think of topics they would like to explore and present later.

Guided Practice

+ Display **Transparency** 46. Remind students that an idea web can help a writer keep track of his or her ideas.

+ Pointing to the Listening Icons, remind students to listen carefully.

+ Have students generate ideas for topics. Suggest that writers can sometimes use their own experiences to help them think of ideas. Ask students if they have had any experiences with windy days.

+ Have students share their ideas or questions about windy days. Choose certain ideas, and write words in the web to represent them, explaining each item to students.

+ Have students vote for their favorite topics. Remind them of their experiences during their inquiries this year, and point out that the topics they choose today might change a little as the inquiry process unfolds.

Fine Art

Discussing Fine Art

Winslow Homer. *Breezing Up (A Fair Wind).* 1873–1876.

✦ Turn to page 48 in the ***Windy Days Big Book.*** Focus students' attention on *Breezing Up (A Fair Wind)* by Winslow Homer. Invite them to talk about the painting, mentioning anything that interests or puzzles them.

✦ Guide students in discussing the painting. Use questions such as the following:

- *What do you see in this painting?*
- *What are the children doing? Do they appear to be having fun? How can you tell?*
- *How does this painting make you feel? Do you like it? Why or why not?*

✦ Discuss how this painting relates to the unit theme Windy Days. Ask students the following:

- *How do you know the wind is blowing in this painting?*
- *Is the wind strong? What details in the painting show you the wind's strength?*

✦ To end the discussion, ask students to pretend to be with the children in the painting and to make up a story about their experiences on the boat that day.

Background Information

Winslow Homer (1836–1910) is best known for his depictions of the sea and of the people who live and work near water. Many of his paintings show hardworking people struggling against powerful forces of nature, while others, such as *Breezing Up,* show children enjoying themselves in happy, peaceful, natural scenes.

Differentiating Instruction **English Learners**

IF . . . students have limited vocabulary, **THEN . . .** help them participate in the discussion by asking questions that can be answered *yes* or *no.* For example, *Do you see the sailboat in the painting?*

Sounds and Letters

OBJECTIVES

Students will

✦ match initial phonemes in groups of words.

✦ replace initial phonemes to make new words.

✦ identify the /ē/ sound in print.

MATERIALS

✦ *Alphabet Letter Card Ee* for each student

✦ *Pickled Peppers Big Book,* p. 10

✦ *Skills Practice 2,* p. 97

Calendar

Su	M	T	W	Th	F	S
		1	2	3	4	5
6	7	8	9	10	11	12
13	14	15	16	17	18	19
20	21	22	23	24	25	26
27	28	29	30	31		

Point to the box that represents today. Review the names of the months in the proper order with students, beginning with January (not the current month). Then have students identify the names of the days in the proper order, beginning with Monday.

Teacher Tip

SAME-SOUND GAME This game is just like the Phonemic Awareness activities in which students match initial phonemes. Now that students are familiar with the concept, this activity lightens the practice by presenting it as a game.

Warming Up

MORNING MESSAGE

Good morning, boys and girls!

Today is _____.

What words begin with the /d/ sound?

Kindergarten News

✦ Copy the text above on the board or on chart paper; however, make several errors when you write the sentences, such as omitting punctuation.

✦ Tell students to check the Morning Message for errors. Have students come to the board and proofread your mistakes.

✦ Ask students to help you brainstorm a list of words that begin with the /d/ sound. As students suggest words, invite them to come and write them in the message under the third sentence.

Phoneme Matching

✦ Play the Same-Sound game with students. Say a series of three words, two of which have the same initial sound. Ask students to listen closely and to identify which words start with the same sound. Call on volunteers to say the words and to give the initial sound.

✦ Try these sets of words:

wish, foolish, **wait** /w/   **gift, garage,** hotel /g/

turnip, tile, mile /t/   **vacuum, vanish,** busy /v/

silly, **jump, jeep** /j/   **zany,** soup, **zoom** /z/

butler, bonus, pain /b/   **California, Colorado,** Hawaii /k/

Phonemic Awareness

Phoneme Replacement: Initial Sounds

✦ Bring out the **Lion Puppet,** and remind students he wants them to make new words by using what they know about sounds and letters.

✦ Say the word *pan.* Have students repeat the word. Then say the /m/ sound, and ask students what word they make when they take away the first sound in *pan,* /p/, and change it to the /m/ sound. *man* Then change the initial sound to /t/. *tan*

✦ Tell students the puppet will say a word and a beginning sound and you want them to use the sound to make a new word from the old one.

✦ Use the following procedure:

Puppet:	*The word is* nap. *The beginning sound is* /t/. *What is the new word?*
Students:	*tap*
Puppet:	*The word is* mass. *The beginning sound is* /p/. *What is the new word?*
Students:	*pass*
Puppet:	*The word is* nip. *The beginning sound is* /s/. *What is the new word?*
Students:	*sip*

Teacher Tip

VOWEL SPELLINGS Note that in this lesson, students are not asked to visually identify the target words in the activities. Some of the words make the long *e* sound using spellings other than *e* or *e_e*, which is a spelling present more in multisyllable words rather than one-syllable words. (Students will use this spelling more in later lessons.) Use this lesson to have students practice their listening identification skills only.

Skills Practice 2, p. 97

Alphabetic Principle

Reviewing the Sound of Long *Ee*

✦ Point to **Alphabet Sound Wall Card** Long *Ee*, and ask a volunteer to say the name of the letter. Ask students why vowels are special. *Every word or syllable in English needs a vowel.*

✦ Have students recite the rhyme for the sounds of *Ee*:

E's my name.

Two sounds for me:

Short e *in* hen,

Long e *in* he.

Listening for Initial /ē/

Give each student an **Alphabet Letter Card** *Ee*. Ask students to raise the cards and say the sound when they hear a word that begins with the /ē/ sound. Try the following words:

elongate	open	oven	**equal**
every	able	**event**	omit
unit	**evening**	idea	**Egypt**

Alphabet Sound Wall Card 5

Listening for Medial /ē/

✦ Distribute to each student **Alphabet Letter Card** *Ee*. Ask students to raise the cards and say the sound when they hear a word with the /ē/ sound in the middle. Try the following words:

seen	when	buck	**cedar**
sack	**week**	**keep**	side
brick	**bees**	happen	**fever**

✦ Give students additional practice with the /ē/ sound. Ask them to open their **Skills Practice 2** to page 97. After you have finished working through the page, review students' work.

Monitor Progress to Differentiate Instruction

Formal Assessment

Letter and Sound Identification Note how easily students identify the /ē/ sound.

APPROACHING LEVEL	IF ... students are still having difficulty,	THEN ... refer to Unit 10 Lesson 2 of the **Intervention Guide.**
ON LEVEL	IF ... students need more practice,	THEN ... have them match **Alphabet Letter Cards** Ee with classroom objects whose names contain the /ē/ sound.
ABOVE LEVEL	IF ... students are comfortable,	THEN ... have them look through **Windy Days Little Big Books** with partners to identify words with the /ē/ sound.

Pickled Peppers Big Book

✦ Display the **Pickled Peppers Big Book.** Ask students to identify the book on sight.

✦ Turn to page 10, "Little Boy Blue." Have students point to the title, and read it aloud. Have students share anything they remember about the rhyme.

✦ Tell students you will play "Little Boy Blue" on the **Listening Library CD** and you would like them to listen for the words with the /ē/ sound. Ask students to close their eyes as they listen.

✦ Invite students to say any /ē/ words they noticed while listening.

✦ Reread the rhyme, pointing to each word as you say it. This time ask students to stop you each time you point to a word with the letter *e* in it. *Little, Blue, Come, sheep's, the, meadow, Where, after, sheep, He's, under, asleep, wake, sure* When you pause, ask students if they hear the /ē/ sound in the word. When you find a word with the /ē/ sound, have students say aloud the letter's name: *EEEEEEEE!*

Pickled Peppers Big Book, p. 10

Technology

Use the **Listening Library CD** to support the **Pickled Peppers Big Book** lessons.

Audio CD

Reading and Responding

OBJECTIVES

Students will

✦ locate the title and the name of the author.

✦ connect their own life experiences to the text.

✦ develop an understanding of vocabulary words.

✦ become familiar with the unit theme Windy Days.

MATERIALS

✦ *Read Aloud Collection: Can You See the Wind?*

✦ Routines 5–7

✦ *Home Connection,* pp. 77–78

Differentiating Instruction **English Learners**

IF . . . students need help understanding vocabulary, **THEN . . .** use pictures and actions to illustrate meanings.

Vocabulary

damage	produce
twisters	flapping

Technology

To promote independent reading, encourage students to use Workshop to listen to the recording of the selection on the **Listening Library CD.** Invite them to follow along and say the words whenever they can.

Read Aloud

Activate Prior Knowledge

Tell students in this unit they will be reading and learning all about the wind. Invite students to look out the classroom window and to share how they can tell whether the wind is blowing. Ask students how they could tell the wind was blowing if the object were not there. Lead students to the understanding that we cannot actually see the wind; we can see only things being moved by the wind.

Preview the Selection

✦ Display the cover of *Can You See the Wind?* Follow Routine 5, the previewing the selection routine, as you introduce the title and the name of the author. Ask students what an author does. Focus students' attention on the cover illustration, and ask them how they know the wind is blowing. Ask students to look at the illustrations for clues as to what the selection might tell them.

✦ Use Routine 7, the reading the selection routine, as you read the Focus Question printed above the **Read Aloud Collection** selection.

Vocabulary

✦ Follow Routine 6, the selection vocabulary routine, as you introduce the vocabulary words for this selection.

✦ Explain to students that the word *damage* means "harm." Ask students what damage a bad storm can cause.

✦ Tell students *twisters* are very bad storms where the wind twirls in a column. Use the following sentence to illustrate: *Several twisters passed through our area last night.*

✦ Explain that the word *produce* means "to make." Ask students what kinds of things they produce in school.

✦ Tell students the word *flapping* means "swaying loosely, especially with noise." Use the following sentence to illustrate: *We could hear the flag flapping as the storm approached.*

Focus Question How can you see the wind?

Can You See the Wind?

by Allan Fowler

Someone once said that wind was air in a hurry.

On a very cold day, you might think it's in too much of a hurry.

Icy wind can seem to blow right through you and make you feel even colder.

Other winds are more welcome. You need wind to fly a kite or fill the sails of a boat to push it along the water.

Doesn't a cool breeze feel good on a hot summer day?

Ask *How can wind be helpful?*

Sometimes people even make their own wind by waving a paper fan or turning on an electric fan.

How are nature's winds turned on? Why does air move from one place to another?

If every place on Earth were the same temperature at the same time, there would be no winds. But some places are warm while others are cold.

When air is warm, it rises. As it rises above land or water, cooler air rushes in to take its place.

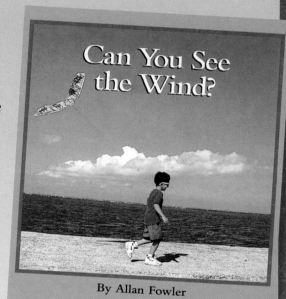

Can You See the Wind?

Teacher Tip

READ ALOUDS Allow students to listen to a variety of texts from various cultures every day. Reading aloud to students provides an opportunity to teach reader responses and problem-solving strategies that adult readers employ. In addition to reading aloud with expression and enthusiasm, model your own reading strategies while reading aloud to students. This makes the use of strategies "real" for students and encourages them to begin to respond to text similarly.

That rush of air is wind.

Light winds are called breezes. Strong winds are called gales.

Tornadoes have the strongest winds and do great damage.

Tornadoes are also known as twisters, because they blow in a circle.

Hurricanes also produce strong winds.

A hurricane is a tropical storm that forms over a warm ocean.

Can you see the wind? You can certainly see some of the things it does.

Pollen is a powder that must be carried from one plant to another to help new plants grow.

Wind carries the pollen of grasses and most trees.

Ask *How does wind help things grow?*

Wind blows desert sand into hills called dunes.

Over a very long time, wind can even change the shape of rocks. Bit by tiny bit, it wears the rocks away.

Before people knew how to use steam, gas, or electricity for power, they used the wind.

They crossed oceans in great ships driven by wind.

People built windmills with big sails that turned in the wind. The windmills ground corn for bread or pumped water off flooded lands.

Many farms still use windmills today.

Ask *How does the wind make power?*

Winds high in the sky often blow much harder than those at ground level.

A jet plane goes slower if it has to fly against the wind.

With the wind pushing it from behind, however, a plane might reach the airport ahead of time.

Scientists send up weather balloons to learn how the wind is blowing.

Can you see the wind? Just look up at the clouds. How fast is the wind moving them along? Where is the wind coming from—north, south, east, or west?

Closer to the ground, look for a flag flapping or a tree swaying in the breeze.

Yes, in a way, you can see the wind!

Teacher Tip

READING ALOUD Before reading a selection, make some predictions aloud. As you read, let students know what questions occur to you, what images pop up in your mind, and how points made in the reading relate to ideas you already know. Toward the end of the reading, summarize the selection for students. If you cannot summarize the selection well, let students see you go back and reread to fill in the gaps in your summary.

Discussing the Read Aloud

✦ After you have finished reading *Can You See the Wind?* invite students to ask questions about what they have heard. Turn through the pages again, and encourage students to discuss what they see in the photographs.

✦ Review the Focus Question with students: How can you see the wind? *You can see the wind by seeing some of the things it does.*

✦ Discuss with students what they learned about the wind from listening to this selection. Ask them the following questions about the unit theme:

• *How do people make their own wind? They wave a paper fan or turn on an electric fan.*

• *How does nature make wind? Warm air rises above land or water, and cooler air rushes in to take its place. This rush of air is wind.*

• *How can wind change the land? It can blow sand into dunes or wear away rocks.*

• *How has the wind helped people travel? It has powered great ships across the ocean.*

• *How might a jet reach the airport ahead of schedule? A strong wind might push it from behind.*

• *How do scientists learn how the wind is blowing? They send up balloons and watch how they move.*

Vocabulary Review

Review with students the selection vocabulary words *damage, twisters, produce,* and *flapping.* Ask students the following questions:

✦ *What kinds of damage can wind cause?*

✦ *Why are some winds called twisters?*

✦ *What are some things we could produce with crayons, paper, and scissors and glue?*

✦ *What does it look like when our arms are flapping?*

From Your Teacher **Home Connection**

Give each student a copy of **Home Connection** page 77. This same information is also available in Spanish on **Home Connection** page 78. Encourage students to discuss "Gilberto and the Wind" with their families and complete the activity provided.

Language Arts

OBJECTIVES

Students will
✦ create a web of ideas.
✦ review spacing between words.
✦ review differences between words and sentences.
✦ participate in a Thinking Story experience.

MATERIALS

✦ **Transparency** 46
✦ **Language Arts Big Book,** p. 37
✦ **Skills Practice 2,** p. 98
✦ **Willy the Wisher,** p. 91

Writing Process

Model: Creating a Web

Teach

Remind students for this writing assignment, the class will work together to write a report about windy days. Tell students before they begin writing, they have to learn about their topic. And before they can research their topic, they have to think about some things they would like to learn about.

Guided Practice

✦ Display **Transparency** 46. Tell students a word web is one easy way to think of and keep track of ideas for writing.

✦ Draw students' attention to the middle circle, and explain that this is where the web begins. Write *spider* in the middle circle, and say it aloud for students. Tell them you will use the topic of spiders to show how a web can be helpful.

✦ Ask a student to say something he or she knows about spiders and write the example into one of the attached circles.

✦ Close by reiterating that word webs can help writers keep track of their ideas. Save the web until the next class.

Grammar, Usage, and Mechanics

Teach

✦ Display page 37 of the **Language Arts Big Book,** and read aloud the heading *We Make Sentences from Words.* Remind students that sentences are groups of words put together in a certain way. Then identify the differences between a word (columns 1 and 2) and a sentence (column 3).

✦ Then draw students' attention to the first sentence, and read it aloud, pointing to each word as you say it. Have students help you count the number of words in the sentence. Ask students *How do we know how many words are in the sentence?* Point to the space between the words *Vicki* and *stands,* and remind students that writers put space between words so readers know where one word ends and another one begins.

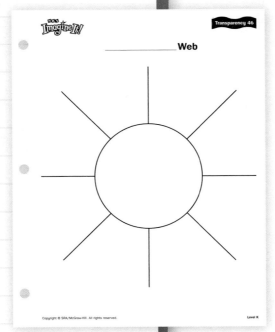

Transparency 46

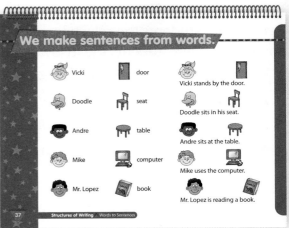

Language Arts Big Book, p. 37

Grammar, Usage, and Mechanics, continued

Guided Practice

✦ Have students open their **Skills Practice 2** to page 98.

✦ Work through the page with students, and review their answers when you finish.

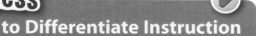
Skills Practice 2, p. 98

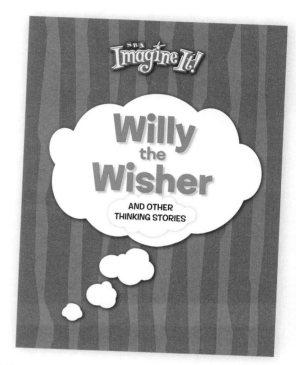

Willy the Wisher

✦ Display the book **Willy the Wisher,** and turn to page 91, "The Lion Who Roared Like a Waterfall."

✦ Before reading the story to students, have them discuss what they remember about Mrs. Nosho. Read the story, pausing at the red text to ask students the questions and encouraging them to share their thinking.

Willy the Wisher, p. 91

✦ After reading the story, discuss it in general. Use questions such as the following:

- *Why did the lion's roar get quieter instead of louder after all his practice?*

- *Do you think the owl's idea was a good one? Why or why not?*

- *What advice would you have given the lion if he had asked you how to make his roar louder?*

Monitor Progress

Formal Assessment

to Differentiate Instruction

Grammar Note how easily students are able to identify space between words.

APPROACHING LEVEL

IF ... students are having difficulty,	**THEN ...** help them complete **Reteach** page 180.

ON LEVEL

IF ... students need more practice,	**THEN ...** help them write simple sentences while noting the space between words.

ABOVE LEVEL

IF ... students are comfortable,	**THEN ...** have them complete **Challenge Activities** page 137.

 Teacher Tip

MAKING PREDICTIONS You might challenge students to make a few predictions about the events in the story "The Lion Who Roared Like a Waterfall." When you pause to ask students the fourth question in red text, also ask them to "guess" how the waterfall had fooled the lion. When you pause for the next question, revisit a few student predictions, and discuss how closely they reflected the information that was revealed.

Sounds and Letters

OBJECTIVES

Students will

✦ identify words in print.

✦ replace final phonemes to make new words.

✦ attach the /ē/ sound to the letter *Ee*.

✦ review writing the letters *Hh, Tt, Nn, Ll,* and *Ii.*

✦ practice writing words they have blended.

MATERIALS

✦ *Pickled Peppers Big Book,* pp. 16–27

✦ *Pocket Chart Picture Cards* 2–11, 14, 30, 54, 103, 121, 125, 131, 135, 142, 193

✦ *Alphabet Letter Card Ee* for each student

✦ *Skills Practice 2,* p. 99

✦ Supply Icons

✦ Routine 2

Calendar

Su	M	T	W	Th	F	S
				1	2	3
4	5					
6	7	8	9	10	11	12
13	14	15	16	17	18	19
20	21	22	23	24	25	26
27	28	29	30	31		

Point to the box that represents today. Review the differences between school days and weekend days, and have students identify examples of each on the calendar.

Warming Up

MORNING MESSAGE

Good morning, boys and girls!

What is the date? Today is _____.

Tommy the taxi driver took ten tiny tots to the tailor.

Kindergarten News

✦ Copy the text above on the board or on chart paper, and invite a volunteer to come up and write today's date in the blank.

✦ Invite volunteers to circle any words they can read. Ask another student to circle the marks that end each sentence.

✦ Read aloud the third sentence to students, and ask them what sound they hear repeated at the beginnings of words in this silly sentence. /t/ Then invite them to find the letters *Tt, h, n, l,* and *i* in the Morning Message as well.

Focusing on Words in Print

✦ Display the **Pickled Peppers Big Book,** opened to "One Hungry Monster," page 16. Reread the poem, pausing to let students read the numbers.

✦ In the **Pocket Chart,** place the **Pocket Chart Picture Cards** for each of the foods mentioned on pages 24–27. Leave space to the left of the food **Picture Cards.** Next have ten volunteers stand in a row facing the class. Give a **Picture Card** for numbers 1–10 to each student.

✦ Point to a food **Picture Card,** and say the name. Tell the class to identify the line and word(s) in the **Big Book** that name the food. Have the student who has the number appearing in the line say the food name. Then ask the student to say the first sound of the food name. Ask the class if that is correct. Finally have the student place his or her number **Picture Card** to the left of the food **Picture Card** in the **Pocket Chart.**

Phonemic Awareness

Phoneme Replacement: Final Sounds

✦ With this lesson, you will switch the focus of students' attention to replacing final phonemes in words to make new words.

✦ Tell students the **Lion Puppet** wants to change the game they have been playing. For this new game, the puppet will say a word and an *ending* sound. Then you want them to use that ending sound to make a new word from the old one.

✦ Say the word *tab,* and then repeat the final sound: */b/.* Have students repeat the word and the sound. Then say the /p/ sound, and ask students what word they make when they replace the ending sound in *tab, /b/,* with /p/. *tap* Change the final sound to /n/, and ask for the new word. *tan*

✦ Use the following procedure:

Puppet:	*The word is* sad. *The new ending sound is /t/. What is the new word?*
Students:	*sat*
Puppet:	*The word is* lip. *The new ending sound is /d/. What is the new word?*
Students:	*lid*
Puppet:	*The word is* hiss. *The new ending sound is /m/. What is the new word?*
Students:	*him*

✦ Continue with these words and sound changes:

pad, /l/ pal, /n/ pan
dip, /m/ dim, /g/ dig
sad, /t/ sat, /m/ Sam
mat, /d/ mad, /p/ map

Teacher Tips

REPLACING SOUNDS If students are still having difficulty replacing sounds, help them identify and write the letters that make up each word, and then have them rewrite the word with the new letter/sound. They can then blend the new word.

PHONEME REPLACEMENT This skill can be difficult for some students. Combined with the fact that final sounds are often more challenging than initial sounds, some students might need extra practice. Take the time to work with these students during Workshop, not during whole-class practice.

Alphabetic Principle

Reviewing the Sound of Long *Ee*

Point to **Alphabet Sound Wall Card** Long *Ee*, and have students recite the rhyme for the sounds of *Ee*:

E's *my name.*

Two sounds for me:

Short e *in* hen,

Long e *in* me.

Listening for Medial /ē/

Give each student an **Alphabet Letter Card** *Ee*. Ask students to raise the cards and say the sound when they hear a word with the /ē/ sound. Try the following words:

bread	**peel**	flame	pies
meet	spend	**zebra**	**squeeze**
deck	mother	**concrete**	**compete**

Linking the Sound to the Letter

Write a pair of similar-looking words on the board, one beginning with the /ē/ sound and one with a different vowel sound. For each pair, say the word with the /ē/ sound, point to each of the words, and have students identify the correct word by signaling thumbs-up when you point to it. Then ask a volunteer to tell the class how he or she knew the correct word. *The word begins with long* e. Try these word pairs:

even ... oven   ailment ... *ecology*

insect ... *Egypt*   *ether* ... other

equal ... able   *evening* ... invert

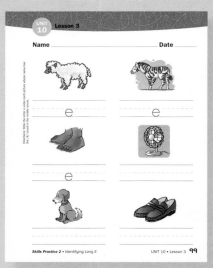

Skills Practice 2, p. 99

Monitor Progress to Differentiate Instruction   Formal Assessment ✓

Letter and Sound Identification Note how easily students identify the /ē/ sound.

APPROACHING LEVEL	**IF** ... students are having difficulty,	**THEN** ... help them match **Alphabet Letter Card** *Ee* with classroom objects whose names contain the /ē/ sound.
ON LEVEL	**IF** ... students need more practice,	**THEN** ... have them complete **Skills Practice 2** page 99.
ABOVE LEVEL	**IF** ... students would enjoy a challenging activity,	**THEN** ... they can work independently to complete **Challenge Activities** page 138.

Penmanship

✦ Distribute a sheet of writing paper and a pencil to each student.

✦ Use the procedure established for writing letters to review how to form the letter *H*. Also review how to form small *h*.

✦ Invite students to practice writing capital *H*s and small *h*'s, alternating across the top row of the paper: *H h H h H h*.

✦ Repeat the procedure for the letters *Tt, Nn, Ll,* and *Ii*.

Guided Practice

✦ Distribute a sheet of writing paper to each student, or use **White Boards** turned to the sides with writing lines. Place the Supply Icon for *pencil* on the board or in the **Pocket Chart.**

✦ Blend the word *hit* using the sound-by-sound blending routine.

✦ Guide students in blending the word sound by sound. /h/ /i/ /t/

✦ After students have blended the word *hit* have them read it again naturally, the way you would speak it. Then have them place their fingers on line 1 and write the word *hit* on their papers or **White Boards.** After students have written the word, have them read it again.

✦ Repeat the procedure with the words *lit* and *hint*.

Monitor Progress

Formal Assessment

to Differentiate Instruction

Penmanship   Note how easily students review the letters.

APPROACHING LEVEL	
IF ... students are having difficulty,	**THEN ...** guide them in completing **Reteach** pages 181 and 182.
ON LEVEL	
IF ... students need more practice,	**THEN ...** use **eSkills** for additional activities.
ABOVE LEVEL	
IF ... students would enjoy a challenging activity,	**THEN ...** have them write and blend additional words using the letters they have reviewed so far.

Students will

✦ locate the title and the names of the author and the illustrator.

✦ develop an understanding of vocabulary words.

✦ use the comprehension strategies Clarifying and Predicting.

✦ identify print and book features.

✦ *Windy Days Big Book,* pp. 4–23

✦ Routines 5–7

Focus Question How does the wind play with Gilberto?

Gilberto and the Wind

by Marie Hall Ets
illustrated by Loretta Krupinski

I hear Wind whispering at the door.

"You-ou-ou," he whispers. "You-ou-ou-ou!"
So I get my balloon, and I run out to play.

4

Windy Days Big Book, p. 4

Preview and Prepare

ROUTINE 5

1st READ

Activate Prior Knowledge

✦ "Gilberto and the Wind" is a fictional account of a boy's experiences with the wind in different seasons and different kinds of weather. Relate what you already know to what you are reading, and encourage students to do the same.

✦ Ask students the following questions: *Have you ever played in the wind? What did you do? Has the wind ever helped you?*

✦ Explain to students that in this story, Gilberto talks to the wind as though it were a person. Tell students writers of make-believe stories sometimes treat animals and objects as real people.

✦ Encourage students to think about what they are learning about the unit theme as they listen to "Gilberto and the Wind." Key concepts include the following:

• The wind is necessary for some activities such as flying a kite.

• The wind can vary in strength and can either help us work and play or prevent us from working and playing.

• Although we cannot see the wind, we can see its effect on the things around us, such as leaves blowing and kites sailing.

Preview the Selection

✦ Open the ***Windy Days Big Book*** to pages 4–5, the opening pages of "Gilberto and the Wind." Follow Routine 5 as you introduce the title and the names of the author and the illustrator. Ask students what an author and an illustrator do.

✦ As you prepare to read the selection, encourage students to comment on anything they find interesting or puzzling. Ask students to predict what the selection is about.

✦ Encourage students to think of reasons to read "Gilberto and the Wind." Ask students to consider what they might learn about the unit theme Windy Days.

Technology

To promote independent reading, encourage students to use Workshop to listen to the recording of the selection on the ***Listening Library CD.*** Invite them to follow along and say the words whenever they can.

Audio CD

Vocabulary

ROUTINE **6**

✦ Follow Routine 6, the selection vocabulary routine, as you introduce the vocabulary words for this selection.

✦ Explain to students that the word *gentle* means "light and soft." Tell students the wind can be gentle or strong.

✦ Explain that in this selection the word *floats* means "carries along in the air." Use the following sentence to illustrate: *A light wind floats the balloon just above my head.*

✦ Tell students a *pasture* is land where cattle graze. Use the following sentence to illustrate: *A herd of cattle grazed calmly in the pasture.*

✦ Explain that the word *unlatched* means "not locked." Tell students if a gate is *unlatched,* pets can escape. Ask students if they have unlatched something.

Read the Selection

ROUTINE **7**

✦ Before beginning the selection, read the Focus Question at the top of the first page. Tell students to keep this question in mind as they listen to the story.

✦ Follow Routine 7, the reading the selection routine, as you read the entire selection. Ask volunteers to point to the face of the wind on the pages it appears.

✦ Before, during, and after the first reading, encourage students to ask questions and to think aloud about the selection.

Comprehension Strategies

✦ You will model the following comprehension strategies:
  • Clarifying
  • Predicting

✦ Think aloud through each strategy, and encourage students to share their ideas as well.

Vocabulary

gentle	pasture
floats	unlatched

Monitor Progress

to Differentiate Instruction
Formal Assessment

Vocabulary Note how easily students grasp vocabulary words.

APPROACHING LEVEL

IF ... students need help with the vocabulary words,

THEN ... refer to Unit 10 Lesson 3 of the *Intervention Guide.*

ON LEVEL

IF ... students need to practice the vocabulary words,

THEN ... have them play Password with other students.

ABOVE LEVEL

IF ... students understand the vocabulary words,

THEN ... have them work in a small group to think of as many words as possible that relate to each vocabulary word.

Comprehension Strategies

Teacher Modeling

❶ Predicting *First the wind played gently with Gilberto, and then it took his balloon. What do you think might happen next? What clues can help us make our prediction?*

❷ Clarifying *I wonder what a* pillow slip *is. How can we figure out what this is? I know* slip *is like* falling, *but I don't think that's what this means. When I look at the picture again and reread the sentences, I can see that a* pillow slip *is what I call a pillowcase. Rereading the page helped me clarify that.*

❸ Predicting *Our prediction about the wind was confirmed. First, Wind pulled out the clothespins; then he broke Gilberto's umbrella. How did your predictions turn out? When we read these pages, we were able to check our predictions.*

Focus Question How does the wind play with Gilberto?

Gilberto and the Wind

by Marie Hall Ets
illustrated by Loretta Krupinski

I hear Wind whispering at the door. "You-ou-ou," he whispers. "You-ou-ou-ou!" So I get my balloon, and I run out to play.

4

At first Wind is gentle and just floats my balloon around in the air. But then, with a jerk, he grabs it away and carries it up to ❶ the top of a tree. "Wind! Oh, Wind!" I say. "Blow it back to me! Please!" But he won't. He just laughs and whispers, "You-ou-ou-ou!"

5

Wind loves to play with the wash on the line. He blows the pillow slips into balloons and shakes the sheets and twists the apron strings. ❷

6

And he pulls out all the clothespins that he can. Then he tries on the clothes— though he knows they're too small.

7

 Teacher Tip

GLOSSARY The words *floats, pasture,* and *unlatched* can be found in the Glossary of the *Windy Days Big Book.*

And Wind loves umbrellas. Once when I took one out in the rain he tried to take it away from me. And when he couldn't, he broke it. **3**

If the gate in the pasture is left unlatched, Wind plays with that, too. He opens it up, then bangs it shut, making it squeak and cry. "Wind! Oh, Wind!" I say, and I go and climb on. "Give me a ride!" But with me on it the gate is too heavy. Wind can't move it at all.

8

9

But he always wins, because he just runs over the top of the grass and I have to run through it and touch the ground with my feet.

When the grass is tall in the meadow Wind and I like to race. Wind runs ahead, then comes back and starts over.

10

11

Windy Days Big Book, pp. 4–11

Print and Book Awareness

Quotation Marks

Identify the quotation marks on page 5, and ask students what they show. If necessary, explain that quotation marks show the words that a person or story character is saying. Ask volunteers to point to the words Gilberto says. *"Wind! Oh, Wind!" "Blow it back to me! Please!"* Ask another volunteer to point to Wind's reply. *"You-ou-ou-ou!"*

Exclamation Points

Have a volunteer point to the exclamation points on page 9, and ask students what an exclamation point means. If necessary, remind students an exclamation point means the speaker is excited. Then read the sentences in a normal voice and an excited voice, and invite students to do the same.

Differentiating Instruction   **English Learners**

IF . . . students are unfamiliar with the words *bangs* and *squeak* on page 9, **THEN . . .** ask English speakers to demonstrate the meaning of each word for their English Learner classmates.

IF . . . students are native speakers of Spanish, **THEN . . .** explain that in English the exclamation point is placed only at the end of the sentence, never at the beginning.

Comprehension Strategies

Teacher Modeling

4 Predicting *Wind knows that the children are having fun with their kites. What prediction can we make?*

5 Predicting *Well, now we see this prediction didn't happen. When we read more of the story, we found out Wind did not let Gilberto fly the kite at all.*

6 Clarifying *Here's a word we may not understand—we'll reread the sentences and look at the picture again and try to figure out what it is. When I reread the sentence, it says the wind is turning the pinwheel very fast. Then the picture shows us the pinwheel is turning so quickly, we can hardly see its different points. Now we can figure it out. A blur is something moving so fast that it's hard to see what it is.*

7 Clarifying *How can the wind carry a bubble? Let's look again at the page to see if we can clarify this. The picture shows the bubbles are floating in the air. So the wind is carrying the bubbles up in the air.*

When the big boys on the hill have kites to fly Wind helps them out. Wind carries their kites way up to the sky and all around. **4**

12

But when I have a kite Wind won't fly it at all. He just drops it. "Wind! Oh, Wind!" I say, "I don't like you today!" **5**

13

When the apples are ripe in the fall, I run with Wind to the pasture and wait under the tree. And Wind always blows one down for me.

14

And when I have a boat with a paper sail Wind comes and sails it for me— just as he sails big sailboats for sailors on the sea.

15

 Teacher Tip

CLARIFYING Remind students readers stop reading when some part of the text does not make sense. Model for students the various ways readers clarify difficult ideas or passages. These include rereading, using charts and other graphic organizers, thinking of other comprehension strategies that might help, and asking someone for help.

And when I have a pinwheel Wind comes and plays, too. First I blow it myself to show him how.

16

Then I hold it out, or hold it up, and Wind blows it for me. And when he blows it, he turns it so fast that it whistles and sings, and all I can see is a blur. **6**

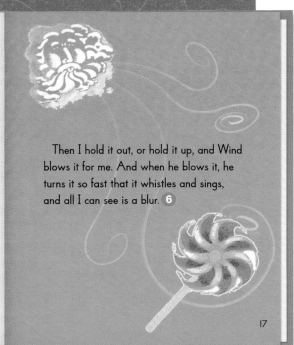

17

Wind likes my soap bubbles best of all. *He* can't make the bubbles—*I* have to do that.

18

7 But he carries them way up into the air for the sun to color. Then he blows some back and makes me laugh when they burst in my eyes or on the back of my hand.

19

Windy Days Big Book, pp. 12–19

Print and Book Awareness

High-Frequency Words

Display pages 10 and 11, and have volunteers point to and read any high-frequency words they have learned. Words they might find include *the, is, and, I, to, of, have,* and *with.*

Picture-Text Relationship

Display page 15, and ask students where this part of the story takes place. *on the beach* Ask them what they see in the picture. Do they see the wind? The lighthouse? The bird? How many boats are in the picture? *two* Are both boats toys? *No; one is a real boat.*

Sentences: Periods

Display pages 16, 17, and 19 of the **Big Book,** and have volunteers point to the first and last words in each sentence: page 16— *And, too; First, how;* page 17—*Then, me; And, blur;* page 19—*But, color; Then, hand.* Have volunteers point to the periods at the ends of sentences and say *This is a period.*

Comprehension Strategies

Teacher Modeling

8 Predicting *We know in the fall leaves are all over the ground. We also know that this wind hasn't been very helpful. I predict Wind will blow these leaves all over the place and ruin Gilberto's neat pile. Who else wants to make a prediction? Let's read some more to find out.*

9 Predicting *We were right! Leaves don't stay in neat piles when the wind is around. The wind scatters them all about.*

When the leaves have fallen off the trees I like to sweep them into a pile. But then Wind comes along. **8**

20

And just to show that he can sweep without a broom, Wind scatters the leaves all about again. And he blows the dirt in my face. **9**

21

Sometimes Wind is so strong he starts breaking the trees and knocking down fences. Then I'm afraid. I run in the house and lock the door. And when Wind comes howling after me and tries to squeeze in through the keyhole, I tell him, "No!"

22

But then comes a day when Wind is all tired out. "Wind," I whisper. "Oh, Wind! Where are you?" "Sh-sh-sh-sh," answers Wind, and he stirs one dry leaf to show where he is. So I lie down beside him and we both go to sleep— under the willow tree.

23

Windy Days Big Book, pp. 20–23

 Teacher Tip

COMPREHENSION Encourage students to be active readers. Active readers interact with the text as they read—by emoting, reacting, responding, and problem solving—in their efforts to construct and maintain meaning.

Print and Book Awareness

Sentences, Directionality

Display page 22 of the **Big Book,** and have volunteers show where to start reading each sentence and where to stop. Have each volunteer run his or her hand under each line of print.

Alphabetic Knowledge

Have volunteers come to the **Big Book** and point to and say the names of any letters or words they recognize on pages 20–23.

Discussing the Selection

✦ Review the Focus Question with students: How does the wind play with Gilberto? *Wind allows Gilberto to sail his toy boat. Wind also turns his pinwheel.*

✦ Have students visit the school library and choose a fiction selection to read for pleasure.

Vocabulary Review

Review with students the selection vocabulary words *gentle, floats, pasture,* and *unlatched.* Ask students the following questions:

- *What does a gentle breeze feel like?*
- *What is something that floats in the wind?*
- *What kinds of animals might we see in a pasture?*
- *Why would we want to keep something unlatched?*

Language Arts

OBJECTIVES

Students will
✦ create a web of prior knowledge.
✦ generate research concepts.
✦ identify the problem in story plot.
✦ identify a minor story line.

MATERIALS

✦ *Transparency* 46
✦ *Story Lines Big Book,* p. 32

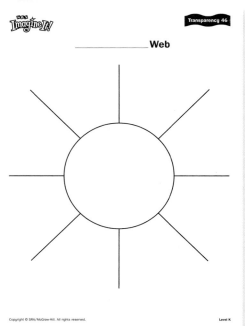

_____ **Web**

Level K

Transparency 46

Traits of Good Writing

Organizing and Ideas Writers use graphic organizers, such as webs, to help organize their ideas before beginning to write.

 Teacher Tip

WORKSHOP PLANNER During Workshop, students can learn about line graphs as another way to generate ideas and give information in writing. Students can participate in the creation of a line graph and use it to create a simple summary of the class's favorite color.

Writing Process

Prewrite: Creating a Web

Teach

✦ Remind students the class is working together to write a report about windy days.

✦ Display **Transparency** 46, the word web you created in the previous lesson as a model. Ask students what they remember about the model. *Webs can help keep track of ideas. This web is about spiders.* Take a few moments to review the model.

Guided Practice

✦ Display **Transparency** 46. Tell students the class will use this web to help them think of and keep track of their ideas for writing the report.

✦ Pointing to the Listening Icons, remind students to listen carefully.

✦ Ask students to look at the middle circle, and ask them what words you should write there to describe the report on windy days. Write in the circle any appropriate words to represent the topic.

✦ Ask students to share anything they already know about windy days, and write one idea in a circle. Then invite students to generate questions or concepts about that aspect of the topic, and write those ideas in an attached circle.

✦ Guide students in keeping the web as simple as possible. Paraphrase their ideas, or combine similar ones. In the next lesson you will use the ideas and concepts recorded in the web to help generate research questions. Save the web for the next class.

Story Crafting 🕐

Story Lines

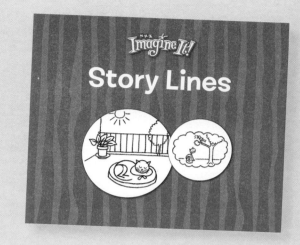

Story Lines Big Book, pp. 32–39

✦ Display the **Story Lines Big Book,** and open it to page 32, "Oliver and the Wind Storm." Tell students you will read aloud the story and they should look at the story frames as you read. As you read the captions, point to each corresponding frame.

✦ When you finish reading, invite a volunteer to come to the **Story Lines Big Book** and to point to a frame in which Oliver runs into a problem.

✦ Take a few moments to discuss how Oliver's dream is like a story within a story. Break down the idea into simple terms for students:

- Point out how the story begins with Oliver taking a nap. Write on the board the words *Frame 1,* and then draw a straight line across the board.

- *Then we learn that Oliver is dreaming about catching the pesky robin, which is another story.* Draw a second line that begins on the first line, travels upward, and then runs parallel to the first line. Where the line begins, write the words *Frame 2.*

- Again point to Frame 3, and discuss how the problem of the wind is introduced here.

- Then point to Frame 4, and discuss how the second story—Oliver's dream—is no longer continued in this frame. Draw an *X* at the end of the second line on the board, and write *Frame 4.*

✦ Explain to students that Oliver's problem with the wind becomes big when he wakes up from his dream. Review the next several frames, and discuss how these frames tell more about the problem.

✦ Tell students they will continue working with Oliver's story in the next lesson.

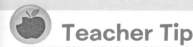 **Teacher Tip**

STORY WITHIN A STORY In real life, events might happen during other events. Tell students if they go home tonight and tell their families about Oliver's story, they are telling a story within a story. The main story they are telling could have the title "What I Did at School Today," and Oliver's story is a part of that story.

Sounds and Letters

OBJECTIVES

Students will
- replace initial phonemes.
- replace final phonemes to make new words.
- attach the /ē/ sound to the letter *Ee.*
- identify the /ē/ sound in print.

MATERIALS
- ***Alphabet Letter Card*** *Ee* for each student
- ***Skills Practice 2,*** p. 100
- ***Pickled Peppers Big Book,*** p. 43

Calendar

Su	M	T	W	Th	F	S
		1	2	3	4	5
6	7	8	9	10	11	12
13	14	15	16	17	18	19
20	21	22	23	24	25	26
27	28	29	30	31		

Point to the box that represents today. Review the names of seasons with students, having them say each aloud with you. Then have students identify the letters and sounds in the words.

Differentiating Instruction English Learners

IF . . . students are native Spanish speakers, **THEN . . .** they may have difficulty pronouncing the /h/ sound. In Spanish, the letter *h* is always silent. Provide native Spanish speakers with extra practice pronouncing /h/ in simple words such as *hot, hail, hoot,* and *high.*

Warming Up

MORNING MESSAGE

Today is ________.

What things make you happy?

Kindergarten News

- Copy the text above on the board or on chart paper. Ask students to identify any words they can read on their own.
- Ask students to share things that make them happy. Assist students in writing their answers on the board below the question.
- Use prompts such as the following to discuss the letters and words in the message: *Can you find any words that begin with the letter* Hh? happy *Come circle them. Can you hear the /ā/ sound in any words?* make *Come underline the letters that make the sound.*

Phoneme Replacement

- Tell students they are going to play the Rhyme game.
- Say the word *turn.* Then ask *What rhymes with* turn *but starts with /l/?* learn
- Continue with these words and sounds:

rink /s/ sink   *hint /m/* mint
rent /l/ lent   *tick /k/* kick

Phonemic Awareness

Phoneme Replacement: Final Sounds

✦ Bring out the **Lion Puppet,** and remind students for his new game, the puppet will say a word and an ending sound. Then they can use that ending sound to make a new word from the old one.

✦ Say the word *can,* and then repeat the final sound: /n/. Have students repeat the word and the sound. Then say the /b/ sound, and ask students what word they make when they replace the ending sound in *can,* /n/, with /b/. *cab* Change the final sound to /p/, and ask for the new word. *cap*

✦ Continue with these words and sound changes:

cut, /b/ cub, */p/* cup	*pill, /n/* pin, */t/* pit
sod, /p/ sop, */b/* sob	*cot, /b/* cob, */d/* cod
man, /t/ mat, */p/* map	

🍎 Teacher Tip

REPLACING SOUNDS If students are still having difficulty replacing sounds, you can continue to help them identify and write the letters that make up each word, and then have them rewrite the word with the new letter/sound. Remember, however, that the goal is to omit the visual step and to have all students succeed with auditory discrimination.

Teacher Tip

HOMEWORK Encourage students to listen for the long *e* sound at home this evening. They might notice their family members or people on television saying words with the sound. Ask students to have a family member help them write three words that use the long *e* sound.

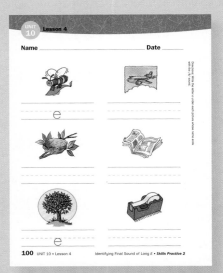

Skills Practice 2, p. 100

Monitor Progress ✓

to Differentiate Instruction
Formal Assessment

Letter and Sound Identification Note how quickly students identify the /ē/ sound.

APPROACHING LEVEL	
IF ... students are still having difficulty,	THEN ... refer to Unit 10 Lesson 4 of the **Intervention Guide** for additional activities.

ON LEVEL	
IF ... students need more practice,	THEN ... have them use **eSkills.**

ABOVE LEVEL	
IF ... students are comfortable,	THEN ... have them work independently to find words with the /ē/ sound in classroom print.

Alphabetic Principle 🕐

Reviewing the Sound of Long *Ee*

Point to **Alphabet Sound Wall Card** Long *Ee*, and have students recite the rhyme for the sounds of *Ee*:

> E's *my name.*
> *Two sounds for me:*
> *Short* e *in* hen,
> *Long* e *in* me.

Listening for Medial /ē/

Give each student an **Alphabet Letter Card** *Ee*. Ask students to raise the cards and say /ē/ when they hear a word with the /ē/ sound. Try the following words:

peck	**Pete**	*feet*	*spell*
these	*rent*	***sneak***	***secret***
tent	***zebra***	*very*	*helpful*

Linking the Sound to the Letter

✦ Write a pair of words on the board, with one of the words including the /ē/ sound. Say the word with the /ē/ sound for each word pair. Then ask students to identify the word you said by signaling thumbs-up and saying the sound when you point to it. Remind students the /ē/ sound is written as *e*, so they should be looking for that letter in the part of the word where they hear /ē/. Have volunteers underline the letter that makes the /ē/ sound.

react ... roast	*prefix* ... private
anvil ... *evil*	*me* ... Ma
cedar ... radar	local ... *legal*

✦ Complete the activity by having students use **Skills Practice 2** page 100. Review their work after they have finished.

Pickled Peppers Big Book

✦ Display the **Pickled Peppers Big Book,** and ask students to say the name of the book.

✦ Turn to page 43, "Little Pine." Point to the title, and read it aloud. Invite students to share anything they remember about the rhyme.

✦ Tell students you will play "Little Pine" on the **Listening Library CD** and you would like them to listen for the words with the /ē/ sound. Ask students to close their eyes as they listen.

✦ Invite students to say any /ē/ words they noticed while listening.

✦ Reread the rhyme, pointing to each word as you say it. This time, ask students to stop you each time you point to a word with the letter *e* in it. *Little, pine, tree, few, feet, doesn't, even, have, yet, keep, measuring, myself, the, more, slower* When you pause, ask students if they hear the /ē/ sound in the word. When you find a word with the /ē/ sound, have students stand up tall like a pine tree and say aloud the letter's name: *EEEEEEEE!*

Pickled Peppers Big Book, p. 43

 Teacher Tip

PRINT AND BOOK AWARENESS Throughout *SRA Imagine It!* various activities are dedicated to teaching students print and book awareness. However, any activity that has students interacting with books and print can be a teaching opportunity. Remember to have students identify print features each time you use a **Big Book** or a trade book. For example, you might ask students to identify capitalized words and punctuation marks in "Little Pine."

Technology

Use the **Listening Library CD** to support the **Pickled Peppers Big Book** lessons.

Audio CD

OBJECTIVES

Students will

✦ develop an understanding of vocabulary words.
✦ review the comprehension strategies Clarifying and Predicting.
✦ use the comprehension skill Cause and Effect.
✦ analyze the author's development of the theme.

MATERIALS

✦ **Windy Days Big Book,** pp. 4–23
✦ Routines 5–7

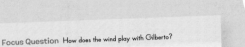

Focus Question How does the wind play with Gilberto?

Gilberto and the Wind

by Marie Hall Ets
illustrated by Loretta Krupinski

I hear Wind whispering at the door.
"You-ou-ou," he whispers. "You-ou-ou-ou!"
So I get my balloon, and I run out to play.

4

Windy Days Big Book, p. 4

Vocabulary

fall	pile
burst	scatters

Preview and Prepare

2nd READ

Preview the Selection ROUTINE 5

✦ Display the **Windy Days Big Book,** opened to the Table of Contents page. Use Routine 5, the previewing the selection routine, to guide students in understanding and using the Table of Contents. Then turn to the selection, and say the title and the names of the author and the illustrator.

✦ As you prepare to reread the selection, have students use the illustrations to retell the main events from the selection.

Vocabulary ROUTINE 6

✦ Follow Routine 6, the selection vocabulary routine, as you introduce the vocabulary words for this selection.

✦ Tell students *fall* is the season following summer. Then have students say the names of all the seasons.

✦ Explain that the word *burst* means "to break open." Use the following sentence to illustrate: *When balloons hit something sharp, they burst.*

✦ Tell students a *pile* is many things lying on top of each other. Use the following sentence to illustrate: *Please pick up the pile of clothes on the floor.*

✦ Explain that the word *scatters* means "spreads around." Tell students the wind scatters leaves all around.

Read the Selection

ROUTINE **7**

Comprehension Strategies

✦ During the first reading of "Gilberto and the Wind," you introduced and modeled the following comprehension strategies:

- Clarifying
- Predicting

✦ In this second reading of the selection, you will revisit each comprehension strategy model from the first reading.

Comprehension Skills

In this lesson of "Gilberto and the Wind," students will focus on the comprehension skill Cause and Effect.

Reading with a Writer's Eye

✦ In this rereading of "Gilberto and the Wind," you will discuss how the author develops the theme of the selection.

✦ As students analyze the author's writing techniques, they become more aware of ways to improve their own writing.

Concept/Question Board

Tell students readers keep thinking about questions generated as they are reading. As they read, tell them to keep in mind the questions on the **Concept/Question Board.** Explain that readers are always thinking about and trying to remember what is important in selections.

Technology

To promote independent reading, encourage students to use Workshop to listen to the recording of the selection on the *Listening Library CD.* Invite them to follow along and say the words whenever they can.

Audio CD

Comprehension Strategies

Teacher Modeling

❶ Predicting *Readers often make predictions about what will happen next in a story. We talked about how the wind moves sometimes and about how it took Gilberto's balloon. Then we predicted Wind would do something that isn't nice. Making predictions helps us think more about the story and makes us want to keep reading to check our predictions.*

❷ Clarifying *When we weren't sure what a pillow slip was, we remembered that readers reread the page and look at the pictures to clarify something. We did that, and it helped us understand that we did know what a pillow slip was, but we called it by a different name.*

❸ Predicting *When we read this page, we were able to check our prediction about the wind. Wind pulled out the clothespins and then broke Gilberto's umbrella. I know that our predictions don't always happen, but this time it did. By making and checking our prediction, we understood the story better.*

Differentiating Instruction **English Learners**

IF ... students have limited vocabulary, **THEN ...** they may not be familiar with the verbs *shake* and *twist*. Ask English speakers to model the meaning of each word for their English Learner classmates.

Focus Question How does the wind play with Gilberto?

Gilberto and the Wind

by Marie Hall Ets
illustrated by Loretta Krupinski

I hear Wind whispering at the door. "You-ou-ou," he whispers. "You-ou-ou-ou!" So I get my balloon, and I run out to play.

4

At first Wind is gentle and just floats my balloon around in the air. But then, with a jerk, he grabs it away and carries it up to ❶ the top of a tree. "Wind! Oh, Wind!" I say. "Blow it back to me! Please!" But he won't. He just laughs and whispers, "You-ou-ou-ou!"

5

Wind loves to play with the wash on the line. He blows the pillow slips into balloons and shakes the sheets and twists the apron strings. ❷

6

And he pulls out all the clothespins that he can. Then he tries on the clothes— though he knows they're too small.

7

 Teacher Tip

GLOSSARY The words *fall*, *burst*, and *pile* can be found in the Glossary of the *Windy Days Big Book.*

And Wind loves umbrellas. Once when I took one out in the rain he tried to take it away from me. And when he couldn't, he broke it. **3**

8

If the gate in the pasture is left unlatched, Wind plays with that, too. He opens it up, then bangs it shut, making it squeak and cry. "Wind! Oh, Wind!" I say, and I go and climb on. "Give me a ride!" But with me on it the gate is too heavy. Wind can't move it at all.

9

When the grass is tall in the meadow Wind and I like to race. Wind runs ahead, then comes back and starts over.

10

But he always wins, because he just runs over the top of the grass and I have to run through it and touch the ground with my feet.

11

Windy Days Big Book, pp. 4–11

Comprehension Skills

Cause and Effect

✦ When one thing makes something else happen, the first thing is called the *cause,* and the second thing is called the *effect.*

✦ Help students use the selection to find the answers to these cause-and-effect questions:

- *What causes Gilberto to have trouble holding his umbrella?* *The wind is trying to blow it away.*

- *What happens when the wind blows against the unlatched pasture gate?* *The gate squeaks and bangs shut.*

Reading with a Writer's Eye

Theme

✦ Explain to students that every story has a *theme*—a message or lesson the author wants readers to take away with them when they finish reading the story.

✦ Ask students what the story is about. Point out that the author has a lot to say about Wind and that she does this by treating Wind as a story character with a personality. Explain that we learn about Wind the same way that we learn about another person—by observing how he behaves.

✦ To help students understand, ask the following questions: *How is the wind gentle? How is the wind mean? How is the wind playful?*

2nd READ

Comprehension Strategies

Teacher Modeling

4 **Predicting** *Here I thought about the way Wind was acting with the big boys and predicted he would act the same way with his friend, Gilberto.*

5 **Predicting** *When I read more of the story, I found out my prediction was not confirmed. Wind did not help Gilberto fly his kite at all. That happens sometimes. It's still a good idea to think about the story and predict what you think will happen next.*

6 **Clarifying** *Does anyone remember how we figured out what* blur *means? When we didn't understand what a* blur *was, we decided to reread the sentences on the page and to look at the picture again. By rereading, we were able to clarify the meaning of the word and to understand the story better. Remember, a* blur *is something moving so fast that it's hard to see what it is.*

7 **Clarifying** *I wasn't sure how the wind could carry the bubbles, so I looked at the picture and saw the bubbles floating in the air. Looking at the picture helped me figure out what was happening. This helped me understand what Gilberto meant.*

When the big boys on the hill have kites to fly Wind helps them out. Wind carries their kites way up to the sky and all around. **4**

12

But when I have a kite Wind won't fly it at all. He just drops it. "Wind! Oh, Wind!" I say, "I don't like you today!" **5**

13

When the apples are ripe in the fall, I run with Wind to the pasture and wait under the tree. And Wind always blows one down for me.

14

And when I have a boat with a paper sail Wind comes and sails it for me—just as he sails big sailboats for sailors on the sea.

15

Vocabulary Tip

Review the meaning of the word *fall*. Then have students use the word in a sentence.

And when I have a pinwheel Wind comes and plays, too. First I blow it myself to show him how.

16

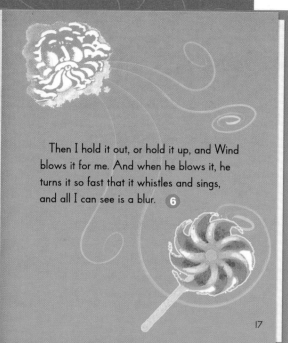

Then I hold it out, or hold it up, and Wind blows it for me. And when he blows it, he turns it so fast that it whistles and sings, and all I can see is a blur. **6**

17

Wind likes my soap bubbles best of all. *He* can't make the bubbles—*I* have to do that.

18

7 But he carries them way up into the air for the sun to color. Then he blows some back and makes me laugh when they burst in my eyes or on the back of my hand.

19

Windy Days Big Book, pp. 12–19

Vocabulary Tip
Review the meaning of the word *burst*. Then have students use the word in a sentence.

Comprehension Skills

Cause and Effect

Help students use the selection to find the answers to these cause-and-effect questions:

- *What causes the big boys' kites to fly high in the sky?* *The wind is blowing.*
- *What causes Gilberto's kite to fall to the ground?* *The wind is not blowing.*
- *What causes Gilberto's boat to move?* *The wind pushes against the sails.*
- *What happens when the wind blows against Gilberto's pinwheel?* *It turns so fast it whistles and sings and looks like a blur.*
- *What happens when the wind blows bubbles into Gilberto's face?* *The bubbles burst and make Gilberto laugh.*

Reading with a Writer's Eye

Theme

The author continues to develop Wind's personality on these pages. Ask students the following questions to help them understand:

- *What do pages 12 and 13 tell you about Wind?*
- *How is Wind helpful on pages 14–17?*
- *How is Wind playful on page 19?*

Comprehension Strategies

Teacher Modeling

8 Predicting *Here we predicted Wind would blow the leaves in Gilberto's pile all over the place. To make this prediction, we used information we already knew about Wind. Making predictions helps us think more about the story. It also makes us more interested in reading on to find out if our prediction is confirmed.*

9 Predicting *Our prediction was confirmed. Wind scattered the leaves all around.*

When the leaves have fallen off the trees I like to sweep them into a pile. But then Wind comes along. **8**

20

And just to show that he can sweep without a broom, Wind scatters the leaves all about again. And he blows the dirt in my face. **9**

21

Sometimes Wind is so strong he starts breaking the trees and knocking down fences. Then I'm afraid. I run in the house and lock the door. And when Wind comes howling after me and tries to squeeze in through the keyhole, I tell him, "No!"

22

But then comes a day when Wind is all tired out. "Wind," I whisper. "Oh, Wind! Where are you?" "Sh-sh-sh-sh," answers Wind, and he stirs one dry leaf to show where he is. So I lie down beside him and we both go to sleep— under the willow tree.

23

Windy Days Big Book, pp. 20–23

 Teacher Tip

COMPREHENSION STRATEGIES Readers are good listeners. Reading aloud to students provides an opportunity to teach the reader responses and problem-solving strategies readers employ. In addition to reading aloud with expression and enthusiasm, model your own comprehension strategies while reading aloud to students. This makes the use of strategies "real" for students and encourages them to begin to respond to text similarly.

Reading with a Writer's Eye

Theme

✦ The author continues to develop Wind's personality on these pages. Ask students the following questions to help them understand:

- *How is Wind not helpful on page 21?*
- *How is Wind strong and mean?*

✦ Ask students what message the author shares about the wind through the different ways the character Wind behaves. Encourage students to express the story's message or theme in one sentence.

Discussing the Selection

Help students summarize the story by naming some of the good things Wind does. Ask students to name some of the bad things Wind does.

Purposes for Reading

✦ Remind students that they listened to this selection to learn more about the wind. Then ask them what new information they learned.

✦ Ask students to share what they liked best about "Gilberto and the Wind."

Vocabulary Review

Review with students the selection vocabulary words *fall, burst, pile,* and *scatters.* Ask students the following questions:

- *What kinds of things can we see in the fall?*
- *When was a time you saw or heard something burst?*
- *What kinds of things can we stack in a pile?*
- *What happens when something scatters?*

BIG Idea

Why do we have wind?

Write the Big Idea question on the board. Ask students what they learned about wind. Ask which selections added something new to their understanding of wind. Encourage students to share their thoughts about the unit so far.

Students will
✦ brainstorm research goals.
✦ formulate research questions.
✦ review capital letters and question marks.
✦ identify the resolution in a story plot.

✦ *Language Arts Big Book,* pp. 56–57
✦ *Skills Practice 2,* p. 101
✦ *Story Lines Big Book,* p. 32

Writing Process

Model: Brainstorming Goals and Generating Questions

Teach

Remind students the class is working together to write a report about windy days. Tell students they must first make a plan for research.

Guided Practice

✦ Display the "spider" word web that the class created. Point to one of the concepts that you recorded, and discuss with students how you might turn that concept into a research question. For example, if the concept is "Spiders have eight legs," you might make a research question that reads *Do all spiders have eight legs?*

✦ Remind students that making a list of questions helps them remember exactly what they want to learn about their topic.

Research in Action

Writing is a self-directed activity that involves deftly juggling a variety of skills, strategies, and knowledge. The writer must make plans, consider the reader, draw ideas from memory, develop new ideas, organize thoughts, consider the conventions of the genre, translate ideas into words, craft sentences, evaluate decisions, make needed revisions, transcribe words into correctly spelled print, and monitor the writing process, among other things. *(Steve Graham and Karen Harris)*

Grammar, Usage, and Mechanics

Teach

✦ Display **Language Arts Big Book** page 56. Ask students if anyone knows what a question is. *It is the kind of sentence that asks something.* Invite a volunteer to come and point to the question on page 56.

✦ Now turn to page 57 of the **Language Arts Big Book,** and read the sentence at the top of the page: *End marks finish sentences.*

✦ Remind students that different kinds of end marks come at the ends of different kinds of sentences. Ask students *What kind of end mark comes at the end of a question?* Have a volunteer come and point to the question mark on the page.

✦ Remind students that capital letters begin sentences. Explain that a capital letter helps show where a new sentence begins. All sentences begin with capital letters. Have a volunteer come and point to the capital letter that begins the question on page 56.

Language Arts Big Book, pp. 56–57

Grammar, Usage, and Mechanics continued

Guided Practice

✦ Have students open their **Skills Practice 2** to page 101.

✦ Work through the page with students, and review their answers when you finish.

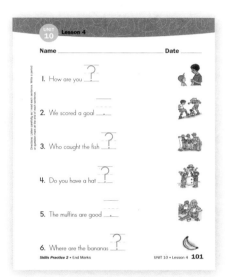

Skills Practice 2, p. 101

Monitor Progress
Formal Assessment ✓

to Differentiate Instruction

Grammar Note how easily students understand what sentences are.

APPROACHING LEVEL

IF ... students are having difficulty,

THEN ... help them complete **Reteach** page 183.

ON LEVEL

IF ... students need more practice,

THEN ... help them create simple sentences.

ABOVE LEVEL

IF ... students are comfortable,

THEN ... have them complete **Challenge Activities** page 139.

Teacher Tip

LINKING PICTURES AND TEXT You might work with students to match key words in the text to the objects in the drawings. For example, in Frame 1, you might call out the words *cat* and *sunny,* and have students point to the cat and the sun in the drawing.

Story Crafting 🕐

Story Lines

✦ In advance of the activity, draw on the board the lines you used in the previous lesson to illustrate the story within a story for "Oliver and the Wind Storm." Display the **Story Lines Big Book,** and open it to page 32. Remind students that this story has a story within a story.

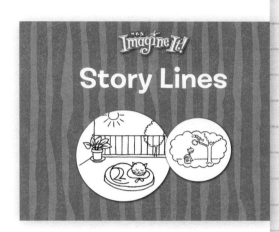

Story Lines Big Book, pp. 32–39

✦ Ask a volunteer to come and point to the story frame in which Oliver gets an idea to solve his problem.

✦ Return to the lines you drew on the board. Below the long line that represents the main story, write the words *Frame 19–Frame 27.* Tell students those frames continue to tell the main story of Oliver and the windstorm.

✦ Now ask students *What happens to the story in Frame 18?* Point out that Oliver's dream is continued. Say *We have another story within a story!*

✦ Return students' attention to the lines on the board. At the end of the line that represents the main story, draw another line that goes up and then parallel.

✦ Turn to page 19 of the **Story Lines Big Book,** and reveal the "Tell Me More" frames to students. Tell them next week they will work to tell more about Oliver's story.

Sounds and Letters

OBJECTIVES

Students will

✦ replace medial phonemes in words to make new words.

✦ attach the /ē/ sound to the letter *Ee*.

✦ review writing the letters *Ss, Mm, Dd, Pp, Aa, Hh, Tt, Nn, Ll,* and *Ii.*

✦ practice writing words they have blended.

✦ read and respond to a **Decodable.**

MATERIALS

✦ *Pocket Chart Letter Cards e, h, m, n, s, t, w*

✦ *Alphabet Letter Card Ee* for each student

✦ Supply Icons

✦ Routines 2, 4

✦ *Skills Practice 2,* p. 102

✦ *Decodable* 20

Calendar

Su	M	T	W	Th	F	S
		1	2	3	4	5
6	7	8	9	10	11	12
13	14	15	16	17	18	19
20	21	22	23	24	25	26
27	28	29	30	31		

Point to the box that represents today. Ask students how many days are in a week. Then ask them how many days are in a month. Discuss how not every month has the same number of days.

Warming Up

MORNING MESSAGE

Today is _____.

Let's write a story!

Once there was a _____.

He/She/It had a very large _____.

One day, he/she/it _____ down the street.

Everyone _____. The end.

Kindergarten News

✦ Copy the text above on the board or on chart paper. Ask students if they can read any words in the message today. Have students point to and say any words they can read.

✦ Ask volunteers to say words to complete the sentences. Have them write the words in the blanks.

✦ Use prompts such as the following to discuss the letters and words in the message: *Can someone find the exclamation point? the second sentence Come circle it. How many syllables are in the word* everyone? *three Let's clap them out.*

Grab Bag of Letters and Words

✦ Put **Pocket Chart Letter Card** *e* in the **Pocket Chart,** or have a student stand in front of the class holding the *e* card. Say /e/, and remind students they can make words by putting letters together. Place on a table where students can reach them the letters *h, m, n, s, t,* and *w.*

Ask *How can we make the word* set? Have a student put the **Letter Card** *s* in the **Pocket Chart** or take it and stand in front of the other students holding the *e* and *t* cards. Ask other students to make *hen, men,* and *wet.*

Phonemic Awareness

Phoneme Replacement: Medial Vowels

✦ Review with students the short-vowel sounds they have been learning. /a/, /e/, /i/, /o/, /u/

✦ Explain to students that the **Lion Puppet** will say a word and that you will say a vowel sound that makes his word into a new word. Tell them you want them to change the sound in the middle to the new vowel and to say that new word.

Puppet:	*sit*
Teacher:	*/a/. What is the new word?*
Students:	*sat*

✦ Continue with these words:

> *hit /a/ hat, /o/ hot, /u/ hut*   *bad /i/ bid, /u/ bud, /e/ bed*
>
> *pat /i/ pit, /e/ pet, /o/ pot*   *dug /o/ dog, /i/ dig*

Differentiating Instruction | **English Learners**

IF ... students have difficulty with the Phonemic Awareness activity, **THEN ...** refer to Unit 10 Lesson 5 of the **English Learner Support Guide.**

 Teacher Tip

PHONEME REPLACEMENT If the class is having difficulty identifying the new words after vowel replacement, write the words on the board, erase the middle phoneme, and then write the new one in its place. Help students blend the new word.

Alphabetic Principle

Reviewing the Sound of Long *Ee*

Point to **Alphabet Sound Wall Card** Long *Ee*, and have students recite the rhyme for the sounds of *Ee*:

E's my name.

Two sounds for me:

Short e *in* hen,

Long e *in* me.

Listening for Medial /ē/

Give each student an **Alphabet Letter Card** *Ee*. Ask students to raise the cards and say /ē/ when they hear a word with the /ē/ sound. Try the following words:

seep	fled	Fred	well
step	**fleet**	belt	spend
lettuce	**cedar**	**complete**	**female**

Blending with the Sound of Long *Ee* **ROUTINE 2**

✦ Remind students when the letter *e* appears at the end of a word, it is often a "signal" that helps us remember that the vowel is long or says its name.

✦ Tell students today they are going to begin blending with the /ē/ sound represented by the letters *e_e*. Write *e_e* on the board. Now write the word *we* on the board. Explain that when the *e* is by itself on the end of a word, it is going to make the long-vowel sound.

✦ Work with students to blend the following words. Refer to the sound-by-sound blending routine.

Eve	*me*
Pete	*he*

✦ Students should reread the words naturally as they would speak them. Have students then say the vowel sound in each word and underline the letter(s) that represents the vowel sound.

✦ When the blending is finished, have students use the words in sentences. Encourage students to extend the sentences by asking them to tell where, why, how, or when. Have them answer in complete sentences.

 Teacher Tip

SUPPLEMENTAL WORDS If additional words are needed for the lesson activity, see the Appendix for a supplemental word list.

Monitor Progress ✓

to Differentiate Instruction
Formal Assessment

Letter and Sound Identification Note how easily students identify the /ē/ sound.

APPROACHING LEVEL

IF ... students are having difficulty,	THEN ... help them complete page 184 in **Reteach.**

ON LEVEL

IF ... students need more practice,	THEN ... make an additional copy of **Skills Practice 2** page 99 for them to use again.

ABOVE LEVEL

IF ... students are comfortable,	THEN ... have them work independently using **eSkills.**

Penmanship

✦ Distribute a sheet of writing paper to each student, or use **White Boards** turned to the sides with writing lines.

✦ Place the Supply Icon for *pencil* on the board or in the **Pocket Chart.**

✦ Using the words *hip, sat, dim, lad,* and *nap,* guide students in blending each word individually. After each word is blended, ask students to practice writing the word on their writing papers. If they need more space, ask them to turn over the papers.

Guided Practice ROUTINE 2

✦ Guide students in completing **Skills Practice 2** page 102 for additional practice blending and writing words.

✦ Read aloud each sentence, and help students blend each word as much as necessary. Allow students time to write the word on the line before moving on to the next word.

✦ When students finish, have them work with partners and proofread their work. Ask each student to circle one word they think they can write better. Have them cross out the word and rewrite it above, below, or next to the first attempt.

✦ After students have finished, review their work, and note which students are struggling with letter formation.

Skills Practice 2, p. 102

 Teacher Tip

MONITOR PROGRESS When working on the **Skills Practice 2** page, you might help students blend words for the first sentence but allow them to attempt reading the others on their own. You might pause before moving on to the next sentence, and ask if students want to blend the word aloud as a class.

Monitor Progress

to Differentiate Instruction
Formal Assessment

Penmanship Note how easily students review the letters.

APPROACHING LEVEL

IF ... students are having difficulty,

THEN ... guide them in completing **Reteach** page 185.

ON LEVEL

IF ... students need more practice,

THEN ... use **eSkills** for additional activities.

ABOVE LEVEL

IF ... students would enjoy a challenging activity,

THEN ... have them work independently to complete **Challenge Activities** page 140.

We Did It!

by Tristan Horrom illustrated by Laura Logan

Decodable 20

 Teacher Tips

PRINT AND BOOK AWARENESS Use *Decodable* 20 to review with students the features of print books. Ask students to identify parts of the book or to locate information in the book on demand. For example, ask them to point to the book's cover or the author's name. Then, ask them to find, point to, and say the page with the word *big* (page 5) or the word *rope* (page 6).

REVIEW Conduct a general review of high-frequency words. Hold up **High-Frequency Flash Cards,** and call on volunteers to read the words on the cards and use them in sentences.

Technology

Use **eDecodable** *We Did It!* with students to reinforce high-frequency words *be* and *she* and the /ē/ sound.

Audio CD

Reading a Decodable

ROUTINE 2   ROUTINE 4

Decodable 20: We Did It!

High-Frequency Words: *be, she*

✦ The high-frequency words introduced are *be* and *she*. Write *be* on the board, and read it aloud. Have students repeat it aloud with you. Then have students say the word on their own. Repeat the process with *she*.

✦ Offer students a few examples of sentences that use *be* and *she*. You might say *We will be happy* or *She has red hair*. Point again to *be* written on the board, and have students read the word independently. Do the same with *she*.

✦ Have students work together in small groups to make sentences using the words *be* and *she*. You might provide frames such as *I can be a _____ .* or *She is _____ .*

✦ Ask them to find and point to the words *be* and *she* on any classroom posters, bulletin boards, or the covers of any books. Review the high-frequency words introduced in previous lessons.

Blending

Before reading **Decodable** 20, blend words from the story that contain the /ē/ sound represented by the letters *e_e*. Words might include *we, Eve,* and *Pete*. After blending, have students make and extend sentences for each word.

Reading Recommendations

✦ Distribute copies of **Decodable** 20. Have students browse the books and look at the pictures, commenting on what they see and making predictions about what they think the story will be about.

✦ Point to the high-frequency words *be* and *she* in the text, and pronounce them. Then have students point to the words and read them aloud.

✦ Hold up your book, and read the title, pointing to each word. Read the names of the author and the illustrator aloud, pointing to each name as you say it. Ask students to explain the jobs of author and illustrator.

✦ Read the **Decodable** with students, following the established procedure. (See Routine 4 for a detailed description.) After you have read the story, reread the title, and have students repeat after you. Then have students read it chorally with you.

We Did It!

by Tristan Horrom   illustrated by Laura Logan

Eve and Pete make a kite.

3

"It can be tan," he said.

4

"It can be big," she said.

5

Here is a rope. Pete tapes it on.

6

She tugs on the kite. Run, Eve, run!

7

The wind takes the kite up! We did it!

8

Decodable 20
We Did It!

High-Frequency Words
Introduced in Decodable 20
be
she

Previously Introduced
High-Frequency Words
a
all
am
and
as
at
boy
but
can
did
do
down
for
girl
go
had
has
have
he
her
him
his
I
in
is
it
little
look
of
on
out

said
see
some
that
the
then
there
they
to
up
was
we
were
what
when
with
you

Sound-Spelling Correspondences in
Decodables
1. /s/, /m/, /d/, /p/, /a/
2. /h/, /t/
3. /n/, /l/
4. /i/
5. /b/, /k/ spelled *c*
6. /o/, /r/
7. /g/
8. /j/, /f/
9. /u/, /ks/ spelled *x*
10. /z/
11. /w/, /k/ spelled *k*
12. /e/, /kw/ spelled *qu*
13. /y/, /v/
14. Long a spelled *a_e*
15. Long i spelled *i_e*
16. Review long a, long i
17. Long o spelled *o, o_e*
18. Long u spelled *u_e*
19. Review long o, long u
20. Long e spelled *e, e_e*

Responding

✦ Display the **High-Frequency Flash Cards** for *be* and *she*. Have students find and point to these high-frequency words in the story. Then have students identify in the story any of the previously introduced high-frequency words.

✦ Ask students to tell about any difficult words they saw in the story. Ask students to explain how they determined the words. Review each word that students identify.

✦ Have students read the words rope, kite, and Pete and point to them. Then have them work as a class to answer the following questions: *On what page does Pete tape the rope on the kite? On what page can you find the word* said?

✦ Have students connect the story to their own experiences. Ask them to share stories about times they flew kites or watched someone do it. They might also enjoy sharing their prior knowledge about how kites use the wind to fly.

✦ Make copies of the story for students to take home after making sure students are comfortable reading their books. A black-and-white version of the story is available in **Pre-Decodable and Decodable Takehomes Blackline Masters.**

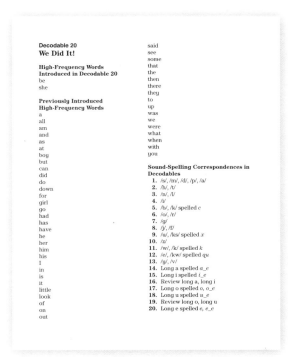

Decodable 20, inside back cover

Reading and Responding

Students will

✦ generate questions about the wind.
✦ conduct experiments with the wind.
✦ record their observations with drawings.
✦ develop an understanding of vocabulary words.

✦ *Windy Days Big Book,* pp. 4–23
✦ Read Aloud Collection: *Can You See the Wind?*

INQUIRY PLANNER

WEEK 1	✦ Begin discussing and sharing ideas. ✦ Think about a question for the **Concept/Question Board.**
WEEK 2	✦ Begin investigating and collecting information. ✦ Generate a question and/or idea for the **Concept/Question Board.**
WEEK 3	✦ Share your findings with others. ✦ Do you have more questions?

Teacher Tip

MATERIALS Activities in this lesson will require drawing paper, markers, and crayons.

Inquiry

✦ Discuss with the class how they could learn more about the wind. If necessary, ask questions such as the following:

  • *What did you learn about how to see the wind in* Can You See the Wind?

  • *What did you learn about things wind can do in "Gilberto and the Wind"?*

  • *How can we find out more about the wind? Whom could we talk to? What experiments could we do?*

✦ Read aloud some of the questions on the **Concept/Question Board,** and encourage the class to think of some possible answers. Using the chart you created, begin writing any answers to their questions they have learned from their reading.

Whole-Group Time Whole Group

✦ Explain to students that they will be investigating the wind in this unit. Using the table you created, review some of the questions. To develop more questions, you may want to ask the following:

  • *What do you wonder about when you feel or hear the wind?*

  • *What do you wonder about when you see the things the wind can do?*

✦ Ask students what kinds of experiments they might do to learn more about the wind and how it works. To help students generate ideas, ask them the following questions:

  • *Where can we find the wind?*

  • *How are wind and other weather related? Is it always windy when it rains?*

✦ Write these new questions on the table as well. Have students identify a question that they would like to investigate. Based upon their answers, have them break into small groups.

Small-Group Time Small Group

✦ Create multiple small groups of three to four students. Review the questions with each group, and have them write what they think the answers might be, given what they already know about the wind. Write their questions on individual sheets of paper, and keep them for use in their presentations. Have groups decide which wind instruments they should make that will help them answer their questions. The instruments might include the following:

- A wind direction indicator (such as a weather vane)
- A pinwheel

✦ Have students take their wind instruments outside and observe what happens. Help them chart what they observe each day when they are outside with their instruments. Discuss what information they get from the different instruments.

✦ Make a chart and collect or record data on the wind each day. The chart could have days down the side and several columns across the top: Weather, Temperature, and Wind. Each day talk about the weather conditions and what the wind is like. At the end of the week, talk about any changes and any surprising things the class observed.

Concept Vocabulary

The first concept vocabulary word for Unit 10, Windy Days, is the word *breezy*. Write the word on an index card, and post it in your classroom. Tell students the word *breezy* means "swept by light, gentle winds." Discuss how the word *breezy* relates to windy days. Use the word in a sentence, and then have students say the word after you. Tell students you will use the word every day, and invite them to do the same.

Differentiating Instruction English Learners

IF ... students have difficulty making oral reports, **THEN ...** encourage them to express their findings and ideas through pictures. Allow them to label their drawings with words from their native languages.

Teacher Tip

RECREATIONAL READING Because it is important to read daily to your students, choose a book from the Additional Reading listed in the Table of Contents, and find a time during the day to read the book aloud to your students.

Concept/Question Board

Remind students the **Concept/Question Board** is a place they can post ideas, questions, drawings, and photographs about the wind. Possibilities include the following:

- Student questions about the wind from the stories or poems
- Student conjectures about the wind
- Student drawings of the effects of the wind
- Pictures from magazines of the wind in action (for example, sailing a boat, blowing clothes on a line, bending trees, and so on)

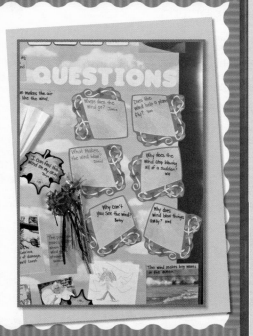

Language Arts

Students will
+ brainstorm research goals.
+ formulate research questions.
+ review extending interrogative sentences.
+ review using sentence frames.
+ review the letters of the alphabet.

+ *Language Arts Big Book,* p. 56
+ Race Track Game Mats
+ *Alphabet Letter Cards*
+ Game markers
+ Number cube

Writing Process

Model: Brainstorming Goals and Generating Questions

Teach

+ Remind students the class is working together to write a report about windy days, and invite a volunteer to say aloud the topic the class has chosen.

+ Tell students today they will begin to make a plan for researching their topic. Again remind them of any relevant experiences they have had this year while performing their unit inquiries.

Guided Practice

+ Display the word web that the class created about the report topic. Review some of the main concepts you explored with the help of the web. Steer students' attention toward concepts you think would work particularly well as research explorations.

+ Help students make a list of questions to explore during the research phase of writing the class report. Write these questions on chart paper, and save it until next week, when the class will continue the writing process.

 ## Teacher Tip

HIGH-FREQUENCY WORDS Ask a volunteer to come to the *Windy Days Big Book* and point to the high-frequency word *be.*

Grammar, Usage, and Mechanics

Teach

Display *Language Arts Big Book* page 56, and ask students to identify the interrogative sentence, or question, on the page. Remind students all sentences begin with capital letters and end with end marks.

Guided Practice

+ Use sentence frames to help students create their own questions. Write the following on the board or on chart paper, and have students fill in the blanks:
  - Do you like _____?
  - What time is _____?
  - How many _____ are in the _____?

+ Continue with other sentence frames that you create. After students have filled in the sentence frames, guide them in extending the sentences by adding more information.

+ For an extra challenge, omit the question marks when you write the sentences on the board. That way, students will have to remember to add them.

Language Arts Big Book, p. 56

GAME Day

Race Track Game

✦ Tell students they will play the Race Track game. Take out the Race Track Game Mats and the **Alphabet Letter Cards.**

✦ Pointing to the Listening Icons, remind students to listen carefully.

✦ Separate the class into several groups, and set up game stations around the room.

✦ Review the rules before students begin playing: To play the game, a player rolls the number cube and moves a marker the correct number of spaces. When a player lands on a space, he or she must draw a card from the pack and identify the letter on the card and the sound the letter makes. If a player cannot correctly identify the letter or sound on the card, the player forfeits the next turn.

✦ If you believe students are ready, you might challenge them to name a word that begins with the letters or the sounds they draw.

✦ If you have adapted the game rules to better suit your class's needs, review these rules instead. Note, however, that students should be required to identify both the letters and the sounds of the cards they choose.

✦ While they play, circulate around the room to make sure students are playing the game properly and to answer any questions that arise.

Teacher Tip

CLASS CHAMPION Remember you can easily organize this Game Day activity into a tournament: The winners from each game station can play a "championship" game as the rest of the class watches. The winner of that game can have the title of Race Track Champion.

Differentiating Instruction **English Learners**

IF ... students have had difficulty with some letter names and sounds, **THEN ...** review these with students before beginning the game. You may also wish to review counting.

Lesson Planner

Day 1

Day 2

Sounds and Letters

MATERIALS

- *Alphabet Letter Cards*
- Routine 2
- *Pickled Peppers Big Book,* pp. 28–41, 44
- *Skills Practice 2,* pp. 103, 104, 107–108

Day 1

Warming Up, pp. T92–T93
Phonemic Awareness
Phoneme Deletion: Initial Sounds, p. T93
Phonics
- Word Building, p. T94
- Oral Language and Sentence Extension, p. T95
Alphabetic Principle
- Reviewing the Short and Long Sounds of *Aa,* p. T96
- Listening for /a/ and /ā/, p. T96
- Blending, p. T96
- Penmanship, p. T97

Day 2

Warming Up, p. T104
Phonemic Awareness
Phoneme Deletion: Initial Sounds, p. T105
Phonics
- Word Building, p. T106
- Oral Language and Sentence Extension, p. T107
Alphabetic Principle
- Reviewing the Short and Long Sounds of *Ii,* p. T108
- Listening for /i/ and /ī/, p. T108
- Blending, p. T108
- Pickled Peppers Big Book, p. T109

Reading and Responding

MATERIALS

- *Windy Days Big Book*
- Routines 5–7
- *Read Aloud Collection: Can You See the Wind?*
- *Home Connection,* pp. 79–80

Poetry
- Activate Prior Knowledge, p. T98
- Preview the Poem, p. T98
Vocabulary, p. T99
Read the Poem, p. T99
Comprehension Strategies, p. T100
Discussing the Poem, p. T101
Vocabulary Review, p. T101

Preview and Prepare, p. T110
Vocabulary, p. T111
Read the Selection, p. T111
Comprehension Strategies, pp. T112, T114, T116
Print and Book Awareness, pp. T113, T115, T117
Discussing the Selection, p. T117
Vocabulary Review, p. T117

1st READ

Language Arts

MATERIALS

- *Language Arts Big Book,* pp. 6, 56
- *Windy Days Big Book,* pp. 5, 48
- *Willy the Wisher,* p. 93
- *Story Lines Big Book,* p. 32
- *Skills Practice 2,* pp. 105–106
- *Transparency* 47
- *Alphabet Sound Cards*

Writing Process
Prewrite: Brainstorming Ideas and Forming Hypotheses, p. T102
Fine Art
Discussing Fine Art, p. T103

Writing Process
Prewrite: Finding and Answering Questions, p. T118
Grammar, Usage, and Mechanics, p. T118
Willy the Wisher, p. T119

Monitor Progress

✓ = Formal Assessment

Ⓑ = Benchmark Assessment

✓ Blending, p. T94
✓ Letter and Sound Review, p. T96

✓ Blending, p. T106

Day 3

Warming Up, p. T120
Phonemic Awareness
Phoneme Deletion: Final Sounds, p. T121
Phonics
• Word Building, p. T122
• Oral Language and Sentence Extension, p. T123
Alphabetic Principle
• Reviewing the Short and Long Sounds of *Aa* and *Ii*, p. T124
• Listening for Medial /ā/ and /ī/, p. T124
• Linking the Sound to the Letter, p. T124
• Penmanship, p. T125

Preview and Prepare, p. T126
Vocabulary, p. T126
Read the Selection, p. T127
Comprehension Strategies, pp. T128, T130, T132
Comprehension Skills, pp. T129, T131
Reading with a Writer's Eye, pp. T129, T131, T133
Discussing the Selection, p. T133
Vocabulary Review, p. T133

Writing Process
Prewrite: Finding Information and Answering Questions, p. T134
Story Crafting
Story Lines Big Book, p. T135

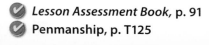 *Lesson Assessment Book,* p. 91
✓ Penmanship, p. T125

Day 4

Warming Up, pp. T136–T137
Phonemic Awareness
Phoneme Deletion: Final Sounds, p. T137
Phonics
• Word Building, p. T138
• Oral Language and Sentence Extension, p. T139
Alphabetic Principle
• Reviewing the Short and Long Sounds of *Oo*, p. T140
• Listening for /o/ and /ō/, p. T140
• Blending, p. T140
• *Pickled Peppers Big Book,* p. T141

Poetry
• Activate Prior Knowledge, p. T142
• Preview the Poem, p. T142
Vocabulary, p. T143
Read the Poem, p. T143
Comprehension Strategies, p. T144
Discussing the Poem, p. T145
Vocabulary Review, p. T145

Writing Process
Model: Summarizing and Sequencing, p. T146
Grammar, Mechanics, and Usage, pp. T146–T147
Story Crafting
Story Lines Big Book, p. T147

✓ Visualizing, p. T145
✓ Punctuation, p. T147

Day 5

Warming Up, pp. T148–T149
Phonemic Awareness
Phoneme Deletion: Internal Sounds, p. T149
Phonics
• Word Building, p. T150
• Oral Language and Sentence Extension, p. T151
Alphabetic Principle
• Reviewing the Short and Long Sounds of *Uu*, p. T152
• Listening for /u/ and /ū/, p. T152
• Blending, p. T152
• Penmanship, p. T153

Inquiry
• Small-Group Time, p. T154
• Whole-Group Time, p. T155
• Concept Vocabulary, p. T155

Writing Process
Draft: Collaborating to Write Report, p. T156
Grammar, Usage, and Mechanics, p. T156
Game Day
Letter Lists, p. T157

Comprehension Observation Log
✓ Blending, p. T153

Big Books   Audio CD

Big Book Selection

Windy Days Big Book

What Happens When Wind Blows?
by Daphne Butler, pp. 26–45

Teacher Support

Language Arts Big Book

Teacher's Resource Book

Willy the Wisher

Curriculum Connections

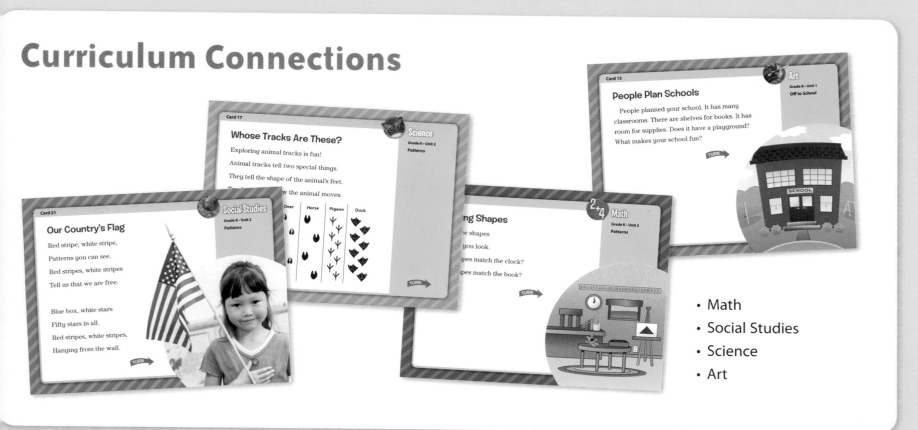

Card 17

Whose Tracks Are These?

Science
Grade K • Unit 2
Patterns

Exploring animal tracks is fun!

Animal tracks tell two special things.

They tell the shape of the animal's feet.

the animal moves.

| Deer | Horse | Pigeon | Duck |

TURN

Card 21

Our Country's Flag

Social Studies
Grade K • Unit 2
Patterns

Red stripe, white stripe,

Patterns you can see.

Red stripes, white stripes

Tell us that we are free.

Blue box, white stars

Fifty stars in all.

Red stripes, white stripes,

Hanging from the wall.

TURN

ing Shapes

2+4 Math
Grade K • Unit 2
Patterns

ee shapes

you look.

pes match the clock?

pes match the book?

TURN

Card 15

Art
Grade K • Unit 1
Off to School

People Plan Schools

People planned your school. It has many classrooms. There are shelves for books. It has room for supplies. Does it have a playground? What makes your school fun?

TURN

SCHOOL

- Math
- Social Studies
- Science
- Art

Additional Skills Practice

Approaching Level	On Level	English Learner	Above Level
Reteach	**Skills Practice 2**	**English Learner Support Activities**	**Challenge Activities**
Blending, pp. 186–187, 190	Blending, pp. 104, 107–108	Lessons 6–10	Blending, p. 143
Penmanship, p. 188	Letter and Sound Review, p. 103		Letter and Sound Review, p. 141
Punctuation, p. 189	Punctuation, pp. 105–106		Punctuation, p. 142

Differentiating Instruction
for Workshop

Day 1

Approaching Level	On Level	English Learner	Above Level
Sounds and Letters			
Alphabetic Principle: Using **Alphabet Sound Card** Long *Aa,* students walk around the classroom, matching the letter with classroom labels, posters, or books and saying the /ā/ sound.	**Alphabetic Principle:** Students look through the **Windy Days Little Big Book** for the letter *Aa* and identify the short and long sounds when possible.	**Alphabetic Principle:** Refer to Unit 10 Lesson 6 of the **English Learner Support Guide.**	**Alphabetic Principle:** Have students work independently to complete **Challenge Activities** page 141.
Reading and Responding			
Comprehension: Browse the poem "Go Wind." Have students look at the illustrations and discuss what items in the poem are being blown around by the wind.	**Comprehension:** Give students a scene in nature in which there is a lot of wind, and have them draw the scene.	**Comprehension:** Refer to Unit 10 Lesson 6 of the **English Learner Support Guide.**	**Comprehension:** Have students create their own poetry about wind. Act as the students' scribe to write down and post their work.
Language Arts			
Writing: Each student signs his or her name to a copy of the line graph.	**Writing:** Students discuss as a group one question they still have about wind.	**Writing:** With your help, each student signs his or her name to a copy of the line graph.	**Writing:** Discuss with students what they have learned about wind.

Approaching Level	On Level	English Learner	Above Level

Sounds and Letters

Alphabetic Principle: Help students make lists of words with the /ī/ sound.	**Alphabetic Principle:** Students listen to the *Pickled Peppers Big Book* poem "Rhyme" on the *Listening Library CD*.	**Alphabetic Principle:** Refer to Unit 10 Lesson 7 of the *English Learner Support Guide.*	**Alphabetic Principle:** Students use the *Alphabet Sound Card Stories CD* to review the /i/ sound.

Reading and Responding

Comprehension: Students browse the selection "What Happens When Wind Blows?" and formulate questions about anything that confuses them or adds to their wonderings about wind.	**Comprehension:** On chart paper, write words that help students visualize the sights and sounds of wind.	**Comprehension:** Refer to Unit 10 Lesson 7 of the *English Learner Support Guide.*	**Comprehension:** Students retell the selection "What Happens When Wind Blows?" to one another.

Language Arts

Writing: With your help, students think of one question they have about wind. **Grammar:** With your help, students look at the poem "Crick! Crack!" and talk about the punctuation they see.	**Writing:** Students discuss ways to get their questions answered. **Grammar:** Students discuss what they remember about punctuation.	**Writing:** Students think of one question they have about wind. Provide help with vocabulary as needed. **Grammar:** Refer to Unit 10 Lesson 7 of the *English Learner Support Guide.*	**Writing:** Students brainstorm questions they still have about wind. **Grammar:** Students correct a simple sentence that is missing its capital letters.

Differentiating Instruction
for Workshop

Day 3

Approaching Level	On Level	English Learner	Above Level
Sounds and Letters			
Alphabetic Principle: Guide students in completing the activity on page 188 in **Reteach.**	**Alphabetic Principle:** Browse the **Alphabet Book Little Big Book** with partners to find the letters *Aa* and *Ii* and identify the /ā/ and /ī/ sounds.	**Alphabetic Principle:** Refer to Unit 10 Lesson 8 of the **English Learner Support Guide.**	**Alphabetic Principle:** Students work independently with the **eGames** activity for this unit to review long- and short-vowel sounds.
Reading and Responding			
Comprehension: Have students retell the selection "What Happens When Wind Blows?" by using the photographs. Encourage them to point out anything that seems confusing.	**Comprehension:** Have students discuss questions the story raises.	**Comprehension:** Refer to Unit 10 Lesson 8 of the **English Learner Support Guide.**	**Comprehension:** Students draw pictures of other situations where wind is present that was not featured in the story.
Language Arts			
Writing: Students discuss ways they could find answers to their questions about wind.	**Writing:** Students choose one research method and use it to find answers to their questions.	**Writing:** Students discuss ways they could find answers to their questions about wind. Provide options, such as asking yes-no questions, as needed.	**Writing:** Students choose one question the group has about wind and form a hypothesis to answer it.

Day 4

Approaching Level	On Level	English Learner	Above Level

Sounds and Letters

Alphabetic Principle: Refer to Unit 10 Lesson 9 of the *Intervention Guide* for activities to help students.

Alphabetic Principle: Students use the *eGames* activity for practice with the long- and short-vowel sounds.

Alphabetic Principle: Refer to Unit 10 Lesson 9 of the *English Learner Support Guide.*

Alphabetic Principle: Students write words with the /ō/ sound.

Reading and Responding

Preview: Students browse the poem "Crick! Crack!" and point to any words in the poem they recognize.

Preview: Write a word from the poem, and have students work together to find out the meaning.

Preview: Refer to Unit 10 Lesson 9 of the *English Learner Support Guide.*

Preview: Have students draw pictures of how they discovered what the word from the poem "Crick! Crack!" meant.

Language Arts

Writing: With your help, students research their questions about wind.

Grammar: With your help, students complete *Reteach* page 189.

Writing: Students continue to research answers to their questions.

Grammar: Students look at the poem "Crick! Crack!" and point out the punctuation.

Writing: With your help, students research their questions about wind. Provide help with vocabulary as needed.

Grammar: Refer to Unit 10 Lesson 9 of the *English Learner Support Guide.*

Writing: Students discuss with you research ideas they have.

Grammar: Have students work independently to complete *Challenge Activities* page 142.

Differentiating Instruction
for Workshop

Lessons 6-10 Overview

Day 5

Approaching Level	On Level	English Learner	Above Level
Sounds and Letters			
Alphabetic Principle: Review sound-by-sound blending with students, using words from the lesson or the supplemental word list in the Appendix.	**Alphabetic Principle:** Using *Alphabet Sound Card* Long *Uu*, students walk around the classroom, matching the letter with classroom labels, posters, or books and saying the /ū/ sound.	**Alphabetic Principle:** Refer to Unit 10 Lesson 10 of the *English Learner Support Guide.*	**Alphabetic Principle:** Students work independently to complete *Challenge Activities* page 143.
Reading and Responding			
Inquiry: Have students browse the selections they have read so far and draw their questions or wonderings.	**Inquiry:** Students look at the **Concept/Question Board** and see if their questions have been answered and if they have any new questions about the wind.	**Inquiry:** With your help, students generate a list of vocabulary and concepts related to wind.	**Inquiry:** Students think of a windy day and describe their windy day to partners.
Language Arts			
Writing: Students discuss with you the answers they found for their questions. **Grammar:** Refer to Unit 10 Lesson 10 of the *Intervention Guide* for additional support for this Grammar activity.	**Writing:** Students share their discoveries about wind with you. **Grammar:** Students look at the poem "Crick! Crack!" and identify the punctuation.	**Writing:** Students answer yes-no and either-or questions about the information they found. **Grammar:** Refer to Unit 10 Lesson 10 of the *English Learner Support Guide.*	**Writing:** Students begin their research for the group's question. **Grammar:** Students correct a few simple sentences that are missing punctuation.

Resources for
Differentiating Instruction R+I

English Learner

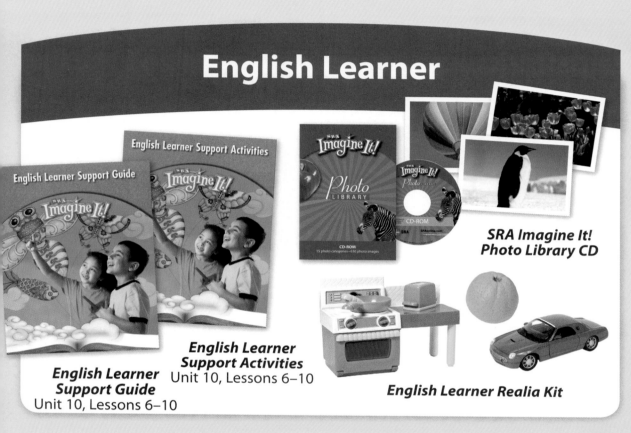

English Learner Support Guide
Unit 10, Lessons 6–10

English Learner Support Activities
Unit 10, Lessons 6–10

SRA Imagine It!
Photo Library CD

English Learner Realia Kit

Approaching Level

Intervention

Intervention Guide

Intervention Workbook

Workshop Kits

- High Frequency Words
- Letter Recognition
- Phonemic Awareness
- Phonics
- Print and Book Awareness
- Sequencing

Technology

Alphabet Sound Card Stories CD
eGames
eSkills & eGames
Listening Library CD

Listening Library Unit 10

Lesson Assessment

Monitor Progress
to Differentiate Instruction

Use these summative assessments along with your informal observations to assess student mastery.

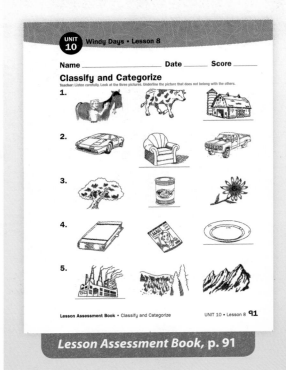

Lesson Assessment Book, p. 91

Lesson Assessment Book

Comprehension Observation Log

Student _____ Date _____

Unit _____ Lesson _____ Selection Title _____

General Comprehension
Concepts discussed: _____

Behavior Within a Group
Articulates, expresses ideas: _____

Joins discussions: _____

Collaborates (such as works well with other students, works alone): _____

Role in Group
Role (such as leader, summarizer, questioner, critic, observer, non-participant): _____

Flexibility (changes roles when necessary): _____

Use of Reading Strategies
Uses strategies when needed (either those taught or student's choice of strategy)/Describes strategies used: _____

Changes strategies when appropriate: _____

Changes Since Last Observation

110   Comprehension Observation Log • **Lesson Assessment Book**

Lesson Assessment Annotated Teacher's Edition, p. 110

The Comprehension Observation Log, found in the **Lesson Assessment Annotated Teacher's Edition,** is a vehicle for recording anecdotal information about individual student performance on an ongoing basis. Information such as students' strengths and weaknesses can be recorded at any time the occasion warrants. It is recommended that you maintain a folder for each student where you can store the logs for purposes of comparison and analysis as the school year progresses. You will gradually build up a comprehensive file that reveals which students are progressing smoothly and which students need additional help.

Sounds and Letters

OBJECTIVES

Students will
✦ manipulate initial phonemes in words.
✦ blend and read words.
✦ review the /a/ and /ā/ sounds.
✦ review writing the letters *Bb, Cc, Oo, Rr,* and *Gg.*
✦ practice writing words they have blended.

MATERIALS
✦ *Alphabet Letter Cards Aa, Mm,* and *Tt* for each student
✦ *Skills Practice 2,* p. 103
✦ Supply Icons
✦ Routine 2

Calendar

Su	M	T	W	Th	F	S
		1	2	3	4	5
6	7	8	9	10	11	12
13	14	15	16	17	18	19
20	21	22	23	24	25	26
27	28	29	30	31		

Point to the box that represents today. Take this opportunity to identify any important events that will happen during the coming week, such as students' birthdays, school functions, and national holidays.

Warming Up

MORNING MESSAGE

Today is _____.

Kate was wearing a cap and a cape.

_____, _____, and _____ rhyme with *bake.*

Kindergarten News

✦ Copy the text above on the board or on chart paper. Make errors in today's Morning Message for students to proofread and correct.

✦ Ask students if they can read any words in today's message. Have them come to the board, point to a word, and say it aloud.

✦ Ask students to proofread any mistakes you might have made in today's message. Invite volunteers to correct your errors.

✦ For the second sentence, ask a volunteer to come and underline the word with the short *a* sound. *cap* Have another volunteer come and circle the words with the long *a* sound. *Kate, cape*

✦ Ask students to think of rhyming words to fill in the blanks.

Phoneme Replacement

✦ Say the name *Willie Winkie,* stressing the initial phoneme: /w/ /w/ /w/ /w/. Say *If your name begins with the same sound as* Willie Winkie, *stand up now.* If necessary, say several names of students in the class, and ask which begins with the /w/ sound. For example, *Does* David *begin with /w/? no /d/ Does* Katie *begin with /w/? no /k/ Does* William *begin with /w/? Yes! Please stand up, William.*

✦ Call on a student whose name does not begin with /w/ to say her or his name. Say the name, then say it again, replacing the initial sound with /w/. If students are sensitive about being given a silly name, then provide names outside those in the class.

Callie, Wallie	*Jimmy, Wimmy*
Paul, Wall	*Stephie, Wephie*

Phonemic Awareness

Phoneme Deletion: Initial Sounds

✦ Bring out the **Lion Puppet,** and tell students he wants to play the game in which he takes away sounds from words to make new words.

✦ Say a word, have students repeat it, and then have the puppet tell students to take away the beginning sound to make a new word. Everyone will then say the new word. For example:

Teacher: *The word is* clip.

Students: *clip*

Puppet: *Say clip without the /k/.*

Everyone: *lip*

✦ Continue with these words:

trail /t/ rail	*swipe /s/ wipe*
mask /m/ ask	*grind /g/ rind*
twin /t/ win	*black /b/ lack*
drink /d/ rink	*crib /k/ rib*
smile /s/ mile	*clap /k/ lap*

Teacher Tips

PHONICS These initial Phonics activities will build on skills students have already been practicing, such as blending and extending sentences.

WRITING AND SPELLING The Word-Building game gives students an opportunity to use the knowledge they gained from the segmentation exercises they completed in earlier lessons. Whereas decoding requires us to blend phonemes to make familiar words, spelling and writing require us to segment familiar words into their separate phonemes. The game is a fast-paced activity in which, under guidance, the students use the **Alphabet Letter Cards** to build related sets of words. Each word in a set differs from the previous one by only one letter sound. To lead this activity, write at the board.

Monitor Progress

to Differentiate Instruction
Formal Assessment

Blending Note how easily students blend the words.

APPROACHING LEVEL

IF ... students are having difficulty,

THEN ... guide them in completing page 186 and 187 in **Reteach.**

ON LEVEL

IF ... students need more practice,

THEN ... have them look through the **Windy Days Little Big Books** to find words they can read to partners.

ABOVE LEVEL

IF ... students would enjoy a challenging activity,

THEN ... have them work independently using **eSkills.**

Phonics

Word Building

✦ Beginning with this lesson, students will take another important step toward becoming independent readers and writers. Up to this point, students have been blending words using their knowledge of sounds and letters. In Word Building, students will combine their ability to segment words into individual sounds and then connect those sounds to letters to spell words.

✦ Give each student the *a, m,* and *t* **Alphabet Letter Cards.** Have them place all the cards in a row at the top of their desk or table.

✦ Say *am,* and then use it in a sentence. Say *I am glad to be here today. The word is* am. Have students say the word.

✦ Ask students what is the first sound they hear in the word *am.* /a/ Then ask the class to check the **Alphabet Sound Wall Card** and tell which letter says /a/. *Aa* Point to the **Alphabet Sound Card Wall Card** Short *Aa.* Have students pull down **Alphabet Letter Card** *a.*

✦ Then ask the class what sound they hear next in *am.* /m/ Ask the class to check the **Alphabet Sound Wall Card** and tell which letter says /m/. *Mm* Point to **Alphabet Sound Wall Card** *Mm.* Have students pull down **Alphabet Letter Card** *m.*

✦ Then write the word *am* on the board, and have students proofread their word. If necessary, they should correct their spelling of the word.

✦ Have students put their letter cards back on the desk or table, and repeat the process with the word *mat.*

✦ Remind students that when they are writing words on their own, they should say the word to themselves, think about the sounds in words, and then write the letters. They should always check the **Alphabet Sound Wall Cards** if they are unsure of the letter for a sound.

Oral Language and Sentence Extension

✦ Say clues for words to use for Sentence Extensions. Try the following clues:

It is the opposite of go. *stop*

It is the opposite of small. *big*

You can ride one of these to school. bus

✦ When the student has identified and said the word, have her or him use it in a sentence.

✦ Help students extend the sentences by asking them such questions as *Where? Which?* and *When?* For example:

Student: *The bus stops.*

Teacher: *Where?*

Student: *The bus stops at the school.*

Teacher: *Which bus?*

Student: *The yellow bus stops at the school.*

Teacher Tip

VOWEL REVIEW To begin this review of vowel sounds, lead students in a few rounds of the "Vowel Song" while you point to the **Alphabet Sound Wall Cards** for *Aa, Ee, Ii, Oo,* and *Uu.* (See the Appendix.)

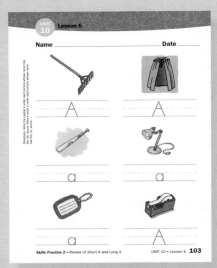

Skills Practice 2 • Review of Short A and Long A   UNIT 10 • Lesson 6 **103**

Skills Practice 2, p. 103

Monitor Progress

to Differentiate Instruction
Formal Assessment

Letter and Sound Review Note how easily students review the sounds of *Aa.*

APPROACHING LEVEL

| IF ... students are having difficulty, | THEN ... refer to Unit 10 Lesson 6 of **Intervention Guide** for activities. |

ON LEVEL

| IF ... students need more practice, | THEN ... use **Skills Practice 2** page 103 for additional activities. |

ABOVE LEVEL

| IF ... students are comfortable, | THEN ... have them work independently to complete **Challenge Activities** page 141. |

Alphabetic Principle

Reviewing the Short and Long Sounds of *Aa*

✦ Focus students' attention on **Alphabet Sound Wall Card** Short *Aa*, and ask them what they remember about Pam the Lamb. Read the story for students, inviting them to join in on the /a/ /a/ /a/ /a/ /a/ part.

✦ Next turn students' attention to **Alphabet Sound Wall Card** Long *Aa*. If necessary, remind them that the picture of the long, thin *A* means that this card is the Long *A* vowel card. Ask students why vowels are special. *Because every word needs a vowel.*

✦ Have students recite the rhyme for the sounds of *Aa:*

A's *my name.*

Two sounds I make:

Short a *in* lamb,

Long a *in* cake.

Listening for /a/ and /ā/

Give each student an **Alphabet Letter Card** *Aa.* Ask students to turn the cards to the capital *A* sides, hold them up, and say /ā/ when they hear the /ā/ sound. When they hear the /a/ sound, have them hold up the cards with the small *a* sides facing you and say /a/. Try the following words:

ate	and	ape	age
stand	shape	fast	plane

Blending ROUTINE **2**

Using Routine 2, the sound-by-sound blending routine, have students practice blending words containing the short and long sounds of the letter *Aa* as you write each word, letter by letter, on the board or chart paper. After blending, have students make and extend sentences for some of the words. Try these words:

ask	at	man	cat
late	same	wave	name

Penmanship

✦ Distribute a sheet of writing paper to each student, or use **White Boards** turned to the sides with writing lines.

✦ Place the Supply Icon for *pencil* on the board or in the **Pocket Chart.**

✦ Use the procedure established for writing letters to review how to form the capital letter *B*. Also review how to form the small *b*.

✦ Invite students to practice writing capital *B*s and small *b*'s, alternating across the top row of the paper or board from left to right: *B b B b B b*.

✦ Repeat the procedure for the letters *Cc, Oo, Rr,* and *Gg*.

Guided Practice ROUTINE 2

✦ Distribute another sheet of writing paper or a **White Board** to each student.

✦ Blend the word *rob* using the sound-by-sound blending routine.

✦ Guide students in blending the word sound by sound. /r/ /o/ /b/

✦ After students have blended the word *rob*, have them read it again naturally, the way they would speak it. Then have them place their fingers on line 1 and write the word *rob* on their papers or boards. After students have written the word, have them read it again.

✦ Repeat the procedure with the words *bog, cob,* and *gob*.

Reading and Responding

Students will

✦ locate the title of the poem and the names of the poet and the illustrator.

✦ connect their own life experiences to the text.

✦ develop an understanding of vocabulary words.

✦ use the comprehension strategy Visualizing.

MATERIALS

✦ *Windy Days Big Book,* pp. 24–25

✦ Routines 5–7

✦ *Home Connection,* pp. 79–80

Focus Question **Why is the girl talking to the wind?**

Go Wind
by Lilian Moore
illustrated by Kathryn Mitter

Go wind, blow
Push wind, swoosh.
Shake things
take things
make things
fly.

Ring things
swing things
fling things
high.

24

Windy Days Big Book, pp. 24–25

Technology

To promote independent reading, encourage students to use Workshop to listen to the recording of the selection on the *Listening Library CD.* Invite them to follow along and say the words whenever they can.

Audio CD

Poetry

Activate Prior Knowledge **ROUTINE 5**

✦ "Go Wind" is a simple, playful poem that conveys a child's joyful experience of a windy day. The many rhyming words and repeated sounds make this poem fun to read and listen to. As you read the poem, relate what you already know to what you are reading, and encourage students to do the same.

✦ Have students discuss their experiences with windy days. Ask them questions such as the following: *What do you like about a windy day? How does a windy day feel on your skin? Have you ever tried to do something on a windy day but couldn't? What happened? How does a windy day make you feel inside?*

✦ Before reading the poem, encourage students to make pictures in their heads of the poem's words.

✦ Have students discuss the knowledge they are building about windy days as they listen to the selection. Ask them how this knowledge might help them appreciate windy days.

Preview the Poem **ROUTINE 5**

✦ Display the *Windy Days Big Book,* opened to pages 24–25. Follow Routine 5, the previewing the selection routine, as you introduce the poem's title and the names of the poet and the illustrator. Ask students what a poet and an illustrator do.

✦ As you prepare to read the poem, invite students to examine the picture and to share what they see. Remind students pictures can give readers clues as to what a poem or story is about.

✦ Encourage students to think about why they are reading this poem. Encourage students to wonder what the poem will say about windy days.

Vocabulary

 ROUTINE **6**

✦ Follow Routine 6, the selection vocabulary routine, as you introduce the vocabulary words for this selection.

✦ Explain to students that the word *ring* has several meanings but that in this poem it means "to make bell sounds." Use the following sentence to illustrate: *Strong winds ring the metal chains on our swings.*

✦ Tell students the word *fling* means "to throw hard." Use the following sentence to illustrate: *Josh tried to fling a rope over the lowest branch.*

Read the Poem

 ROUTINE **7**

✦ Before reading the poem, read the Focus Question above it. Tell students to keep this question in mind as they listen to the poem.

✦ Follow Routine 7, the reading the selection routine, as you read aloud "Go Wind." Dramatize the rhythm and playfulness of this poem by stressing the rhyming words and repeated sounds. Encourage students to listen for rhyming words as you read.

✦ Invite students to ask questions or to think aloud about anything in the poem that interests or puzzles them.

Comprehension Strategies

For this poem, model the comprehension strategy Visualizing to help students make mental pictures of settings, characters, and actions.

Vocabulary

ring	fling

 Teacher Tip

WRITING POETRY Some students may enjoy writing or dictating poems about the wind.

Focus Question Why is the girl talking to the wind?

Go Wind
by Lilian Moore
illustrated by Kathryn Mitter

Go wind, blow
Push wind, swoosh.
Shake things
take things
make things
fly.

Ring things
swing things
fling things
high.

Go wind, blow
Push things—wheee.
No, wind, no.
Not me —
not *me*.

24   25

Windy Days Big Book, pp. 24–25

Differentiating Instruction   **English Learners**

IF . . . students are unfamiliar with the word *push, shake,* or *swing* from the poem,
THEN . . . ask English speakers to demonstrate the meaning of each word for their English Learner classmates.

Comprehension Strategies

Teacher Modeling

❶ Visualizing *Let's pretend we're in a park with trees and swings on a windy day. Make a picture in your head of the wind pushing the swings high into the air. Hear their chains clang against the metal frame of the swing set. Hear the swoosh of the tree branches as they sway in the wind. Feel your hair blowing in your face and your dress or pant legs flapping in the wind. Ahhhh . . . to be as free as the wind!*

Discussing the Poem

ROUTINE **7**

✦ Review the Focus Question with students: Why is the girl talking to the wind? *She's having fun watching what the wind is doing and is cheering it on.*

✦ Invite students to share their feelings and ideas about the poem. Ask students if the poem has helped them think differently about windy days. Encourage them to share how their ideas about windy days have changed after listening to this poem.

✦ Visit the school library, and choose a variety of genres, such as nursery rhymes, fairy tales, and picture books. Have students discuss the characters, setting, and sequence of events of each selection.

✦ Have students make connections between the text and themselves, as well as connections to the world around them.

Purposes for Reading

✦ Remind students they were listening to find out what the poem says about windy days. Invite students to share what they learned about this subject.

✦ Ask students what they liked best about the poem and why they liked it.

Vocabulary Review

ROUTINE **6**

Review with students the selection vocabulary words *ring* and *fling*. Ask students the following questions:

- *What are some things that ring?*
- *How would you fling a ball?*

 Differentiating Instruction **English Learners**

IF ... students have difficulty discussing their feelings about the poem, **THEN ...** invite them to share one-word responses about their thoughts on the poem.

 From Your Teacher **Home Connection**

Give each student a copy of *Home Connection* page 79. This same information is also available in Spanish on *Home Connection* page 80. Encourage students to discuss "What Happens When Wind Blows?" with their families and complete the activity provided.

Language Arts

Students will
+ brainstorm methods of research.
+ form hypotheses about what their research might yield.
+ view, appreciate, and react to fine art.

+ *Language Arts Big Book,* p. 6
+ *Windy Days Big Book,* p. 48

Language Arts Big Book, p. 6

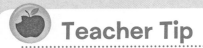

Teacher Tip

PLAN AHEAD In preparation for the following activity, have art supplies and drawing paper on hand.

Differentiating Instruction   English Learners

IF ... students have difficulty brainstorming, **THEN ...** ask them yes-no and either-or questions, using words they can add to their report.

Writing Process

Prewrite: Brainstorming Ideas and Forming Hypotheses

Teach

+ Display **Language Arts Big Book** page 6, and remind students the class is working together to write a report on a topic related to the wind.

+ Point to the list, and read aloud the title *Getting Ideas*. Tell students the items on this list can also help them get ideas for the best ways to get information for the report.

+ Review each item on the list, and discuss how students can *look* at pictures and print materials, *think* about the information they learn, *talk* to people who know something about their topic, and *listen* to what experts have to say about it.

Guided Practice

+ Display the list of research questions that students created in the previous lessons. Review each question with students, and ask if anyone is confused by any items or if they have something they would like to add to or delete from the list.

+ Next choose a few of the research questions to explore in more depth. Reread each question, and then ask students *What do you think you will find when you investigate this question?* Record students' hypotheses on a clean sheet of chart paper.

+ Repeat the process with two or three other research questions. When you are finished, store students' hypotheses until the next lesson, when they will reflect on how their original conjectures changed over the course of their inquiry into the topic.

Vocabulary

ROUTINE **6**

✦ Follow Routine 6, the selection vocabulary routine, as you introduce the vocabulary words for this selection.

✦ Explain to students that the word *steadily* means "not changing." Use the following sentence to illustrate: *The men worked steadily through the night.*

✦ Tell students when something is *still,* it is not moving. Ask a volunteer to demonstrate being very still.

✦ Explain that in this selection the word *swept* means "moved or carried." Use the following sentence to illustrate: *I swept the floor to clean it.*

✦ Tell students when birds *soar,* they fly upward.

Vocabulary

steadily	swept
still	soar

Read the Selection

ROUTINE **7**

✦ Before beginning the selection, read the Focus Question at the top of the first page. Tell students to keep this question in mind as they listen to the story.

✦ Follow Routine 7, the reading the selection, to read the entire selection.

✦ Before, during, and after the first reading, invite students to ask questions and to think aloud about anything in the selection.

Comprehension Strategies

✦ During the reading of "What Happens When Wind Blows?" you will model the following comprehension strategies:

- Asking Questions
- Clarifying
- Predicting

✦ Think aloud through each strategy, and encourage students to share their ideas as well.

 Teacher Tip

PRETEACH For English learners or students who may need extra help, you may wish to read this selection a day or so in advance of when you read it to the entire class. As you read, give students the opportunity to discuss the selection and to clarify any problems they have with it. Model asking questions for them. When students hear the selection again with the class, they may feel more comfortable asking questions they may have.

Differentiating Instruction   English Learners

IF . . . students need additional help with vocabulary, **THEN . . .** refer to Unit 10 Lesson 7 of the *English Learner Support Guide.*

Comprehension Strategies

Teacher Modeling

1 Predicting *The first sentence tells us wind is always changing. What do you predict this selection will be about? Let's read on to find out if our prediction is confirmed.*

2 Clarifying *Look at these special titles on these pages. They help us understand what kind of information to expect in each section. By looking again at these pages, I was able to clarify what I needed to know.*

3 Asking Questions *I wonder why some of these words are in dark type. Sometimes new words or special words are printed in dark type. By thinking about what we already know, we can sometimes answer our own questions.*

4 Asking Questions *Are there different kinds of storms? Are the winds different in different kinds of storms? Let's keep reading to see if the selection tells us about this.*

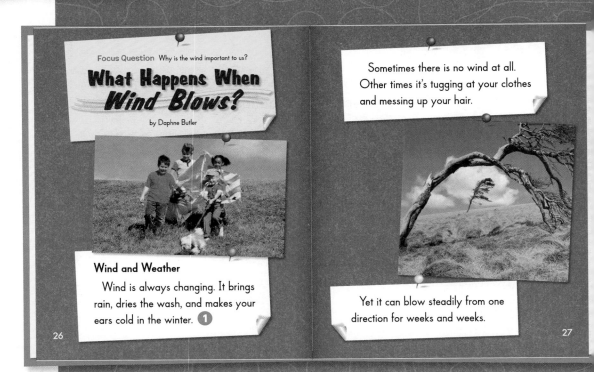

Focus Question Why is the wind important to us?

What Happens When Wind Blows?
by Daphne Butler

Wind and Weather
Wind is always changing. It brings rain, dries the wash, and makes your ears cold in the winter. **1**

26

Sometimes there is no wind at all. Other times it's tugging at your clothes and messing up your hair.

Yet it can blow steadily from one direction for weeks and weeks.

27

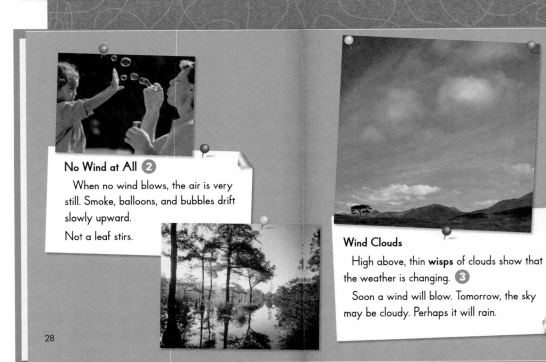

No Wind at All **2**
When no wind blows, the air is very still. Smoke, balloons, and bubbles drift slowly upward.
Not a leaf stirs.

28

Wind Clouds
High above, thin **wisps** of clouds show that the weather is changing. **3**
Soon a wind will blow. Tomorrow, the sky may be cloudy. Perhaps it will rain.

29

IF ... students have difficulty understanding the Asking Questions strategy used with indirect questions such as *I wonder...*,
THEN ... model asking direct questions that begin with the words *who, what, when, where, why,* and *how.* Make sure students know what kind of information each word asks for.

 Teacher Tip

GLOSSARY The word *swept* can be found in the Glossary of the ***Windy Days Big Book.***

Windy Days Big Book, pp. 26–33

English Learners

IF ... students have difficulty understanding the verbs on pages 30–33, **THEN ...** ask English speakers to demonstrate the meaning of each word for their English Learner classmates.

Print and Book Awareness

Headings

Point to and read the words *Wind and Weather* on page 26. Remind students these words are called a *heading* and authors use headings to let readers know what they will be reading about in a section of the text. Ask what this section of text is about.

Sentences: Periods

Have students come to the **Big Book** and point to the first and last words in each sentence on page 27. Have them point to the periods at the ends of sentences and say *This is a period.*

Initial /s/

Reread page 31, and ask students to listen for words that begin with the /s/ sound. *Smoke, swept, soar, Sailboats* Have volunteers come to the **Big Book** and point to words beginning with the letter that represents the /s/ sound. As volunteers point to the letter *s,* have the class say the /s/ sound.

Comprehension Strategies

Teacher Modeling

5 **Asking Questions** *Our questions about storms were answered on these pages. Now we know there are different kinds of storms and different kinds of winds.*

6 **Clarifying** *I'm not sure why we would have to stay inside during a blizzard. Let's look at the page and the picture again. Can you explain why being outside is not a good idea?*

7 **Asking Questions** *What does the title of this page mean? Rocks are very hard. How can the wind hurt them? Maybe we'll find the answer as we read.*

8 **Asking Questions** *Our question was answered here. Now we know the wind carries the sand. Then the sharp sand smooths the rocks. By reading more, we were able to answer one of our questions.*

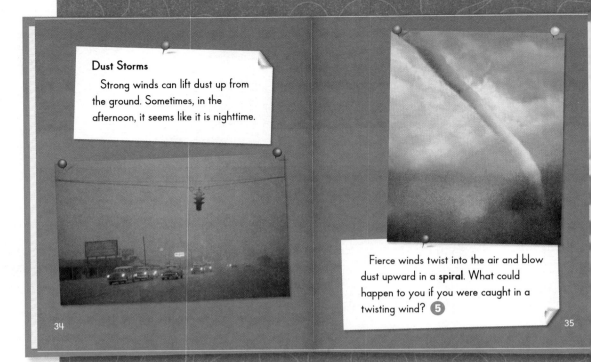

Dust Storms

Strong winds can lift dust up from the ground. Sometimes, in the afternoon, it seems like it is nighttime.

Fierce winds twist into the air and blow dust upward in a **spiral**. What could happen to you if you were caught in a twisting wind? **5**

34

35

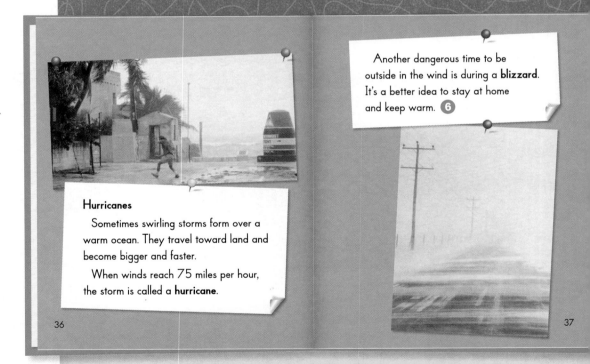

Hurricanes

Sometimes swirling storms form over a warm ocean. They travel toward land and become bigger and faster.

When winds reach 75 miles per hour, the storm is called a **hurricane**.

Another dangerous time to be outside in the wind is during a **blizzard**. It's a better idea to stay at home and keep warm. **6**

36

37

Differentiating Instruction **English Learners**

IF ... students would benefit from practice with words that express time of day,
THEN ... review or introduce the following words: *morning, afternoon, evening, night, daytime,* and *nighttime.*

 Teacher Tip

ASKING QUESTIONS Inform students they should keep asking questions and trying to answer them as they read.

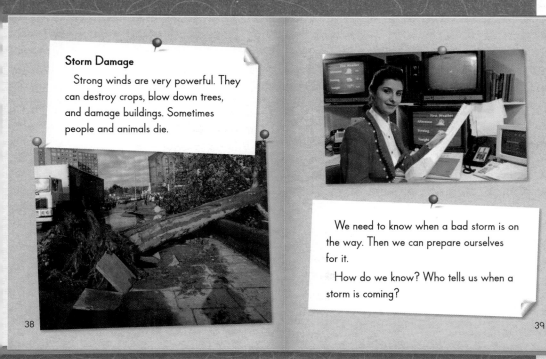

Windy Days Big Book, pp. 34–41

English Learners

IF ... students are not familiar with the word *damage* on page 38, **THEN ...** rephrase the sentence by saying *They can destroy crops, blow down trees, and hurt or break buildings.*

Print and Book Awareness

Picture-Text Relationship

Ask students to look closely at page 37 and tell what they see. What is happening in the picture? *a blizzard* Reread the text that accompanies the picture, and ask what the picture adds to the text. *Why is it better to stay at home during a blizzard? Roads are dangerous; it is difficult to see very far; strong winds can blow cars off the road.* Remind students that a picture often helps make the text clearer or easier to understand.

Question Marks

Have a volunteer point to the question marks on page 39, and ask students what a question mark means. If necessary, remind students a question mark means a question is being asked. Then read the question with the appropriate expression, and invite students to do the same.

Exclamation Points

Have a volunteer point to the exclamation point on page 40, and ask students what an exclamation point means. If necessary, remind students an exclamation point means something is being said with feeling. Then read the sentence with feeling, and invite students to do the same.

Comprehension Strategies

Teacher Modeling

9 **Asking Questions** *How does the temperature of Earth make air move? This page doesn't explain. Let's read on to find out more.*

10 **Asking Questions** *Our question was answered here. When hot air rises, it leaves room for cooler air to move in. That movement of air is wind. By reading on, we were able to find an answer to our question.*

Power from the Wind

In the past, windmills have used the power of the wind to grind corn and to pump water.

Today's windmills make electricity. They are silent and clean. All they need to run is a strong, steady wind.

42
43

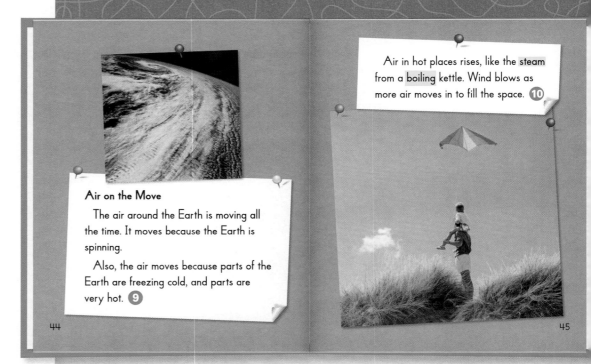

Air in hot places rises, like the steam from a boiling kettle. Wind blows as more air moves in to fill the space. **10**

Air on the Move

The air around the Earth is moving all the time. It moves because the Earth is spinning.

Also, the air moves because parts of the Earth are freezing cold, and parts are very hot. **9**

44
45

Windy Days Big Book, pp. 42–45

Concept/Question Board

Tell students that readers continue to think about questions generated as they are reading. As they read, tell them to keep in mind the questions on the **Concept/Question Board.** Explain that readers are always thinking about and trying to remember what is important in selections.

Print and Book Awareness

Headings

Ask volunteers to come to the ***Big Book*** and to point to the headings on pages 40, 42, and 44. Ask students why authors use headings. *to let the reader know what a section is about* Read each heading, and ask students what the text that follows each heading is about.

Discussing the Selection

✦ Review the Focus Question with students: Why is the wind important to us? *The wind cools us on hot days and provides energy.*

✦ Have students retell the main idea, identify supporting details, and arrange the events in sequence.

✦ Have students identify the purpose of this non-fiction text.

Vocabulary Review

Review with students the selection vocabulary words *steadily, still, swept,* and *soar.* Ask students the following questions:

- *What does it mean to work steadily through the day?*
- *When was a time you had to stay still?*
- *Who do you know that has swept the floor?*
- *What kinds of animals can soar?*

Differentiating Instruction **English Learners**

IF . . . students have difficulty answering the Focus Question, **THEN . . .** rephrase the question so it can be answered *yes* or *no*. For example, *Is the wind important to us? yes*

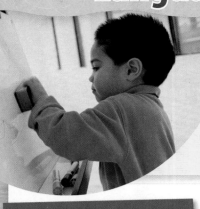
OBJECTIVES

Students will
✦ collaborate to find information.
✦ answer research questions.
✦ review the proper spacing between sentences.
✦ participate in a Thinking Story experience.

MATERIALS
✦ *Windy Days Big Book,* p. 5
✦ *Willy the Wisher,* p. 93

Writing Process

Prewrite: Finding and Answering Questions

Teach

In advance of the lesson, gather various reference materials related to the topic of the class report. Schedule a visit to the school library, and guide students in finding reference materials. Tell students today they will begin researching their topic.

Guided Practice

✦ Organize the class into groups of four or five students, and give each group a few of the reference materials you have gathered for them.

✦ Display the list of research questions you helped the class prepare. Read aloud the first question, and ask each group to look through the reference materials for pictures or words they think might help answer the questions.

✦ Have students raise their hands if they find something they think is useful. You should visit the group and review the reference material. If it is useful information, carry the book to the front of the room, read aloud the important information, and write it on a clean sheet of chart paper.

✦ After you have reviewed each group's findings for the first question, tell students you will continue this research in the next lesson. Save the chart paper on which you take notes of valuable information.

Grammar, Usage, and Mechanics

Teach

✦ Display page 5 of the *Windy Days Big Book,* and read the sentences aloud, pausing noticeably between each sentence.

✦ Have students help you count the number of sentences on the page. Ask students *How do we know how many sentences there are?* Review with students that a capital letter begins a sentence and that an end mark ends a sentence.

✦ Next point to the space between the first two sentences. Explain that spaces between sentences also show readers where one sentence ends and another one begins.

Guided Practice

✦ Write the following sentences on the board, but do not use spaces between the words, and do not include capitalization or punctuation:

- Is it a windy day? *(isitawindyday)*
- We can fly a kite. *(wecanflyakite)*
- I love to listen to the wind! *(ilovetolistentothewind)*

✦ Guide students in identifying where the spaces, capitalization, and punctuation should be placed in each sentence. Use slashes to indicate where the spaces should be. Below the compressed sentences, help students rewrite the sentences correctly.

Willy the Wisher

✦ Display the book ***Willy the Wisher,*** and turn to page 93, "I Know All about Mr. Muddle."

✦ Pointing to the Listening Icons, remind students to listen carefully.

✦ Before reading the story to students, invite them to share what they remember about Portia and Ferdie. In this story students will be able to recognize Ferdie's impulsiveness as well as Portia's reasoning abilities.

✦ You might also discuss Loretta the Mail Carrier, who is an important character in this story. Students might remember her from when she delivered all of Portia's valentines.

✦ Use the established procedure for reading the ***Willy the Wisher*** stories. Read the story, pausing at the red text to ask students the questions. If necessary, model the thinking process, and ask specific students to share their thinking.

✦ After reading the story, discuss it in general. Use questions such as the following:

- *Does Portia do a good job remembering the things Loretta explains?*
- *Does Ferdie do a better or worse job remembering than Portia?*
- *What would you have done if you were Portia or Ferdie to help you remember these things about Mr. Muddle?*
- *What are three things you remember about Mr. Muddle?*

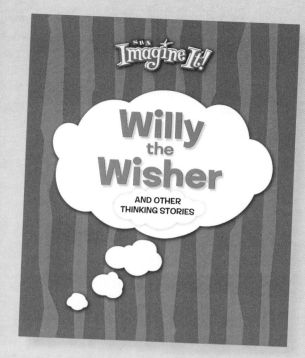

Willy the Wisher, p. 93

🍎 Teacher Tip

PRINT AND BOOK AWARENESS Lessons that include any print book, such as the ***Willy the Wisher*** book, present an opportunity to teach print and book awareness. For example, invite a volunteer to come to the book and to point to each word in the story's title as you say it. Ask the class to help you count the words and the spaces in the title, or have them identify the first and the last words on page 93.

Differentiating Instruction **English Learners**

IF ... students have difficulty tracking print, **THEN ...** bear in mind that some languages are written and read vertically or from right to left. Make sure students know how to track English print, and provide extra practice as needed.

Sounds and Letters

Students will

✦ manipulate final phonemes.

✦ make and extend oral sentences.

✦ review the long- and short-vowel sounds of *Aa* and *Ii.*

✦ review writing the letters *Jj, Ff, Uu, Xx,* and *Zz.*

✦ practice writing words they have blended.

✦ ***Pickled Peppers Big Book,*** p. 28

✦ ***Alphabet Letter Cards*** *Aa, Ff, Nn, Pp, Tt, Ww,* and *Ii* for each student; miscellaneous cards for other exercises

✦ Routine 2

Calendar

Su	M	T	W	Th	F	S
		1	2	3	4	5
6	7	8	9	10	11	12
13	14	15	16	17	18	19
20	21	22	23	24	25	26
27	28	29	30	31		

Point to the box that represents today. Ask students to tell the name of the current season. Then ask students in which season each of the following national holidays is: Thanksgiving, Memorial Day, New Year's Day, and Independence Day. If possible, point to each holiday on a yearly calendar.

Warming Up

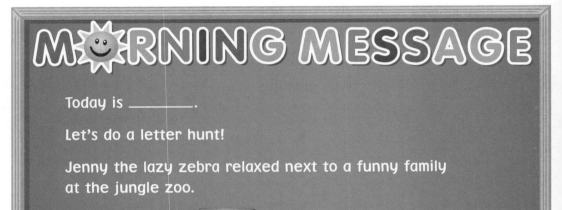

M☀RNING MESSAGE

Today is _____.

Let's do a letter hunt!

Jenny the lazy zebra relaxed next to a funny family at the jungle zoo.

Kindergarten News

✦ Copy the text above on the board or on chart paper, and invite a volunteer to come up and write today's date in the blank.

✦ Ask the class to identify any letters or sounds. *Jj, Ff, Xx, Zz, Uu; /j/, /f/, /ks/, /z/, /u/* They will review writing these letters in the Penmanship lesson.

✦ Invite students to tell which sentences end with periods and which sentence ends with an exclamation point. *first, third; second* Have students count the letters and words in the last sentence.

Phoneme Blending

Bring out the **Lion Puppet,** and tell students he wants to play a blending game. Remind them that you will say the beginning sound of each word, and they will repeat it. Then the puppet will give the rest of the word. Make sure you emphasize the beginning phoneme. Start with the following words: */s/ . . . imple, /l / . . . ake, /t/ . . . umble, /k/ . . . rack, /h / . . . ighway.*

Phonemic Awareness

Phoneme Deletion: Final Sounds

✦ Bring out the **Lion Puppet,** and tell students he wants to play the game in which he takes away sounds from words again but this time the game will be a little different. In this game, the puppet will ask to take away the ending sound in a word to make a new word.

✦ Say a word, have students repeat it, and then have the puppet tell students to take away the ending sound to make a new word. Everyone will then say the new word. For example:

Teacher: *The word is* keep.

Students: *keep*

Puppet: *Say* keep *without the /p/.*

Everyone: *key*

✦ Continue with these words:

bake /k/ *bay*	*mist* /t/ *miss*
find /d/ *fine*	*plump* /p/ *plum*
flute /t/ *flew*	*tent* /t/ *ten*
grain /n/ *gray*	*serve* /v/ *sir*
carp /p/ *car*	*date* /t/ *day*

Differentiating Instruction **English Learners**

IF ... students have difficulty with the Phonemic Awareness activity, **THEN ...** refer to Unit 10 Lesson 8 of the *English Learner Support Guide.*

Teacher Tip

THE WORD-BUILDING GAME If you feel that your students are ready, you may want to have them use pencil and paper, slates, or **White Boards.**

Differentiating Instruction **English Learners**

IF ... students are native Spanish speakers, **THEN ...** they may need extra help producing the /w/ sound and associating it with the letter *w*. The letter *w* does not appear in Spanish words, although Spanish speakers use /w/ occasionally for words borrowed from other languages.

Phonics

Word Building

✦ Give each student **Alphabet Letter Cards** *i, f, n, p, t,* and *w*. Have them place all the cards in a row at the top of their desks or tables.

✦ Say *in,* and then use it in a sentence. Say *The girl sleeps in her bed. The word is in.* Have students say the word.

✦ Ask students what the first sound is that they hear in the word *in. /i/* Then ask the class to check the **Alphabet Sound Wall Card** and tell which letter says /i/. *Ii* Point to the **Alphabet Sound Card Wall Card** Short *Ii.* Have students pull down **Alphabet Letter Card** *i.*

✦ Then ask the class what the next sound is that they hear in *in. /n/* Ask the class to check the **Alphabet Sound Wall Card** and tell which letter says /n/. *Nn* Point to **Alphabet Sound Wall Card** *Nn.* Have students pull down **Alphabet Letter Card** *n.*

✦ Then write the word *in* on the board, and have students proofread their words. If necessary, they should correct their spellings of the words.

✦ Have students put their letter cards back on the desk or table, and repeat the process with the words *fin, win, pin,* and *pit.*

✦ Remind students that when they are writing words on their own, they should say the words to themselves, think about the sounds in words, and then write the letters. They should always check the **Alphabet Sound Wall Cards** if they are unsure of the letter for a sound.

Oral Language and Sentence Extension

✦ Say clues for words for the Sentence Extension activity. Try the following clues:

It is the opposite of save. *spend*

It rhymes with stick. *wick*

It is another word for wet. *damp*

✦ When the student has identified and said the word, have her or him use it in a sentence.

✦ Help students extend the sentences by asking them questions such as *When? Where?* and *Which?* For example:

Student: *I got my coat damp.*

Teacher: *When?*

Student: *I got my coat damp yesterday.*

Teacher: *Where?*

Student: *I got my coat damp in the rain yesterday.*

Alphabetic Principle

Reviewing the Short and Long Sounds of *Aa* and *Ii*

✦ Focus students' attention on **Alphabet Sound Wall Card** Short *Aa*, and read the story for students again. Ask them to say the /a/ /a/ /a/ /a/ /a/ part.

✦ Point to **Alphabet Sound Wall Card** Long *Aa*, and ask a volunteer to say the name of the letter. Have students recite the rhyme for the sounds of *Aa*.

✦ Point to **Alphabet Sound Wall Card** Short *Ii*, and read the story about Pickles the Pig again, inviting students to say the /i/ /i/ /i/ /i/ /i/ part.

✦ Next turn students' attention to **Alphabet Sound Wall Card** Long *Ii*. Have students recite the rhyme for the sounds of *Ii*.

Listening for Medial /ā/ and /ī/

Give each student one **Alphabet Letter Card** *Aa* and one **Alphabet Letter Card** *Ii*. Ask students to raise the *Aa* cards and say /ā/ when they hear a word with the /ā/ sound. They should raise the *Ii* cards and say /ī/ when they hear the /ī/ sound. Try the following words:

bike	*save*	*wake*	*bite*
base	*fade*	*nine*	*tape*
pipe	*wipe*	*slide*	*Grace*

Linking the Sound to the Letter

Write a pair of similar-looking words on the board, one with the /a/ sound and one with the /i/ sound. Say one of the words in each pair, and have students identify the correct word by signaling thumbs-up when you point to it. Then have a volunteer tell you how they know the correct word. They should recognize the letter and sound correspondence. Try these word pairs:

bit ... bat	*rap ... rip*
fast ... fist	*than ... thin*
trick ... track	*drift ... draft*

Technology

Use the **Alphabet Sound Card Stories CD** to review the /a/ and /i/ sounds.

Audio CD

Penmanship

✦ Distribute a sheet of writing paper to each student, or use **White Boards** turned to the sides with writing lines.

✦ Place the Supply Icon for *pencil* on the board or in the **Pocket Chart.**

✦ Use the procedure established for writing letters to review how to form the capital letter *J.* Also review how to form the small *j.*

✦ Invite students to practice writing capital *J*s and small *j*'s, alternating across the top row of the paper or board from left to right: *J j J j J j.*

✦ Repeat the procedure for the letters *Ff, Uu, Xx,* and *Zz.*

Guided Practice ROUTINE 2

✦ Distribute another sheet of writing paper to each student.

✦ Blend the word *fun* using the sound-by-sound blending routine.

✦ Guide students in blending the word sound by sound. */f/ /u/ /n/*

✦ After students have blended the word *fun,* have the class read the word again naturally. Then have students write the word *fun* on their papers or boards. After students have written the word, have them read it again.

✦ Repeat the procedure with the words *jut, fix, fuzz,* and *jazz.*

Monitor Progress to Differentiate Instruction

Formal Assessment

Penmanship Note how easily students review the letters.

APPROACHING LEVEL

IF ... students are having difficulty,   THEN ... help them to complete **Reteach** page 188.

ON LEVEL

IF ... students need more practice,   THEN ... use **Alphabet Letter Cards** to review the letters again, and have students write another row of each letter using the cards as a model.

ABOVE LEVEL

IF ... students would enjoy a challenging activity,   THEN ... have them work independently with **eSkills.**

Teacher Tip

SPACING Review students' writing to make sure they are leaving the proper spacing between words. To help them conceptualize the proper distance between words, you might tell students to imagine an invisible letter is between the words they write.

Reading and Responding

OBJECTIVES

Students will

✦ review the comprehension strategies Asking Questions, Clarifying, and Predicting.

✦ use the comprehension skill Classify and Categorize.

✦ analyze the author's use of text structure.

MATERIALS

✦ *Windy Days Big Book,* pp. 26–45

✦ Routines 5–7

Focus Question Why is the wind important to us?

What Happens When Wind Blows?

by Daphne Butler

Wind and Weather

Wind is always changing. It brings rain, dries the wash, and makes your ears cold in the winter.

26

Windy Days Big Book, p. 26

Vocabulary

fierce	steam
stings	boiling

Teacher Tip

VOCABULARY Encourage students to use a variety of sources to build their vocabulary, such as making word banks, discussing characters and events from a story, talking with other people, and thinking about their own life experiences.

 2nd READ

Preview and Prepare 🕐

Activate Prior Knowledge **ROUTINE 5**

✦ Display the **Windy Days Big Book,** opened to the Table of Contents page. Use Routine 5, the previewing the selection routine, to guide students in understanding and using the Table of Contents. Then turn to the selection, and say the title and the name of the author.

✦ As you prepare to reread the selection, have students use the illustrations to retell important facts in the story.

Vocabulary **ROUTINE 6**

✦ Follow Routine 6, the selection vocabulary routine, as you introduce the vocabulary words for this selection.

✦ Tell students in this selection the word *fierce* means "very, very strong or powerful." Use the following sentence to illustrate: *Fierce winds blew the boats out to sea.*

✦ Explain to students that the word *stings* means "makes a sharp pain." Use the following sentence to illustrate: *The bee stings the boy, and it hurt.*

✦ Tell students *steam* is a hot mist that rises from water heated to a high temperature. Use the following sentence to illustrate: *The steam from the kettle made the ceiling wet.*

✦ Explain that the word *boiling* means "heating something like water, until bubbles form." Use the following sentence to illustrate: *Dad lifted the boiling pot of soup off the stove.*

Read the Selection

ROUTINE **7**

Comprehension Strategies

✦ During the first reading of "What Happens When Wind Blows?" you modeled the following reading comprehension strategies:

- Asking Questions
- Clarifying
- Predicting

✦ In this second reading of the selection, you will revisit each comprehension strategy model from the first reading.

Comprehension Skills

In this lesson of "What Happens When Wind Blows?" students will focus on the comprehension skill Classify and Categorize.

Reading with a Writer's Eye

✦ In this rereading of "What Happens When Wind Blows?" you will discuss how the author uses text structure to share information.

✦ By discussing the author's writing strategies, students learn how they can be better writers.

Technology

To promote independent reading, encourage students to use Workshop to listen to the recording of the selection on the **Listening Library CD.** Invite them to follow along and say the words whenever they can.

Audio CD

Comprehension Strategies

Teacher Modeling

① Predicting *Readers think about what they have read and make predictions about what might happen next. The first page says the wind is always changing, so we predicted the selection would tell us about the kinds of changes the wind can make.*

② Clarifying *When we're confused about something in a selection, we know we can reread pages to help us figure out what is happening. We were confused about the special titles on these pages. But when we reread some pages, we remembered these titles help us understand what kind of information to expect in each section.*

③ Asking Questions *When we ask questions about what we're reading, it makes us think more about it. Here we wondered why some of these words are in dark type. Then we remembered that new words or special words are sometimes printed in dark type. We were able to answer our own question by thinking about what we already knew.*

④ Asking Questions *Here we wondered if there were different kinds of storms and if the winds were different in each kind of storm. Asking questions keeps us interested in what we're reading. As we read on, we looked for answers to our questions.*

Focus Question Why is the wind important to us?

What Happens When Wind Blows?
by Daphne Butler

Wind and Weather
Wind is always changing. It brings rain, dries the wash, and makes your ears cold in the winter. ①

26

Sometimes there is no wind at all. Other times it's tugging at your clothes and messing up your hair.

Yet it can blow steadily from one direction for weeks and weeks.

27

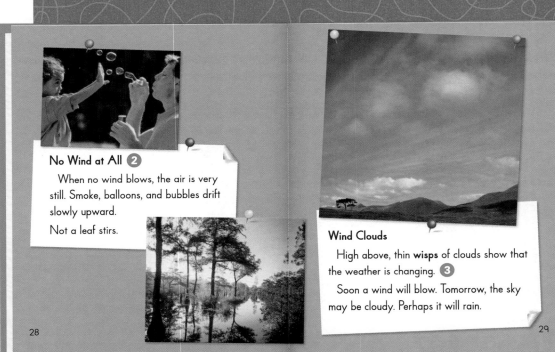

No Wind at All ②
When no wind blows, the air is very still. Smoke, balloons, and bubbles drift slowly upward.
Not a leaf stirs.

28

Wind Clouds
High above, thin **wisps** of clouds show that the weather is changing. ③
Soon a wind will blow. Tomorrow, the sky may be cloudy. Perhaps it will rain.

29

 **Teacher Tip**

GLOSSARY The words *steam* and *boiling* can be found in the Glossary of the **Windy Days Big Book.**

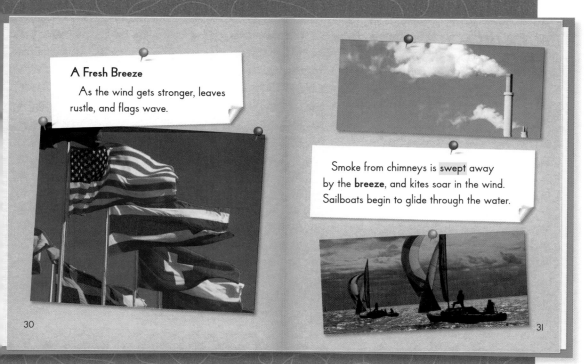

A Fresh Breeze

As the wind gets stronger, leaves rustle, and flags wave.

Smoke from chimneys is swept away by the **breeze**, and kites soar in the wind. Sailboats begin to glide through the water.

30

31

Storm Clouds Gather

The wind grows stronger, and dark **storm** clouds gather high up in the air. The ocean forms **peaks**, and the water becomes rough. ④

On land trees sway, and it is difficult to walk in the wind.

32

33

Windy Days Big Book, pp. 26–33

Comprehension Skills

Classify and Categorize

✦ Point out to students that "What Happens When Wind Blows?" tells about many kinds of winds. Explain that some winds are gentle; others are strong. Some are helpful; others are harmful.

✦ Help students categorize the kinds of winds mentioned in the selection by creating a chart with the column headings Strong Winds and Gentle Winds.

✦ Ask students where to put *no wind, breeze,* and *storms.* Tell students you will add to this chart as you read the rest of the selection.

Reading with a Writer's Eye

Text Structure: Types

✦ Explain to students that authors who write to share information often organize the information in ways that make it easier to understand. Tell students one way to do this is to use headings that group information by how it is alike.

✦ Tell students we can group things according to how they are alike, the kinds of things they do, or other characteristics.

✦ Reread the headings on page 26–33, and ask students how the author has grouped the information. *by the different kinds of winds*

Comprehension Strategies

Teacher Modeling

5 Asking Questions *When I read these pages, I found the answers to my questions about storms. By reading on, I learned more about the topic.*

6 Clarifying *I was confused about what a blizzard really was like and why we should stay indoors. When we looked at the picture, it helped me clarify that a blizzard is a dangerous and windy snowstorm. Clarifying that helped me understand what the words really meant.*

7 Asking Questions *I was curious as to how wind could change a hard rock. Readers ask questions about what they read and then read to find the answer.*

8 Asking Questions *This is where we found the answer to my question. We learned it's the sand carried by the wind that smooths the rocks. By reading more, I was able to answer one of my questions. But sometimes the answers aren't in the selection. Then we can look in another book or ask someone to help us find the answer.*

Differentiating Instruction **English Learners**

IF ... students are accustomed to using the metric system to measure distance, **THEN ...** explain that 75 miles per hour is the same as 121 kilometers per hour.

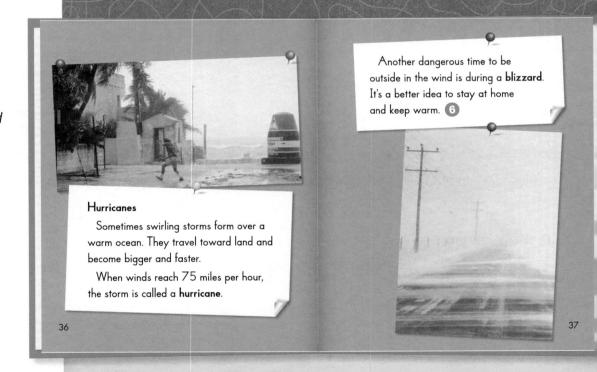

Dust Storms

Strong winds can lift dust up from the ground. Sometimes, in the afternoon, it seems like it is nighttime.

34

Fierce winds twist into the air and blow dust upward in a **spiral**. What could happen to you if you were caught in a twisting wind? **5**

35

Hurricanes

Sometimes swirling storms form over a warm ocean. They travel toward land and become bigger and faster.

When winds reach 75 miles per hour, the storm is called a **hurricane**.

36

Another dangerous time to be outside in the wind is during a **blizzard**. It's a better idea to stay at home and keep warm. **6**

37

Vocabulary Tip

Review the meaning of the word *fierce*. Then have students use the word in a sentence.

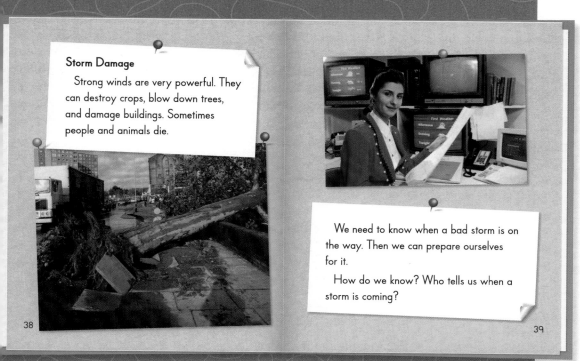

Windy Days Big Book, pp. 34–41

Comprehension Skills

Classify and Categorize

✦ Reread pages 34–37, and have volunteers repeat words that tell what a *dust storm, twisting wind, hurricane,* and *blizzard* are like. Then have students tell where on the chart you should place these storms.

✦ Reread pages 40–41, and have volunteers repeat words that tell about the winds that wear away rocks. Then have students tell where on the chart you should place *winds that carry sand.*

Reading with a Writer's Eye

Text Structure: Types

Reread the headings on pages 34–41, and ask students how the author has grouped the information. *by the different kinds of damaging winds*

Vocabulary Tip

Review the meaning of the word *stings*. Then have students use the word in a sentence.

🍎 Teacher Tip

CLASSIFY AND CATEGORIZE To help students with this skill, encourage them to group objects, such as blocks, in various ways. Then have them discuss the different ways they might categorize the blocks.

Comprehension Strategies

Teacher Modeling

9 Asking Questions *Here I wondered how the temperature of Earth could make air move. When this page didn't explain, I read on to find an answer.*

10 Asking Questions *This page answered my question. Now I know when hot air rises, cooler air moves in. I learned that this movement of air is wind. Reading on helped me understand.*

Vocabulary Tip

Review the meanings of the words *steam* and *boiling*. Then have students use the words in sentences.

Power from the Wind

In the past, windmills have used the power of the wind to grind corn and to pump water.

42

Today's windmills make electricity. They are silent and clean. All they need to run is a strong, steady wind.

43

Air on the Move

The air around the Earth is moving all the time. It moves because the Earth is spinning.

Also, the air moves because parts of the Earth are freezing cold, and parts are very hot. **9**

44

Air in hot places rises, like the steam from a boiling kettle. Wind blows as more air moves in to fill the space. **10**

45

Windy Days Big Book, pp. 42–45

 ## Teacher Tip

DISCUSSING THE SELECTION Tell students after reading, they should always ask *What did I find interesting? What is important here?* Later remind students again whenever they conclude a reading, they should ask themselves questions about what was in the text.

Reading with a Writer's Eye

Text Structure: Types

Reread the heading on page 42, and ask students how the author has grouped the information. *by one way that the wind is useful—in creating power*

Discussing the Selection

Ask students to list and describe the kinds of winds they learned about in this selection.

Purposes for Reading

✦ Ask students to share any new information they learned in "What Happens When Wind Blows?"

✦ Ask students if they would recommend this selection to their friends, and encourage them to explain why.

Vocabulary Review

Review with students the selection vocabulary words *fierce, stings, steam,* and *boiling.* Ask students the following questions:

• *When was a time you saw or heard fierce wind?*

• *What is something that stings you?*

• *When was a time you have seen steam?*

• *What happens when something is boiling?*

BIG Idea

Why do we have wind?

Write the Big Idea question on the board. Ask students what they learned about wind. Ask which selections added something new to their understanding of wind. Encourage students to share their thoughts about the unit so far.

Students will

✦ find information and answer research questions.

✦ extend a story line through words and illustrations.

Story Lines Big Book, p. 32

Writing Process

Traits of Good Writing

Voice Writers often choose topics that allow them to use personal experiences to highlight their voice in the writing.

Teacher Tips

PLAN AHEAD In preparation for the following activity, have reference materials available.

HIGH-FREQUENCY WORDS Ask a volunteer to come to the ***Windy Days Big Book*** and point to the high-frequency word *when* on the pages of the story "What Happens When Wind Blows?"

Prewrite: Finding Information and Answering Questions

Teach

Remind students they are working together to write a report about a topic related to the wind. Tell students today they will continue researching their topic to find answers to research questions.

Apply

✦ Organize the class into the groups you created in the previous lesson. If possible, give each group a different set of reference materials from those they explored in the previous lesson.

✦ Display the list of research questions you helped the class prepare. Continue the research procedure you established in the previous lesson: Read aloud a question, and ask each group to look through the reference materials for pictures or words they think might help answer the question.

✦ Ask students to raise their hands if they find something they think is useful. Review the information, and write it on chart paper if it is relevant to the topic or, more specifically, if it answers the given research question.

✦ After you have researched each question on the list, tell students you will save their research until the next lesson, when they will work together to organize it.

Story Crafting

Story Lines

✦ Display the **Story Lines Big Book,** and open it to page 32, "Oliver and the Wind Storm." Review the story, pointing to each story frame as you read its accompanying text.

✦ When you finish reading, review Frame 18, and discuss how the existing story ends.

✦ Draw students' attention to the "Tell Me More" extender frames on pages 38–40. Remind students these boxes are just like the story frames they see on the previous pages, except these frames are empty so students can help tell more of the story.

✦ Point out that because Oliver is asleep in the story's final frame, the story that the class continues should be about another dream that Oliver has. Give students a few moments to consider what Oliver might dream about. Use questions such as the following to spur students' thinking:

- *Does Oliver dream about the "pesky robin" again? What other problem might the robin cause Oliver?*

- *What other things do cats like to do? What were the three things Oliver did when he came into the house after the windstorm?*

- *Oliver is sleeping on a girl's lap. Will the girl be in Oliver's dream?*

✦ Invite students to share their ideas for the story extension. Write ideas that students offer, and guide the class in choosing a workable direction for the story extension.

✦ Tell students they will finish the story in the next lesson. Encourage them to think about new ideas for the story for homework.

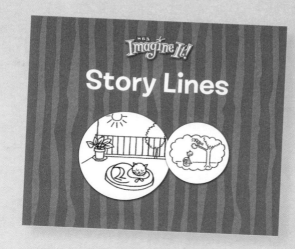

Story Lines Big Book, pp. 32–39

🍎 Teacher Tip

THINKING CROWNS Students might enjoy wearing the **Thinking Crowns** while they create an ending for "Oliver and the Wind Storm."

Differentiating Instruction **English Learners**

IF . . . students are unable to generate sentences to extend the story, **THEN . . .** encourage them to make suggestions by saying words or phrases or by drawing.

Sounds and Letters

Students will
- review word order in sentences.
- manipulate final phonemes to make new words.
- blend and read words.
- make and extend oral sentences.
- review the /o/ and /ō/ sounds.

- *Pickled Peppers Big Book,* p. 44; pp. 29–39
- *Alphabet Letter Cards Bb, Cc, Hh, Nn, Rr, Tt, Uu,* and *Oo* for each student

Calendar

Su	M	T	W	Th	F	S
		1	2	3	4	5
6	7	8	9	10	11	12
13	14	15	16	17	18	19
20	21	22	23	24	25	26
27	28	29	30	31		

Point to the box that represents today. Ask a volunteer to describe today's weather. Review the differences among various types of weather, and talk about how the weather differs in the various seasons.

Warming Up

Good morning, students!

Today is _____ .

_____ and _____ are things that are tall.

Kindergarten News

- Copy the text above on the board or on chart paper, and invite a volunteer to come up and write today's date in the blank.

- Have students tell a few items that are normally tall, such as trees, roller coasters, and skyscrapers. Invite students to come to the board to write their ideas.

- To discuss the letters and words in the message, you might ask students *What is the longest word in the message? Come point to it. How many letters does it have? Let's count them.*

Reviewing Word Order

- Have students play the Word Order game. Display the **Pickled Peppers Big Book** opened to page 44, "Houses."

- Reread the poem several times until students can say it with you. Point to each word as you read it.

✦ Assign to individual students the words in the first line. Have them stand in a row and repeat their words in order several times until they can do it with fluency.

✦ Ask these students to rearrange themselves and then say their words again. Point out how the sentence is just a group of words that does not work together to produce meaning.

✦ Discuss the importance of the order of words, both spoken and written. Remind students a word has meaning of its own, regardless of where it is used, but the meaning of a sentence depends on the order of its words.

✦ Repeat the activity with the last line of the poem and other students.

Phonemic Awareness

Phoneme Deletion: Final Sounds

✦ Bring out the **Lion Puppet,** and tell students he wants to play the game in which he takes away the ending sounds from words to make new words again.

✦ Remember to say a word, have students repeat it, and then have the puppet tell students to take away the ending sound to make a new word. Everyone will then say the new word. For example:

Teacher:	*The word is* pant.
Students:	*pant*
Puppet:	*Say* pant *without the /t/.*
Everyone:	*pan*

✦ Continue with these words:

mend /d/ men	*tried /d/ try*
clamp /p/ clam	*peep /p/ pea*
dent /t/ den	*band /d/ ban*
beep /p/ bee	*cattle /l/ cat*

Teacher Tip

LETTER/SOUND FLUENCY Review the letters of the alphabet with students by writing on the board six to eight different letters, chosen randomly and presented in both small and capital forms. Have students identify the letters and name the sounds they have learned. Then continue with several other letters also out of alphabetical order.

Phonics

Word Building

✦ Give each student **Alphabet Letter Cards** *b, c, h, n, r, t,* and *u*. Have them place all the cards in a row at the top of their desks or tables.

✦ Say *cut*, and then use it in a sentence. Say *I can cut paper with scissors. The word is* cut. Have students say the word.

✦ Ask students what the first sound is that they hear in the word *cut*. /k/ Then ask the class to check the **Alphabet Sound Wall Card** and tell which letter says /k/. *Cc* Point to the **Alphabet Sound Card Wall Card** *Cc*. Have students pull down **Alphabet Letter Card** *c*.

✦ Then ask the class what the next sound is that they hear in *cut*. /u/ Ask the class to check the **Alphabet Sound Wall Card** and tell which letter says /u/. *Uu* Point to **Alphabet Sound Wall Card** Short *Uu*. Have students pull down **Alphabet Letter Card** *u*.

✦ Finish by asking the class what the last sound is that they hear in *cut*. /t/ Ask the class to check the **Alphabet Sound Wall Card** and tell which letter says /t/. *Tt* Point to **Alphabet Sound Wall Card** *Tt*. Have students pull down **Alphabet Letter Card** *t*.

✦ Then write the word *cut* on the board, and have students proofread their words. If necessary, they should correct their spellings of the words.

✦ Have students put their letter cards back on the desk or table, and repeat the process with the words *hut, rut, but,* and *bun*.

✦ Remind students that when they are writing words on their own, they should say the words to themselves, think about the sounds in words, and then write the letters. They should always check the **Alphabet Sound Wall Cards** if they are unsure of the letter for a sound.

Oral Language and Sentence Extension

✦ Say clues for words to use with sentence extension. Try the following clues:

This is a doctor for animals. vet

This is a place for a baby. crib

✦ When the student has identified and said the word, have her or him use it in a sentence.

✦ Help students extend the sentences by asking them questions such as *Where? Which?* and *When?* For example:

Student:	*The dog went to the vet.*
Teacher:	*Which dog?*
Student:	*The big dog went to the vet.*
Teacher:	*Which big dog?*
Student:	*The big brown dog went to the vet.*
Teacher:	*Which vet?*
Student:	*The big brown dog went to the friendly vet.*

Differentiating Instruction **English Learners**

IF ... students are unable to generate sentences, **THEN** ... for oral practice and vocabulary building, ask them to repeat the sentences their classmates say.

Alphabetic Principle

Reviewing the Short and Long Sounds of *Oo*

✦ Focus students' attention on **Alphabet Sound Wall Card** Short *Oo,* and ask them what they remember about Bob the Fox. Read the story for students, inviting them to join in on the /o/ /o/ /o/ /o/ /o/ part.

✦ Next turn students' attention to **Alphabet Sound Wall Card** Long *Oo.* Have students recite the rhyme for the sounds of *Oo:*

O's my name.

Two sounds I know:

Short o in stop,

Long o in go.

Listening for /o/ and /ō/

Give each student an **Alphabet Letter Card** *Oo.* Ask students to turn the cards to the capital *O* sides and to hold them up when they hear the /ō/ sound. When they hear the /o/ sound, have them hold up the cards with the small *o* sides facing you. Try the following words:

not	ode	rock	nose
pole	stop	rope	rock
joke	drove	spoke	copy
drop	clock	phone	explode

Blending ROUTINE 2

Using Routine 2, the sound-by-sound blending routine, have students practice blending words containing the short and long sounds of the letter *Oo* as you write each word, letter by letter, on the board or chart paper. Remind students that when the letter *o* is by itself at the end of a word, it is going to make the /ō/ sound. After blending, have students make and extend sentences for some of the words. Try these words:

got	fox	not	top
go	joke	no	bone

Technology

Use the **Alphabet Sound Card Stories CD** to review the /o/ sound.

Audio CD

Pickled Peppers Big Book

✦ Display the **Pickled Peppers Big Book,** and ask students to identify the book on sight.

✦ Turn to page 29, "Who Said Red?" Point to the title, and read it aloud. Invite students to share anything that they remember about the rhyme.

✦ Either read aloud "Who Said Red?" or play it on the **Listening Library CD.** Ask students to listen for the words that have the /o/ sound and the /ō/ sound. Encourage them to close their eyes as they listen.

✦ Invite students to say any words with the /o/ sound and the /ō/ sound that they noticed while listening.

✦ Reread the rhyme, pointing to each word as you say it. This time, ask students to stop you each time you point to a word that has the letter *o* in it. *you, stop, don't, look, frog, NO, who, Could, bow, hello, yellow, mellow, Lemonade, Not, Or, brown, orange* Write each word on the board. (Some may appear more than once.)

✦ Then work with students to evaluate the words and to separate the words into two lists: words with short *o* and words with long *o. stop, frog; note, don't, NO, bow, hello, yellow, mellow*

Pickled Peppers Big Book, pp. 29–39

 **Teacher Tip**

VOWEL SPELLINGS Note that several of the *Oo* words in "Who Said Red?" display vowel sounds other than the /o/ sound and the /ō/ sound. If students are curious about these other sounds/spellings, tell them that they will learn all about these special sounds later—after they become "experts" at the /o/ sound and the /ō/ sound.

Technology

Use the **Listening Library CD** to support the **Pickled Peppers Big Book** lessons.

Audio CD

Reading and Responding

Students will

✦ locate the title and the names of the poet and the illustrator.

✦ connect their own life experiences to the text.

✦ develop an understanding of vocabulary words.

✦ use the comprehension strategy Visualizing.

✦ **Windy Days Big Book,** pp. 46–47

✦ Routines 5–7

Focus Question How does the poem make sounds like the wind?

Crick! Crack!

by Eve Merriam
illustrated by Todd Bonita

Crick! Crack!
Wind at my back.
Snit! Snat!
Snatched off my hat.

Whew! Whew!
It blew and it blew.

46

Windy Days Big Book, pp. 46–47

Technology

To promote independent reading, encourage students to use Workshop to listen to the recording of the selection on the **Listening Library CD.** Invite them to follow along and say the words whenever they can.

 Audio CD

Poetry

Activate Prior Knowledge [Routine 5]

✦ "Crick! Crack!" is another playful poem about a windy day with lots of rhyming words, repeated sounds, and words that sound like the actions they are describing.

✦ Invite students to discuss how a windy day sounds. Ask them questions such as the following: *What sounds do you hear when the wind is blowing hard? Can you make the sounds yourself? What causes some of the sounds? How do the sounds make you feel?*

✦ Have students discuss what they are learning about windy days. Ask them how this knowledge might help them appreciate windy days.

✦ Tell students you will be reading them a poem about a windy day. As you read the poem, relate what you already know to what you are reading, and encourage students to do the same.

Preview the Poem [Routine 5]

✦ Display the **Windy Days Big Book,** opened to pages 46–47. Follow Routine 5, the previewing the selection routine, as you introduce the poem's title and the names of the poet and the illustrator. Ask students what a poet and an illustrator do.

✦ As you prepare to read the poem, invite students to examine the picture and to share what they see. Ask them to identify what is real and what is make-believe in the picture.

✦ Encourage students to think about why they are reading this poem. Invite students to listen closely as you read to learn what the poem says about windy days.

Vocabulary

Routine **6**

✦ Follow Routine 6, the selection vocabulary routine, as you introduce the vocabulary words for this selection.

✦ Tell students the word *snatched* means "grabbed quickly." Use the following sentence to illustrate: Jake snatched the ball before it rolled into the water.

✦ Explain that in this poem the word *flapped* means "moved quickly up and down or side to side." Use the following sentence to illustrate: The waves flapped at the side of the boat. Point out that the word *flapped* can also mean the loose movement something like the flag makes in the wind.

Read the Poem

Routine **7**

✦ Before reading the poem, read the Focus Question above it. Tell students to keep this question in mind as they listen to the poem.

✦ Follow Routine 7, the reading the selection routine, as you read aloud "Crick! Crack!" Dramatize the sound words, which are followed by exclamation points and create rhythm in the poem. Ask students to listen for sound words and rhyming words as you read.

✦ Invite students to ask questions or to think aloud about anything in the poem that interests, puzzles, or amuses them.

Comprehension Strategies

For this poem, model the comprehension strategy Visualizing to help students make mental pictures of settings, characters, and actions.

Vocabulary

| snatched | flapped |

 Teacher Tip

VISUALIZING Encourage students to listen for sounds in the poem that resemble the wind. Invite them to think about how the wind would make these sounds.

Differentiating Instruction **English Learners**

IF ... students need help understanding vocabulary, **THEN ...** invite classmates who are proficient English speakers to role-play the words. Have English Learners mimic the actions and say the words.

Focus Question How does the poem make sounds like the wind?

Crick! Crack!

by Eve Merriam
illustrated by Todd Bonita

Crick! Crack!
Wind at my back.
Snit! Snat!
Snatched off my hat.

Whew! Whew!
It blew and it blew.

Snapped at my ears,
Flapped at my shoes,

And now I've got only
One mitten to lose. ❶

46

47

Windy Days Big Book, pp. 46–47

Comprehension Strategies

Teacher Modeling

❶ **Visualizing** *Let's think about the sounds the wind is making in this poem. Let's try to visualize the windy day in the poem. The wind is so strong that it's lifting up the man. Maybe that's why it makes the crick-crack sound. Would your back crack if you were suddenly lifted up? The wind snatched the man's hat with a "Snit! Snat!" Say the sounds aloud. Don't they sound like what the wind did? Now say the sounds "Whew! Whew!" Isn't that what the wind sounds like when it blows really hard?*

Discussing the Poem

✦ Review the Focus Question with students: How does the poem make sounds like the wind? *Sounds like crick-crack, snit-snat, and whew-whew all sound like a strong wind.*

✦ Invite students to share their feelings and ideas about the poem.

Purposes for Reading

✦ Remind students they were listening to find out what the poem tells them about windy days. Ask students what they learned about windy days from listening to this poem.

✦ Ask them what they liked best about the poem and why they liked it.

Vocabulary Review

Review with students the selection vocabulary words *snatched* and *flapped*. Ask students the following questions:

• *When was a time the wind snatched your hat?*

• *What would it look like if you flapped your arms?*

Monitor Progress

to Differentiate Instruction
Formal Assessment

Visualizing Note how easily students grasp visualizing.

APPROACHING LEVEL

| IF ... students need help visualizing, | THEN ... refer to Unit 10 Lesson 9 of the ***Intervention Guide.*** |

ON LEVEL

| IF ... students need to practice visualizing, | THEN ... have them play the guessing game I'm Thinking of Something ... with partners. |

ABOVE LEVEL

| IF ... students understand visualizing, | THEN ... ask them to visualize a favorite outdoor place on a windy day, and have them draw what they see. |

Differentiating Instruction **English Learners**

IF ... students have limited vocabulary, **THEN ...** help them participate in the discussion by asking them to imitate the sounds in the story or demonstrate how they think the wind sounds.

OBJECTIVES

Students will
+ learn how to summarize information.
+ learn how to sequence ideas for a report.
+ review that capital letters begin sentences.
+ review that exclamation points end exclamatory sentences.
+ collaborate to extend a story line.

MATERIALS
+ *Transparency* 47
+ *Language Arts Big Book,* p. 56
+ *Skills Practice 2,* pp. 105–106
+ *Story Lines Big Book,* p. 32

Writing Process

Model: Summarizing and Sequencing

Teach

Display *Transparency* 47. Remind students that when telling about events, it is important to tell about each part of an event in the correct order, or people might be confused.

Guided Practice

+ Display the chart paper on which you have written the notes from students' research.

+ Guide students in choosing four or five main points, ideas, or facts to include in the class report. Write these ideas or facts on a clean sheet of chart paper. Read each with students. Have volunteers make suggestions for the order of the final ideas or facts for the report.

+ Work with the class to decide on the final order. Number the ideas on the chart paper, and save it until the next lesson.

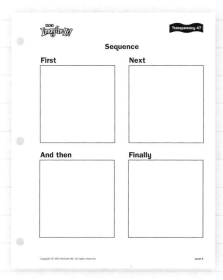

Transparency 47

Grammar, Usage, and Mechanics

Teach

+ Display *Language Arts Big Book* page 56, and ask a volunteer to come up and identify the exclamation on the page. Ask students what an exclamation is. *It is the kind of sentence that shows strong feeling.*

+ Remind students that just like statements and questions, exclamations must end with an end mark. Ask students *What kind of end mark comes at the end of an exclamation?* Have a volunteer come and point to the exclamation point on the page.

+ Remind students capital letters must begin exclamations. Have a volunteer come and point to the capital letter that begins the exclamation on page 56.

Language Arts Big Book, p. 56

Grammar, Usage, and Mechanics continued

Guided Practice

✦ Have students open their *Skills Practice 2* to pages 105–106.

✦ Work through the pages with students, and review their answers when you finish.

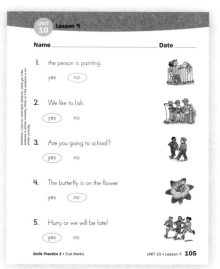
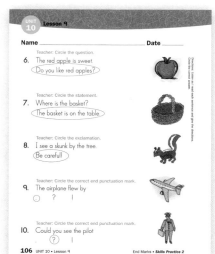

Skills Practice 2, pp. 105–106

 Teacher Tip

REVIEWING SKILLS You might test students' understanding of Oliver or any other story characters they have added by using thought clouds to ask them what a character might be thinking or feeling in a given frame.

Story Crafting

Story Lines

✦ Display the *Story Lines Big Book,* and open it to page 32, "Oliver and the Wind Storm."

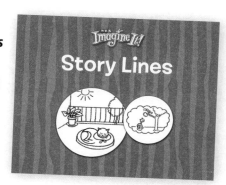

Story Lines Big Book, pp. 32–39

✦ Review the story again, pointing to each story frame as you read its accompanying text.

✦ When you reach page 38, spend some additional time discussing the extender frames that students completed in the previous lesson. Ask students *Would you like to change or add anything in this frame?* Have volunteers tell why they think their suggestions will make the story better.

✦ Then draw students' attention to the next empty frame, and tell them today they will complete the story. Guide students toward a story resolution by asking questions that will lead them there.

✦ Fill in the remaining extender frames, and guide the class in crafting story text to accompany the drawings.

✦ When students have completed the story, review it, beginning with Frame 1 all the way through the frames that students created.

Monitor Progress to Differentiate Instruction

Formal Assessment

Grammar Note how quickly students are able to distinguish between statements, questions, and exclamations.

APPROACHING LEVEL	**IF …** students are having difficulty,	**THEN …** help them complete *Reteach* page 189.
ON LEVEL	**IF …** students need more practice,	**THEN …** have them look at *Language Arts Big Book* page 56, and talk with them about the different types of sentences.
ABOVE LEVEL	**IF …** students are comfortable,	**THEN …** have them complete *Challenge Activities* page 142.

Sounds and Letters

Students will

✦ manipulate internal phonemes to make new words.

✦ make and extend oral sentences.

✦ review the /u/ and /ū/ sounds.

✦ review writing the letters *Bb, Cc, Oo, Rr, Gg, Jj, Ff, Uu, Xx,* and *Zz.*

✦ practice writing words they have blended.

✦ **Alphabet Letter Cards** one of each letter; *Bb, Gg, Hh, Ll, Rr, Tt,* and *Uu* for each student

✦ Routine 2

✦ **Skills Practice 2,** pp. 107–108

Calendar

Su	M	T	W	Th	F	S
		1	2	3	4	5
6	7	8	9	10	11	12
13	14	15	16	17	18	19
20	21	22	23	24	25	26
27	28	29	30	31		

Point to the box that represents today. Ask a volunteer to describe today's weather. Have another volunteer tell about yesterday's weather. Discuss the similarities and differences between the two days' weather.

Warming Up

Good morning, boys and girls!

Today is _____.

I can see a _____ and a _____ at the circus.

Kindergarten News

✦ Copy the text above on the board or on chart paper, and make several errors in the message today.

✦ Invite a volunteer to write today's date in the blank.

✦ Then invite students to find the mistakes you made in the message and to come up to the board to correct the errors.

✦ Ask students if they can read any words in the message today. Invite students to point to and say any words they can read. Help students identify some high-frequency words such as *is, I, can, see, a,* and others in the third sentence.

✦ Discuss the letters, words, and sentences in the message. For example, you might have students count the words and the spaces in the third sentence.

Catching the Letter Train Game

✦ Have students sit in a circle. Give each student an **Alphabet Letter Card** (excluding *Xx*). Remind students that the cards are their tickets to get on the Letter Train and that to catch the train, they must say a word that starts with the sound of their letter.

✦ Walk around the circle, and ask for a ticket. When a student says a word, she or he gets up and joins you as part of the "train." As the train goes around the circle, have students make the beginning sounds of the words.

✦ Ask for another ticket, and continue the game until all students are on the Letter Train.

Phonemic Awareness

Phoneme Deletion: Internal Sounds

✦ Bring out the **Lion Puppet,** and tell students he wants to play the game in which he takes away sounds from words to make new words but this time the sound will be in the middle of the word. You may need to provide extra support for this activity as it is more difficult than deleting initial or final phonemes.

✦ Say a word, have students repeat it, and then have the puppet tell students to take away an internal sound to make a new word. Everyone will then say the new word. For example:

Teacher: *The word is* bloom.
Students: *bloom*
Puppet: *Say* bloom *without the /l/.*
Everyone: *boom*

✦ Continue with these words:

slip /l/ sip	*field /l/ feed*
stand /t/ sand	*clamp /m/ clap*
glaze /l/ gaze	*slow /l/ so*
past /s/ pat	*blank /l/ bank*
bleach /l/ beach	*blend /l/ bend*
spent /p/ sent	*spry /r/ spy*
blow /l/ bow	*broom /r/ boom*

Teacher Tip

ADDITIONAL SUPPORT This activity may be challenging for some students. Provide support as needed by modeling several more words.

Phonics

Word Building

✦ Give each student **Alphabet Letter Cards** *b, g, h, l, r, t,* and *u.* Have them place all the cards in a row at the top of their desks or tables.

✦ Say *bug,* and then use it in a sentence. Say *I see a bug in the grass. The word is* bug. Have students say the word.

✦ Ask students what the first sound is that they hear in the word *bug.* /b/ Then ask the class to check the **Alphabet Sound Wall Card** and tell which letter says /b/. *Bb* Point to the **Alphabet Sound Card Wall Card** *Bb.* Have students pull down **Alphabet Letter Card** *b.*

✦ Then ask the class what the next sound is that they hear in *bug.* /u/ Ask the class to check the **Alphabet Sound Wall Card** and tell which letter says /u/. *Uu* Point to **Alphabet Sound Wall Card** Short *Uu.* Have students pull down **Alphabet Letter Card** *u.*

✦ Finish by asking the class what the last sound is that they hear in *bug.* /g/ Ask the class to check the **Alphabet Sound Wall Card** and tell which letter says /g/. *Gg* Point to **Alphabet Sound Wall Card** *Gg.* Have students pull down **Alphabet Letter Card** *g.*

✦ Then write the word *bug* on the board, and have students proofread their words. If necessary, they should correct their spellings of the words.

✦ Have students put their letter cards back on the desk or table, and repeat the process with the words *lug, rug, tug,* and *tub.*

✦ Remind students that when they are writing words on their own, they should say the words to themselves, think about the sounds in words, and then write the letters. They should always check the **Alphabet Sound Wall Cards** if they are unsure of the letter for a sound.

✦ Close today's activity by telling students they have done an excellent job. Applaud, and congratulate them on becoming excellent readers and writers!

Oral Language and Sentence Extension

✦ Say clues for words to use in sentence extension. Try the following clues:

This is what you do to clothes after they are washed. fold

This ocean creature has two shells. clam

This word rhymes with crab. *grab*

✦ When the student has identified and said the word, have her or him use it in a sentence.

✦ Help students extend the sentences by asking them questions such as *Where?* *Which?* and *When?* For example:

Student: *The clam dug a hole.*

Teacher: *Which clam?*

Student: *The white clam dug a hole.*

Teacher: *Where?*

Student: *The white clam dug a hole in the sand.*

Differentiating Instruction **English Learners**

IF . . . students are native speakers of Spanish, Tagalog (Filipino), or certain other languages, **THEN . . .** they may need extra practice saying /u/ and associating it with the letter *u.* These languages lack the /u/ sound found in English.

Alphabetic Principle

Reviewing the Short and Long Sounds of *Uu*

- Focus students' attention on ***Alphabet Sound Wall Card*** Short *Uu*, and ask them what they remember about Tubby the Tugboat. Read the story for students, inviting them to join in on the /u/ /u/ /u/ /u/ /u/ part.
- Next turn students' attention to ***Alphabet Sound Wall Card*** Long *Uu*. Have students recite the rhyme for the sounds of *Uu:*

  U*'s my name.*

  Two sounds I use:

  Short u *in* cub,

  Long u *in* fuse.

Listening for /u/ and /ū/

Give each student an ***Alphabet Letter Card*** *Uu*. Ask students to turn the cards to the capital *U* sides and to hold them up and say */ū/* when they hear the /ū/ sound. When they hear the /u/ sound, have them hold up the cards with the small *u* sides facing you and say */u/*. Try the following words:

hut	*mule*	*hunt*	*jump*
pun	*run*	*must*	*cube*
cute	*just*	*huge*	*study*
fume	*much*	*immune*	*accuse*

Blending ROUTINE 2

Using Routine 2, the sound-by-sound blending routine, have students practice blending words containing the short and long sounds of the letter *Uu* as you write each word letter by letter on the board or chart paper. After blending, have students make and extend sentences for some of the words. Try these words:

up	*run*	*us*	*cut*
cute	*tune*		

Technology

Use the ***Alphabet Sound Card Stories CD*** to review the /u/ sound.

Audio CD

Penmanship

✦ Distribute a sheet of writing paper to each student, or use **White Boards** turned to the sides with writing lines. Place the Supply Icon for *pencil* on the board or in the **Pocket Chart.**

✦ Write on the board the words *fog, rub, cub, jog,* and *rob.*

✦ Guide students in reading each word individually. After each word is blended, ask students to practice writing the word on their writing papers. If they need more space, ask them to turn over the papers.

Guided Practice

✦ Guide students in completing **Skills Practice 2** pages 107–108, for additional practice blending and writing words.

✦ Read aloud each sentence, and help students blend each word if necessary. Allow students time to write the word on the line before moving on to the next word.

✦ When students finish both pages, have them work with partners to proofread their work. Ask each student to circle one word on each page they think they can write better. Have them cross out the word and rewrite it above, below, or next to the first attempt.

✦ After students have finished, review their work, and note which students are struggling with letter formation.

Monitor Progress
to Differentiate Instruction

Formal Assessment ✓

Blending Note how easily students write and blend the words.

APPROACHING LEVEL	
IF ... students have difficulty,	THEN ... guide them in completing **Reteach** page 190.

ON LEVEL	
IF ... students need more practice,	THEN ... have students write and blend additional words such as *cob, jig,* and *rug.*

ABOVE LEVEL	
IF ... students would enjoy a challenging activity,	THEN ... have them work independently to complete page 143 in **Challenge Activities.**

Teacher Tip

STUDENT MONITORING Check students' writing to make sure they are forming all their letters correctly. Provide extra practice for those students who are still having difficulty during this review lesson.

Skills Practice 2, pp. 107–108

Reading and Responding

OBJECTIVES

Students will

✦ conduct experiments with the wind.

✦ describe and record their observations.

✦ develop an understanding of vocabulary words.

MATERIALS

✦ *Windy Days Big Book,* pp. 4–45

✦ *Read Aloud Collection: Can You See the Wind?*

INQUIRY PLANNER

WEEK 1	✦ Begin discussing and sharing ideas. ✦ Think about a question for the **Concept/ Question Board.**
WEEK 2	✦ Begin investigating and collecting information. ✦ Generate a question and/or idea for the **Concept/Question Board.**
WEEK 3	✦ Share your findings with others. ✦ Do you have **more questions?**

Differentiating Instruction · **English Learners**

IF ... students have limited proficiency, **THEN ...** be sure to place them in a group with at least two native English-speaking students. Encourage proficient English speakers to help their English Learner partners compose descriptive phrases and sentences for their drawings.

Inquiry

✦ Discuss with the class the selections you have read so far. Ask questions such as the following:

- *What good things does the wind do?*
- *What does the wind do that we don't like?* (You should try to connect this to wind events students can relate to, such as tornadoes in the Midwest, hurricanes on the East and Gulf Coasts, or the Santa Ana winds in California.)
- *Does the wind always come from the same place?* (Students should be able to connect this to their findings from the wind direction instruments. Wind can come from different directions and different places.)

✦ Begin writing any answers to their questions that they have learned from their reading. Discuss all the new information that the class has learned about the wind.

Small-Group Time `Small Group`

✦ Have groups decide how to share what they have learned about the wind. They might want to write about what they learned using their wind instruments, or they might want to talk about the information on their class chart and what they learned from their observations. Some may want to take pictures of what the wind can do and create a photo essay.

✦ During the coming days, take time for students to continue their observations and develop their presentations.

Whole-Group Time `Whole Group`

Discuss the use of the wind instruments. What have students learned about the wind? How have the instruments helped students answer their questions about the wind? Some students may want to switch instruments and use different ones for the next few days to help them collect information for their conjectures.

Concept Vocabulary

The word *stormy* is the second concept vocabulary word for Unit 10. Write the word on an index card, and post it in your classroom. Explain to students that the word *stormy* means "having high winds and rain, sleet, hail, snow, or lightning and thunder." Discuss how the word *stormy* relates to windy days. Use the word daily, and students will feel comfortable using it too. Invite students to bring in pictures and drawings that illustrate the word *stormy* to post on the **Concept/Question Board.**

Concept/Question Board

Explain to students that like scientists, they will discover new questions as they do research. Encourage students to share any new questions they have about the wind. Explain that as they think of new ideas, they will discover new questions. Remind students to bring in additional items to post on the Board, such as photographs they have taken or drawings they have made of the wind in action.

IF ... students have difficulty thinking of a presentation for their findings, **THEN ...** help them prepare presentations appropriate for them, such as murals or picture books about the effects of the wind.

IF ... students would benefit from added exposure to the vocabulary and themes of the unit, **THEN ...** encourage them to copy information from the **Concept/Question Board** into notebooks for reference.

 Teacher Tips

MAKING A KITE A natural activity to do in this unit is to build kites and fly them, but this can be done only when sufficient wind is available to keep the kites afloat. Making kites is easy, and directions are available on the Internet. When you try to fly the kites, have the students use their wind instruments to see if there is enough wind and from which direction the wind is coming.

RECREATIONAL READING Because it is important to read daily to your students, choose a book from the Additional Reading listed in the Table of Contents, and find a time during the day to read the book aloud to students.

Language Arts

Students will
✦ begin writing the class report.
✦ review exclamatory sentences.
✦ review letters and sounds through game play.

✦ *Language Arts Big Book,* p. 56
✦ *Alphabet Sound Cards*

Writing Process

Draft: Collaborating to Write Report

Teach

Remind students they are working as a class to write a report about a topic related to the wind.

Guided Practice

✦ Write on the board the list of sequenced ideas the class chose and organized in the previous lesson. Review the list with students, reminding them of the order they chose to present the ideas in the report. Ask students if they would like to make any changes to this writing plan.

✦ When students are satisfied with the writing plan, begin writing the report, having students suggesting or generating sentences, with you translating their ideas to paper. Focus on drafting one sentence at a time.

✦ Continue until you have written sentences for the first few ideas in the report. Tell students that in the next lesson they will continue drafting the class report. Save this first draft for the next lesson.

Grammar, Usage, and Mechanics

Teach

Display *Language Arts Big Book* page 56, and ask a volunteer to identify the exclamation on the page. Ask the student to tell how he or she knew it was the exclamation. *An exclamation point is at the end of the sentence.*

Guided Practice

✦ Use sentence frames to help students create their own exclamations. For example, write the following on the board or on chart paper, and have students fill in the blanks:
  - I love to _____ !
  - Please do not _____ !
  - I wish I _____ !

✦ When students have filled in the sentence frames, guide them in extending the sentences by adding more information.

Language Arts Big Book, p. 56

GAME Day

Letter Lists

✦ In advance of Game Day, gather the individual **Alphabet Sound Cards** in a stack, out of alphabetical order.

✦ On Game Day, organize the class into teams of three or four students per team. Have teams sit together so other teams cannot hear them talk. Write a name for each team on the board. Under these names you will write each team's score for each round of play.

✦ Distribute to each group several sheets of writing paper and one pencil. Ask students to decide on one "secretary" for the group. This student will be responsible for writing words in a list, so the student should have neat handwriting.

✦ Explain the game to students. You will choose an **Alphabet Sound Card** from the stack. The class will say the letter aloud and then work within their groups to think of and write as many words as possible that begin with that letter or sound.

✦ After each round, have groups share the words they generated, and count the words that are correct. Invite one student from each group (other than the secretary) to write the number on the board under their group's name.

✦ Continue until one team reaches a predetermined total of points. Or if time permits, practice each letter of the alphabet.

Lesson Planner

Day 1

Day 2

Sounds and Letters

MATERIALS

- ✦ *Alphabet Letter Cards:* Aa, Ee, Ii, Oo and Uu
- ✦ Routine 2
- ✦ *Pickled Peppers Big Book,* pp. 16–19, 40, 46
- ✦ *Skills Practice 2,* pp. 109, 111–112, 115–116
- ✦ *High-Frequency Flash Cards*
- ✦ *Alphabet Sound Cards*

Day 1

Warming Up, p. T170
Phonics
Blending and Sentence Extension, p. T171
Alphabetic Principle
- Reviewing the Short and Long Sounds of *Oo* and *Uu*, p. T172
- Listening for Medial /ō/ and /ū/, p. T172
- Linking the Sound to the Letter, p. T172
- Penmanship, p. T173

Day 2

Warming Up, p. T180
Phonics
Blending and Sentence Extension, p. T181
Alphabetic Principle
- Reviewing the Short and Long Sounds of *Ee*, p. T182
- Listening for /e/ and /ē/, p. T182
- Blending, p. T182
- *Pickled Peppers Big Book,* p. T183

Reading and Responding

MATERIALS

- ✦ *Windy Days Big Book,* p. 48
- ✦ *Science Lap Book,* pp. 36–43
- ✦ Routines 5–7
- ✦ *Story Time Collection:* Wind Says Good Night
- ✦ *Home Connection,* pp. 81–82

Science Link, p. T174
Vocabulary, p. T175
Read the Selection, p. T175
Comprehension Strategies, p. T176
Print and Book Awareness, p. T177
Vocabulary Review, p. T177

Science Link, p. T184
Vocabulary, p. T184
Read the Selection, p. T185
Comprehension Strategies, p. T186
Reading with a Writer's Eye, p. T187
Discussing the Selection, p. T187
Vocabulary Review, p. T187

Language Arts

MATERIALS

- ✦ *Language Arts Big Book,* pp. 9, 22, 39, 46, 51, 54
- ✦ *Windy Days Big Book*
- ✦ *Willy the Wisher,* p. 96
- ✦ *Skills Practice 2,* pp. 110, 113–114
- ✦ *Transparency* 44
- ✦ *Read Aloud Collection:* Can You See the Wind?
- ✦ *Story Time Collection:* Wind Says Good Night

Writing Process
Draft: Collaborating to Write Report, p. T178
Fine Art
Discussing Fine Art, p. T179

Writing Process
Revise: Revising Class Report, p. T188
Grammar, Usage, and Mechanics, pp. T188–T189
Willy the Wisher, p. T189

Monitor Progress

- ✔ = **Formal Assessment**
- Ⓑ = **Benchmark Assessment**

✔ Penmanship, p. T173

✔ Blending, p. T181
✔ Order Words, p. T189

Day 3

Warming Up, pp. T190–T191
Phonics
Blending and Sentence Extension, p. T191
Alphabetic Principle
• Reviewing the Short and Long Sounds of *Aa, Ii,* and *Oo,* p. T192
• Differentiating Vowel Sounds, p. T192
• Linking the Sound to the Letter, p. T192
• Penmanship, p. T193

Preview and Prepare, p. T194
Vocabulary, p. T195
Read the Selection, p. T195
Comprehension Strategies, pp. T196, T198, T200, T202
Print and Book Awareness, pp. T197, T199, T201, T203
Discussing the Selection, p. T203
Vocabulary Review, p. T203

Writing Process
Draft: Drawing and Illustrating Findings, p. T204
Story Crafting, p. T205

✓ *Lesson Assessment Book,* p. 92
✓ Blending, p. T193

Day 4

Warming Up, pp. T206–T207
Phonics
Blending and Sentence Extension, p. T207
Alphabetic Principle
• Reviewing the Short and Long Sounds of *Ee* and *Uu,* p. T208
• Listening for Medial /ē/ and /ū/, p. T208
• *Pickled Peppers Big Book,* p. T209

Preview and Prepare, p. T210
Vocabulary, p. T210
Read the Selection, p. T211
Comprehension Strategies, pp. T212, T214, T216, T218
Comprehension Skills, pp. T213, T215, T217
Reading with a Writer's Eye, pp. T213, T215, T217, T219
Discussing the Selection, p. T219
Vocabulary Review, p. T219

Writing Process
Reflect: Comparing Report to Conjectures Made Prior to Research, p. T220
Grammar, Usage, and Mechanics, pp. T220–T221
Story Crafting, p. T221

✓ *Lesson Assessment Book,* pp. 92–93
✓ Pronouns, p. T221

Day 5

Warming Up, pp. T222–T223
Phonics
Blending and Sentence Extension, p. T223
Alphabetic Principle
• Reviewing the Short and Long Sounds of *Aa, Ee, Ii, Oo,* and *Uu,* p. T224
• Differentiating Vowel Sounds, p. T224
• Penmanship, p. T225

Theme Wrap-Up and Review, p. T226

Writing Process
Publish: Presenting Report and Sharing Drawings, p. T227
Grammar, Usage, and Mechanics, p. T227
Benchmark Assessment, pp. T228–T229
Unit Celebration
• Celebrate the Wind!, p. T230
• Inquiry Wrap-Up, p. T231

✓ *Lesson Assessment Book,* pp. 94–96
Comprehension Observation Log
✓ Blending, p. T225
✓ Action Words, p. T227
Ⓑ *Benchmark Assessment,* Benchmark 6

Student Resources

StoryTime Selection

Wind Says Good Night

by Katy Rydell

Wind Says Good Night

It was late at night. All little children were in their beds, fast asleep. All except one.

The night wind brushed against a window. *"Shh-h-h,"* whispered the wind. "Go to sleep."

But the child could not fall asleep. Outside, on the branch of a tree, Mockingbird was singing.

Katy Rydell   *illustrated by* David Jorgensen

SRA
Columbus, OH

Audio CD

Big Books

Imagine It!
Science Lap Book

Imagine It! Unit 10
Windy Days

Imagine It!
Pickled Peppers

Teacher Support

Language Arts Big Book
SRA Imagine It!

Language Arts Big Book

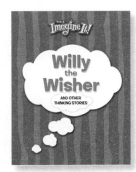

SRA Imagine It!
Willy the Wisher
AND OTHER THINKING STORIES

Willy the Wisher

Curriculum Connections

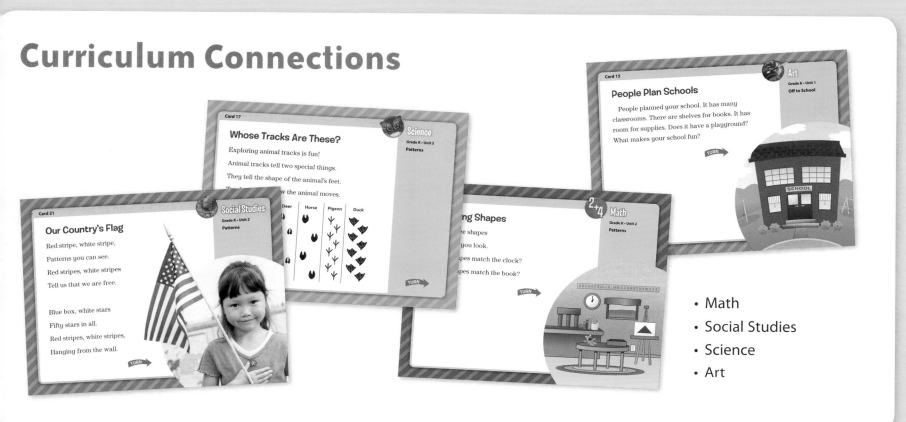

Card 17

Whose Tracks Are These?

Exploring animal tracks is fun!
Animal tracks tell two special things.
They tell the shape of the animal's feet.

Science
Grade K · Unit 2
Patterns

Deer | Horse | Pigeon | Duck

Card 21

Our Country's Flag

Red stripe, white stripe,
Patterns you can see.
Red stripes, white stripes
Tell us that we are free.

Blue box, white stars
Fifty stars in all.
Red stripes, white stripes,
Hanging from the wall.

Social Studies
Grade K · Unit 2
Patterns

Card 15

People Plan Schools

People planned your school. It has many
classrooms. There are shelves for books. It has
room for supplies. Does it have a playground?
What makes your school fun?

Art
Grade K · Unit 1
Off to School

Math
Grade K · Unit 2
Patterns

- Math
- Social Studies
- Science
- Art

Additional Skills Practice

Approaching Level	On Level	English Learner	Above Level
Reteach	**Skills Practice 2**	**English Learner Support Activities**	**Challenge Activities**
Action Words, p. 196	Blending, pp. 109, 111–112, 115–116	Lessons 11–15	Blending, pp. 145, 147
Blending, pp. 193, 195	Position Words, p. 110		Position Words, p. 144
Penmanship, p. 191	Pronouns, pp. 113–114		Pronouns, p. 146
Position Words, p. 192			
Pronouns, p. 194			

Differentiating Instruction

Lessons 11-15 Overview

for Workshop Planner

Day 1

Approaching Level	On Level	English Learner	Above Level
Sounds and Letters			
Alphabetic Principle: Refer to Unit 10 Lesson 11 of the **Intervention Guide** for additional support activities.	**Alphabetic Principle:** Students think of words with the /ō/ sound as you write them on the board or chart paper, and then choose one word to illustrate.	**Alphabetic Principle:** Refer to Unit 10 Lesson 11 of the **English Learner Support Guide.**	**Alphabetic Principle:** Students use the **eGames** activity for this unit to review vowels and their sounds.
Reading and Responding			
Comprehension: Students browse the selection "So Much Is Moving," and point out any pictures that confuse or interest them.	**Comprehension:** Have students discuss how different things move in the selection.	**Comprehension:** Refer to Unit 10 Lesson 11 of the **English Learner Support Guide.**	**Comprehension:** Students use the Internet and magazines to locate pictures of people making things move and post them to the **Concept/Question Board.**
Language Arts			
Writing: With your help, students discuss the books they have read this year.	**Writing:** Students brainstorm lists of their favorite books.	**Writing:** Students answer yes-no and either-or questions about the books they have read this year.	**Writing:** Students continue their research on their questions about wind.

Day 2

Approaching Level	On Level	English Learner	Above Level
Sounds and Letters			
Alphabetic Principle: Work with students to use **eGames** for practice identifying vowels and their sounds.	**Alphabetic Principle:** Have students use **eSkills** to review the /ē/ sound.	**Alphabetic Principle:** Refer to Unit 10 Lesson 12 of the **English Learner Support Guide.**	**Alphabetic Principle:** Students write down all the words they can think of with the /ē/ sound and each choose one word to illustrate.
Reading and Responding			
Comprehension: Students browse the selection "So Much Is Moving," and make connections between how the people in the pictures are making things move.	**Comprehension:** Have students create their own stories about things they move and how they make these things move.	**Comprehension:** Refer to Unit 10 Lesson 12 of the **English Learner Support Guide.**	**Comprehension:** Students find pictures in magazines of people making things move.
Language Arts			
Writing: With your help, students create lists of their top five favorite books of the year. **Grammar:** With your help, students complete the activity on **Reteach** page 192.	**Writing:** Each student chooses a favorite book. **Grammar:** Review with students what they remember about pronouns.	**Writing:** Students choose their top five favorite books of the year from a list you generate. **Grammar:** Refer to Unit 10 Lesson 12 of the **English Learner Support Guide.**	**Writing:** Students discuss the results of their research about wind. **Grammar:** Have students work independently to complete **Challenge Activities** page 144.

Day 3

Approaching Level	On Level	English Learner	Above Level
Sounds and Letters			
Alphabetic Principle: Refer to Unit 10 Lesson 13 of the *Intervention Guide* for activities to help students.	**Alphabetic Principle:** Students use the *eGames* activities for a comprehensive review of vowels and their long and short sounds.	**Alphabetic Principle:** Refer to Unit 10 Lesson 13 of the *English Learner Support Guide.*	**Alphabetic Principle:** Have students work independently to complete page 145 in *Challenge Activities.*
Reading and Responding			
Comprehension: Have students browse *Wind Says Good Night,* and point to any illustrations that interest them.	**Comprehension:** Students retell the story *Wind Says Good Night* to one another in their own words.	**Comprehension:** Refer to Unit 10 Lesson 13 of the *English Learner Support Guide.*	**Comprehension:** Students discuss and draw pictures about what might happen next in the story *Wind Says Good Night.*
Language Arts			
Writing: Students draw pictures to summarize their favorite books.	**Writing:** Students tell why these books are their favorites.	**Writing:** Each student chooses a favorite book and draws a picture to summarize it.	**Writing:** Students plan presentations about their questions, hypothesis, and research.

Day 4

Approaching Level	On Level	English Learner	Above Level
Sounds and Letters			
Alphabetic Principle: Help students review the /ē/ sound using *eSkills.*	**Alphabetic Principle:** Students listen to the **Alphabet Sound Card Stories CD** to review the short-vowel sounds.	**Alphabetic Principle:** Refer to Unit 10 Lesson 14 of the **English Learner Support Guide.**	**Alphabetic Principle:** Students review sound-letter correspondences by rereading **Decodables** 18 and 19.
Reading and Responding			
Comprehension: Encourage students to browse *Wind Says Good Night* and point to pages that could be real and pages that could be fantasy.	**Comprehension:** Have students practice sequencing by retelling what happened first, next, and last in the story.	**Comprehension:** Refer to Unit 10 Lesson 14 of the **English Learner Support Guide.**	**Comprehension:** Have students discuss which characters they liked best in Unit 10 and why.
Language Arts			
Writing: Students sign their names to their pictures and present them to their groups. **Grammar:** With your help, students complete **Reteach** page 194.	**Writing:** Students draw pictures about their favorite books. **Grammar:** Review with students what they remember about verb tenses.	**Writing:** Students sign their names to their pictures. **Grammar:** Refer to Unit 10 Lesson 14 of the **English Learner Support Guide.**	**Writing:** Students present their findings about wind to you. **Grammar:** Have students complete **Challenge Activities** page 146.

Differentiating Instruction
for Workshop Planner

Day 5

Approaching Level	On Level	English Learner	Above Level
Sounds and Letters			
Reading a *Decodable:* Reread **Decodable** 20 with students, reviewing what is happening in the illustrations and having individual students read pages independently.	**Reading a *Decodable:*** Have students reread using **eDecodable** *We Did It!*	**Reading a *Decodable:*** Review **Decodable** 20 with students, pointing to the high-frequency words *be* and *she* as you read aloud to them.	**Reading a *Decodable:*** Students reread **Decodable** 20 with partners and track print from left to right.
Reading and Responding			
Comprehension: Have students discuss which character they liked best in Unit 10 and why.	**Review:** Have students retell the selections to one another in their own words.	**Review:** Students listen to one of the Unit 10 selections on the **Listening Library CD.**	**Review:** Students discuss similarities and differences between the characters in the Unit 10 selections and post their ideas and wonderings on the **Concept/Question Board.**
Language Arts			
Writing: With your help, students complete **Reteach** page 196. **Grammar:** Refer to Unit 10 Lesson 15 of the **Intervention Guide** for additional support for this Grammar activity.	**Writing:** Students sign their names to their pictures and present them to their groups. **Grammar:** With your help, students each create one sentence using each pronoun.	**Writing:** With your help, students present their drawings first to a partner and then to the group. **Grammar:** Refer to Unit 10 Lesson 15 of the **English Learner Support Guide.**	**Writing:** Students discuss with you how they felt about this activity. **Grammar:** Students each create one sentence, using each verb tense and each pronoun.

Resources for
Differentiating Instruction

English Learner

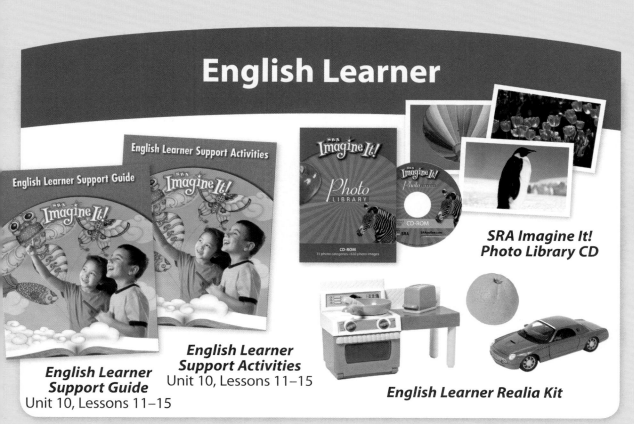

English Learner Support Guide
Unit 10, Lessons 11–15

English Learner Support Activities
Unit 10, Lessons 11–15

SRA Imagine It! Photo Library CD

English Learner Realia Kit

Approaching Level

Intervention

Intervention Guide

Intervention Workbook

Workshop Kits

- High Frequency Words
- Letter Recognition
- Phonemic Awareness
- Phonics
- Print and Book Awareness
- Sequencing

Technology

Alphabet Sound Card Stories CD
eGames
eSkills & eGames
Listening Library CD

Listening Library Unit 10

Lesson Assessment

Monitor Progress to Differentiate Instruction

Use these summative assessments along with your informal observations to assess student mastery.

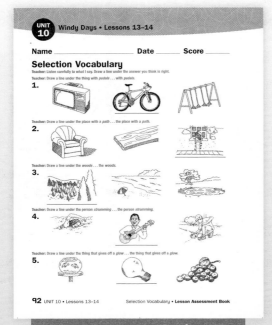

Lesson Assessment Book, p. 92

Lesson Assessment Book, p. 93

Lesson Assessment Book, p. 94

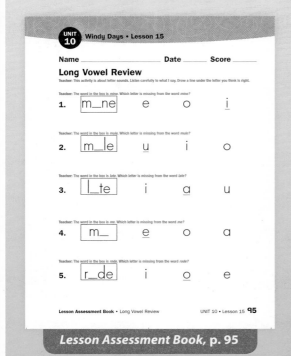

Lesson Assessment Book, p. 95

Lesson Assessment Book, p. 96

Comprehension Observation Log form:

Lesson Assessment Book

Comprehension Observation Log

Student _____ Date _____
Unit _____ Lesson _____ Selection Title _____

General Comprehension
Concepts discussed: _____

Behavior Within a Group
Articulates, expresses ideas: _____

Joins discussions: _____

Collaborates (such as works well with other students, works alone): _____

Role in Group
Role (such as leader, summarizer, questioner, critic, observer, non-participant): _____

Flexibility (changes roles when necessary): _____

Use of Reading Strategies
Uses strategies when needed (either those taught or student's choice of strategy)/Describes strategies used: _____

Changes strategies when appropriate: _____

Changes Since Last Observation

110   Comprehension Observation Log • **Lesson Assessment Book**

Lesson Assessment Annotated Teacher's Edition, p. 110

The Comprehension Observation Log, found in the *Lesson Assessment Annotated Teacher's Edition,* is a vehicle for recording anecdotal information about individual student performance on an ongoing basis. Information such as students' strengths and weaknesses can be recorded at any time the occasion warrants. It is recommended that you maintain a folder for each student where you can store the logs for purposes of comparison and analysis as the school year progresses. You will gradually build up a comprehensive file that reveals which students are progressing smoothly and which students need additional help.

Use *Benchmark Assessment,* Benchmark 6, to target students at risk for reading failure.

Sounds and Letters

Students will

+ blend and read words.
+ make and extend oral sentences.
+ review the long- and short-vowel sounds of *Oo* and *Uu*.
+ review writing the letters *Ww, Kk,* and *Ee*.
+ practice writing words they have blended.

+ Routine 2
+ **Alphabet Letter Cards** *Oo* and *Uu* for each student

Calendar

Su	M	T	W	Th	F	S
		1	2	3	4	5
6	7	8	9	10	11	12
13	14	15	16	17	18	19
20	21	22	23	24	25	26
27	28	29	30	31		

Point to the box that represents today. Take this opportunity to identify any important events that will happen during the coming week, such as students' birthdays, school functions, and national holidays. You might have students count with you the days until the last day of school this year.

Warming Up

MORNING MESSAGE

Today is _____.

We will practice writing the letters _____,
_____, and _____.

Kindergarten News

+ Copy the text above on the board or on chart paper, and invite a volunteer to come up and write today's date in the blank.

+ Give students clues to help them identify the letters for the blanks in the second sentence. For example: *The first letter we will review begins the word* water. *Ww The second letter we will review is in the middle of the word* men. *Ee The third letter we will review is at the end of the word* hook. *Kk*

Phoneme Matching

+ Play the Same-Sound game with students. This time, say a series of three words, two of which have the same initial sound. Ask students to listen closely and to identify which words start with the same sound. Call on volunteers to say the words and to give the initial sounds.

+ Try these sets of words:

banjo, *dollar,* **bumper** /b/   **finger, fasten,** *garage* /f/

teapot, **younger, yellow** /y/   **zipper, zero,** *singer* /z/

puppy, *baby,* **pocket** /p/   *bandit,* **danger, donkey** /d/

Phonics

Blending and Sentence Extension

✦ Using Routine 2, the sound-by-sound blending procedure, have students blend the following words sound by sound as you write them letter by letter on the board:

pen　　　*hot*　　　*take*　　　*like*

✦ On the board, write sentences that contain the words. For example:

Do not take the pen.

Do you like the dog?

✦ Ask students to use their knowledge of high-frequency words and sounds and letters to read each sentence. Be sure to have them reread the sentences until they can do so as they would say or speak them.

✦ Say clues for words from the blending activity. Call on a student to come to the board to underline the word that answers the clue. When the student has identified and said the word, have her or him use it in a sentence. Help students extend the sentences by asking them questions such as *Where? Which?* and *When?*

Alphabetic Principle

Reviewing the Short and Long Sounds of *Oo* and *Uu*

✦ Focus students' attention on **Alphabet Sound Wall Card** Short *Oo*, and read aloud the story about Bob the Fox again. Ask them to say the /o/ /o/ /o/ /o/ /o/ part.

✦ Point to **Alphabet Sound Wall Card** Long *Oo*, and ask a volunteer to say the name of the letter. Remind students vowels sometimes say their names in words.

✦ Have students recite the rhyme for the sounds of *Oo*.

✦ Point to **Alphabet Sound Wall Card** Short *Uu*, and read the story about Tubby the Tugboat once more, inviting students to say the /u/ /u/ /u/ /u/ /u/ part.

✦ Next turn students' attention to **Alphabet Sound Wall Card** Long *Uu*. Have students recite the rhyme for the sounds of *Uu*.

Listening for Medial /ō/ and /ū/

Give each student one **Alphabet Letter Card** *Oo* and one **Alphabet Letter Card** *Uu*. Ask students to raise the *Oo* cards *and say /ō/* when they hear a word with the /ō/ sound. They should raise the *Uu* cards *and say /ū/* when they hear the /ū/ sound. Try the following words:

use	robe	note	fume
huge	mode	muse	home
hope	cute	globe	wrote

Linking the Sound to the Letter

Write a pair of similar-looking words on the board, one with the /o/ sound and one with the /u/ sound. Say one of the words in each pair, and have students identify the correct word by signaling thumbs-up when you point to it. Then have them tell how they knew the correct word and underline the letter that makes the sound they heard. Try these word pairs:

cob ... cub	hut ... hot
bus ... boss	dock ... duck
hunk ... honk	cluck ... clock

Penmanship

✦ Distribute a sheet of writing paper to each student, or use **White Boards** turned to the sides with writing lines.

✦ Place the Supply Icon for *pencil* on the board or in the **Pocket Chart.**

✦ Use the procedure established for writing letters to review how to form the capital letter *W*. Also review how to form the small *w*.

✦ Invite students to practice writing capital *W*s and small *w*'s, alternating across the top row of the paper or board: *W w W w W w.*

✦ Repeat the procedure for the letters *Kk* and *Ee*.

Guided Practice

ROUTINE 2

✦ Distribute another sheet of writing paper or a **White Board** to each student.

✦ Blend the word *wed* using the sound-by-sound blending routine.

✦ Guide students in blending the word sound by sound. */w/ /e/ /d/*

✦ After students have blended the word *wed,* have them read it again naturally, the way they would speak it. Then have students write the word *wed* on their papers or boards. After students have written the word, have them read the word again.

✦ Repeat the procedure with the words *kin, kelp,* and *wet*.

Monitor Progress

Formal Assessment

to Differentiate Instruction

Penmanship Note how easily students review penmanship.

APPROACHING LEVEL

IF ... students are having difficulty,   THEN ... help them complete **Reteach** page 191.

ON LEVEL

IF ... students need more practice,   THEN ... have them make a collage using cut-out letters.

ABOVE LEVEL

IF ... students would enjoy a challenging activity,   THEN ... have them practice the strokes in watercolors on chart paper.

Teacher Tip

SLANTING Review students' writing to make sure they are using the proper slant when writing letters. If necessary, provide extra practice while looking at or tracing model letters.

Reading and Responding

Students will

✦ develop an understanding of vocabulary words.

✦ use the comprehension strategies Asking Questions and Making Connections.

✦ identify print and book features.

✦ make connections to the unit theme.

✦ *Science Lap Book,* pp. 36–43

✦ Routines 5–7

Science Link

ROUTINE
5

Activate Prior Knowledge

✦ Remind students that readers relate what they already know to what they are reading. Explain that this approach will help them better understand what they read.

✦ Tell students they are going to listen to a selection about how things move. To prompt a discussion, ask students the following questions: *How can you make a bike move? A sled? A wagon? A chair? A kite? What controls how fast or slow each thing moves?*

✦ Encourage students to think about the things they have tried to move as they listen to the selection "So Much Is Moving."

Preview the Selection

✦ Open the *Science Lap Book* to pages 36–37, the opening pages of "So Much Is Moving." Follow Routine 5, the previewing the selection routine, as you introduce the title of the selection.

✦ As you prepare to read the selection, ask students if the photos help them predict what the selection might say.

✦ Encourage students to suggest reasons for reading the selection. Ask them to think about what the story might teach them about how things move.

✦ Have students discuss what they are learning about how things move as you read the selection. Ask students how the ways things move connects with the unit theme Windy Days.

Focus Question What makes things move?

So Much Is Moving

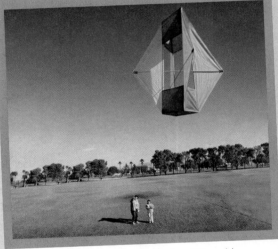

Look at the girl flying her kite. Whoosh!
A big gust of wind pushed her kite up high.

36

1st READ

Science Lap Book, p. 36

Technology

To promote independent reading, encourage students to use Workshop to listen to the recording of the selection on the *Listening Library CD.* Invite them to follow along and say the words whenever they can.

Audio CD

Vocabulary

ROUTINE **6**

+ Follow Routine 6, the selection vocabulary routine, as you introduce the vocabulary words for this selection.

+ Explain to students that a *gust* is a sudden rush of wind. Use the following sentence to illustrate: *Suddenly a gust blew my hat across the yard.*

+ Explain to students *pedals* are parts of a bicycle on which you put your feet. Ask students if they or someone they know can ride a bicycle.

+ Tell students the word *passing* means "going by." Use the following sentence to illustrate: *We'll be passing some farms on our trip.*

Read the Selection

ROUTINE **7**

+ Before beginning the selection, read the Focus Question at the top of the first page. Tell students to keep this question in mind as they listen to the story.

+ Follow Routine 7, the reading the selection routine, to read the entire selection.

+ Before, during, and after this first reading, invite students to ask questions or to think aloud about anything in the selection that interests or puzzles them.

Comprehension Strategies

+ As you read, model the following comprehension strategies:
  - Asking Questions
  - Making Connections

+ Think aloud through each strategy, and encourage students to share their ideas as well.

Vocabulary

gust   passing

pedals

 Teacher Tip

VOCABULARY Encourage students to use a variety of sources to build their vocabulary, such as making word banks, discussing characters and events from a story, talking with other people, and thinking about their own life experiences.

Differentiating Instruction **English Learners**

IF ... students need additional help with vocabulary, **THEN ...** refer to Unit 10 Lesson 11 of the *English Learner Support Guide.*

Comprehension Strategies

Teacher Modeling

❶ Making Connections *We can understand better when we think about the times we have done something like what the character is doing. I remember when the wind gets hold of my kite, it's hard to control. I've had to pull and pull to keep my kite away from trees and rooftops. Flying a kite can be hard work.*

❷ Making Connections *When my friends and I race our bikes, I push my pedals as hard and as fast as I can. My friends do the same. Sometimes I win, and sometimes someone else does. Thinking about how I've made my bike go faster helps me understand what the story is saying here.*

❸ Asking Questions *Why are the bikes passing the stroller? What are some clues that might help us answer our question?*

❹ Asking Questions *On another page we learned the faster you push a bike's pedals, the faster the bike goes. But if a bike or car had no wheels, it would rub against the ground. That would make it move very slowly. We answered our question by thinking about what we knew about how bikes and cars move.*

Focus Question What makes things move?

So Much Is Moving

Look at the girl flying her kite. Whoosh!
A big gust of wind pushed her kite up high.

36

She is pulling hard to keep her kite away from the treetops! ❶

37

These children are riding bikes.
They are pushing the pedals with their feet.

38

The faster they push the pedals, the faster their bikes will go. ❷

39

 Teacher Tip

GLOSSARY The word *gust* can be found in the Glossary of the *Science Lap Book.*

They are passing a mother and her baby. **3**

40

The mother is slowly pushing a stroller down a lovely path in a park.

41

Things can move fast or slow.
We can push or pull to make things move.

42

How would the movement change if this wagon did not have wheels? **4**

43

Science Lap Book, pp. 36–43

Science Link

Help students understand what influences an object's movement by placing a wooden chair on the classroom floor and having volunteers push it across the room, first with their hands and then with one finger. Invite students to discuss what made the movement of the chair harder or easier in each situation.

Print and Book Awareness

Exclamation Points

Have a volunteer identify the exclamation point on page 37, and ask students what an exclamation point means. If necessary, remind students an exclamation point means that the words before it should be said with strong feeling or excitement. Then read the sentence in a normal voice and an excited voice, and invite students to do the same.

Question Marks

Have a volunteer point to the question mark on page 43, and ask students what a question mark means. If necessary, remind students a question mark means a question is being asked. Then read the question with the appropriate expression, and invite students to do the same.

Vocabulary Review

Review with students the selection vocabulary words *gust, pedals,* and *passing.* Ask students the following questions:

- *When was a time you felt a gust of wind?*
- *How do you use pedals to ride your bicycle?*
- *What kinds of things would we see if we were passing by a school?*

OBJECTIVES

Students will
+ continue working as a class to write a report.
+ view, appreciate, and react to fine art.
+ interpret fine art.

MATERIALS

Windy Days Big Book, p. 48

Writing Process 🕐

Draft: Collaborating to Write Report

Teach

Remind students they are working together to write a report about a topic related to the wind.

Guided Practice

+ Pointing to the Listening Icons, remind students to listen carefully.

+ Write on the board the list of sequenced ideas the class chose and organized last week. Also display the sentences students have written so far (with your help).

+ Review the list of ideas again, pointing out how the first few ideas connect to the first few sentences of the report.

+ Continue writing the report, with students making writing suggestions and you transcribing their ideas to paper.

+ Continue until all the ideas have been represented in sentence form. Do not be concerned about sentence structure now; indeed, it would be best for there to be much room for improvement when students return to the text for revising.

+ Tell students in the next lesson they will have the opportunity to revise the report. For homework, encourage them to think of how to make the report better.

Fine Art

Discussing Fine Art

✦ Pointing to the Listening Icons, remind students to listen carefully.

✦ Turn to page 48 in the **Windy Days Big Book.** Focus students' attention on *Breath of Fresh Air* by Daniel Hernández.

✦ Invite students to give their initial impressions of the painting, saying what they like and do not like about it. Encourage students to freely express their feelings, interpretations, and opinions about the painting. In particular, have them discuss what they think it has to do with the unit theme.

✦ Guide students in discussing what they see in the painting. Use questions such as the following:

* *What do you see in the picture? Where are they? How do you know?*
* *What colors are used? Are they bright or dull?*
* *How would you describe the main woman? Does she seem happy or sad? How do you know?*

Daniel Hernández. *Breath of Fresh Air*
(Una brisa fresca).

 **Teacher Tip**

FINE ART You might want to share with students other examples of Peruvian art, such as those from fellow master José Sabogal or the contemporary artists Gerardo Chávez and José Tola.

Background Information

Daniel Hernández (1856–1932) is considered one of Peru's "Great Masters" of fine art. Motivated by a grant from the Peruvian government, he traveled to Europe in 1875, where he lived for more than forty years. In 1918, he returned to his country to establish the National School of Fine Arts. He also founded the Graduates Hall to exhibit new painters' works of his time.

Sounds and Letters

OBJECTIVES

Students will
+ blend and read words.
+ review knowledge of letters and sounds.
+ review the /e/ and the /ē/ sounds.
+ identify the /e/ and /ē/ sounds in print.

MATERIALS
+ Routine 2
+ *Skills Practice 2,* p. 109
+ *Alphabet Letter Card Ee* for each student
+ *Pickled Peppers Big Book,* p. 46

Calendar

Su	M	T	W	Th	F	S
		1	2	3	4	5
6	7	8	9	10	11	12
13	14	15	16	17	18	19
20	21	22	23	24	25	26
27	28	29	30	31		

Point to the box that represents today. Ask students to count aloud with you how many Thursdays are in this month. Point to each day as you count aloud. You can repeat for other days of the week.

Warming Up 🕐

M☀RNING MESSAGE

Today is _____.

(Child's name) thinks _____ is fun!

Can you hear or feel the wind today?

Kindergarten News

+ Copy the above text on the board or on chart paper, and make several errors in your writing today.

+ Ask a volunteer to write the date in the first blank.

+ Ask students to proofread the message, and have volunteers come to the board to correct them.

+ Challenge students to identify the /ē/ sound in the words in the message as you reread them. *hear, feel*

Phoneme Blending

Bring out the **Lion Puppet,** and tell students he wants to play another blending game. Tell them the puppet will say the beginning of each word and then you will give the ending sound of the word. Make sure you emphasize the ending phoneme. Start with the following words: *daydrea… /m/, lan… /d/, frien… /d/, deligh… /t/, fin… /d/, dow… /n/.*

Phonics

Blending and Sentence Extension

✦ Using Routine 2, have students blend the following words sound by sound as you write them letter by letter on the board:

bag   *man*   *run*   *dog*

✦ On the board, write sentences that contain the words. For example:

He has a bag.

The man and his dog run.

✦ Ask students to use their knowledge of high-frequency words and sounds and letters to read each sentence. Be sure to have them reread the sentences until they can do so as they would speak them.

✦ Say clues for words from the blending activity. Call on a student to come to the board to underline the word that answers the clue. When the student has identified and said the word, have her or him use it in a sentence. Help students extend the sentences by asking them questions such as *Where? Which?* and *When?*

Monitor Progress
to Differentiate Instruction
Formal Assessment

Blending Note how easily students blend the words.

APPROACHING LEVEL

| IF ... students are still having difficulty, | THEN ... use Unit 10 Lesson 12 of the *Intervention Guide.* |

ON LEVEL

| IF ... students need more practice, | THEN ... continue blending using *Skills Practice 2* page 109. |

ABOVE LEVEL

| IF ... students would enjoy a challenging activity, | THEN ... give them additional words to write and blend such as *pad, nap,* and *tap.* |

Skills Practice 2, p. 109

Alphabetic Principle

Reviewing the Short and Long Sounds of *Ee*

✦ Focus students' attention on **Alphabet Sound Wall Card** Short *Ee*, and ask them what they remember about Jen's pet hen. Read the story for students, inviting them to join in on the /e/ /e/ /e/ /e/ /e/ part.

✦ Next turn students' attention to **Alphabet Sound Wall Card** Long *Ee*. Have students recite the rhyme for the sounds of *Ee*:

E's my name.

Two sounds for me:

Short e *in* hen,

Long e *in* he.

Listening for /e/ and /ē/

Give each student an **Alphabet Letter Card** *Ee*. Ask students to turn the cards to the capital *E* sides and to raise them when they hear the /ē/ sound. When they hear the /e/ sound, have them raise the cards with the small *e* sides facing you. Try the following words:

we	*wet*	*went*	*bee*
red	*left*	*help*	*spent*
set	*rent*	*swell*	*check*
need	*these*	*cheese*	*sneeze*

Blending ROUTINE **2**

Using Routine 2, the sound-by-sound blending routine, have students practice blending words containing the short and long sounds of the letter *Ee* as you write each word on the board or chart paper. Remind students that when the vowel is by itself at the end of a word, it is going to make the long-vowel sound. After blending, have students make and extend sentences for some of the words. Try these words:

bed	*red*	*met*
be	*we*	*me*

Technology

Use the **Alphabet Sound Card Stories CD** to review the /e/ sound.

Audio CD

Pickled Peppers Big Book

✦ Display the **Pickled Peppers Big Book,** and ask students to identify the book on sight.

✦ Turn to page 46, "Keep a Poem in Your Pocket." Point to the title, and read it aloud. Invite students to share anything they remember about the rhyme.

✦ Either read aloud the poem or play it on the **Listening Library CD.** Ask students to listen for the words with the /e/ sound and the /ē/ sound. Encourage them to close their eyes as they listen.

✦ Have students say any words with the /e/ sound or the /ē/ sound they noticed while listening.

✦ Reread the rhyme, pointing to each word as you say it. This time, ask students to stop you each time you point to a word with the letter *e* in it. *Keep, poem, pocket, picture, head, never, feel, lonely, when, you're, bed, The, little, dozen, dreams, dance* Reread the word, and ask students to give you a thumbs-up if they hear the /e/ sound or to say *E* if it has the /ē/ sound.

Pickled Peppers Big Book, p. 46

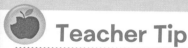 **Teacher Tip**

THE SCHWA Remind students that every time they see the letter *e* it will *not* make the /e/ sound or the /ē/ sound. Sometimes the letter *Ee* makes the schwa sound (uh). Explain to students that they will learn more about other sounds when they become "masters" of the sounds they have so far learned in kindergarten.

OBJECTIVES

Students will

✦ develop an understanding of vocabulary words.

✦ review the comprehension strategies Asking Questions and Making Connections.

✦ discuss the author's purpose in writing the selection.

MATERIALS

✦ **Science Lap Book,** pp. 36–43

✦ Routines 5–7

Science Link

Preview the Selection   ROUTINE **5**

✦ Display the **Science Lap Book** opened to the Table of Contents page. Use Routine 5, the previewing the selection routine, to guide students in understanding and using the Table of Contents. Then turn to the selection, and say the title.

✦ As you prepare to reread the selection, have students use the photographs to retell important facts from the selection.

Vocabulary   ROUTINE **6**

✦ Follow Routine 6, the selection vocabulary routine, as you introduce the vocabulary words for this selection.

✦ Explain to students that a *path* is a place to walk. Tell them most parks have at least one *path*.

✦ Explain to students a *park* is an area of land with trees within a city or town. Ask students if they have ever visited a park and what kinds of things they saw there.

✦ Tell students the word *movement* means "the act of moving." Use the following sentence to illustrate: *The movement of the roller coaster made me feel sick.*

Focus Question What makes things move?

So Much Is Moving

Look at the girl flying her kite. Whoosh!
A big gust of wind pushed her kite up high.

36

2nd READ

Science Lap Book, p. 36

Vocabulary

path   movement

park

Read the Selection

ROUTINE
7

Comprehension Strategies

✦ During the first reading of "So Much Is Moving," you modeled the following comprehension strategies:

- Asking Questions
- Making Connections

✦ In this second reading of the selection, you will revisit each comprehension strategy model from the first reading.

Reading with a Writer's Eye

✦ In this rereading of "So Much Is Moving," students will discuss the author's purpose in writing the selection.

✦ By discussing the writing strategies an author uses, students learn how to be better writers themselves.

Concept/Question Board

Tell students readers keep thinking about questions generated as they are reading. As they read, tell them to keep in mind the questions on the **Concept/Question Board.** Explain that readers are always thinking about and trying to remember what is important in selections.

Technology

To promote independent reading, encourage students to use Workshop to listen to the recording of the selection on the *Listening Library CD.* Invite them to follow along and say the words whenever they can.

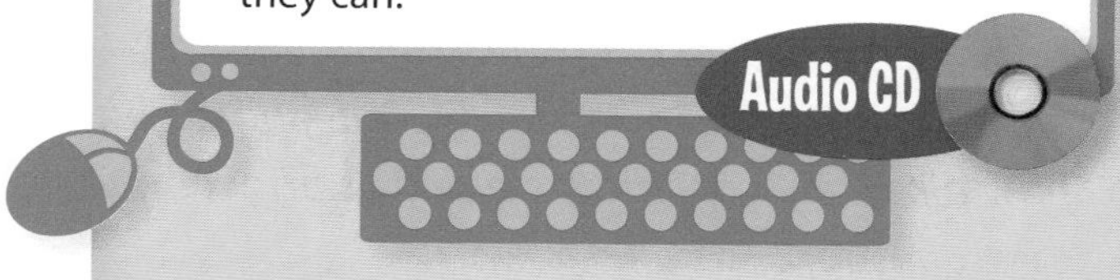

Audio CD

Comprehension Strategies

Teacher Modeling

1 **Making Connections** *Let's think about flying a kite. What experiences have you had? I remembered how the wind would blow my kite around and how I'd have to pull and pull to keep it away from trees and rooftops. This helped me understand how hard the girl in the photo was working.*

2 **Making Connections** *Here I thought about when my friends and I would race our bikes. We'd push our bike pedals as hard and as fast as we could. When was a time you rode your bike with a friend? Did you race?*

3 **Asking Questions** *We wondered why the bikes were passing the stroller. So we looked at the picture and noticed the bike's wheels were turning faster than the stroller's wheels. Asking questions helps us check our understanding.*

4 **Asking Questions** *We know wheels help a bike or a car move. So we decided that with no wheels a bike or car would rub against the ground and move more slowly. Thinking about how bikes and cars move helped us answer my own question.*

Focus Question What makes things move?

So Much Is Moving

Look at the girl flying her kite. Whoosh! A big gust of wind pushed her kite up high.

36

She is pulling hard to keep her kite away from the treetops! **1**

37

These children are riding bikes. They are pushing the pedals with their feet.

38

The faster they push the pedals, the faster their bikes will go. **2**

39

 Teacher Tip

GLOSSARY The word *path* can be found in the Glossary of the ***Science Lap Book.***

They are passing a mother and her baby. **3**

40

The mother is slowly pushing a stroller down a lovely path in a park.

41

Things can move fast or slow.
We can push or pull to make things move.

42

How would the movement change if this wagon did not have wheels? **4**

43

Science Lap Book, pp. 36–43

Science Link

Tell students to consider what they know about how objects move. Remind students of the chair activity and their conclusions that an object's size, weight, and resistance with the surface all influence how easily it will move. Then ask students how cars should be built so they move more easily and require less power.

Reading with a Writer's Eye

Author's Purpose

✦ Ask students why they think the author wrote "So Much Is Moving." Model the following questions: *Did the author write the story to make us laugh? Did he or she write it to share an experience? Did the author write the story to share information? Did the author write the story to help us feel an emotion like love or sadness? Did he or she write it to share a message?*

✦ Help students realize the author wrote the story to share information about what makes things move. Ask students what information the author shares about this subject.

Discussing the Selection

Review the Focus Question with students: What makes things move? *the pushing or pulling of the wind and other forces*

Vocabulary Review

Review with students the selection vocabulary words *path, park,* and *movement.* Ask students the following questions:

• *Where is a place we might see a path?*

• *What kinds of things might we see in a park?*

• *What kind of movement does the wind make?*

OBJECTIVES

Students will
✦ work together to revise the class report.
✦ review words that show position.
✦ review words that show order.
✦ participate in a Thinking Story experience.

MATERIALS

✦ *Language Arts Big Book,* pp. 9, 39, 51
✦ *Windy Days Big Book,* p. 4
✦ *Skills Practice 2,* p. 110
✦ *Willy the Wisher,* p. 96

Writing Process

Revise: Revising Class Report

Teach

Display *Language Arts Big Book* page 9, and read the sentence *How Can I Make It Better?* Remind students that revising is an important step in the writing process. Review each item on the revising checklist, and relate it to the picture Tanisha is holding.

Guided Practice

✦ Take out the chart paper you have been using to draft the class report. Read the sentences you have helped the class write as they are written in the order they appear on the paper.

✦ Encourage students to look for ways to revise the text by moving items, adding ideas, and deleting text. Help students make the changes that they suggest.

✦ On a clean sheet of chart paper, create a final draft of the class report. Tell students they will continue the writing process in the next lesson.

Grammar, Usage, and Mechanics

Teach

✦ Pointing to the Listening Icons, remind students to listen carefully.

✦ Display *Language Arts Big Book* page 51, and read the sentence *Where is Doodle?* Remind students words that describe position tell us where something is.

✦ Guide students in choosing words to describe Doodle's position in each picture. *in front of; between; under*

✦ Then, turn to page 39 in the *Language Arts Big Book,* and ask students to identify on the page the words that show order. *First, Next, Last* Remind students words that show order can tell us the best way to complete a task with more than one step, or part.

Language Arts Big Book, pp. 9, 39, 51

Grammar, Usage, and Mechanics continued

Guided Practice

✦ Have students open their **Skills Practice 2** to page 110.

✦ Work through the page with students, and review their work when they finish.

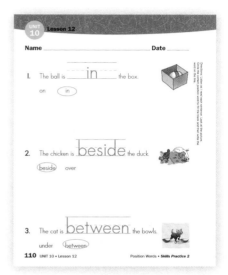

Skills Practice 2, p. 110

Monitor Progress

Formal Assessment ✓

to Differentiate Instruction

Grammar Note how easily students are able to identify order words.

APPROACHING LEVEL

IF ... students are having difficulty,

THEN ... help them complete **Reteach** page 192.

ON LEVEL

IF ... students need more practice,

THEN ... have students look at the **Windy Days Big Book** story "Gilberto and the Wind" and with your help circle the order words.

ABOVE LEVEL

IF ... students are comfortable,

THEN ... have them complete **Challenge Activities** page 144.

 Teacher Tip

ACTIVITY EXTENSION Students might enjoy drawing pictures of the characters and events from the **Willy the Wisher** stories. Students can illustrate many scenes for this story. Invite volunteers to present their drawings and to explain why they made the pictures look the way they do.

Willy the Wisher

✦ Display the book **Willy the Wisher.** Ask students to identify the book on sight. Then invite a volunteer to come up and open the book to the Table of Contents. Have students help you find the story on page 96, "Willy's Lost Kitten."

Willy the Wisher, p. 96

✦ Before you read the story to the students, invite them to discuss Willy and his particular characteristics. Identify the title, and ask students what they would do to find a lost kitten. In this story, Willy characteristically wishes for things to happen but never takes any steps to make them happen.

✦ Read aloud the story, following the established procedure for reading from the **Willy the Wisher** book. Remember that your pauses to discuss the red text should not be too long, as students may lose the flow of the story.

✦ After you have read the story, discuss it in general. Use questions such as the following:

• *Why does Willy end up lost, hungry, and tired?*

• *What did Willy do in this story that he has never done before?*

• *Is this a good change for Willy to make, or will this change make things even harder for Willy?*

• *Do you think Willy will change his "wishing ways" for good? Why or why not?*

Students will

+ identify high-frequency words in print.
+ make and extend oral sentences.
+ review the long and short vowel sounds of *Aa, Ii,* and *Oo.*
+ review writing the letters *Qq, Yy,* and *Vv.*
+ practice writing words they have blended.

+ ***Pickled Peppers Big Book,*** p. 40
+ Routine 2
+ ***High-Frequency Flash Cards***
+ ***Alphabet Letter Cards*** *Aa, Ii,* and *Oo* for each student
+ ***Skills Practice 2,*** pp. 111–112

Calendar

Su	M	T	W	Th	F	S
		1	2	3	4	5
6	7	8	9	10	11	12
13	14	15	16	17	18	19
20	21	22	23	24	25	26
27	28	29	30	31		

Point to the box that represents today. Ask students to count aloud with you how many days are in this month. Begin with the first day of the month, and point to each day as you count aloud.

Warming Up

MORNING MESSAGE

Today is _____.

What color are your eyes?

Let's play a game!

Kindergarten News

+ Copy the text above on the board or on chart paper. Use a self-sticking note to cover the word *game* in the third sentence; it can be today's Secret Word.

+ Ask a volunteer to come to the board and to write today's date in the first blank.

+ Read all three sentences, saying the word *blank* in place of the word *game* in the third sentence. Tell students today's Morning Message has a Secret Word. Read the third sentence again, and have students tell the Secret Word. Discuss the clues that led them to find the correct word.

+ Ask students what long-vowel sound they hear in the Secret Word. *long a* Have a volunteer underline the letters in the word that make the sound. *a, e*

+ Then ask a student to come to the board and to make a star next to the question, a check mark next to the exclamatory sentence, and an *X* next to the statement. Discuss with students how they can identify the three types of sentences. *end marks*

High-Frequency Words

✦ Look through the poem "Rhyme" on **Pickled Peppers Big Book** page 40, and choose several high-frequency words students have learned. Words you might choose include *I, to, see, a, it, the, at,* and *and*.

✦ Point to the high-frequency words, and have students read them. You may choose to have **High-Frequency Flash Cards** ready to distribute to students.

✦ Pair students, and have each pair walk around the room to find the words in print. Tell students to look for the words in storybooks, poems, and old magazines and on signs, calendars, posters, bulletin board notes, and messages.

Phonics

ROUTINE
2

Blending and Sentence Extension

✦ Using Routine 2, have students blend the following words sound by sound as you write them letter by letter on the board:

cap   kite   Kate   Pete

✦ On the board, write sentences that contain the words. For example:

Pete has a kite.
Kate likes her cap.

✦ Ask students to use their knowledge of high-frequency words and sounds and letters to read each sentence. Be sure to have them reread the sentences until they can do so as they would speak them.

✦ Say clues for words from the blending activity. Call on a student to come to the board to underline the word that answers the clue. When the student has identified and said the word, have her or him use it in a sentence. Help students extend the sentences by asking them questions such as *Where? Which?* and *When?*

Teacher Tip

FOSTERING SUCCESS Even though students have had much practice discerning the differences in vowel sounds, students might still have difficulty with the Differentiating Vowel Sound activity simply because they have the long and short vowels of three letters from which to choose. To foster successful answers, repeat each word a few times, and pause before moving on to the next word. Allowing students to hear the word over and over as they make their decisions will render them more likely to identify the correct sound and to choose the correct card to illustrate their knowledge.

Alphabetic Principle ✷

Reviewing the Short and Long Sounds of *Aa, Ii,* and *Oo*

To briefly review vowels, lead students in singing the "Vowel Song" or "Apples and Bananas," both available on the **Listening Library CD** and in the Appendix.

Differentiating Vowel Sounds

Give each student one **Alphabet Letter Card** *Aa*, one *Ii* **Alphabet Letter Card** *Ii*, and one **Alphabet Letter Card** *Oo*. Ask students to raise the *Aa* cards when they hear a word with the /a/ or the /ā/ sounds. Have them raise the *Ii* cards if the word has the /i/ or the /ī/ sounds. They should raise the *Oo* cards if the word has the /o/ or the /ō/ sounds. Try the following words:

cone	kite	fake	wire
band	made	bat	lone
rope	rob	side	pack
bit	take	hop	cane

Linking the Sound to the Letter

Write sets of similar-looking words on the board that display the long and short vowels *a, i,* or *o.* Say one of the words in each set, and have students identify the correct word by signaling thumbs-up when you point to it. As each word is identified, ask students how they know the correct word, and have them underline the letter that makes the sound they heard. Try these word sets:

bag ... big ... bog	pat ... pot ... pit
hot ... hit ... hat	sip ... sop ... sap
lock ... lack ... lick	tick ... tack ... tock

Technology

Have students use the **eGames** activity for this unit to practice vowel sounds.

Audio CD

Penmanship

✦ Distribute a sheet of writing paper to each student, or use **White Boards** turned to the sides with writing lines.

✦ Place the Supply Icon for *pencil* on the board or in the **Pocket Chart.**

✦ Use the procedure established for writing letters to review how to form the capital letter *Q*. Also review how to form the small *q*.

✦ Have students practice writing capital *Q*s and small *q*'s, alternating across the top row of the paper or board from left to right: *Q q Q q Q q*.

✦ Repeat the procedure for the letters *Yy* and *Vv*.

Guided Practice ROUTINE 2

✦ Distribute another sheet of writing paper or a **White Board** to each student.

✦ Blend the word *vet*.

✦ Blend the word sound by sound. */v/ /e/ /t/*

✦ After students have blended the word *vet,* have the class read the word again naturally, the way they would speak it. Then have students write the word *vet* on their papers or boards. After students have written the word, have them read it again.

✦ Repeat the procedure with the words *yet, van, vote,* and *yak*.

✦ End the activity by guiding students to complete **Skills Practice 2** page 111.

Monitor Progress to Differentiate Instruction

Formal Assessment ✓

Blending Note how easily students write and blend the words.

APPROACHING LEVEL

IF ... students have difficulty,

THEN ... guide them in completing **Reteach** page 193.

ON LEVEL

IF ... students need more practice,

THEN ... use **Skills Practice 2** page 112 to continue the activity.

ABOVE LEVEL

IF ... students would enjoy a challenging activity,

THEN ... have them work independently to complete page 145 in **Challenge Activities.**

 Teacher Tips

PENMANSHIP NEATNESS Remember to call attention to and praise students for penmanship that is especially neat.

STUDENT MONITORING Check students' writing to make sure they are forming all their letters correctly. Provide extra practice for those students who are still having difficulty during this review lesson.

Skills Practice 2, pp. 111–112

OBJECTIVES

Students will
+ connect their own life experiences to the text.
+ develop an understanding of vocabulary words.
+ use the comprehension strategy Clarifying.
+ identify print and book features.

MATERIALS

+ **Story Time Collection:** *Wind Says Good Night*
+ **Routines 5–7**
+ **Home Connection,** pp. 81–82

Wind Says Good Night

Technology

To promote independent reading, encourage students to use Workshop to listen to the recording of the selection on the **Listening Library CD.** Invite them to follow along and say the words whenever they can.

1st READ

Preview and Prepare 🕐

ROUTINE 5

Activate Prior Knowledge

+ *Wind Says Good Night* is fiction about a child who is having trouble falling asleep because of the outdoor sounds. As you read aloud the selection, relate what you already know to what you are reading, and encourage students to do the same.

+ Encourage students to talk about times that night noises have kept them awake. Ask students the following questions: *What makes some of the sounds we hear at night? Which sounds help you fall asleep? Which sounds keep you awake?*

+ Tell students you will read them a story about a child who is kept awake by gentle night noises. Invite students to listen for how the problem gets solved.

+ Encourage students to think about what they are learning about the unit theme as they listen to the selection. This story demonstrates that events in nature, especially changes in weather, are often dependent on the wind. Key concepts include the following:
  • Wind influences many events in nature.
  • Wind plays a major role in changing the weather.

Preview the Selection

+ Display the cover of *Wind Says Good Night*. Follow Routine 5, the previewing the selection routine, as you introduce the title and the names of the author and the illustrator. Ask students what an author and an illustrator do.

+ As you prepare to read the selection, encourage students to comment about anything they find interesting or puzzling.

+ Encourage students to think of reasons for reading *Wind Says Good Night*. Ask students to consider what they might learn about the unit theme Windy Days.

Vocabulary

ROUTINE **6**

✦ Follow Routine 6, the selection vocabulary routine, as you introduce the vocabulary words for this selection.

✦ Explain to students if something *spilled,* it came out. Ask students if they or anyone they know has ever spilled something.

✦ Explain to students that a *woods* is a whole group of trees growing closely together. Use the following sentence to illustrate: *Rabbits, squirrels, and deer live in our woods.*

✦ Tell students when they are *cheerful,* they are happy. Ask students to demonstrate a cheerful face.

✦ Tell students a *melody* is a tune. Ask a volunteer to hum or sing a popular melody.

✦ Tell students a fiddle is another name for a violin. Point out the fiddle in the story *Wind Says Good Night,* and ask students whether they have ever heard anyone playing a fiddle.

✦ Tell students if they are *strumming* an instrument, they are moving their fingers back and forth across the strings. Demonstrate strumming for the class.

Read the Selection

ROUTINE **7**

✦ Before reading *Wind Says Good Night,* read the Focus Question at the top of the first page. Tell students to keep this question in mind as they listen to the story.

✦ Follow Routine 7, the reading the selection routine, as you read the entire story.

✦ Before, during, and after the first reading, encourage students to ask questions and to think aloud about anything that interests or puzzles them.

Comprehension Strategies

✦ You will introduce and model the Clarifying comprehension strategy.

✦ Think aloud through each comprehension strategy, and encourage students to share their ideas as well.

Vocabulary

spilled	melody
woods	fiddle
cheerful	strumming

 Teacher Tip

ACTIVATING PRIOR KNOWLEDGE Tell students readers relate what they know to a reading. As you are reading, make certain you relate what you already know to what you are reading. As students read the selections, they encounter familiar ideas as well as new ideas. When they read something they already know, encourage them to make a note of the information. When they learn something new, have them be sure to notice that too. This will help students learn as they are reading.

 Give each student a copy of *Home Connection* page 81. This same information is also available in Spanish on *Home Connection* page 82. Encourage students to discuss *Wind Says Good Night* with their families and complete the activity provided.

Comprehension Strategies

Teacher Modeling

1 Clarifying *I'm not sure what the mockingbird is talking about. The mockingbird is the only one making noise. Let's look at the page again. Does anyone see anything that will help clarify this? What do you see? By looking carefully at the pages again, we were able to clarify something that was confusing.*

2 Clarifying *We've seen this word—*fiddle. *Readers sometimes use the pictures to help them learn about new words. When we look at the picture of the cricket, it looks like he's playing a violin. Now we understand that* fiddle *is another word for* violin. *The picture helped us clarify that.*

Focus Question How did the night wind help the child fall asleep?

It was late at night. All little children were in their beds, fast asleep. All except one.

The night wind brushed against a window. *"Shh-h-h,"* whispered the wind. "Go to sleep."

But the child could not fall asleep. Outside, on the branch of a tree, Mockingbird was singing.

4   5

"Mockingbird," said the night wind, "will you stop singing so the child can go to sleep?"

But Mockingbird loved to sing. Music spilled from deep in his throat, as he sang of green woods, bright flowers, and warm summer nights.

"No," said Mockingbird, "I can't stop singing until Cricket stops playing." **1**

6   7

Wind Says Good Night, pp. 4–11

Print and Book Awareness

Quotation Marks

Have a volunteer point to the quotation marks on page 6, and ask students what they show. If necessary, explain that quotation marks show the words a person or story character is saying. Have volunteers locate the beginning and the end of each line of dialogue on the page.

Initial /s/

Reread page 9, and ask students to listen for words that begin with the /s/ sound. *steps, stop, singing, sleep, strings, strumming* Have volunteers come to the **Big Book** and point to words beginning with the letter that represents the /s/ sound. As volunteers point to the letter *s*, have the class say the /s/ sound.

Question Marks

Reread page 11, exaggerating the question asked by the wind. Then ask students what kind of mark goes at the end of the sentence. Show students the page, and have a volunteer point to the question mark. If necessary, remind students a question mark means a character in the story is asking a question.

Comprehension Strategies

Teacher Modeling

❸ Clarifying *The word* widespread *may be a new word for you. How can we figure out this word? Let's look at the picture of the moth. Her wings are open very far apart. Then, when we look at the word, we can see two smaller words,* wide *and* spread. *I know what these two words mean. By using the picture and looking carefully at the word, we can figure out a new word.* (It may be helpful to demonstrate what the words *wide* and *spread* mean.)

❹ Clarifying *This is a surprise. All of a sudden it started to rain. The night was very clear. Let's look back at the pages. How can we figure this out? When the wind scooped up the cloud, the cloud must have had some rain in it. That's why it's raining now. By rereading these pages, we can clarify what is happening in the story.*

English Learners

IF . . . students have limited vocabulary,
THEN . . . explain that the word *hard* on page 15 means "difficult" or "tough" rather than "solid" or "firm."

 Teacher Tip

CLARIFYING Remind students readers stop reading when some part of the text does not make sense. Model for students the various ways readers clarify difficult ideas or passages. These include rereading, using charts or graphic organizers, thinking of other comprehension strategies that might help, and asking someone for help.

Far to the west hovered a small dark shadow.

"Cloud," called the night wind, "will you cover the earth
so Moon will stop shining
so Moth will stop dancing
so Frog will stop strumming
so Cricket will stop playing
so Mockingbird will stop singing
so the child can go to sleep?"

"Only if you will carry me," said Cloud.

16   17

In a rush of cool air the night wind scooped up Cloud. Soon
a mist spread over the meadow. A gentle rain began to fall,
tumbling down through the dark, splashing on the flat bay
waters, skipping on the warm green earth.

18   19

Wind Says Good Night, pp. 12–19

Print and Book Awareness

Initial /m/

Reread page 14, and ask students to listen for words that begin with the /m/ sound. *Moth, Mockingbird, Moon* Have volunteers come to the **Big Book** and point to words beginning with the letter that represents the /m/ sound.

Quotation Marks

Have a volunteer point to the quotation marks on pages 14–15, and ask students what they show. If necessary, explain that quotation marks show the words a person or story character is saying. Have volunteers locate the beginning and the end of each line of dialogue on the page.

Sentences: Periods

Display page 18 of the **Big Book,** and have volunteers point to the first and last words of each sentence. *In, Cloud; Soon, meadow; A, earth* Have them point to the periods at the ends of sentences and say *This is a period.*

Comprehension Strategies

Teacher Modeling

5 **Clarifying** *How can we figure out why the moth fell asleep? We can look back to figure it out. It says she liked to dance in the moonlight. When the moon stopped shining, the moth had no more moonlight to dance in. Then she was able to fall asleep. By looking at earlier pages, I could figure out why something happened.*

6 **Clarifying** *Why is Cricket sleeping? The sky looks clear, but the moonlight isn't keeping him awake. Let's look back at the pages. We see now that Frog has stopped playing. Frog's playing was keeping Cricket awake. Now that Frog is sleeping, Cricket can also sleep. Rereading the pages helps us to clarify what is happening on this page.*

Moon stopped shining.

20

21

Moth stopped dancing.

22

23

🍎 Teacher Tip

COMPREHENSION Readers constantly evaluate their understanding of what they are reading. Stop often to make sure students are doing this.

Frog stopped strumming.

24

25

Cricket stopped playing. **6**

26

27

Wind Says Good Night, pp. 20–27

Print and Book Awareness

Picture-Text Relationship

Show students the picture of the sleeping moon on page 21. Ask them to talk about what they see in the picture. Reread the text *Moon stopped shining,* and then ask what the picture shows that explains why Moon stopped shining. *It is being covered by clouds.*

Word Length

Display page 24, and reread the text. Write the three words on the board, and ask students which word is the longest and which is the shortest. Have students count and say the names of the letters in each word.

Comprehension Strategies

Teacher Modeling

7 Clarifying *Well, this is confusing. Everyone is asleep. How can we figure this out? We can reread a few pages when we are confused about story events. Let's look back a little bit to help figure this out. Let's see. The wind carried the cloud across the sky. That's what started the rain. Then everything else happened, which made everyone fall asleep. We can figure it out by rereading a few pages.*

8 Clarifying *How can we figure out why the wind said "Good Night"? We can look back at the last picture. Oh, that's right—the little child finally fell asleep. By looking back, we can clarify what we didn't understand.*

Mockingbird stopped singing.

28   29

At last the night was dark, and quiet, and still. The child snuggled under warm blankets, closed tired eyes, and fell asleep. **7**

30   31

Concept/Question Board

Tell students readers keep thinking about questions generated as they are reading. As they read, tell them to keep in mind the questions on the **Concept/Question Board.** Explain that readers are always thinking about and trying to remember what is important in selections.

✦ Practice with the following word:

Puppet: ... *elper*

Teacher: /h/ (Emphasize the /h/ sound.)

Puppet: *What's the word?*

Everyone: *helper*

✦ Continue with the following words:

backyar ... /d/ backyard   *bathroo ... /m/* bathroom

cartwhee ... /l/ cartwheel   *ebra ... /z/* zebra

umber ... /n/ number   *coconu ... /t/* coconut

irthday ... /b/ birthday   *inger ... /f/* finger

Phonics

ROUTINE **2**

Blending and Sentence Extension

✦ Using Routine 2, have students blend the following words sound by sound as you write them letter by letter on the board:

car   *bus*   *big*   *kid*

✦ On the board, write sentences that contain the words. For example:

Look at the car.

The kid can ride the bus.

✦ Ask students to use their knowledge of high-frequency words and sounds and letters to read each sentence. Be sure to have them reread the sentences until they can do so as they would speak them.

✦ Say clues for words from the blending activity. Call on a student to come to the board to underline the word that answers the clue. When the student has identified and said the word, have her or him use it in a sentence. Help students extend the sentences by asking them questions such as *Where? Which?* and *When?*

Differentiating Instruction **English Learners**

IF ... students have difficulty with the Phonics activity, **THEN ...** refer to Unit 10 Lesson 14 of the *English Learner Support Guide.*

Alphabetic Principle

Reviewing the Short and Long Sounds of *Ee* and *Uu*

✦ Focus students' attention on **Alphabet Sound Wall Card** Short *Ee*, and read aloud the story about Jen's pet hen again. Ask them to say the /e/ /e/ /e/ /e/ /e/ part.

✦ Point to **Alphabet Sound Wall Card** Long *Ee*, and ask a volunteer to say the name of the letter. Have students recite the rhyme for the sounds of *Ee*:

E's my name.

Two sounds for me:

Short e in hen,

Long e in he.

✦ Point to **Alphabet Sound Wall Card** Short *Uu,* and read the story about Tubby the Tugboat again, inviting students to say the /u/ /u/ /u/ /u/ /u/ part.

✦ Next turn students' attention to **Alphabet Sound Wall Card** Long *Uu.* Have students recite the rhyme for the sounds of *Uu*:

U's my name.

Two sounds I use:

Short u in cub,

Long u in fuse.

Listening for Medial /ē/ and /ū/

Give each student one **Alphabet Letter Card** *Ee* and one **Alphabet Letter Card** *Uu*. Ask students to raise the *Ee* cards and say /ē/ when they hear a word with the /ē/ sound. They should raise the *Uu* cards and say /ū/ when they hear the /ū/ sound. Try the following words:

mute	Steve	peep	seed
Pete	fuse	cube	mule
these	excuse	delete	complete

Pickled Peppers Big Book

✦ Display the **Pickled Peppers Big Book,** and turn to page 16, "One Hungry Monster." Point to the title, and read it aloud. Ask students to share anything they remember about the rhyme.

✦ Either read aloud the poem or play it on the **Listening Library CD.** Ask students to listen for the words with the /u/ sound and the /ū/ sound. Encourage them to close their eyes as they listen.

✦ Invite students to say any words with the /u/ sound or the /ū/ sound they noticed while listening.

✦ Reread the first four pages of the rhyme (pages 16–19), pointing to each word as you say it. This time, ask students to stop you each time you point to a word with the letter *u* in it. *hungry, underneath, up, upstairs, 'round, out, munching, crunching, rug, bug, our, sauerkraut*

✦ Work with students to evaluate the words as you read them. If students hear the /u/ sound, have them raise their hands. *hungry, underneath, up, upstairs, munching, crunching, rug, bug* Ask students to also evaluate the words to identify the long *u* sound, and congratulate them when they realize that none of the words use the /ū/ sound.

✦ If time permits, repeat the activity with a focus on the /e/ sound and the /ē/ sound.

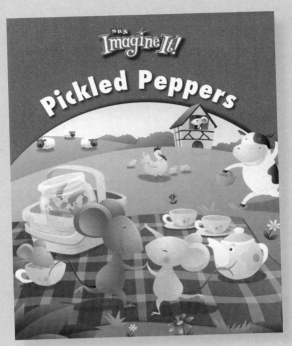

Pickled Peppers Big Book, pp. 16–19

Reading and Responding

OBJECTIVES

Students will
✦ develop an understanding of vocabulary words.
✦ review the comprehension strategy Clarifying.
✦ use the comprehension skill Reality and Fantasy.
✦ analyze the author's use of characterization.

MATERIALS

✦ *Story Time Collection: Wind Says Good Night*
✦ Routines 5–7

2nd READ

ROUTINE **5**

Preview and Prepare

Preview the Selection

✦ Show students the front cover of *Wind Says Good Night*. Use Routine 5, the previewing the selection routine, as you say the title and the names of the author and the illustrator.

✦ Follow Routine 5 as you prepare to reread the story. As you turn through the pages, have students use the illustrations to retell the main events in the story.

ROUTINE **6**

Vocabulary

✦ Follow Routine 6, the selection vocabulary routine, as you introduce the vocabulary words for this selection.

✦ Explain to students a *beat* is a repeated sound. Demonstrate by tapping a beat and then have students tap their own beats with you.

✦ Explain to students that the word *rhythm* means "a pattern of sounds." Tell students the words *beat* and *rhythm* mean the same thing. Demonstrate the word *rhythm* by clapping in rhythm, and invite students to join in.

✦ Tell students the word *glow* means "brightness." Use the following sentence to illustrate: *The moon's glow lit up the sky*.

✦ Explain that the word *hovered* means "floated in the air over a certain spot." Use the following sentence to illustrate: *The hummingbird hovered over the flower for several seconds*.

✦ Tell students a *mist* is a light spray of moisture. Demonstrate what a mist looks like by filling a water bottle and spraying it for the class. Ask students if they have ever seen or felt a mist.

✦ Tell students the word *snuggled* means "lay comfortably." Use the following sentence to illustrate: *Katie snuggled under the covers as her father read a story*.

Wind Says Good Night

Vocabulary

beat	hovered
rhythm	mist
glow	snuggled

Read the Selection

ROUTINE **7**

Comprehension Strategies

✦ During the first reading of *Wind Says Good Night,* you modeled the Clarifying comprehension strategy.

✦ In this second reading of the selection, you will revisit each comprehension strategy model from the first reading.

Comprehension Skills

In this lesson for *Wind Says Good Night,* students will focus on the comprehension skill Reality and Fantasy.

Reading with a Writer's Eye

✦ In this rereading of *Wind Says Good Night,* you will discuss how the author develops characterization.

✦ By discussing the writing strategies the author uses, students become more aware of how they can be better writers.

Teacher Tip

COMPREHENSION STRATEGIES Readers are also listeners. Reading aloud to students provides an opportunity to teach the reader responses and problem-solving strategies that readers employ. In addition to reading aloud with expression and enthusiasm, model your own comprehension strategies while reading aloud to students. This makes the use of strategies "real" for students and encourages them to begin to respond to text similarly.

Technology

To promote independent reading, encourage students to use Workshop to listen to the recording of the selection on the *Listening Library CD.* Invite them to follow along and say the words whenever they can.

Audio CD

Comprehension Strategies

Teacher Modeling

❶ Clarifying *We were confused about what Mockingbird meant by these words. So we looked again at the picture on this page. That's when we saw a tiny cricket that seemed to be making noise. Looking again at the picture helped us figure out what Mockingbird was talking about.*

❷ Clarifying *This time we needed to clarify the meaning of a word. Again we looked back at a picture to help. We recognized the violin, and then read Cricket was playing something. By rereading the words and looking at the pictures, we clarified the meaning of a new word,* fiddle.

Focus Question How did the night wind help the child fall asleep?

Wind Says Good Night, pp. 4–11

The illustrations contain the following text:

From the tall grass by the back steps came the cheerful ring of Cricket's tune.

"Cricket," said the night wind, "will you stop playing
so Mockingbird will stop singing
so the child can go to sleep?"

But Cricket didn't want to stop playing. His toes were tapping, his coattails flapping, as the melody flowed from his fiddle strings.

"No," said Cricket, "I can't stop playing until Frog stops strumming."

"Frog," said the night wind, "will you stop strumming
so Cricket will stop playing
so Mockingbird will stop singing
so the child can go to sleep?"

But Frog was deep in the swing, lost in the beat, with a night full of rhythm in his hands and feet.

"No," said Frog, "I can't stop strumming until Moth stops dancing."

Vocabulary Tip

Review the meanings of the words *beat* and *rhythm*. Then have students use the words in sentences.

Comprehension Skills

Reality and Fantasy

✦ Ask students to name stories they know that are make-believe and stories they know that are true.

✦ Remind students that some make-believe stories are called *fantasy*. Fantasy stories have things that could not be real, such as talking animals, made-up creatures, and so on. Remind students that even fantasy has many real details.

✦ Help students begin to separate reality from fantasy by asking questions such as the following:

- *Do pages 4–7 have anything that could not be real?*
- *How can we tell what is real on pages 4–7?*
- *Do birds, crickets, and frogs really make musical sounds at night?*
- *What makes this story a fantasy?*

Reading with a Writer's Eye

Characterization

✦ Tell students in a fantasy or make-believe story, animals and objects are often treated as people with personalities. Explain to students that the author of this story creates several make-believe characters and develops these characters through what they say and how they behave.

✦ Ask students to describe the personality of the night wind and personalities of the other characters on these pages.

Comprehension Strategies

Teacher Modeling

❸ Clarifying *When we saw the word* widespread, *we needed to clarify what it meant. The picture of Moth helped us understand what her wings looked like. Then we saw the two smaller words. By looking again at the word and using the picture clue, we were able to figure out the meaning.*

❹ Clarifying *This part of the story confused us. We couldn't understand why it started to rain, and the words on this page didn't tell us. Then we looked back a few more pages. We reread the page that tells about the wind carrying the cloud. That helped us clarify that the cloud must have had rain in it. By going back to reread earlier pages, we were able to figure this out.*

"Moth," said the night wind, "will you stop dancing
so Frog will stop strumming
so Cricket will stop playing
so Mockingbird will stop singing
so the child can go to sleep?"

❸ But Moth loved to dip and twirl on widespread wings by moonlight.
"Impossible," said Moth. "The night is too, too beautiful. I can't stop dancing until Moon stops shining."

12   13

"Moon," said the night wind, "will you stop shining
so Moth will stop dancing
so Frog will stop strumming
so Cricket will stop playing
so Mockingbird will stop singing
so the child can go to sleep?"

But Moon's glow was so strong, it turned the green meadow grass to silver.
"Hard to do," said Moon, "hard to do. I can't stop shining unless there's a change in the weather."

14   15

Vocabulary Tip

Review the meaning of the word *glow*. Then have students use the word in a sentence.

Teacher Tip

COMPREHENSION SKILLS When you reread the selection, model the strategies only if your students need additional help. Otherwise, focus on comprehension skills.

Far to the west hovered a small dark shadow.

"Cloud," called the night wind, "will you cover the earth
so Moon will stop shining
so Moth will stop dancing
so Frog will stop strumming
so Cricket will stop playing
so Mockingbird will stop singing
so the child can go to sleep?"

"Only if you will carry me," said Cloud.

16   17

In a rush of cool air the night wind scooped up Cloud. Soon
a mist spread over the meadow. A gentle rain began to fall,
tumbling down through the dark, splashing on the flat bay
waters, skipping on the warm green earth. 4

18   19

Wind Says Good Night, pp. 12–19

Vocabulary Tip

Review the meanings of the words *hovered*
and *mist*. Then have students use the words
in sentences.

Comprehension Skills

Reality and Fantasy

✦ Help students determine reality and
fantasy by asking questions such as the
following:

- *Does a moth usually have a face like a
  person?* No, that is fantasy.

- *Did you ever see a moon with a face
  like the one in the picture on pages
  14–15?* Students should recognize that
  although sometimes the moon has
  features that seem to be a face, it does
  not have a face like this one.

- *Do clouds have faces?* No, that is fantasy.

- *Does the wind carry clouds in real life?*
  Yes, the wind blows clouds across the sky.
  This brings changes in weather.

Reading with a Writer's Eye

Characterization

✦ Ask students to describe the characters
of Moth, Moon, and Cloud. *Moth is too
busy enjoying the beautiful night and won't
stop dancing when asked. Moon also won't
cooperate with the night wind's request.
Cloud is willing to help out if the night wind
carries him.*

✦ Ask students what they would add to their
descriptions of the night wind's character.
*He is very patient with the other characters
and helpful to Cloud.*

Comprehension Strategies

Teacher Modeling

5 **Clarifying** *When we saw Moth sleeping, we were confused. She has really been dancing a lot. Then we looked back a few pages and realized Moon had stopped shining, so there was no light. That helped clarify for us why Moth has stopped dancing. By looking back a few pages, we were able to figure out what happened.*

6 **Clarifying** *This is another place that confused us. Cricket didn't care about the moonlight. We used the rereading strategy and looked back at what else had happened. Then we understood that Frog had gone to sleep and wasn't making any music. That allowed Cricket to sleep. Rereading helped us clarify why things happened in the story.*

Moon stopped shining.

20   21

Moth stopped dancing. **5**

22   23

Frog stopped strumming.

24   25

Cricket stopped playing. **6**

26   27

Wind Says Good Night, pp. 20–27

Teacher Tip

REALITY AND FANTASY Remind students to distinguish *reality* from *fantasy*. They should ask themselves *Could this really happen?*

Comprehension Skills

Reality and Fantasy

✦ Help students continue to determine reality and fantasy by asking the following questions:

- *Could a cloud cover the moon?* yes
- *Would this cause the moon to stop shining?* No, but its glow might be hidden by the cloud.

✦ Ask students to look at the illustrations of Frog and Cricket and describe the real elements and the make-believe elements. *Frogs and crickets are real, but they don't wear clothing or glasses and don't look like this when they are sleeping. The grass, flowers, and other parts of the natural world are real.*

Reading with a Writer's Eye

Characterization

Explain to students that on these pages, the illustrations tell more about the characters than the words do. Ask students how they would describe Moon, Moth, Frog, and Cricket. *All four characters have honored the night wind's request to stop what they were doing and have fallen comfortably asleep.*

Comprehension Strategies

Teacher Modeling

7 Clarifying *We needed to clarify why everyone had fallen asleep. We looked back one page, but that didn't really help. We knew that readers look back as far as they need to figure out what is happening. After we looked back some more pages, we were able to clarify how everything had happened and why everyone had fallen asleep.*

8 Clarifying *We didn't know why the wind said "Good night." By looking back at the last couple of pages, we were able to clarify that the wind was saying this to the little child.*

Mockingbird stopped singing.

28   29

At last the night was dark, and quiet, and still. The child snuggled under warm blankets, closed tired eyes, and fell asleep. **7**

30   31

Vocabulary Tip

Review the meaning of the word *snuggled*. Then have students use the word in a sentence.

 Teacher Tip

REALITY AND FANTASY Distinguishing between *reality* and *fantasy* may be difficult for kindergarten students. Keep a light touch here. For example, say *Have you ever seen a cricket with clothes on?* When students reply *no*, tell them that is fantasy.

"Good night," said the wind. **8**

Wind Says Good Night, pp. 28–32

Reading with a Writer's Eye

Characterization

Ask students what they would add to their description of the night wind.

Discussing the Selection

Have students retell the sequence of story events by using the words *and then.* Tell students to include why each character will not stop its activity.

Purposes for Reading

✦ Ask students what they liked best about *Wind Says Good Night.*

✦ Ask them what they learned about the wind from this selection.

Vocabulary Review

Review with students the selection vocabulary words *beat, rhythm, glow, hovered, mist,* and *snuggled.* Ask students the following questions:

- *What does a beat sound like?*
- *How do I make a rhythm?*
- *What is something that has a glow?*
- *What would it look like if something hovered over your head?*
- *When might you see a mist?*
- *When was a time you snuggled with something?*

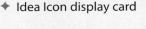

OBJECTIVES

Students will

✦ compare the ideas in their final report to their pre-research ideas.

✦ review the pronouns *I, you, he, she, it, we,* and *they.*

✦ review identifying problems, ideas, and solutions in a story plot.

✦ review sequence of events.

MATERIALS

✦ *Language Arts Big Book,* p. 54

✦ *Skills Practice 2,* pp. 113–114

✦ *Transparency* 44

✦ Thought Cloud display card

✦ Idea Icon display card

Writing Process

Reflect: Comparing Report to Conjectures Made Prior to Research

Teach

Congratulate students on all their hard work while writing the class report. Remind them of some of the steps the class went through to create the report: *brainstorming ideas, planning the research, researching information, putting ideas in the best order, writing sentences to explain the information, and drawing pictures to show the important information.*

Guided Practice

Ask students to think about their experiences writing the class report. Ask students the following questions:

• *What did you think about the wind before writing the report?*

• *How did your ideas change from then to now?*

• *What did you learn about the wind that surprised you?*

• *What did you already know about the wind that you also saw in your research?*

Differentiating Instruction   English Learners

IF . . . students are native Spanish speakers, **THEN . . .** they may drop personal subject pronouns. In Spanish, personal pronouns are often dropped when they are the subject of a sentence. Explain that in English, subject pronouns are always stated, except in commands such as *Close the door,* in which *you* is dropped.

Grammar, Usage, and Mechanics

Teach

✦ Display page 54 of the *Language Arts Big Book,* and read the sentences aloud, pointing to each corresponding picture.

✦ Draw students' attention to the word *I* in the first sentence, and point out that it is taking the place of Vicki's name. Have students identify the names of the characters the other pronouns are replacing in the other sentences on the page.

✦ Remind students that the words *I* and *you* are called pronouns. Say *A pronoun can be used to take the place of a person's name.*

✦ Tell students the words *he, she,* and *it* are also called pronouns. *He* replaces a boy's name, *she* replaces a girl's name, and *it* replaces a noun that is neither a boy nor a girl.

✦ Finally explain that the words *we* and *they* are also called pronouns. *We* and *they* take the place of more than one name or of a group.

Language Arts Big Book, p. 54

Grammar, Usage, and Mechanics continued

Guided Practice

✦ Have students open their **Skills Practice 2** to pages 113 and 114.

✦ Work through the pages with students, and review their answers when you finish.

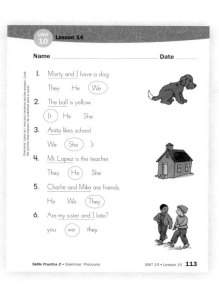

Skills Practice 2, pp. 113–114

Monitor Progress to Differentiate Instruction

Formal Assessment ✓

Grammar Note how easily students are able to use pronouns.

APPROACHING LEVEL

IF ... students are having difficulty,

THEN ... help them complete **Reteach** page 194.

ON LEVEL

IF ... students need more practice,

THEN ... with your help, have them create a list of pronouns.

ABOVE LEVEL

IF ... students are comfortable,

THEN ... have them complete **Challenge Activities** page 146.

 Teacher Tip

ACTIVITY PREPARATION In advance of the following activity, make one photocopy of **Transparency** 44, "Wind Says Good Night," for each student. Cut the individual frames of each copy, and place them in an envelope with a student's name on it.

Story Crafting ☀

✦ Display **Transparency** 44, "Wind Says Good Night," and lead students in a brief retelling of the story.

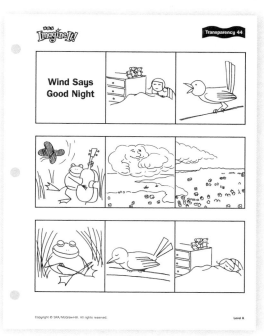

Transparency 44

✦ Pointing to the Listening Icons, remind students to listen carefully.

✦ Point to the drawing of the child at the beginning of the story. Ask students to describe the child's problem. Draw another thought cloud over the child's head, and have students help you think of words to write that tell about the problem that is introduced. *The child cannot fall asleep because of the mockingbird's singing.*

✦ Next draw students' attention to Frame 5, in which the wind has an idea to make everyone quiet. Show students the Idea Icon display card, and remind them the lightbulb shows that the story character has an idea to solve the problem.

✦ Draw the Idea Icon (lightbulb) above the frame, and have students tell you what words to write to explain wind's idea.

✦ Invite a volunteer to come up and point to the frame that shows the problems were solved.

✦ Remove from view the working copy of **Transparency** 44, "Wind Says Good Night," and distribute to students the envelopes with the cut-up transparency frames.

✦ Ask students to work independently to arrange the frames in the proper sequence of events of the story. Then supply students with drawing paper and glue, and have them paste the frames onto the paper to "capture" their sequencing work.

Sounds and Letters

Students will

✦ make and extend oral sentences.

✦ review the long- and short-vowel sounds of *Aa, Ee, Ii, Oo,* and *Uu.*

✦ review writing the letters *Ww, Kk, Ee, Qq, Yy,* and *Vv.*

✦ practice writing words they have blended.

✦ Routine 2

✦ **Alphabet Letter Cards** *Aa, Ee, Ii, Oo* and *Uu* for each student

✦ **Skills Practice 2,** pp. 115–116

Calendar

Su	M	T	W	Th	F	S
			1	2	3	4	5
6	7	8	9	10	11	12
13	14	15	16	17	18	19
20	21	22	23	24	25	26
27	28	29	30	31		

Point to the box that represents today. Ask a student to identify on the calendar the Fourth of July holiday. Then have the class count aloud with you the days until that special day. Point to each day as you count aloud.

Warming Up

MORNING MESSAGE

Today is _____.

Next year we will begin the _____ grade!

Have a wonderful summer, boys and girls!

Kindergarten News

✦ Copy the above text on the board or on chart paper. Ask a volunteer to come up and write today's date in the first blank.

✦ Ask students to say what grade they will be in next year. Help a student write the numeral in the second blank. If the school year ends in a different season for your class, then replace *summer* with the appropriate time of year.

✦ Discuss in broad terms some of the things students have learned in your class this year, such as the letters of the alphabet, the sounds of the letters, how to count, how to tell time, and so on.

Phoneme Segmentation

✦ Do a quick review of segmentation with students, using counters. Tell students you will say a word. Explain that you want them to count how many sounds they hear in the word.

✦ Say the word *map*, stretching the sounds: */m-m-m-m/ /a-a-a-a/ /p/*. Have students place a counter in front of them for each sound they hear.

✦ Call on volunteers to tell how many sounds the word has. Then guide the class in blending and saying aloud the word *map*.

✦ Continue the activity with the following words: *tap, tag, rag, ran, pan, pin*. Have students identify which sound is different in each word change.

Phonics

Blending and Sentence Extension

✦ Using the established procedure, have students blend the following words sound by sound as you write them letter by letter on the board:

jam   job   pig   five

✦ On the board, write sentences that contain the words. For example:

I am five.

Do you have a job?

✦ Ask students to use their knowledge of high-frequency words and sounds and letters to read each sentence. Be sure to have them reread the sentences until they can do so as they would speak them.

✦ Say clues for words from the Blending activity. Call on a student to come to the board to underline the word that answers the clue. When the student has identified and said the word, have her or him use it in a sentence. Help students extend the sentences by asking them questions such as *Where? Which?* and *When?*

 **Teacher Tip**

BLENDING To include all of your students, you may want to create shorter example sentences.

Alphabetic Principle

Reviewing the Short and Long Sounds of *Aa, Ee, Ii, Oo,* and *Uu*

To briefly review vowels, lead students in singing the "Vowel Song" or "Apples and Bananas," both available on the **Listening Library CD** and in the Appendix.

Differentiating Vowel Sounds

✦ Give each student one **Alphabet Letter Card** *Aa,* one **Alphabet Letter Card** *Ee,* one **Alphabet Letter Card** *Ii,* one **Alphabet Letter Card** *Oo,* and one **Alphabet Letter Card** *Uu.* Ask students to raise the cards with the letter that matches the vowel sound in the word you say. Tell students they should be listening for the short-vowel sounds of each vowel. Say each aloud: /a/, /e/, /i/, /o/, /u/. Try the following words:

bad	tip	nut	nod	led
win	ham	sat	bib	hug
ten	rob	pen	sun	fit
bug	puff	pig	yam	rod
dot	met	top	set	bat

✦ Continue the activity, this time asking students to listen for the long-vowel sounds of each vowel. Say each aloud: /ā/, /ē/, /ī/, /ō/, /ū/. Try the following words:

cube	we	rope	nine	wave
bee	mule	fuse	feet	post
kite	date	fade	hole	eve
game	nose	keep	huge	ride
joke	hide	five	lake	use

Technology

Have students use the **eGames** phonics activity for this unit to review long and short vowels.

Penmanship

✦ Distribute a sheet of writing paper to each student, or use **White Boards** turned to the sides with writing lines.

✦ Place the Supply Icon for *pencil* on the board or in the **Pocket Chart.**

✦ Write on the board the words *wave, vine,* and *woke.*

✦ Guide students in blending each word individually. After each word is blended, ask students to practice writing the word on their writing papers. If they need more space, ask them to turn over the papers.

Guided Practice

✦ Guide students in completing **Skills Practice 2** pages 115 and 116 for additional practice writing and blending words.

✦ Read aloud each sentence, and help students blend each word as much as necessary. Allow students time to write the word on the line before moving on to the next word.

✦ When students finish both pages, have them work with partners to proofread their work. Ask each student to circle one word on each page that they think they can write better. Have them cross out the word and rewrite it above, below, or next to the first attempt.

✦ After students have finished, review their work, and note which students are struggling with letter formation.

Monitor Progress

Formal Assessment

to Differentiate Instruction

Blending Note how easily students write and blend the words.

APPROACHING LEVEL

IF ... students have difficulty,   THEN ... help them complete **Reteach** page 195.

ON LEVEL

IF ... students need more practice,   THEN ... have them use **Alphabet Letter Cards** of various consonants and vowels to blend words you write on the board.

ABOVE LEVEL

IF ... students would enjoy a challenging activity,   THEN ... have them work independently to complete **Challenge Activities** page 147.

 Teacher Tip

PENMANSHIP PRACTICE Remind students to keep practicing their penmanship over the break. You might suggest they each get a new writer's notebook and learn how to write a new word every day until they return to school.

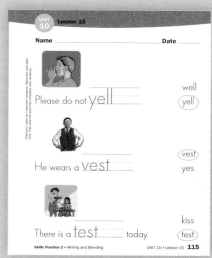

Skills Practice 2, p. 115

Skills Practice 2, p. 116

OBJECTIVES

Students will
- ✦ present the class report.
- ✦ share the drawings that illustrate ideas.
- ✦ review the present, past, and future tenses of action words.
- ✦ participate in a celebration of the unit theme.

MATERIALS

- ✦ **Language Arts Big Book,** pp. 22, 46
- ✦ Final draft of class report
- ✦ Student drawings to accompany class report
- ✦ **Windy Days Big Book,** pp. 4–54
- ✦ **Read Aloud Collection:** *Can You See the Wind?*
- ✦ **Story Time Collection:** *Wind Says Good Night*

Theme Wrap-Up and Review

✦ Discuss the chart you kept, how students kept thinking about new questions, and how their reading and inquiry helped them find answers to their questions. *What else would you like to learn about the wind?*

✦ Talk with the class about inquiry in general. Ask *What did you learn from inquiry? Ask Why is asking questions important for learning? What are some special inquiry words? How can we investigate things that interest us? How can we keep track of what we are learning? What are some things you can investigate during summer vacation?*

✦ Have students identify the purpose of informational text and distinguish between informational text and text read for pleasure.

✦ Have students use the **Listening Library CDs** to review selections that interest them. Encourage students to use online tools and games to enhance their learning.

Teacher Tip

SCHEDULING Students may need additional time to complete their final product. If possible, set aside another part of the day to devote to this activity.

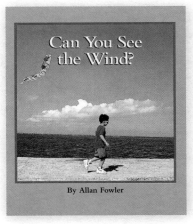

Read Aloud Collection:
Can You See the Wind?

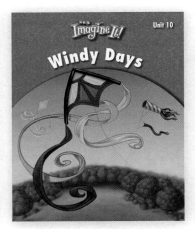

Windy Days Big Book

Story Time Collection:
Wind Says Good Night

Writing Process

Publish: Presenting Report and Sharing Drawings

Teach

In advance of the activity, invite a guest to visit your classroom. Begin the lesson by telling students today the class will work together to present the report. Explain that they will show their drawings while you read the final report that the class wrote.

Apply

✦ Distribute each student's drawings. Then work with the class to plan and practice the presentation.

✦ If you believe students are ready, assign lines of text, and have them recite the report aloud while other students display their drawings.

✦ Welcome the guest to the classroom, and lead the class in presenting the report.

✦ After the presentation, collect the drawings, and display them in the classroom.

Monitor Progress to Differentiate Instruction

Formal Assessment ✓

Grammar Note how easily students are able to use action words.

APPROACHING LEVEL	
IF ... students are having difficulty,	THEN ... have them complete **Reteach** page 196.

ON LEVEL	
IF ... students need more practice,	THEN ... have them help create a list of action words.

ABOVE LEVEL	
IF ... students are comfortable,	THEN ... have them reread "Go Wind" and find the action words.

Grammar, Usage, and Mechanics

Teach

Display page 22 of the **Language Arts Big Book.** Read aloud the sentence at the top of the page, and ask students whether it is in the past, present, or future. *present* Guide students in turning the sentences into the past tense and into the future tense.

Guided Practice

✦ Display page 46 of the **Language Arts Big Book,** and ask students to tell what is pictured on the page. *a calendar*

✦ Use sentence frames to guide students in forming sentences with past-, present-, and future-tense verbs based on the items in the calendar. Use the following sentence frames:

• Today we _____ a soccer game. *play*

• Last week my family _____ a birthday cake for me. *baked*

• On Saturday my friends _____ _____ a sleepover. *will enjoy*

Language Arts Big Book, *pp. 22, 46*

Monitor Progress ✓
Formal Assessment Options

You will need the following materials, along with your informal observations and Lesson Assessment results, to monitor student progress throughout the year.

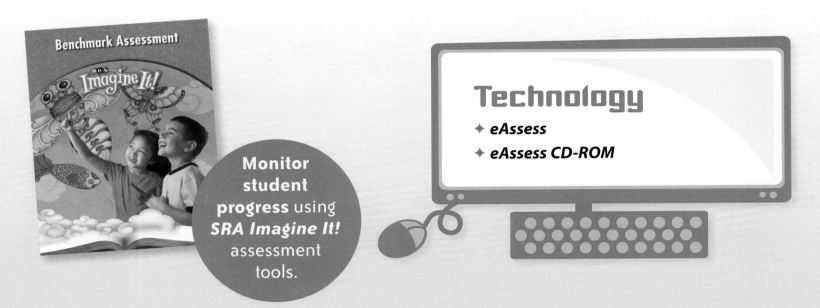

Monitor student progress using *SRA Imagine It!* assessment tools.

Technology
- ✦ *eAssess*
- ✦ *eAssess CD-ROM*

Benchmark Assessment for Unit 10 addresses the following skills:

- **Phonemic Awareness**
- **Letter Recognition**
- **Phonics/Word Reading**
- **Comprehension**
- **Grammar, Usage, and Mechanics**

Results on **Benchmark Assessment** will serve as a performance indicator that shows how well students are prepared to take an end-of-the-year standardized test. **Benchmark Assessment** results also will allow you to intervene with students who are at risk for failure.

Monitor Progress with Benchmark Assessment

Below are two sets of **Benchmark Assessment** cutoffs that can be used for predicting student performance—one for Benchmark Skills Assessments and the other for Oral Fluency Assessments. Each cutoff begins with a baseline score under Benchmark 1, which is given at the beginning of the year and ends with Benchmark 6, which is given at the end of the year. The cutoffs are determined by finding the amount of growth a student must make over the course of the year to ensure he or she will not be at risk for reading failure.

Benchmark Skills Assessment

The Benchmark Skills Assessment is a 100-point test, consisting of questions covering phonemic awareness; letter recognition; phonics/word reading; comprehension; and grammar, usage, and mechanics. The table below shows how many points out of 100 kindergarten students should score on a particular Benchmark Skills Assessment over the course of the year. The highlighted score indicates where your students should be at this time.

Benchmark 1	Benchmark 2	Benchmark 3	Benchmark 4	Benchmark 5	Benchmark 6
7	23	38	54	70	85

Oral Fluency Assessment: Letter Sounds

The Oral Fluency Assessment is an individually administered assessment, consisting of letter sounds, phonetically regular words, and high-frequency words that students read aloud to the teacher to assess fluency. The table below shows how many letter sounds and words kindergarten students should read on a particular Oral Fluency Assessment over the course of the year. The highlighted score indicates where your students should be at this time.

Benchmark 1	Benchmark 2	Benchmark 3	Benchmark 4	Benchmark 5	Benchmark 6
0	6	12	18	24	30

Independent Tools to Monitor Progress

DIBELS and TPRI

Based on your DIBELS or TPRI scores, use manipulatives from the **Workshop Kit** to practice letter sounds and letter recognition.

Unit Celebration

 Teacher Tip

UNIT CELEBRATION Remember, the goal of this celebration is to allow students to take ownership of their learning. Your role is to guide them toward success. You must take the lead for certain elements of the celebration, but rely on student input for all major decisions.

Why do we have wind?

Write the Big Idea question on the board or on chart paper. Ask students what they have learned about the wind. Ask which selections added something new to their understanding about the wind.

Celebrate the Wind!

✦ In advance of the activity, prepare the materials students will need to share the final product of their inquiry. The necessary materials will depend on the method students chose for sharing.

✦ Congratulate students on all their hard work in this unit as they learned about the wind. Remind them the unit celebration is a reward for all their hard work.

✦ Help students decide on a forum for sharing the final product of their inquiry. Encourage them to think of new ideas for sharing their inquiry with people outside the classroom. If students need help sparking their creativity, make suggestions for how students might share their celebration with others.

✦ Encourage students to include in their planning some tasks for you to complete. Remind them they are in charge of the celebration and they should decide what they can handle on their own and what they will need your help with. You might even help them create a "To-Do List" for you.

✦ Support students through each step of their preparation for the celebration. For example, if students have decided to present a science experiment exploring the wind, help them research the process, plan for safety, assign roles, and gather necessary materials.

Inquiry Wrap-Up

✦ In this lesson, students will share their investigations of wind. Be sure they begin their presentations by telling the class the inquiry question and conjecture: *Our question is _____. Our conjecture is _____.*

✦ Take a few minutes to talk about evaluating their inquiry activities.

- *What did you learn from our inquiry activities?*
- *How did the instruments help us? Which ones were most helpful in learning about wind?*
- *What problems did you have? How can we solve those problems?*
- *How did you like working in groups? How did this help with your inquiries?*
- *How were your conjectures supported?*

✦ Allow time for students to share their final products not only with your class but with other classes in the school. You may want to invite family members for the presentations.

✦ Go fly a kite, and enjoy the wind!

Teacher Tip

RECREATIONAL READING Because it is important to read daily to your students, choose a book from the Additional Reading listed in the Table of Contents, and find a time during the day to read the book aloud to students.

Concept/Question Board

Encourage students to discuss what they have learned about the wind. Invite them to share how their ideas about the wind have changed since the unit began. Focus students' attention on the **Concept/Question Board** postings, and peel back the layers of self-sticking notes to see how their knowledge has changed. Read each question aloud, and determine if it has been answered and can be moved to the Concept side of the Board. Invite volunteers to add ideas to the questions that still need answers.

B

boiling
The water in the pan is **boiling**.

burst
My balloon **burst**.

50

F

fall
We like to pick apples in the **fall**.

floats
The leaf **floats** in the breeze.

51

P

pasture
Cows eat grass in the **pasture**.

pile
Paul stacks the wood into a **pile**.

52

S

steam
Steam is coming out of the teapot.

swept
Rob **swept** the floor with the broom.

53

U

unlatched
I **unlatched** the gate.

54

Appendices

Program Appendix

Level Appendix

Index

Imagine It!

The Program Appendix includes a step-by-step explanation of procedures for research-based, effective practices in reading instruction that are repeatedly used throughout **SRA Imagine It!** These practices may also be used in other instructional materials.

Table of Contents

Phonological and Phonemic Awareness

The key to learning to read is the ability to identify different sounds and to connect those sounds to the letters of the alphabet. The basic purpose of providing structured practice in phonemic awareness is to help students hear and understand the sounds from which words are made. Before students can be expected to understand the sound/symbol correspondence that forms the base of written English, they need to have a strong working knowledge of the sound relationships that make up the spoken language. This understanding of spoken language lays the foundation for the transition to written language.

Phonological awareness is an umbrella term. It incorporates a range of oral language skills that involve the ability to notice, think about, and manipulate individual sounds in words. Phonological awareness involves working with sentences, words, rhyme, syllables, and sounds. The objective is for students to be able to manipulate words, word parts, and sounds without regard to meaning.

Phonological and phonemic awareness activities initially provide students with the opportunity to think about sentences and to break them into words and then to play with words and to break them into parts. It involves easy and fun activities that engage students in playing with and exploring the parts and sounds of language. The goal of these gamelike activities is to help students understand that speech is made of distinct, identifiable sounds. The playful nature of the activities makes them appealing and engaging, while giving students practice and support for learning about language. When students begin reading and writing, this experience with manipulating sounds will help them use what they know about sounds and letters to sound out and spell unfamiliar words when they read and write.

Developing phonological awareness engages students in activities that move from working with words and syllables — the larger units of language — to individual sounds (phonemes). Students progress by

- Identifying sentences
- Identifying words
- Working with rhymes
- Exploring compound words
- Listening for syllables
- Blending syllables
- Oral blending
- Deleting and substituting sounds
- Segmenting phonemes

As students progress through various phonemic awareness activities, they will become proficient at listening for and reproducing the sounds they hear. It is essential for their progression to phonics and reading that they are able to hear the sounds and the patterns used to make up recognizable words. The phonemic awareness activities support the phonics instruction. Initially students are not expected to read the words they are exploring and manipulating, so any consonant and vowel sounds may be used, even if students have not been formally taught the sounds and their spellings.

> *As students progress through various phonemic awareness activities, they will become proficient at listening for and reproducing the sounds they hear.*

After students have an awareness of phonemes, they can begin to connect sounds to letters and to engage in a variety of activities in which sounds and letters are substituted to make new words. Students begin to understand that if a sound changes, a letter must change, and a new word is created. As students move into phonics, research suggests that connecting sounds to spellings actually heightens their awareness of language. Phonological and phonemic awareness is both a prerequisite for and a consequence of learning to read.

Research suggests that the majority of instructional time should be focused on two critical phonemic awareness formats: phoneme or oral blending and phoneme segmentation. These are supported by discrimination and elision activities (deleting and substituting sounds) and general wordplay. Oral blending encourages students to combine sounds to make words and lays the foundation for decoding and reading. Segmentation, conversely, requires students to break words into discrete sounds and lays the foundation for spelling. Other activities support discrimination, or recognition, of particular sounds. Sometimes simple songs, rhymes, or games engage students in wordplay. In these, students manipulate words in a variety of ways. From these playful activities, students develop serious knowledge about their language.

Oral Blending
Purpose

In oral blending, students are led through a progression of activities designed to help them hear how sounds are put together to make words.

Until students develop an awareness of the component parts of words, they have no tools with which to decode words or to put letters together to form words. Oral blending helps students understand these component parts of words, from syllables down to single sounds, or phonemes. Oral blending is not to be confused with the formal blending of specific sounds whose spellings students will be taught through phonics instruction. Oral blending does not depend on the recognition of written words; it focuses instead on hearing the sounds.

Oral blending focuses on hearing sounds through a sequence that introduces the most easily distinguished word parts and then systematically moves to oral blending of individual sounds that contains all the challenges of phonic decoding (except letter recognition). This sequence provides support for the least-prepared student—one who comes to school with no concept of words or sounds within words. At the same time, the lively pace and playful nature of oral blending activities hold the interest of students who already have some familiarity with words and letters.

Oral blending prepares students for phonics instruction by developing an awareness of the separate sounds that make up speech. Oral blending activities then continue in concert with phonics instruction to reinforce and extend new learning. And because these activities involve simply listening to and reproducing sounds, oral blending need not be restricted to the sounds students have been or will be taught in phonics.

The tone of the activities should be playful and informal and should move quickly. Although these activities will provide information about student progress, they are not diagnostic tools. Do not expect mastery. Those students who have not caught on will be helped more by varied experiences than by more drilling on the same activity.

Procedure

The following is a description of the progression of oral blending activities.

Word-Part Blending

Syllables are easier to distinguish than individual sounds (phonemes), so students can quickly experience success in forming meaningful words. Tell students that you are going to say some words in two parts. Tell them to listen carefully so they can discover what the words are. Read each word, pronouncing each part distinctly with a definite pause between syllables. The lists of words that follow are arranged in sequence from easy to harder. They cover different types of cues. Whenever they fit into the sequence, include multisyllabic names of students in the class.

Model

Teacher: dino . . . saur. What's the word?
Students: dinosaur

Example Words

✦ First part of the word cues the whole word:
  vita . . . min
  vaca . . . tion
  hippopot . . . amus
  ambu . . . lance

✦ Two distinct words easily combined:
  butter . . . fly
  straw . . . berry
  surf . . . board
  basket . . . ball

✦ Two distinct words, but first word could cue the wrong ending:
  tooth . . . ache
  tooth . . . paste
  water . . . fall
  water . . . melon

✦ First part, consonant + vowel, not enough to guess whole word:
  re . . . member
  re . . . frigerator
  bi . . . cycle
  bi . . . ology

✦ Identifying cues in second part:
  light . . . ning
  sub . . . ject
  in . . . sect

✦ Last part, consonant + vowel sound, carries essential information:
  yester . . . day
  rain . . . bow
  noi . . . sy
  pota . . . to

✦ Changing the final part changes the word:
  start . . . ing
  start . . . er
  start . . . ed

Initial Consonant Sounds

Initial consonant blending prepares students for consonant replacement activities that will come later. Tell students that you will ask them to put some sounds together to make words. Pronounce each word part distinctly, and make a definite pause at the breaks indicated. When a letter is surrounded by slash marks, pronounce the letter's sound, not its name. When you see /s/, for example, you will say "ssss," not "ess." The words that follow are arranged from easy to harder. Whenever they fit into the sequence, include names of students in the class.

Model

Teacher: /t/ . . . iger. What's the word?
Students: tiger

Example Words

✦ Separated consonant blend, with rest of word giving strong cue to word identity:
  /b/ . . . roccoli   */k/ . . . racker*
  /f/ . . . lashlight   */k/ . . . reature*

✦ Held consonant that is easy for students to hear, with rest of word giving strong cue:
  /s/ . . . innamon   */l/ . . . adybug*
  /s/ . . . eventeen   */n/ . . . ewspaper*

✦ Stop consonant that is harder for students to hear preceding vowel, with rest of word giving strong cue:
  /t/ . . . adpole   */p/ . . . iggybank*
  /d/ . . . ragonfly   */b/ . . . arbecue*

✦ Single-syllable words and words in which the second part gives a weaker cue:
  /s/ . . . ing   */l/ . . . augh*   */v/ . . . ase*

Final Consonant Sounds

In this phase of oral blending, the last sound in the word is separated.

Model

Teacher: cabba . . . /j/. What's the word?
Students: cabbage

Example Words

✦ Words that are easily recognized even before the final consonant is pronounced:
  bubblegu . . . /m/   *Columbu . . . /s/*
  crocodi . . . /l/   *submari . . . /n/*

✦ Multisyllabic words that need the final consonant for recognition:
  colle . . . /j/ (college)   *come . . . /t/ (comet)*

✦ Single-syllable words:
  sa . . . /d/   *gra . . . /s/ (grass)*   *snai . . . /l/*

Initial Consonant Sound Replacement

This level of oral blending further develops awareness of initial consonant sounds. The activity begins with a common word then quickly changes its initial consonant sound. Most of the words produced are nonsense words, which helps keep the focus on the sounds in the word. Note that the words are written on the board, but students are not expected to read them. The writing is to help students see that when the sounds change, the letters change, and vice versa.

Model

Teacher: [Writes word on board.] This word is *magazine*. What is it?
Students: magazine
Teacher: Now I'm going to change it. [Erases initial consonant.] Now it doesn't start with /m/; it's going to start with /b/. What's the new word?
Students: bagazine
Teacher: That's right . . . [Writes *b* where *m* had been.] It's *bagazine*. Now I'm going to change it again. . . .

Repeat with different consonant sounds. Then do the same with other words such as *remember, Saturday, tomorrow, lotion,* and *million*. Continue with single-syllable words such as *take, big, boot, cot, seat, look, tap, ride,* and *late*. There are two stages in using written letters:

✦ The replacement letter is not written until ***after*** the new "word" has been identified.

◆ Later, the replacement letter is written at *the same time* the change in the initial phoneme is announced. For example, erase *d* and write *m* while you say, "Now it doesn't start with /d/; it starts with /m/."

When the consonants used have already been introduced in phonics, you may wish to alter the procedure by writing the replacement letter and having students sound out the new word. Feel free to switch between the two procedures within a single exercise. If students are not responding orally to written spellings that have been introduced in phonics, do not force it. Proceed by saying the word before writing the letter, and wait until another time to move on to writing before pronouncing.

One-Syllable Words

Students now begin blending individual phonemes to form words. This important step can be continued well into the year. Continued repetitions of this activity will help students realize how they can use the sound/spellings they are learning to read and write real words.

At first, the blended words are presented in a story context that helps students identify the words. They soon recognize that they are actually decoding meaningful words. However, the context must not be so strong that students can guess the word without listening to the phonemic cues. Any vowel sounds and irregularly spelled words may be used because there is no writing involved.

Model

Teacher: When I looked out the window, I saw a /l/ /ī/ /t/. What did I see?
Students: A light.
Teacher: Yes, I saw a light. At first I thought it was the /m/ /o͞o/ /n/. What did I think it was?
Students: The moon.
Teacher: But it didn't really look like the moon. Suddenly I thought, maybe it's a space /sh/ /i/ /p/. What did I think it might be?
Students: A spaceship!

When students are familiar with this phase of oral blending, they can move to blending one-syllable words without the story context.

Example Words

◆ CVC (consonant/vowel/consonant) words beginning with easily blended consonant sounds (/sh/, /h/, /r/, /v/, /s/,

/n/, /z/, /f/, /l/, /m/):
  nip   nap
◆ CVC words beginning with any consonant:
  ten   bug   lip
◆ Add CCVC words:
  flap   step
◆ Add CVCC words:
  most   band   went
◆ Add CCVCC words:
  stamp   grand   scuffs

Final Consonant Sound Replacement

Final consonant sounds are typically more difficult for students to use than initial consonants.

✦ Begin with multisyllabic words, and move to one-syllable words.

✦ As with initial consonants, first write the changed consonant after students have pronounced the new word.

✦ Then write the consonant as they pronounce it.

✦ For sound/spellings introduced in phonics instruction, write the new consonant spelling, and have students identify and pronounce it.

Model

Teacher: [Writes word on board.] This word is *teapot*. What is it?
Students: teapot
Teacher: Now I'm going to change it. [Erases final consonant.] Now it doesn't end with /t/; it ends with /p/. What's the word now?
Students: teapop
Teacher: That's right . . . [Writes *p* where *t* had been.] It's *teapop*. Now I'm going to change it again. . . .

Example Words

✦ Words that are easily recognized even before the final consonant is pronounced:
  picnic   picnit   picnis   picnil   picnid
  airplane   airplate   airplabe   airplafe
✦ Multisyllabic words that need the final consonant for recognition:
  muffin   muffil   muffim   muffip   muffit
  amaze   amate   amake   amale   amade
✦ Single-syllable words:
  neat   nean   neap   neam   neaj   nead   neaf
  broom   broot   brood   broof   broop   broon

Initial Vowel Replacement

Up to now, oral blending has concentrated on consonant sounds because they are easier to hear than vowels. As you move to vowel play, remember that the focus is still on the sounds, not the spellings. Use any vowel sounds.

Model

Teacher: [Writes word on board.] This word is *elephant*. What is it?
Students: elephant
Teacher: Now I'm going to change it. [Erases initial vowel.] Now it doesn't start with /e/; it starts with /a/. What's the word now?
Students: alephant
Teacher: That's right . . . [Writes *a* where *e* had been.] It's *alephant*. Now I'm going to change it again. . . .

Example Words

✦ Multisyllabic words:
  angry   ingry   oongry   ungry   engry
  ivy   avy   oovy   evy   ovy   oivy
✦ One-syllable words:
  ink   ank   oonk   unk   onk   oink
  add   odd   idd   oudd   edd   udd

Segmentation

Purpose

Segmentation and oral blending complement each other: Oral blending puts sounds together to make words, while segmentation separates words into sounds. Oral blending will provide valuable support for decoding when students begin reading independently.

Procedure

Syllables

The earliest segmentation activities focus on syllables, which are easier to distinguish than individual sounds, or phonemes. Start with students' names, and then use other words. As with the oral blending activities, remember to move quickly through these activities. Do not hold the class back waiting for all students to catch on. Individual progress will vary, but drilling on one activity is less helpful than going on to others. Return to the same activity often. Frequent repetition is very beneficial and allows students additional opportunities to catch on.

- Say, for example, "Let's clap out Amanda's name. A-man-da."
- Have students clap and say the syllables along with you. Count the claps.
- Tell students that these word parts are called syllables. Don't try to explain; the idea will develop with practice. After you have provided the term, simply say, "How many syllables?" after students clap and count.
- Mix one-syllable and multisyllabic words: *fantastic   tambourine   good imaginary   stand   afraid*

> *Oral blending will provide valuable support for decoding when students begin reading independently.*

Comparative Lengths of Words

Unlike most phonemic awareness activities, this one involves writing on the board or on an overhead transparency. Remember, though, that students are not expected to read what is written. They are merely noticing that words that take longer to say generally look longer when written.

- Start with students' names. Choose two names, one short and one long, with the same first letter (for example, *Joe* and *Jonathan*).
- Write the two names on the board, one above the other, so that the difference is obvious.
- Tell students that one name is *Jonathan* and that one is *Joe*. Have them pronounce and clap each name. Then have them tell which written word they think says *Joe*.
- Move your finger under each name as students clap and say it syllable by syllable.
- Repeat with other pairs of names and words such as *tea/telephone, cat/caterpillar, and butterfly/bug*. Be sure not to give false clues. For example, sometimes write the longer word on top, sometimes the shorter one; sometimes ask for the shorter word, sometimes the

longer; sometimes ask for the top word, sometimes the bottom; and sometimes point to a word and ask students to name it, and sometimes name the word and ask students to point to it.

Listen for Individual Sounds

Activities using a puppet help students listen for individual sounds in words. Use any puppet you have on hand. When you introduce the puppet, tell students that it likes to play word games. Each new activity begins with the teacher speaking to and for the puppet until students determine the pattern. Next, students either speak for the puppet or correct the puppet. To make sure all students are participating, alternate randomly between having the whole group or individuals respond. The activities focus on particular parts of words, according to the following sequence:

I. Repeating last part of word. Use words beginning with easy-to-hear consonants such as *f, l, m, n, r, s,* and *z*. The puppet repeats only the rime, the part of the syllable after the initial consonant.

Model

Teacher: farm
Puppet: arm
After the pattern is established, students respond for the puppet.
Teacher: rope
Students: ope

Example Words
Use words such as the following:
mine . . . ine   soup . . . oup   feet . . . eet

2. Restoring initial phonemes. Now students correct the puppet. Be sure to acknowledge the correction.

Model

Teacher: lake
Puppet: ake
Teacher: No, lllake. You forgot the /l/.
Teacher: real
Puppet: eal
Teacher: What did the puppet leave off?
Students: /r/. It's supposed to be *real*.
Teacher: That's right. The word is *real*.

Example Words
Use words such as the following:
look . . . ook   mouse . . . ouse sand . . . and

3. Segmenting initial consonants. The puppet pronounces only the initial consonant.

Model

Teacher: pay
Puppet: /p/

Example Words
Use words such as the following:
moon . . . /m/   nose . . . /n/   bell . . . /b/

4. Restoring final consonants. Students correct the puppet. Prompt if necessary: "What's the word? What did the puppet leave off?"

Model

Teacher: run
Puppet: ru
Students: It's run! You left off the /n/.
Teacher: That's right. The word is *run*.

Example Words
Use words such as the following:
meet . . . mee   cool . . . coo   boot . . . boo

5. Isolating final consonants. The puppet pronounces only the final consonant.

Model

Teacher: green
Puppet: /n/

Example Words
Use words such as the following:
glass . . . /s/   boom . . . /m/   mice . . . /s/

6. Segmenting initial consonant blends. The sounds in blends are emphasized.

Model

Teacher: clap
Puppet: lap
Next have students correct the puppet.
Teacher: stain
Puppet: tain
Students: It's stain! You left off the /s/.
Teacher: That's right. The word is *stain*.

Example Words
Use words such as the following:
blaze . . . laze   draw . . . raw proud . . . roud

Discrimination

Purpose

Discrimination activities help students focus on particular sounds in words.

Listening for long-vowel sounds is the earliest discrimination activity. Vowel sounds are necessary for decoding, but young students do not hear them easily. This is evident in students' invented spellings, where vowels are often omitted. Early in the year, students listen for long-vowel sounds, which are more easily distinguished than short-vowel sounds:

✦ Explain to students that vowels are special because sometimes they say their names in words.

✦ Tell students which vowel sound to listen for.

✦ Have them repeat the sound when they hear it in a word. For example, if the target-vowel sound is long *e,* students will say long *e* when you say *leaf,* but they should not respond when you say *loaf.*

✦ Initially students should listen for one long vowel sound at a time. Later they can listen for two vowel sounds. All Example Words, however, should contain one of the target vowels.

Procedure

Listening for short-vowel sounds

These discrimination activities should be done after the short vowels /a/ and /i/ have been introduced. Short vowels are very useful in reading. They are generally more regular in spelling than long vowels, and they appear in many short, simple words. However, their sounds are less easily distinguished than those of long vowels. Thus, the activities focus only on /a/ and /i/. All the words provided have one or the other of these sounds. Either have students repeat the sound of a specified vowel, or vary the activity as follows: Write an *a* on one side of the board and an *i* on the other. Ask students to point to the *a* when they hear a word with the /a/ sound and to point to the *i* when they hear a word with the /i/ sound. Use words such as the following:

> bat   mat   sat   sit   spit
> pit   pat   pan   pin   spin

Consonant sounds in multisyllabic words

Discriminating these sounds helps students attend to consonant sounds in the middle of words.

✦ Say the word *rib,* and have students repeat it. Ask where they hear the /b/ in *rib.*

✦ Then say *ribbon,* and ask students where they hear the /b/ in *ribbon.*

✦ Tell students that you will say some words and that they will repeat each word.

✦ After they repeat each word, ask what consonant sound they hear in the middle of that word. Use words such as the following:
*famous   message   picky
jogger   flavor   zipper*

Phonemic Play

Purpose

Wordplay activities help students focus on and manipulate sounds, thus supporting the idea that words are made of specific sounds that can be taken apart, put together, or changed to make new words. Through wordplay, students gain important knowledge about language.

Procedure

Producing rhymes

Many phonemic play activities focus on producing rhymes. A familiar or easily learned rhyme or song is introduced, and students are encouraged to substitute words or sounds. An example is "Willaby Wallaby Woo," in which students change the rhyming words in the couplet "Willaby Wallaby Woo/ An elephant sat on you" so that the second line ends with a student's name and that the first line ends with a rhyme beginning with *W;* for example, "Willaby Wallaby Wissy/An elephant sat on Missy."

Generate alliterative words

Students can also say as many words as they can think of that begin with a given consonant sound. This is a valuable complement to discrimination activities in which the teacher produces the words and students identify them.

The Alphabetic Principle: How the Alphabet Works

The Alphabetic Principle

Purpose

A major emphasis in the kindergarten program is on letter recognition and attending to sounds. Students need to learn the alphabetic principle: that letters work together in a systematic way to connect spoken language to written words. This understanding is the foundation for reading. Students are not expected to master letter/ sound correspondence at the beginning of kindergarten, nor are they expected to blend sounds into words themselves. They are expected to become an "expert" only on their Special Letters as they learn how the alphabet works. Through this introduction to the alphabetic principle, students will have the basic understanding required to work through the alphabet letter by letter, attaching sounds to each.

Key concepts of the alphabetic principle include the following:

✦ A limited number of letters combine in different ways to make many different words.

✦ Words are composed of sounds, and letters represent those sounds.

✦ Anything that can be pronounced can be spelled.

✦ Letters and sounds can be used to identify words.

✦ Meaning can be obtained by using letters and sounds to determine words.

Procedures for Kindergarten

The following steps can be used for introducing letters and sounds in kindergarten. These steps may be adapted for students at other grades if they do not understand the alphabetic principle. The tone of these activities should be informal, fun, and fast-paced. The purpose of these activities is to familiarize students with how the alphabet works by having them participate in group play with letters and sounds.

I Can Spell Anything

✦ Reinforce the idea that anything that can be pronounced can be spelled with the letters of the alphabet.

✦ Tell students that you can spell any word. Have them give you words to spell.

✦ Write the words on the board, naming each letter as you write it. This shows students that the words contain the letters displayed on the **Alphabet Sound Wall Cards.**

✦ Have students help you spell the words again by pointing to letters as you say them.

✦ Encourage students to spell each word letter by letter.

> *The alphabetic principle is the understanding that speech sounds can be mapped onto print.*

Letter Expert Groups

✦ Have **Alphabet Letter Cards** (Levels K and 1) available for the following set of letters: *b, d, f, h, l, m, n, p, s, t.* You will need two or three cards for each letter. (You will not need the **Alphabet Sound Cards** until later.)

✦ You will be the letter expert for the vowels.

✦ Organize the class into groups of two or three, and assign each group a letter. Give each student the appropriate **Alphabet Letter Card.**

✦ Tell students that they are now in their Letter Expert groups and that they are going to become experts on their Special Letter's name, shape, and sound.

Making Words

✦ Begin each lesson with a rehearsal of each group's letter name.

✦ Demonstrate how letters work by writing a word in large letters on the board.

✦ Tell students the experts for each letter in the word should hold up their **Alphabet Letter Cards** and name the letter. One member of the group should stand in front of their letter on the board.

✦ Continue until all letters in the word are accounted for. Remember that you are responsible for the vowels.

✦ Demonstrate that you can make different words by changing a letter or by changing the letter order.

Identifying Sounds in Words

✦ Use the **Alphabet Sound Cards** to demonstrate that every letter has at least one sound.

✦ Give each student the **Alphabet Sound Card** for his or her Special Letter.

✦ Point out the pictures on the cards. Explain that each card has a picture of something that makes the letter's sound. The picture will help them remember the sound.

✦ Tell each group the sound for its letter. (Remember, you are the expert for the vowels.)

✦ Quickly have each group rehearse its letter's name and sound.

✦ Write a word on the board in large letters. First say the word sound by sound, and then blend the word.

✦ For each letter/sound in the word, have one student from each Letter Expert group come forward, stand in front of the appropriate letter, and hold his or her card. Although only one member of the group may come forward with the **Alphabet Letter Card** or **Alphabet Sound Card,** all students in a Special Letter group should say the name or sound of their letter when it occurs in words.

✦ Say the word again, pointing to the **Alphabet Sound Cards.**

✦ Ask students who are not already standing to help you hold the vowel cards.

✦ Vary the activity by changing one letter sound and having an expert for that letter come forward.

✦ End the activity for each word by saying the sounds in the words one by one and then saying the entire word. Encourage students to participate.

Tips

✦ Remind students to use the picture on the **Alphabet Sound Card** for their Special Letter to help them remember the letter's sound. Students are expected to "master" only their own Special Letter and to share the information with their classmates. At this point in the year, they are not expected to blend and read the words by themselves. These are group activities in which you work with students to help them gain insight into the alphabet.

✦ Be sure to connect what students learn about the letters and words to the words they work with in **Big Book** selections.

✦ Occasionally, have students find their special letters in a **Big Book** selection. Play some of the letter replacement and rearrangement games with words encountered in the **Big Books.**

Developing the Alphabetic Principle

Purpose

The alphabetic principle is the understanding that speech sounds can be mapped onto print. It is the association of sounds with letters and the understanding that speech can be turned into print and that print can be turned into speech sounds. Activities associated with the alphabetic principle help kindergarten students develop a more thorough understanding of how sounds "work" in words. In this group of activities, students are introduced to specific letter/sound correspondences, consonants, and short vowels. While students have previously been introduced to vowels and their special characteristics, students' understanding is extended by introducing students to the convention that a vowel has a short sound in addition to its long sound. With this information and a carefully structured set of activities, students can begin to explore and understand the alphabetic principle in a straightforward and thorough manner. Students not only listen for sounds in specified positions in words, they also link sounds to their corresponding letters. The

activities in this group of lessons lay the groundwork for students to work their way through the entire alphabet as they learn letter-sound associations and to understand the purpose and the value of this learning.

Move students quickly through these activities. Do not wait for all students to master each letter/sound correspondence before going on. They will have more opportunities to achieve mastery. The goal of these activities is for students to obtain a basic understanding of the alphabetic principle.

> *Students need to learn the alphabetic principle: that letters work together in a systematic way to connect spoken language to written words. This understanding is the foundation for reading.*

Procedures

Introducing Consonant Letters and Sounds

✦ Point to the **Alphabet Sound Wall Card** and ask students what they know about the card (the letter name, the capital and lowercase letter, and so on).

✦ Turn the card, and point to the picture. Name the picture, and point to and name the letter. Tell students the sound of the letter and how the picture helps them remember the sound. Repeat the sound several times.

✦ Tell students you will read them the short story or an alliterative sentence to help them remember the sound of the letter. Read the story several times, emphasizing the words with the target sound. Have students join in and say the sound.

✦ After introducing and reviewing a letter/sound correspondence, summarize the information on the **Alphabet Sound Wall Card:** the name of the card, the sound, and the letter.

Generating Words with the Target Sound

Brainstorm to create a list of words that begin with the target sound. Write the words on the board or on a chart. Include any of the students' names that begin with the target sound.

Listening for Initial Sounds

✦ Give each student an **Alphabet Letter Card** for the target sound.

✦ Point to the picture on the **Alphabet Sound Wall Card,** and have students give the sound.

✦ Tell students to listen for the first sound in each word you say. If it is the target sound, they should hold up their cards. Establish a signal so that students know when to respond.

✦ Read the list of words, some beginning with the target sound and some beginning with other sounds.

Listening for Final Sounds

The procedure for listening for the final sound of a word is the same as that for listening for the initial sound. Students may need to be reminded throughout the activity to pay attention to the final sound.

Read a list of words, some ending with the target sound and some ending with other sounds. Avoid words that begin with the target sound.

Linking the Sound to the Letter

✦ **Word Pairs (initial sounds).** Write pairs of words on the board. One of each pair should begin with the target sound. Say the word beginning with the target sound, and ask students to identify it. Remind them to listen for the target sound at the beginning of the word, to think about which letter makes that sound, and to find the word that begins with that letter. For example,
Target sound: /s/
Word pair: *fit sit*
Which word is *sit?*

✦ **Word Pairs (final sounds).** Follow the same procedure used for initial sounds, and direct students to think about the sound that they hear at the end of the word. Because it is often more difficult for students to attend to the ending sound, you may need to lead them through several pairs of words. Remind students to listen for the target sound and to think about which letter makes that sound.

✦ **Writing Letters.** Using either of the handwriting systems outlined in this Program Appendix or the system in use at your school, have students practice writing uppercase and lowercase letters. Remind students about the letter sound, and have them repeat it.

Other activities that support the development of the alphabetic principle include the following:

Comparing Initial Consonant Sounds

This activity is exactly like Listening for Initial Sounds except that students must discriminate between two sounds. They are given *Alphabet Letter Cards* for both sounds and must hold up the appropriate card when they hear the sound.

Comparing Final Consonant Sounds

This activity is exactly like Listening for Final Sounds except that students must discriminate between two sounds. They are given *Alphabet Letter Cards* for both sounds and must hold up the appropriate card when they hear the sound.

Linking the Consonant Sound to the Letter

In these activities students will link beginning and ending sounds and letters.

✦ **I'm Thinking of Something That Starts (Ends) with ___ Game.** Begin with the target sound, and add clues until students guess the word. If students give a word that does not begin with the target sound, emphasize the beginning sound, and ask if the word begins with the target sound.

✦ **Silly Sentences.** Make silly sentences with students that include many words with the target sound. Encourage students to participate by extending the sentences: Mary mopes. Mary mopes on Monday. Mary and Michael mope on Monday in Miami. For older students, have them make silly sentences using the sound at the beginning of their first

name. Have them use the dictionary to find more words beginning or ending with the target sound.

Introducing Short-Vowel Sounds

✦ Tell students that the vowels are printed in red to remind them that they are special letters. (They are not special because they are printed in red.) They are special because they have more than one sound, and every word in English must have a vowel sound.

✦ Point to the long *Aa* **Alphabet Sound Wall Card,** and remind students that this letter is called a vowel. Tell them vowels sometimes say their names in words (for example, *say, day, tray*). When the vowel says its name, the sound is long. Tell them this vowel sound is called long *a.*

✦ Have students repeat the sound.

✦ Tell students sometimes vowels say different sounds. Point to the picture of the lamb on the short *Aa* card, and tell students that *a* also makes the sound heard in the middle of *lamb.* This is the short *a.* Read the short vowel story to help students remember the short *a.*

✦ Have all students join in saying /a/ /a/ /a/.

Listening for Short-Vowel Sounds Versus Long-Vowel Sounds

✦ Tell students that you will read words with long *a* and short *a.* Review the two sounds.

✦ Give students a signal to indicate when they hear the vowel sound. You may want one signal for short *a,* such as scrunching down, and another for long *a,* such as stretching up tall.

✦ Continue with lists of words such as *add, back, aid, tan, bake,* and *tame.*

Linking the Vowel Sound to the Letter

✦ **Writing Letters.** Have students practice writing the letter and review the sound of the letter.

✦ In this activity to help students link sounds and letters, students will make words either by adding initial consonants to selected word parts or by adding a different final consonant to a consonant-vowel-consonant

combination. Change the beginning of the word or the word ending, but retain the vowel sound to make new words:

at	hat	mat	pat
ap	map	tap	sap
am	Sam	Pam	ham

Comparing Short-Vowel Sounds

This activity requires students to discriminate between short-vowel sounds in the middle of words. Review the short-vowel sounds.

✦ Say a word, and have students repeat it. Establish a signal to indicate whether they hear short *a* or short *o* in the middle of the word. For example, they can hold up the appropriate **Alphabet Letter Card** when they hear a sound. Sample words: *cap, cot, rat, rot, rack,* and *rock.*

Linking the Sound to the Letter

✦ In this activity, write a word on the board, and help students say it.

✦ Change the word by changing the vowel. Help students say the new word, for example, *map, mop; hot, hat; pot, pat.*

✦ For a variation of this activity, write the pairs of words, and simply have students say which word is the target word. For example, students see *tap* and *top.* Ask which word *top* is, directing students' attention to the vowel.

Introducing Long-Vowel Sounds

The introduction of short vowels and consonants helps students internalize the alphabetic principle—a sound can be mapped onto a letter. In English, however, some sounds are represented by more than one letter, for example, the /ē/ can be represented by the letter *e* as in *me* but also represented by e_e as in *Pete.* Toward the end of kindergarten, students will be introduced to long vowels and two common representations of those sounds. These include the single vowel such as *a* or *e* and the vowel consonant silent *e* (VCe). The introduction of the VCe pattern or unit gives students a wide range of common words to read by the end of kindergarten and sets a solid foundation for first grade.

✦ If necessary, remind students that vowels are written in red. Point to the long *Aa* card, and tell students that the sound of long *a* is /ā/.

✦ Have students say the sound with you.

✦ Tell students that long *a* can be written in more than one way; it can be written as *a* just like short *a* but it can also be written as *a_e*. When we see the blank, it is a clue that another sound and letter needs to be put on the blank or line to make a word.

✦ Write *a_e*, and have students give the sound: /ā/. Then write a *t* on the blank, say the sound, and blend the word: *ate*.

✦ The goal is to have students see the *a_e* or any of the other VCe patterns as a unit.

✦ While students have been blending and reading short-vowel words, long vowels create a shift in thinking: Combinations of letters can be used to represent a sound. Here are some easy tips when you are first working with the VCe patterns:

• The VCe patterns are not written on the **Alphabet Sound Cards.** You may want to write the *a_e, e_e, i_e, o_e,* and *u_e* units on the respective long-vowel cards as a reminder for students. Do this as you introduce each long vowel unit. Use an erasable marker so you can reintroduce these special patterns each year.

• Provide maximum support when first using the long-vowel units in blending.

• Write the letter for the first sound, for example, /m/, and have students give the sound.

• Write the unit for /ā/: *a_e*. Tell students this says /ā/. Be sure to write the whole unit.

• Write the final letter ON the blank, for example, *k*. Give the sound for the *k*, and then blend the word.

• Let students hear your voice during the blending, but gradually reduce it so they are doing more of the thinking.

• Help students blend long vowel words as they are reading their **Decodables.**

Tips

✦ Model and support the activities as necessary until students begin to catch on and can participate with confidence.

✦ To keep students focused on the various activities, have them tell you the task for each activity. For example, after telling students to listen for final sounds, ask students what they will be listening for.

✦ Actively involve students by giving them opportunities to tell what they know rather than supplying the information for them. *What is the letter name? What is the sound? What words begin with the sound?*

✦ Keeping students focused on the idea that they are learning about sounds and letters so they can read books themselves makes the lessons more relevant for students.

Introducing Sounds and Letters

Purpose

In **SRA Imagine It!** students learn to relate sounds to letters in kindergarten through the use of thirty-one **Alphabet Sound Wall Cards.** In the upper grade levels, **Sound/Spelling Wall Cards** (Levels 1–3) are used to relate sounds and spellings. The purpose of the **Alphabet Sound Wall Cards** is to remind students of the sounds of the English language and their letter correspondences. These cards are a resource for students to use to remember sound-letter associations for both reading and writing.

Each card contains the capital and small letter and a picture that shows the sound being produced. For instance, the Sausage card introduces the /s/ sound and shows sausages sizzling in a pan. The sound the sausages make sizzling in the pan is /s/ /s/ /s/. The name of the picture on each card contains the target sound at the beginning of the word for the consonants and in the middle for the vowels. Vowel letters are printed in red, and consonants are printed in black. In addition, the picture associates a sound with an action. This action-sound association is introduced through a short, interactive story found in the **Teacher's Edition,** in which the pictured object or character "makes" the sound of the letter. Long vowels are represented by a tall—or "long"—picture of the letters themselves rather than by a picture for action-sound association. Short vowels have a green background, and long vowels have a yellow background.

Procedures

✦ Display Cards 1–26 with the picture sides to the wall. Initially post the first twenty-six cards in alphabetical order so that only the alphabet letters on the back show. The short-vowel cards may be posted as they are introduced later. As you introduce the sound of each letter, you will turn the card to show the picture and the letter on the other side. Because students will be referring to these cards for reading and writing, post them where all students can easily see them.

✦ Before turning a card, point to the letter. Ask students to tell what they know about the letter. For example, they are likely to know its name if the letter is one with which they have already worked. They might also note that there is an upper- and lowercase for the letter or that the letter is a consonant or a vowel.

✦ Turn the card, and point to the picture. Tell students the name of the picture (card), and explain that it will help them remember the sound the letter makes.

✦ Tell students the name and the sound of the letter.

✦ Read the story that goes with the card. Read it expressively, emphasizing the words with the target sound and the isolated sound when it occurs. Have students join in to produce the sound.

> The purpose of the **Alphabet Sound Wall Cards** is to remind students of the sounds of the English language and their letter correspondences.

✦ Repeat the story a few times, encouraging all students to say the sound along with you.

✦ Repeat the name of the letter and the sound.

✦ Follow the story with the cards for the target sound. (These are listed within the lessons.)

✦ Name each picture, and have students listen for the target sound at the beginning of the word. Ask students to repeat the words and the sound.

✦ Listening for the sound in different positions in words provides additional work with phonemic awareness. Give each student the letter card for the introduced sound and letter. Read the words from Listening for the Sound, and have students raise their letter card if they hear the target sound at the beginning of the word. For many letters, students will also listen for the sound at the end of words as well.

✦ To link the sound and the letter, demonstrate how to form the uppercase and lowercase letters by writing on the board or on an overhead transparency. Have students practice forming the letter and saying the sound as they write.

Alphabet Sound Cards

The pictures and letters on the **Alphabet Sound Wall Cards** also appear on the small sets of individual **Alphabet Sound Cards.** The **Teacher's Edition** specifically suggests that you use the individual **Alphabet Sound Cards** for Workshop and small-group activities for review, reteaching, and practice sessions. Place sets of the cards in the appropriate Workshop area for students to use alone or with partners. Add each small card to the Activity Center after you have taught the lesson in which the corresponding individual **Alphabet Sound Card** is introduced. Here are some suggestions for activities using the individual **Alphabet Sound Cards:**

1. **Saying sounds from pictures.** The leader flashes pictures as the others say the sound each picture represents.

2. **Saying sounds.** The leader flashes the letters on the cards as the others say the sound that the letters represent.

3. **Naming words from pictures.** The leader flashes pictures. The others say the sound and then say a word beginning with that sound.

4. **Writing letters from the pictures.** Working alone, a student looks at a picture and then writes the letter for the sound that picture represents.

5. **Making words using the pictures.** A student uses the pictures (Sausages, Pig, Timer for *sit*) or the letters to make words.

Tips

✦ Throughout the beginning lessons, help students remember that vowels are special by reminding them that vowels sometimes say their names in words. For example, tell them the picture of the *a* on the long *a* **Alphabet Sound Wall Card** is long because the long *a* says its name. The short *a* **Alphabet Sound Wall Card** pictures the lamb because the lamb makes the short *a* sound, and you can hear the sound in the word *lamb*.

✦ From the very beginning, encourage students to use the **Alphabet Sound Wall Cards** as a resource to help them with their work.

✦ Mastery of letter recognition is the goal students should reach so that they will be prepared to link each letter with its associated sound. If students have not yet mastered the names of the letters, it is important to work with them individually in Workshop, or at other times during the day.

✦ Both the *Cc* and the *Kk* cards have the same picture—a camera. A camera makes the /k/ sound when it clicks, and the word *camera* begins with the /k/ sound. However, the word *camera* is not spelled with a *k*. Remember, the first sound of the word helps students remember the sound of the letter.

✦ The picture on the *Qq* card depicts quacking ducks. Make sure that students consistently call them quacking ducks, not ducks, and that they focus on the /kw/ sound.

Explicit, Systematic Phonics

The purpose of phonics instruction is to teach students the association between the sounds of the language and the written symbols—spellings—that have been chosen to represent those sounds.

As with all alphabetic languages, English has a limited number of symbols—twenty-six—that are combined and recombined to make the written language. These written symbols are a visual representation of the speech sounds we use to communicate. This is simply a code. The faster students learn the code and how it works, the faster the whole world of reading opens up to them.

Beginning at the kindergarten level, students are introduced to sounds and letters. Students learn that sounds can be mapped onto letters and that those sounds and letters can be blended to read words.

In Grade 1, students make the shift from mapping sounds onto letters to mapping sounds onto spellings. The introduction of both sounds and letters in kindergarten and the sounds and spellings in Grade 1 is done in a very systematic, sequential manner. This allows students to continually build on what they learned the day before. As each sound/symbol relationship is introduced, students learn about and practice with words containing the target sound and letter in kindergarten and sound/spelling in Grade1. This new knowledge is then reinforced through the use of engaging text specifically written for this purpose.

It can be very difficult for students to hear the individual sounds, or phonemes, that make up words. When phonics instruction is explicit—students are told the sounds associated with the different written symbols—there is no guesswork involved. They know that the sound /b/ is spelled *b*. Therefore, students in an **SRA Imagine It!** classroom spend time learning to discriminate individual speech sounds, and then they learn the spellings of those sounds. This systematic, explicit approach affords students the very best chance for early and continuing success.

Sound/Spelling Wall Cards

(Grade 1 on) See The Alphabetic Principle for information on the introduction of sounds and letters in pre-kindergarten and kindergarten.

Purpose

The purpose of the **Sound/Spelling Wall Cards** (Levels 1–3) is to remind students of the sounds in English and their spellings. The name of the picture on each card contains the target sound at the beginning of the name for consonants and in the middle for the short vowels. Long vowels are represented by elongated pictures of the vowel. The variant vowels such as /aw/ and /oi/ contain the vowel sound in the name as well. In addition, the picture associates a sound with an action. This association is introduced through an interactive story in which the pictured object or character "makes" the sound. This "action" cue is particularly helpful for students whose primary language is not English. In some cases, the name of the card and the initial sound may be similar to words in other languages. For example, the word for *lion* in Spanish is *león,* which begins with the same sound as the English word. This is not true for other languages. In Russian the word for *lion* is *лев* and in Japanese it is *raion.* The word for *zipper* in Spanish is *cremallera,* in Russian it is *застежка-молния* and in Japanese it is *jippa.* But all students can remember the actions and sounds and use them as a resource for both reading and writing.

> *The faster students learn the code and how it works, the faster the whole world of reading opens up to them.*

Procedure

Posting the Cards

In Grade 1, initially post the first twenty-six cards with the picture to the wall so that only the alphabet letters on the backs show. As you introduce each card, you will turn it to show the picture and the spellings on the front of the card. Some Grade 1 teachers who have students who are familiar with the cards from kindergarten choose to place the first twenty-six cards (the alphabet) with the pictures facing the class. Because students are familiar with the cards and how to use them, this provides support for writing. Even these first-grade teachers, however, cover the spellings not introduced in kindergarten. In second- or third-grade classrooms in which students are reviewing what they learned the year before, place all the cards with the pictures and the spellings facing forward so students can use these as a resource from the beginning of the school year. Make sure that the cards are positioned so that you can touch them with your hand or with a pointer when you refer to them and so that all students can see them easily. The cards should be placed where students can readily see and reference them throughout the day.

Special Devices

+ Vowel spellings are printed in red to draw attention to them. It is the vowels and their different spellings that challenge us all. Consonants are printed in black. The blank line in a spelling indicates that a letter will take the place of the blank in a word. For example, the replacement of the blank with *t* in the spelling *a_e* makes the word *ate.* The blank lines may also indicate the position of a spelling in a word or a syllable. The blank in *h_,* for example, means that the sound /h/ spelled *h_* occurs at the beginning of a word or a syllable.

+ The blanks in *_ie_* indicate that the *ie* spelling will not come at the beginning or the end of a word or a syllable as in *babies,* while the blank in *_oy* shows that the *oy* spelling comes at the end of a word or a syllable as in *toy.* Uses of blanks in specific spellings are discussed in the lessons. Please note now, however, that when you write a spelling of a sound on the board or an overhead transparency, you should include the blanks.

✦ The color of the background behind the spellings also has a meaning. Consonants have a white background. The colors behind vowel spellings are pronunciation clues. Short-vowel spellings have a green background, which corresponds to the green box that appears before some consonant spellings. Thus, before *ck, tch,* or *x,* you will see a green box, which indicates that a short vowel always precedes that spelling. Long-vowel spellings have a yellow background; other vowel spellings such as *r*-controlled vowels, diphthongs, and variant vowels have a blue background. The color code reinforces the idea that vowels are special and have different pronunciations.

Introducing the Sound/ Spelling Wall Cards

In first grade, each sound and spelling is introduced by using a see/hear/say/write sequence. In Grades 2 and 3 the same sequence is used in the review of the cards.

1. *See:* Students see the spelling or spellings on the **Sound/Spelling Wall Card** and the board or an overhead transparency.

2. *Hear:* Students hear the sound used in words and in isolation in the story. The sound is, of course, related to the picture (and the action) shown on the **Sound/ Spelling Wall Card.**

3. *Say:* Students say the sound.

4. *Write:* Students write the spelling(s) for the sound.

There are a number of important points to remember about this routine.

✦ Take down the **Sound/Spelling Wall Card,** tell the class the name of the card, the sound, and the spelling.

✦ Read the alliterative story so students hear the sound used in words as well as in isolation, and say the sound.

✦ After you present the sound and spelling, have several students go to the board to write the spelling. Have them say the sound as they write the spelling. After they have written the spelling of the sound, give them an opportunity to proofread their own work. Then give

the other students the opportunity to help with proofreading by noting what is good about the spelling and then suggesting how to make it better.

✦ Difficulty in blending may be the result of not knowing the sounds or not being able to pronounce the sounds. Teach the sounds thoroughly during the introduction of the **Sound/Spelling Wall Card** and during initial sounding and blending. To help ensure success for all students, make certain that every student is able to see the board or screen.

Introducing the Sound /s/ spelled *s*

✦ Point to the back of **Sound/Spelling Wall Card** 19—Sausages, and have students tell you what they know about the card: it is a consonant and there is an upper and lowercase *s* on the card. Turn the card, and tell the class the name of the card: Sausages. Point to the sausages in the picture, and say the word *sausages,* emphasizing the initial consonant sound—*sssssausages.* Note: teachers usually place a sticky note over the other spellings of /s/—the *ce, ci_,* and *cy*—in order to help students focus on the single spelling being introduced in the lesson.

✦ Point to the spelling *s.* Tell students that /s/ is spelled *s.*

✦ Read the alliterative story. In Grades 2 and 3, the stories for the card are printed in the Level Appendix of the **Teacher's Edition.** If your students in Grades 2 and 3 are familiar with the cards, have them tell you the name of the card, the sound, and the spelling and tell the story.

✦ If students had **SRA Imagine It!** before, you can ask them if they learned an action to help them remember the sound. If your students do not already have an action they associate with the sound, make some up with your students. They will have fun, and it will be another way for them to remember the sound/spelling relationships.

✦ Write *s* on the board or on an overhead transparency, and say the sound. Write the spelling again and ask students to say the sound with you as they write the spelling on slates, on paper, or with their index fingers in the air or in the palm of their hands. Repeat this activity several times.

✦ Have several students come to the board and write the upper- and lowercase spelling while the others continue to write them on slates or with their fingers. Be sure to encourage students to say the sound as they make the spelling. For students writing at the board, take time to have them proofread their work.

✦ Have students listen for words beginning with /s/, indicating by some signal, such as thumbs-up or thumbs-down, whether they hear the /s/ sound and saying /s/ when they hear it in a word. Repeat with the sound in various positions in words. Encourage students to tell you and the class words with /s/ at the beginning, as well as at the ends of words.

✦ Check students' learning by pointing to the card. Have students identify the sound, name the spelling, and discuss how the card can help them remember the sound.

Remember that saying the sound, listening to the alliterative story, and listening for the sound (discriminating it from other sounds) in different positions in words are all phonemic awareness activities that have been integrated into phonics.

Individual Sound/Spelling Cards

Use the individual **Sound/Spelling Cards** for review and for small-group reteaching and practice sessions. Students can use them alone or with partners. Here are some suggestions for activities using the individual **Sound/Spelling Cards:**

1. **Saying sounds from pictures.** The leader flashes pictures as the others say the sound each picture represents.

2. **Saying sounds.** The leader flashes the spellings on the cards as the others say the sound that the spellings represent.

3. **Naming spellings from pictures.** The leader flashes pictures. The others name the card, say the sound, and then name as many spellings as they can.

4. **Writing spellings from the pictures.** Working alone, a student looks at a picture and then writes as many spellings for that **Sound/Spelling Card** as he or she can remember.

5. **Saying words from pictures.** The leader presents a series of individual cards, for example, Sausages, Lamb, Timer. The others tell the word by blending the sounds represented—*sat.*

Blending

Purpose

The purpose of blending is to teach students a strategy for figuring out unfamiliar words. Initially students will be blending sound by sound as they learn how to blend. After they understand the process, they will move to whole-word blending and develop the strategy they will use to read unfamiliar words. Ultimately students will sound and blend only those words that they cannot read. Eventually the blending process will become quick and comfortable for them.

Procedure

Learning the sounds and their spellings is only the first step in learning to read and write. The second step is learning to blend the sounds into words.

Blending Techniques

Blending lines are written on the board or an overhead transparency as students watch and participate. The lines and sentences should not be written out before class begins. It is through the sound-by-sound blending of the words and the sentences that students learn the blending process.

Sound-by-Sound Blending

+ Write the spelling of the first sound in the word. Point to the spelling, and say the sound. For example, the word students will be blending is *sat*.

+ Have students say the sound with you as you say the sound again. Write the spelling of the next sound. Point to the spelling, and say the sound. Have students say the sound with you as you say the sound again. After you have written the vowel spelling, blend through the vowel (unless the vowel is the first letter of the word), making the blending motion—a smooth sweeping of the hand beneath the sounds, linking them from left to right, for example, *sa*. As you make the blending motion, make sure that your hand is under the letter that corresponds to the sound you are saying at the moment.

+ Write the spelling of the next sound—*t*. Point to the spelling, and have students, say the sound with you as you touch the spelling. If this is the last sound and spelling in the word, then have students

blend and read the word—*sat*. If this is not the final sound and spelling, continue pointing to the spelling and asking for the sound. For example, in the word *sand,* you would blend through the vowel then ask for the sounds for the spellings *n* and *d* before blending the word. After pronouncing the final sound in the word, make the blending motion from left to right under the word as you blend the sounds. Then have students blend the word. Let them be the first to pronounce the word normally.

+ Ask a student to read the word again naturally, as he or she would say or speak it. Then have a student use it in a sentence. Ask another student to extend the sentence, that is, make it more interesting by giving more information. Help the student by asking an appropriate question about the sentence, using, for example, *How? When? Where?* or *Why?* Continue blending the rest of the words in the blending line. At the end of each line, have students reread the words naturally.

> *Blending is the heart of phonics instruction and the key strategy students must learn to open the world of written language.*

Whole-Word Blending

When students are comfortable with sound-by-sound blending, they are ready for whole-word blending.

+ Write the whole word to be blended on the board or display the overhead transparency.

+ Ask students to blend the sounds as you point to each spelling.

+ Then have students say the whole word.

+ Ask students to use the word in a sentence and then to extend the sentence.

+ After blending each line, have students read the words naturally, as they would say them.

+ When all of the words have been blended, point to words randomly, and ask individuals to read them.

Blending Syllables

In reading the **Student Readers,** students will often encounter multisyllabic words. Some students are intimidated by long words, yet many multisyllabic words are easily read by reading and blending the syllables rather than the individual sounds. Beginning in first grade, students will learn about different syllable generalizations, open and closed syllables, consonant -*le*, and the like. Following a set of rules for syllables is difficult because so many of the rules have exceptions. Students need to remember that each syllable in a word contains one vowel sound. Early in the process, you will need to provide support.

+ Have students identify the vowel sounds and spellings in the word.

+ Have students blend the first syllable sound by sound if necessary or read the first syllable.

+ Handle the remaining syllables the same way.

+ Have students blend the syllables together to read the word.

Blending Sentences

Blending sentences is the logical extension of blending words. Blending sentences helps students develop fluency, which is critical to comprehension. Encourage students to reread sentences with phrasing and natural intonation.

Write the sentence on the board, underlining any high-frequency sight words—words that students cannot decode either because they are irregular or because they contain sounds or spellings that students have not yet learned or reviewed—or display the transparency. High-frequency sight words are taught before blending. Write the word or words on the board or the overhead transparency, and introduce them before writing the sentence. Read the word, and have students repeat the word then spell the word. Use each word in a sentence. Point to the word or words, and have students read them again. These words should not be blended but read as whole words.

Tips

+ The goal of blending in first grade is not to have students blend words sound by sound for the whole year. Sound-by-sound instruction should begin with maximum instructional support—with teachers and students blending together. As students understand the sound-by-sound blending routine, drop the verbal cues (sound, sound, blend, sound, blend), and simply point to the spellings after they are written, and have the class give the sounds.

✦ How do you know when to move from sound-by-sound to whole-word blending? When you are writing the final spelling and students are reading the word, it is time to move on to whole-word blending. This often occurs around Unit 3 in first grade.

✦ Keep in mind, however, that when you introduce more complex long-vowel and variant vowel spellings, you can always drop back to sound-by-sound blending for the first couple of blending lines in the lesson.

✦ Even though the entire class may be doing whole-word blending, sound-by-sound blending is an excellent preteaching tool for students needing extra help. After all the sounds and spellings have been introduced, students may be ready to move just to reading the words in the blending line. Have them read the words, stopping to blend only words they cannot read fluently and automatically.

✦ In Grades 2 and 3, teachers often begin the phonics review in the Getting Started lessons with sound-by-sound blending and then quickly move into whole-word blending. Again, the goal is to have students reading the words as quickly and automatically as possible. If the majority of the class can do this, then use whole-word blending. Use sound-by-sound blending to preteach the blending lines with students who need more support.

Building for Success

A primary cause of students' blending failure is their failure to understand how to use the **Sound/Spelling Cards.** Students need to practice sounds and spellings when the **Sound/Spelling Cards** are introduced and during initial blending. They also need to understand that if they are not sure of how to pronounce a spelling, they can check the cards. You may need to lead the group almost constantly. Soon, however, leaders in the group will take over. Watch to see whether any students are having trouble

during the blending. Include them in small-group instruction sessions. At that time you may want to use the vowel-first procedure to reteach blending lines.

Extra Help

In working with small groups during Workshop, you may want to use some of the following suggestions to support students who need help with blending.

Vowel-First Blending

Vowel-first blending is an alternative to sound-by-sound and whole-word blending for students who need special help. Used in small-group sessions, this technique helps students who have difficulty with the other two types of blending focus on the most important part of each word—the vowels—and do only one thing at a time. These students are not expected to say a sound and blend it with another at virtually the same time. The steps to use in vowel-first blending follow:

1. Across the board or on an overhead transparency, write the vowel spelling in each of the words in the line. For a short vowel, the line may look like this:
   a   a   a
   For a long vowel, the line may look like this: *ee   ea   ea*

2. Point to the spelling as students say the sound for the spelling.

3. Begin blending around the vowels. In front of the first vowel spelling, add the spelling for the beginning sound of the word. Make the blending motion, and have students blend through the vowel, adding a blank to indicate that the word is still incomplete. Repeat this procedure for each partial word in the line until the line looks like this:
   ma__   sa__   pa__
   see__   mea__   tea__

4. Have students blend the partial word again as you make the blending motion, and then add the spelling for the ending sound.

5. Make the blending motion, and have students blend the completed word—for example, *mat* or *seed.*

6. Ask a student to repeat the word and to use it in a sentence. Then have another student extend the sentence.

7. Repeat steps 4, 5, and 6 for each word in the line, which might look like this:
   mat   sad   pan
   or
   seed   meat   team

Tips

✦ In the early lessons, blend with as much direction and dialogue as is necessary for success. Reduce your directions to a minimum as soon as possible. You have made good progress when you no longer have to say, "Sound—Sound—Blend," because students automatically sound and blend as you write.

✦ Blending is more than just reading words; it is an opportunity to build vocabulary and to develop oral language.

Always ask students to use less familiar words in sentences and then to extend the sentences. This sentence extension is a technique that can be applied to writing as well. Students will naturally extend sentences by adding phrases to the ends of the sentences. Encourage them to add phrases at the beginning or in the middle of the sentence as well.

✦ Use the vowel-first procedure in small-group preteaching or reteaching sessions with students who are having a lot of trouble with blending. Remember that you must adapt the blending lines in the lessons to the vowel-first method.

✦ The sight words in the sentences cannot be blended. Students must approach them as sight words to be memorized. If students are having problems reading sight words, tell them the words.

✦ Cue marks written over the vowels may help students.

  • Straight line cue for long vowels
   EXAMPLES: āpe, mē, fīne, sō, ūse

  • Curved line cue for short vowels
   EXAMPLES: căt, pĕt, wĭn, hŏt, tŭg

  • Tent cue for variations of *a* and *o*
   EXAMPLES: âll, ôff

  • Dot cue for schwa sound with multisyllabic words
   EXAMPLES: saląd, planėt, pencil, wagón

Dictation and Spelling

Purpose

The purpose of dictation is to teach students to segment words into individual sounds and to spell words by connecting sounds to spellings. In addition, learning dictation gives students a new strategy for reflecting on the sounds they hear in words to help them with their own writing.

As students learn about sounds and spellings, they begin to learn the standard spellings that will enable others to read their writing. As students learn to encode, they develop their visual memory for spelling patterns and words (spelling ability) and hence increase their writing fluency. Reinforcing the association between sounds and spellings and words through dictation gives students a spelling strategy that provides support and reassurance for writing independently. Reflecting on the sounds they hear in words will help students develop writing fluency as they apply the strategy to writing unfamiliar words.

A dictation activity is a learning experience; it is not a test. Students should be encouraged to ask for as much help as they need. The proofreading technique is an integral part of dictation. Students' errors lead to self-correction and, if need be, to reteaching. The dictation activities must not become a frustrating ordeal. Students should receive reinforcement and feedback.

There are two kinds of dictation: Sounds-in-Sequence Dictation and Whole-Word Dictation. The two types differ mainly in the amount of help they give students in spelling the words. The instructions vary for each type.

Procedure

Sounds-in-Sequence Dictation

Sounds-in-Sequence Dictation gives students the opportunity to spell words sound by sound, left to right, checking the spelling of each sound as they write. (Many students write words as they think they hear and say the words, not as the words are actually pronounced or written.)

✦ Pronounce the first word to be spelled. Use the word in a sentence, and say the word again (word/sentence/word). Have students say the word.

✦ Tell students to think about the sounds they hear in the word. Ask, "What's the first sound in the word?"

✦ Have students say the sound.

✦ Point to the *Sound/Spelling Card,* and direct students to check the card. Ask what the spelling is. Students should say the spelling and then write it.

✦ Proceed in this manner until the word is complete.

✦ **Proofread.** You can write the word on the board as a model, or have a student do it. Check the work by referring to the *Sound/Spelling Cards.* If a word is misspelled, have students circle the word and write it correctly, either above the word or next to it.

Whole-Word Dictation

Whole-Word Dictation gives students the opportunity to practice this spelling strategy with less help from the teacher.

✦ Pronounce the word, use the word in a sentence, and then repeat the word (word/sentence/word). Have students repeat the word. Tell students to think about the word and each sound in the word. Remind students to check the *Sound/Spelling Cards* for spellings and to write the word.

✦ **Proofread.** Write or have a volunteer write the word on the board as a model. Check the word by referring to the *Sound/Spelling Cards.*

Sentence Dictation

Writing dictated sentences. Help students apply this spelling strategy to writing sentences. Dictation supports the development of fluent and independent writing. Dictation of a sentence will also help students apply conventions of written language, such as capitalization and punctuation.

✦ Say the complete sentence aloud.

✦ Dictate one word at a time, following the procedure for Sounds-in-Sequence Dictation.

Continue this procedure for the rest of the words in the sentence. Remind students to put a period at the end. Then proofread the sentence sound by sound or word by word. When sentences contain sight words, the sight words should be dictated as whole words, not sound by sound. Students should be encouraged to check the high-frequency sight words posted in the room if they are unsure how to spell them. As students learn to write more independently, the whole sentence can be dictated word by word.

Proofreading

Whenever students write, whether at the board or on paper, they should proofread their work. Proofreading is an important technique because it allows students to learn by self-correction, and it gives them an immediate second opportunity for success. It is the same skill students will use as they proofread their writing. Students should proofread by circling—not by erasing—each error. After they circle an error, they should write the correction beside the circle. This type of correction allows you and students to see the error as well as the correct form. Students also can see what needs to be changed and how they have made their own work better.

You may want to have students use a colored pencil to circle and write in the correction. This will make it easier for them to see the changes.

Procedure for Proofreading

✦ Write—or have a student write—the word or sentence on the board or on an overhead transparency.

✦ Have the other students tell what is good; for example, it is spelled correctly.

✦ Have students check their words and identify whether anything can be made better, the word needs to be spelled differently, or the handwriting needs to be improved.

✦ If there is a mistake, have the student circle it and write it correctly—make it better.

✦ Have the rest of the class proofread their own work.

The Word Building Game (Grades K and 1)

The major reason for developing writing alongside reading is that reading and writing are complementary communicative processes. Decoding requires that students blend the phonemes together into familiar cohesive words. Spelling requires that students segment familiar cohesive words into separate phonemes. Both help students develop an understanding of how the alphabetic principle works.

The Word Building game gives students a chance to exercise their segmentation abilities and to practice using the sounds and spellings they are learning. The game is a fast-paced activity in which students spell related sets of words with the teacher's guidance. (Each successive word in the list differs from the previous one by one sound.)

For the Word Building game, students use their **Alphabet Letter Cards** (Levels K and 1) to build the words. (As an alternative they can use pencil and paper.) You will be writing at the board.

Give students the appropriate **Alphabet Letter Cards.** For example, if the list for the Word Building game is *am, at,* and *mat,* they will need their *a, m,* and *t* **Alphabet Letter Cards.**

✦ Say the first word, such as *am.* (Use it in a sentence if you wish.) Have students repeat the word. Say the word slowly sound by sound. Tell students to look at the **Alphabet Sound Cards** to find the letters that spell the sounds. Touch the first sound's card, in this case the Lamb card, and have students say the sound. Continue the process with the second sound. Write the word on the board while students use their **Alphabet Letter Cards** to spell it. Have students compare their words with your word, make changes as needed, and then blend and read the word with you.

✦ Students will then change the first word to make a different word. Say the next word in the list, (at). Segment the sounds of the word, and have students find the **Alphabet Letter Cards** that correspond. Write the new word *(at)* under the first word *(am)* on the board, and have students change their cards to spell the new word. Have them compare their words to yours and make changes as needed. Blend and read the word with students. Continue in a like manner through the word list.

Word Structure

Purpose

As students move into the upper grades, there is a shift from Phonics to Word Structure. Phonology is the study of the sounds that make up words. In the early grades, students learn to map sounds with spellings to read words. However, as students move into the upper grades and encounter more complex and longer words, the understanding of morphology and the morphological units that make up words is important for fluent reading, vocabulary development, and comprehension.

Morphology is the study of Word Structure. Word Structure activities support the development of fluency as students learn to identify and read meaningful chunks of words rather than individual spellings. Word Structure also supports the development of vocabulary as students learn how inflectional endings change a word's tense, number, and so on and how affixes can be added to a base word to create or derive a new but related meaning.

Morphemes are the smallest units that have semantic meaning. Morphemes may be free or bound. A free morpheme can stand alone, such as the words *dog, man,* or *woman.* A bound morpheme, on the other hand, is a unit of meaning that must be combined with another morpheme to make a meaningful word. For example, in *rewrite* the prefix *re-* means "to do again", and in *dogs* the *-s* changes the meaning to plural. Both r*e-* and *-s* are bound morphemes because they must combine with other words to create new words.

Learning about word structure helps the reader on several levels. Being able to identify key-word parts not only helps with the pronunciation of longer, unfamiliar words but it also helps with meaning. In Word Structure, students learn how to deconstruct words—to identify the root of the word as well as the affixes. When affixes occur at the beginning of a word, they are called prefixes, and when they occur at the end of a word they are called suffixes. The prefix, root word, and suffix are all morphemes.

In the word *restatement,* there are three morphemes: the prefix *re-,* the root *state* and the suffix *-ment.*

prefix	root	suffix
re-	state	-ment

Suffixes, in particular, can impact the root word in different ways. Suffixes such as *-s* and *-ed* can change the tense of a verb; suffixes such as *-s* can change the number of a noun to make it a plural. Derviational morphemes, in contrast, can be added to words to create or derive another word, for example the addition of *-ness* to *sad* creates the new word *sadness,* or the addition of *-ly* changes *sad* to an adverb, *sadly.*

Word structure includes the study of the following:

✦ **Compound words** are made of two words that combine to form a new word. Compounds can be open or closed.

✦ **Root words** focus on learning about the basic element of words. Root words are the foundations upon which the meaning of a word is formed. A root may be a real word as in *audio,* meaning "sound," but it can also used with a suffix to become *audible,* changing the noun to an adjective. Although *audible* can have other elements, it does not need other elements to be complete. Most roots, however, do need other elements. Roots such as *duct, anthrop,* and *cred* require affixes to form the words *deduct, anthropology,* and *incredible,* respectively. Knowledge of root words and affixes provides students with critical tools for understanding derived words.

✦ **Prefixes** include any morpheme that is attached to the beginning of a root or word and changes the meaning of that word. Prefixes do not change the form of the word, only the meaning. Common prefixes include: *con-, com-, ad-, de-, di-, dis-, per-, re-, sub-, hyper-, un-,* and so on as well as numbers *(bi-, tri-, uni-, mono-, octo-,* and so on.)

✦ **Suffixes** include any morpheme that is attached to the end of a word or root and that changes the meaning of that word. Suffixes often change the function of the word and often require a spelling change in the root as well. For example, the addition of *-ial* to *colony* changes a noun to an adjective.

Common Latin Roots

Aud: auditory, auditorium, inaudible, audible, audition

Dict: dictate, predict, contradict, prediction

Ject: reject, inject, project, object, projection, objection

Port: transport, import, export, portable, support, report

Rupt: rupture, erupt, eruption, disrupt, interruption

Scrib/script: scribe, describe, manuscript, inscription, transcript, description, prescription

Spect: spectator, inspect, inspector, respect, spectacle, spectacular

Struct: structure, construct, instruct, destruction, reconstruction

Tract: tractor, traction, attract, subtraction, extract, retract, attractive

Vis: vision, visual, visit, supervisor, invisible, vista, visualize, visionary

Common Greek Roots

Auto: automatic, autograph, autobiography, automobile

Bio: biology, biography

Graph: graphite, geography, graphic, photograph, phonograph

Hydr: hydrogen, hydrant

Meter: speedometer, odometer, thermometer, metronome

Ology: geology, zoology, phonology

Photo: photography, photocopy, photosynthesis, photogenic

Scope: telescope, stethoscope, microscope, microscopic, periscope

Tele: telephone, television, telegraph

Therm: thermos, thermostat

Other examples of suffixes that change the word form include the following:

- Noun suffixes: *-age, -al, -ance, -ant, -ate, -ee, -ence, -ent, -er, -or, -ar, -ese, -ess, -hood, -ice, -isn, -ist, -ment, -ness, -sion, -tain, -tion, -ure*
- Suffixes that form adjectives: *-able, -al, -er, -est, -ette, -let, -ful, -fully, -ible, -ic, -ical, -ish, -ive, -less, -ous, -some, -worthy*
- Suffixes that form adverbs: *-ly, -wards, -ways, -wide, -wise*
- Suffixes that create verb forms: *-ate, -ed, -en, -ing, -ise, -ize, -yze*
- Inflectional endings are a special set of suffixes that change the number (singular to plural), case, or gender when added to nouns and change tense when added to verbs.

Teaching Word Structure

✦ *Have students read the words in a line.
✦ Tell students that words can be made of several individual parts.
✦ Examine the words in each line for meaningful parts, roots, and affixes.
✦ Identify the root or base word, and discuss the meaning.
✦ Underline and discuss the meaning of the prefix or suffix or both. If there is a prefix and a suffix, begin with the prefix. Tell students a prefix is a group of letters that is attached to the beginning of a base or root word. These letters have a specific meaning. For example, *un-* means "not" or "the opposite of," *non-* means "not," and *re-* means "again." A suffix is a group of letters that comes at the end of the base or root word and changes the meaning of the word. For example, *-er* changes a verb to a noun or the person doing the action as in *sing* and *singer,* or *-al* or *-ial* change nouns to adjectives as in *colony* and *colonial.*
✦ Reassemble the word, thinking about the meaning of the word parts.
✦ Say the word.
✦ Use the word in a sentence.

---

*Sometimes students are intimidated by longer words. Understanding syllable breaks helps when reading these longer words. The following chart includes information on syllable "generalizations." These may help your students when reading longer words during Word Structure activities and in the reading.

Word	Break into Syllables	Syllable Generalizations
Puppet	Pup-pet	Closed. If a word has two consonants in the middle, divide the word between the two consonants. The first syllable is closed, and the vowel pronunciation is short.
Music	Mu-sic	Open. If a word has a VCV pattern, break the syllables before the consonant, which makes the first syllable an open syllable and the first vowel long.
Closet	Clos-et	Some VCV patterns have the break after the consonant, which makes the first syllable a closed syllable and the vowel pronunciation short.
Hundred	Hun-dred	When there is a VCCCV pattern, the break is usually between the consonants. The first syllable is closed, and the vowel pronunciation is short.
Coward	Cow-ard	When there are two diphthongs, the syllable break comes between them.
Chaos	Cha-os	When there is a VV pattern, the syllable break comes between the vowels, and the first vowel is usually long.
Handle	Han-dle	Consonant plus *-le*. If a word has an *-le* (or *-el*) at the end, it usually forms a separate syllable and is pronounced with the consonant and /ə/ /l/.
Excitement Reform	Ex-cite-ment Re-form	Prefixes and suffixes are separate syllables.
Entertain Hurdle	En-ter-tain Hur-dle	*R*-controlled vowels. In most syllables where the vowel is followed by an *r*, the vowel sound is *r*-controlled.
Complete	Com-plete	Final *e*. When there is a vowel, consonant, and then an *e* at the end, the vowel before the consonant is pronounced long, and the *e* is silent.

Developing Vocabulary

For students to develop a deeper understanding of words, they should have multiple experiences with them. There are any number of activities that students can do to help them use words and internalize their meanings. The following activities can be used with the whole class or in small groups during Workshop.

✦ Give a word, and ask the student to find it in the line and to give a definition.
✦ Give a word, and ask the student to add a prefix or a suffix and to tell the meaning of the new word and the new part of speech.

✦ If the word is a multiple-meaning word, have the student point to the word, and then have the student give one meaning and use it in a sentence. Then have a second student give another meaning and use it in a sentence. (Be sure that the words that are used are truly multiple-meaning words and not words that can be used as different parts of speech, for example, a verb and a noun that have the same basic meaning.)
✦ Give two words, and have the student point to them. Ask what is the difference between these two words. For example, *hot* and *cold* are antonyms. The same could be done for synonyms, homonyms,

and homophones. This gets students to use the vocabulary and do the thinking. Point to two words, and have students tell how they are alike and different. For example, *history, historical,* and *historian* all have the same roots. All three words have a common root, but *history* and *historian* are nouns, and *historical* is an adjective.

✦ Give students a word, and have them point to the word. If it is a singular noun, have them change it to a plural or vice versa. If it is a verb, have students change the tense, or if it is an adjective, change it into an adverb if appropriate. In all cases, be sure that students spell the new word.

✦ Give students a word, have them point to and read the word, and then give the part of speech.

✦ Give a student a word, and have him or her use the word in a sentence. Have the class decide if the sentence truly shows the meaning of the word. For example, if the word is *camouflage,* and the student says, "Animals use camouflage," have the class add to the sentence to show the meaning: "Animals use camouflage to protect themselves from predators."

✦ Give students a word with a base word, and ask them to point to the word and read it and then to tell the root of the word.

✦ Give students a word with a Greek or Latin root. Have them point to and read the word, and then have them identify the root. Challenge students to think of other words that have the same root.

✦ Give students a word with a prefix or suffix. Have a student point to and read the word and then identify the prefix or suffix and tell the meaning of the affix. Then, if appropriate, have the student or a different student replace the affix with a different one and tell the meaning of the new word.

✦ When appropriate, give students a word, and have them give a synonym or antonym. When appropriate, work on gradations of words. For example, if the word is *hot* then the opposite is *cold.* Gradations would be *hot, warm, tepid, cool, cold.* These kinds of activities expand vocabulary.

✦ Give two words that are connected in some way, for example, *colony* and *colonial.* Have students come to the board, point to the words, and read them. Then have them tell why or how the words are connected.

✦ Have students find other words that follow comparable patterns to those taught in the lesson. If *colony, colonial, colonist* is a line in Word Structure, many students could find related nouns and use them with affixes, *(history, historical, historian).* Challenge students to think more about words.

Tips

✦ Be sure students understand the limits of structural analysis. The *un-* in *unhappy* is a prefix, but the *un* in *under* and *uncle* is not.

✦ Help students realize that many words are related and that using their knowledge of a word can help them understand related words.

✦ Encourage students to use their knowledge of word structure during all reading to clarify unfamiliar words.

Fluency

Fluency is the ability to read or access words effortlessly with seemingly little attention to decoding. Fluent readers decode words not only automatically but accurately. In addition, fluent readers group words into meaningful units, utilize punctuation to guide their voices, and use expression appropriately to help them comprehend what they are reading. Fluent readers also adjust their reading rate as necessary.

To become proficient readers who fully understand what they read, the whole process of decoding must become automatic. Readers need to be so familiar with the sound/spellings, with common meaningful units like prefixes and suffixes and with the most common nondecodable sight words that they automatically process the spellings and word chunks. This enables them to read the word effortlessly and expend most of their energy on comprehending the meaning of the text. Automaticity is a key component of fluency.

The concept of fluency is introduced in the early grades, even before students are reading. When reading aloud, teachers are modeling fluency and using expression and intonation to support meaning. In pre-kindergarten and kindergarten, emergent readers learn about concepts of print that support fluency: learning about spaces and ending punctuation, reading from left to right, and automatically recognizing high-frequency sight words. Students apply this knowledge to reading *Pre-Decodables.* These skills are then applied to reading *Decodables.* While fluency begins in first grade, many students will continue to need practice in building fluency in second and third grades. Initially students can use the *SRA Imagine It! Decodable Stories* in Grades 2 and 3, but fluency practice should include using materials from a variety of different sources, including selections from the *Student Readers, Leveled Readers,* and the *Leveled Science* and *Social Studies Readers.* At all grade levels using *Pre-Decodables, Decodables, Readers,* or any other materials, students need to appreciate that fluency is about meaning. Take time to ask questions after students have read, talk about new and interesting words, and discuss any problems students encountered.

Building Fluency: Reading Pre-Decodables (K–1)

Purpose

Pre-Decodables play an important role in students' early literacy development by providing them with meaningful "reading" experiences before they are actually reading on their own and by expanding their awareness of the forms and uses of print. By following along as you read aloud a *Pre-Decodable,* students learn about the left-to-right and top-to-bottom progression of print on a page, the clues that indicate the beginnings and endings of sentences, the connections between pictures and words, and important book conventions such as front and back covers, authors' and illustrators' names, title pages, and page numbers.

The *Pre-Decodables* provide students with opportunities to apply their growing knowledge of letter names, shapes, and sounds and to become familiar with individual words. In addition, students practice reading high-frequency sight words. The automatic recognition of these words, the identification of ending punctuation, and reading with expression support the development of foundational fluency skills.

Through retelling the story in a *Pre-Decodable,* predicting or wondering about what will happen, and asking and responding to questions about the book, students not only learn about the relationship between spoken and written language, they learn to think about what they have read.

About the Pre-Decodables

Each *Pre-Decodable* contains a story that engages students' interest as it provides them with opportunities to practice what they are learning in their lessons. These "pre-decodable" stories each contain several high-frequency words that most students already have in their spoken vocabularies and that are a basic part of all meaningful stories. Learning to identify high-frequency words quickly, accurately, and effortlessly is a critical part of students' development as fluent, independent readers. The inside back cover of each *Pre-Decodable* contains a list of high-frequency words.

How to Use the Pre-Decodables

✦ Before reading a *Pre-Decodable,* take time to familiarize students with any new high-frequency words in the book and to review previously introduced words. To reinforce the idea that it is important to know these words because they are used so often in print, always point out the words in context. For example, focus students' attention on the words in *Big Book* selections or on signs and posters around the classroom.

✦ Give each student a copy of the book. Tell students that you will read the book together. Hold up your book. Read the title. If the title has a rebus picture, point to it, and tell students what it is. Then point to the word beneath it, and explain that the picture represents that word. Point to and read the names of the author and illustrator, reminding students that an author writes a book, and an illustrator draws the pictures. Page through the book, pointing to and naming the rebus pictures. Have students say the name of each rebus. To avoid confusion, always tell them the exact word that a rebus represents. Do not encourage them to guess at its meaning.

✦ Allow students time to browse through the book on their own, commenting on what they see in the illustrations and making predictions about what they think the book will be about. Encourage them to comment on anything special they notice about the story, the illustrations, or the words in the book.

✦ Help students find page 3. Read the book aloud without stopping. As you read, move your hand beneath the words to show the progression of print. Pause at each rebus as you say the word it represents, pointing first to the rebus then to the word beneath it.

✦ Reread the book. This time, ask students to point to and read the high-frequency words.

✦ Tell students to follow along in their books as you read the story again. Read the title aloud, and then have students read it with you. Reread page 3. Point to each rebus picture, and ask a volunteer to "read" it. Point to the word beneath the picture, and remind students that the picture shows what the word is. Continue through each page of the book, calling on volunteers to "read" and stopping as necessary to clarify and help students with words.

✦ After reading, answer any questions students might have about the book. Encourage them to discuss the illustrations and to explain what is happening in each one.

Building Fluency: Reading Decodables (K–3)

Purpose

The most urgent task of early reading instruction is to make written thoughts intelligible to students. This requires a balanced approach that includes systematic instruction in phonics as well as experiences with authentic literature. Thus, from the very beginning, **SRA Imagine It!** includes the reading of literature. At the beginning of first grade, when students are learning phonics and blending as a tool to access words, the teacher reads aloud. During this time students are working on using comprehension strategies and skills and discussing stories. As students learn to code and blend words, recognize critical sight words, and develop some level of fluency, they take more responsibility for the actual reading of the text.

This program has a systematic instruction in phonics that allows students to begin reading independently. This instruction is supported by **SRA Imagine It! Decodables.**

About the Decodables

The **SRA Imagine It! Decodables** are designed to help students apply, review, and reinforce their expanding knowledge of sound/spelling correspondences. Each story supports instruction in new phonic elements and incorporates elements and words that have been learned earlier. There are eight-page and sixteen-page **Decodables.** Grade K has eight-page **Decodables.** In Grade 1, the eight-page books focus on the new element introduced in the lesson, while the sixteen-page books review and reinforce the elements that have been taught since the last sixteen-page book. They review sounds

from several lessons and provide additional reading practice. Grades 2–3 have eight-page **Decodable Stories** in Getting Started, and eight- and sixteen-page stories in Units 1–3 in Grade 3 and Units 1–6 in Grade 2. The primary purpose is to provide practice reading the words. It is important that students also attach meaning to what they are reading. Questions are often included in the **Teacher's Edition** to check both understanding and attention to words.

How to use Decodables

Preparing to Read

✦ Introduce and write on the board or cards any nondecodable high-frequency or story words introduced or reviewed in the story. Tell students how to pronounce any newly introduced high-frequency words. Then point to each new word, and have students spell and say it. Have them read any previously introduced sight words in the Word Bank list. All the **SRA Imagine It! Decodables** contain high-frequency words that may not be decodable. For example, the word *said* is a common high-frequency word that is not decodable. Including words such as *said* makes the language of the story flow smoothly and naturally. Students need to be able to recognize and read these words quickly and smoothly.

✦ Read the title. At the beginning of the year, you may need to read the title of the book to students, but as the year goes on, you should have a student read it whenever possible. In Grade 1, selected sixteen-page **SRA Imagine It! Decodables** contain two related chapters, each using the same sounds and spellings. In such cases, read the title of the **Decodable,** and then point out the two individual chapter titles. Have volunteers read the title of the chapter you are about to read.

✦ Browse the story. Have students look through the story, commenting on whatever they notice in the text or illustrations and telling what they think the story will tell them.

Reading the Story

After this browsing, students will read the story a page at a time. Again, these stories are designed to support the learning of sounds and spellings. The focus should not

be on comprehension. Students should understand what they are reading, and they should feel free to discuss anything in the story that interests them. Any areas of confusion are discussed and clarified as they arise, as described below.

✦ Have students read a page to themselves. Then call on one student or groups of students to read the page aloud, or have the entire group read it aloud.

✦ If a student has difficulty with a word that can be blended, help her or him blend the word. Remind the student to check the **Sound/Spelling Cards** for help. If a word cannot be blended using the sound/spellings learned so far, pronounce the word for the student.

✦ If a student has trouble with a word or sentence, have the reader call on a classmate for help and then continue reading after the word or sentence has been clarified. After something on a page has been clarified or discussed, have a different student reread that page before moving on to the next page.

✦ Repeat this procedure for each page.

✦ Reread the story twice more, calling on various students to read or reading it in unison. These readings should go more quickly, with fewer stops for clarification.

Responding to the Story

After the story has been read aloud a couple of times, have students respond as follows:

✦ Ask students which difficult words they found in the story and how they figured them out. They may mention high-frequency words they did not recognize, words they had to blend, and words whose meanings they did not know.

✦ Have students tell about the story, retelling it in their own words, describing what they liked about it, or citing what they found interesting or surprising. Specific suggestions to use are listed in the **Teacher's Edition.**

✦ Questions are often provided in the **Teacher's Edition.** They are designed to focus students' attention on the words and not just the pictures. Ask students the questions, and have all students point to the answer in the story rather than having one student respond orally. Having students point to the answers is important. First, it ensures that all students are engaged in finding the answer, not just one. Second, by pointing to the answer, you know that students know the answer from reading and not just from having heard it read. Third, locating information in a text is an important skill. Finally, by pointing to the answer, you can quickly monitor who is understanding the story and who may still need more support during Workshop.

✦ Have students reread the story with partners. Circulate among the pairs, listening to individual students read. This allows you to monitor students' reading and to identify any students who may need additional help during Workshop.

Building Fluency beyond Decodables (middle of grade 1 on)

For some students, fluency develops naturally, seemingly without instruction. Other students, however, can benefit from more explicit instruction. There are students who can decode and read words but lack the critical phrasing, intonation, and expression that support meaning. Teach the text characteristics that support fluency, model them for students, and then provide students regular opportunities to practice fluency. Instruction can focus on any or all of the following areas:

✦ Discuss and model ending punctuation and what this means in terms of expression and intonation. This should be modeled and then discussed with students. Begin with ending punctuation, and then move to internal punctuation such as commas and semicolons. During modeling,

- pause longer at a period or other ending punctuation.
- raise your voice at a question mark.
- use expression when you come to an exclamation point.
- pause at commas or other internal punctuation such as semicolons.
- when you come to quotation marks, think of the character and how he or she might say his or her words.
- pause at an ellipsis.
- pause at dashes.

✦ Discuss and model words written in a

special way—typographical signals such as underlined words, boldfaced words, or those in all caps—need to be read with expression and changed in intonation for emphasis.

✦ Talk about reading rate. Oral reading should be done at a normal speaking rate. Students should not be reading so fast that someone listening could not hear the individual words and make sense of what is being read.

✦ Discuss and model intonation. Let students hear how voices change with different ending punctuation, how voices change when reading dialogue, and how intonation changes with cues from the author. In dialogue, think of the difference between "screamed Jennifer" versus "pleaded Jessie."

✦ Work on phrase cue boundaries. A good way to teach this is by using an overhead of what students are reading. Mark natural phrase boundaries—for example, clauses, prepositional phrases, subject phrases, verb phrases, and so on, with slashes. For example, *In the summertime,/Josh likes to play baseball/ at the park/down the street from his house.* Have students listen to you read the text, noticing how you paused at the markers. Then have students read the sentences naturally, using the markers as guides. Scaffold the instruction. In the beginning, mark the boundaries, and have students practice reading using the already marked passages. As students become comfortable, have them mark what they are reading with boundary markers. Gradually fade out the markers or slashes.

Fluency develops over time, and students should be given repeated opportunities to practice fluency with a variety of different texts. After students have read a text, take time to go back and discuss any new vocabulary or interesting words that students encountered while reading. Fluency is not an isolated activity; it is about supporting comprehension.

There are a number of techniques for practicing fluency: repeated readings, partner reading, tape-assisted reading, and Reader's Theater. All of these techniques can be done with a variety of different reading materials, including selections from the **Student Readers,** the **Leveled Readers,** and the **Science** and **Social Studies Leveled Readers.**

✦ Repeated readings increase reading rate, accuracy, and comprehension by providing students with multiple exposures to words and spelling patterns. In addition, it helps students improve their ability to break sentences into meaningful phrases and to use intonation. It is effective with both older and younger students. Repeated readings involve the students reading segments of text between 50 to 200 words, depending upon students' ability. Students should practice repeated readings with a variety of different text types. While repeated readings can be done with materials from **SRA Imagine It!** using segments from science and social studies texts helps students in the upper grades apply their reading knowledge across the curriculum. The goal is to have students read the text fluently and automatically at a per-minute rate commensurate with grade-level norms.

✦ CD-assisted readings help build confidence and are excellent support for second-language learners. Tape-assisted reading allows students to hear good models of reading and to develop their awareness of phrasing and prosody, or expressive reading. Tapes should provide students with experiences from a variety of text types. Tape selections should be read at approximately 80–100 words per minute by fluent readers with natural intonation, phrasing, and expression. Students read along with the text, aloud or subvocalizing. When the student is comfortable with the text, the student should practice reading the text independently and then read a portion of it to the teacher. The CDs in **SRA Imagine It!** can help students develop fluency with selections in the **Student Readers.**

✦ Reader's Theater legitimizes practicing fluency because it involves reading a script. While students do not memorize the script the way actors do in a play, they must be able to read the script fluently so the audience—the rest of the class—can enjoy the play. Several students can work together on a single play or playlet. They will need to practice reading the script several times before presenting it to the class. Reader's Theater also provides students with a writing opportunity. They can use a selection from their **Student Readers,** write a playlet, and then practice it for Reader's Theater.

✦ Radio Reading, like Reader's Theater, connects reading aloud to real-life situations. Students, with copies of the text, read aloud in front of the class as if they were news broadcasters. Expository text works particularly well for this. Students can practice, and then once a week, several students can be the radio announcers. Students can also write weekly news reports and read them.

✦ Partner Reading involves students reading with a partner. They can take turns reading pages or the entire selection. While one student reads, the listening-partner should note misread words and then discuss them with the partner after the reading. If the pairs are reading for one-minute-fluency checks, the nonreading partner can be responsible for timing the reading. Selections should be read multiple times with the goal being that students achieve a higher fluency rate on successive readings.

Assessing Fluency

Fluency should be assessed periodically to determine students' growth and to monitor progess. Listening to students read regularly is key. Fluency assessment should include not just reading rate but decoding accuracy, prosody (phrasing and intonation), and expression. In addition, checks should be done using various text types.

Generally accepted procedures for assessment include the following:

✦ Use a passage of approximately 250 words at student's reading level. In the first half of first grade, use the appropriate **Decodable** in the Practice set. Have two copies—one for the student and one for you to mark.

✦ Have the student read the passage for one minute. Use a timer, if possible, so you do not have to keep watching a stopwatch or the minute hand on a clock. You can also tape-record the reading. The goal is to have students read the text aloud in a natural way, the

way they would speak the words. This is not a race! Use the following scoring conventions. Mark any errors made by the reader.

✦ Draw a line through any misread word, and count it as an error.

✦ Circle any words the student omits or refuses to read, and count them as errors.

✦ Indicate with a caret any extra words the student inserts.

✦ Draw an arrow between words that student reverses, and count as one error.

✦ Put two check marks above a word that a student repeats, but do not count it as an error.

✦ Draw a box around the last word student reads in the one-minute time frame.

To calculate the student's accuracy rate, count the total number of words read in one minute. Subtract the number of errors from the total number of words read, and use that number to find the number of correct words read per minute.

For example, to calculate the rate:
Total words read – errors = words correct per minute
75 words read – 10 errors = 65 words per minute

For example, to calculate the accuracy:
Number of words ÷ the total number of words = percent of accuracy
145 (words correct) ÷ 156 (total number of words) = 93%

		Fall	Winter	Spring
Grade	Percentile	WCPM[2]	WCPM	WCPM
1	75		46.75	82
	50		23	53
	25		6	15
2	75	79	100	117
	50	51	72	89
	25	25	42	61
3	75	99	120	137
	50	71	92	107
	25	44	62	78
4	75	119	139	152
	50	94	112	123
	25	68	87	98
5	75	139	156	168
	50	110.25	127	139
	25	85	99	109
6	75	153	167	177
	50	127	140	150
	25	98	111	122

Descriptive Statistics for Oral Reading Fluency by Season for Grades 1–6 (Medians)

[2]WCPM = words correct per minute

SOURCE
From "Curriculum-Based Oral Reading Fluency Norms for Students in Grades 1 Through 6" (2005) by Jan E. Hasbrouck and Gerald Tindal. *Behavioral Research and Teaching.*

In addition, watch for and note the following:

✦ Expression

✦ Ability of the reader to read words in natural syntactic clusters

Assessing accuracy, pace or rate, and expression provide information for instruction.

In addition to the qualitative information, some teachers like to use rubrics in their evaluation of fluency.

✦ **Level 1:** Reads basically word by word with limited phrasing, little expression. Reading is labored with difficulty in reading words automatically and fluently.

✦ **Level 2:** Reads in limited phrases of two words, but grouping of words is not natural. There is little or no appropriate expression or intonation.

✦ **Level 3:** Reads in phrases with most having appropriate breaks. Most of the reading has appropriate expression and intonation. There is limited comprehension.

✦ **Level 4:** Reads with appropriate phrasing, intonation, and expression and demonstrates understanding of the piece.

Interpreting Fluency Data

First compare the student's number of correct words per minute with accepted fluency norms.

Then examine the student's accuracy percentage. Reading accuracy should remain constant or gradually increase within and between grades until it stabilizes at 90 percent or higher. Compare the student's accuracy percentage after each assessment to ensure that his or her accuracy percentage is holding constant or improving.

Next examine the types of errors the student made, and consider what they mean for instruction.

✦ Inserting extra words suggest that the student understands what is being read but is reading perhaps impulsively or carelessly.

✦ Refusing to attempt to read words suggests that the student may be uncertain of his or her abilities, unwilling to take risks, or needs additional work with decoding at the sound/spelling or morpheme level. Look at the words the student does not read. Are they one-syllable words or multisyllabic words?

✦ Misreading routine CVC and CVCe words suggest that the student may need more work with the sounds and spellings. In some cases, a student may be able to read words with common sounds and spellings but needs more work with long vowels, diphthongs, and diagraphs.

✦ Looking for patterns in errors is key.

✦ Using or not using intonation, expression, and phrasing but reading quickly and accurately suggests that students need to think about how words combine to make meaning and how our expression can support understanding.

Tips

✦ Use Workshop time for building fluency. Introduce different ways to practice fluency one at a time.

✦ Set up a listening area for Workshop that students can use for tape-assisted instruction.

✦ Make sure *Pre-Decodables, Decodables,* and *Leveled Readers* are available to students.

✦ Have simple timers available for students to check their fluency rate.

✦ Encourage students to chart their fluency growth. If students are doing repeated reading, have them chart the number of words read each day for several days so they can see their fluency improving.

✦ When students have developed some degree of fluency with a *Pre-Decodable, Decodable,* or *Leveled Reader,* send the materials home for additional practice.

✦ Use a range of materials to practice building fluency throughout the day. Remember, fluency practice can be as short as one minute several times a day.

Reading Aloud

Purpose

Adults read aloud a variety of materials to students. In this program there are *Big Books,* picture books, novels, and excerpts for reading aloud. Research has shown that students who are read to are more likely to develop the skills they need to read successfully on their own.

In kindergarten and Grade 1, there are *Big Books.* In every grade level of *SRA Imagine It!* there are opportunities for teachers to read aloud to students. At the beginning of each unit is a Read Aloud selection tied to the unit theme. This Read Aloud selection allows students the opportunity to think about the unit theme before reading selections on their own.

Reading aloud at any age serves multiple purposes. Reading aloud

+ provokes students' curiosity about text.
+ conveys an awareness that text has meaning.
+ demonstrates the various reasons for reading text (to find out about the world, to learn useful new information and new skills, or simply for pleasure).
+ exposes students to the "language of literature," which is more complex than the language they ordinarily use and hear.
+ provides an opportunity to teach the problem-solving strategies that good readers employ. As students observe you interacting with the text, expressing your own enthusiasm, and modeling your thinking aloud, they perceive these as valid responses and begin to respond to text in similar ways.

Procedures

The following set of general procedures for reading aloud is designed to help you maximize the effectiveness of any Read Aloud session.

+ **Read-Aloud sessions.** Set aside time each day to read aloud.
+ **Introduce the story.** Tell students that you are going to read a story aloud to them. Tell its title, and briefly comment on the topic. To allow students to anticipate what will happen in the story, be careful not to summarize.
+ **Activate prior knowledge.** Ask whether anyone has already heard the story. If so, ask them to see if this version is the same as the one they have heard. If not, activate prior knowledge by saying, "First, let's talk a little about _____." If the story is being read in two (or more) parts, before reading the second part, ask students to recall the first part.
+ **Before reading.** Invite students to interrupt your reading if there are any words they do not understand or ideas they find puzzling or to ask questions. Throughout the reading, encourage them to do this.
+ **Read the story expressively.** Occasionally react verbally to the story by showing surprise, asking questions, giving an opinion, expressing pleasure, or predicting events. Expressive reading not only supports comprehension but serves as a model for fluency. Think-aloud suggestions are outlined below.
+ **Use Comprehension Strategies.** While reading aloud to students, model the use of comprehension strategies in a natural, authentic way. Remember to try to present a variety of ways to respond to text. These include visualizing, asking questions, predicting, making connections, clarifying, and summarizing.
+ **Retell.** When you have finished reading the story, call on volunteers to retell it.
+ **Discuss.** After reading, discuss with students their own reactions: how the story reminded them of things that have happened to them, what they thought of the story, and what they liked best about the story.
+ **Reread.** You may wish to reread the selection on subsequent occasions, focusing the discussion on the unit theme.

Think-Aloud Responses

The following options for modeling thinking aloud will be useful for reading any story aloud. Choose responses that are most appropriate for the selection you are reading.

+ React emotionally by showing joy, sadness, amusement, or surprise.
+ Ask questions about ideas in the text. This should be done when there are points or ideas that you really do wonder about.
+ Identify with characters by comparing them to yourself.
+ Show empathy with or sympathy for characters.
+ Relate the text to something you already know or something that has happened to you.
+ Show interest in the text ideas.
+ Question the meaning or clarity of the author's words and ideas.

Questions to Help Students Respond

At reasonable stopping points in reading, ask students general questions to get them to express their own ideas and to focus their attention on the text. These types of generic questions will help students discuss their reactions to the reading and demonstrate their comprehension.

+ What do you already know about this?
+ What seems really important here? Why do you think so?
+ Was there anything that you did not understand? What?
+ What did you like best about this?
+ What did you not like about this?
+ What new ideas did you learn from this?
+ What does this make you wonder about?
+ What surprised you in the story?

Vocabulary

Purpose

Strong vocabulary skills are correlated to achievement throughout school. The purpose of vocabulary instruction is to introduce students to new words (and ideas) and to teach students a range of strategies for learning, remembering, and incorporating unknown vocabulary words into their existing reading, writing, speaking, and listening vocabularies.

Words chosen for inclusion in **SRA Imagine It!** are based upon the vocabulary research of Andrew Biemiller, who has developed a comprehensive database of words students with large vocabularies know by the end of sixth grade. Biemiller's work identifies words that all students need to know and provides evidence that students from various backgrounds acquire these word meanings in roughly the same order. It appears that for students with small vocabularies, improving vocabulary mainly means moving them through the sequence faster. Because vocabulary knowledge is so critical to comprehension, vocabulary instruction is integrated throughout **SRA Imagine It!**

Vocabulary is taught throughout every part of the lesson.

Part 1: Preparing to Read

✦ In Grades 2–6, Word Structure develops vocabulary and the understanding that words can be deconstructed and related through known elements to determine meaning. In addition, students are learning about Greek and Latin roots, antonyms, synonyms, and multiple-meaning words. The emphasis on root words and affixes, in particular, serves to expand students' knowledge of words and their vocabulary.

✦ In Grades K–1, students are using words they blend in sentences to develop vocabulary and oral language. Learning about inflectional endings also helps children see the relationship between root words and various forms of the root. Reviews of blending lines focus on using words based on teacher clues as well as finding synonyms and antonyms.

Part 2: Reading and Responding

✦ The selection vocabulary instruction in this part of the lesson focuses on teaching specific vocabulary necessary for understanding the literature selection more completely.

✦ In kindergarten and the first half of Grade 1, the teacher introduces the selection vocabulary orally before reading the selection. Suggestions are made throughout the reading to discuss new and interesting words as the class reads the **Big Books.** Work from Biemiller suggests that clarifying words in the context of reading is an effective technique for expanding student vocabulary. Suggestions for which words to stop and clarify are suggested throughout the lessons. Vocabulary review activities are found throughout the lesson.

✦ From the middle of Grade 1 on, critical word meanings needed to understand the story are pre-taught as students read the Vocabulary Warm-Up in the **Student Reader.** This provides an initial exposure to the selection vocabulary. This is followed by guided vocabulary practice in which students discuss the definitions of critical words; learn to apply critical skills such as context, structure and apposition; use the vocabulary words in a variety of activities, and then return to the Vocabulary Warm-Up to reread the sentences containing the vocabulary words and to discuss the words. The clarification of additional vocabulary words is highlighted throughout the reading of each selection. Vocabulary review activities are found throughout the lesson.

✦ Students write the words and their definitions in their Writer's Notebooks.

✦ Vocabulary words, along with any other words students find interesting, are posted on charts to remind students to use these words in discussion of their reading as well as in their writing.

Part 3: Language Arts

During writing, students are encouraged to use their new vocabulary.

General Strategies

There is no question that having students read and reading to students are effective vocabulary instructional strategies. Most word learning occurs through exposure to words in listening and reading. Multiple exposures to words, particularly when students hear, see, say, and write words, is also effective. Wordplay, including meaning and dictionary games, helps develop a word consciousness as well.

Vocabulary Strategies for Unknown Words

Different strategies have been shown to be particularly effective for learning completely new words. These strategies are included in the Vocabulary Warm-Up lessons and **Skills Practice** activities.

Key Word This strategy involves providing or having students create a mnemonic clue for unknown vocabulary. For example, the word *mole* is defined in chemistry as a "gram molecule." By relating *mole* to *molecule*, students have a key to the meaning of the word.

Definitions Copying a definition from a dictionary is somewhat effective in learning new vocabulary. Combining this with using the word in writing and speaking adds to the effectiveness of this strategy. Requiring students to explain a word or to use it in a novel sentence helps ensure that the meaning is understood. It is not uncommon when students use words in sentences that the meaning of the vocabulary word is not clear. For example, a typical sentence a student might give for the word *camouflage* is "The octopus uses camouflage." The word *camouflage* is correctly used, but there is no real indication that the student knows the meaning of the word. Having students extend the sentence to explain why or how in the sentence helps: "The octopus uses camouflage to protect itself from predators." Or "The camouflage an octopus uses when it is in danger is to change its shape and color."

Context Clues Some words can be inferred from context and can be learned with repeated exposure to words in reading and listening. While using context can be useful, it is not the most effective way to learn new words. Also, as students move into content area reading, context becomes a less effective tool for determining the meaning of unfamiliar words.

✦ **Syntax** How a word is used in a sentence may provide some clue as to its meaning. This is particularly effective with homographs. "The lead pipe is a hazard to the community." Here lead is an adjective and is pronounced with a short e. In the sentence "He will lead the troops into battle," *lead* has a very different meaning, is a verb, and is pronounced with a long e.

✦ **Apposition** Sometimes the word is actually defined within the text. In an appositive, the definition of a word is often set off by commas for the reader.

Word Structure Examining the affixes and roots of a word often provides clues to its meaning. Knowing the meaning of at least part of the word can provide a clue as to its meaning. For example, *unenforceable* can be broken down into meaningful word parts. This is a particularly important tool in content area reading.

Developing Vocabulary

Purpose

Vocabulary is closely connected to comprehension. Considerable vocabulary growth occurs incidentally during reading. A clear connection exists between vocabulary development and the amount of reading a person does, and there are strong indications that vocabulary instruction is important and that understanding the meanings of key words helps with comprehension.

In **SRA Imagine It!** vocabulary is addressed before, during, and after reading. Before reading, the teacher presents vocabulary words from the selection. Students use skills such as context clues, apposition, and structural analysis to determine the meanings of the words. These selection vocabulary words are not only important to understanding the text but are also high-utility words that can be used in discussing and writing about the unit theme.

During reading, students monitor their understanding of words and text. When they do not understand something, they stop and clarify what they have read. Students will use these same skills—context clues, apposition, structural elements, and so on—to clarify the meanings of additional words encountered while reading. Determining the meanings of words while reading prepares students for the demands of independent reading both in and out of school.

After reading, students review the vocabulary words that they learned before reading the selection. They also review any interesting words that they identified and discussed during reading. Students record in their Writer's Notebooks both the selection vocabulary words and the interesting words they identified during their reading and are encouraged to use both sets of words in discussion and in writing.

Procedure

Before students read the selection, they read the Vocabulary Warm-Up in the **Student Reader.** As they read, students use context clues, word structure, or apposition to figure out the highlighted selection vocabulary. If students cannot determine the meaning of a word using one of the skills, they can consult the glossary or dictionary. After reading the Vocabulary Warm-Up, the teacher displays an overhead transparency to review the selection vocabulary.

Below are suggestions for modeling the use of context clues, apposition, or word structure to determine the meaning of a word.

Modeling Using Context Clues

Write the following sentences on the board or on a transparency. Explain to students that they will use context clues, or other words in the sentence, to determine the meaning of the underlined word.

1. Mrs. Frisby must undertake a <u>treacherous</u> journey to take her son some medicine.

2. We took a <u>treacherous</u> walk near a swamp filled with crocodiles.

Have students look for clues in the sentences that might help them understand the meaning of the underlined word. Point out that a good clue in the second sentence is "near a swamp filled with crocodiles." This clue should help them understand that *treacherous* probably has something to do with danger. Guide students until they can give a reasonable definition of *treacherous*. To consolidate understanding of the word, ask another student to use the definition in a sentence.

Modeling Using Apposition

Write the following sentences on the board or on a transparency. Explain to students that they will use apposition to determine the meaning of the underlined word. In apposition, the word is followed by the definition, which is set off by commas.

1. The conductor thought he was an <u>abolitionist,</u> a person who wanted to end slavery.

2. John Brown was a famous <u>abolitionist</u>, a person who wanted to end slavery.

It should be clear to students using apposition that the definition of the word *abolitionist* is "a person who wanted to end slavery."

Modeling Using Word Structure

Write the following sentences on the board or on a transparency. Explain to students that they will use word structure, or parts of the word, to determine the meaning of the underlined word.

1. The strong wind blew Ivan's ship away into <u>uncharted</u> seas.

2. The explorers Lewis and Clark went into <u>uncharted</u> territory.

Have students look at the word *uncharted* and break it into parts: the prefix *un-*, *chart*, and the suffix *-ed*. Students should know that the suffix *un-* means "not" and that the suffix *-ed* usually indicates the past tense of a verb. However, you may need to remind students about the meanings of these affixes. Ask students for the meaning of the word *chart*. Students should know that a chart could be a map or a table. Guide them as they put together the definitions of the word parts: *un-* (not), *charted* (mapped or tabled). They should be able to come up with the definition "not mapped" or "unmapped" or even "unknown." Have them substitute their definition in the sentences to see if the definition makes sense. For instance, the first sentence would read, "The strong wind blew Ivan's ship away into unmapped (or unknown) seas." Confirm with students that the new sentence makes sense, and then repeat the same process for the second sentence.

Everything students learn about phonemic awareness, phonics, word structure and decoding has one primary goal—to help them understand what they are reading. Without comprehension, there is no reading.

Take time to review words and their meanings. Help students connect new words to familiar words. Each unit in **SRA Imagine It!** revolves around a theme, and there are key words. In every lesson, there is a concept.

Semantic Mapping Having students create a semantic map of an unknown word after learning its definition helps them learn it. Have students write the new word and then list in a map or web all words they can think of that are related to it.

Semantic Feature Analysis A semantic feature analysis helps students compare and contrast similar types of words within a category to help secure unknown words. Have students chart, for example, the similarities and differences between various types of sports, including new vocabulary such as *lacrosse* and *cricket*.

Reading Comprehension

Purpose

The primary aim of reading is comprehension. Without comprehension, neither intellectual nor emotional responses to reading are possible—other than the response of frustration. Reading is about problem solving. Expert readers bring their critical faculties to bear on everything they read. They generally understand most of what they read, but just as importantly, they recognize when they do not understand, and they have at their command an assortment of strategies for monitoring and furthering their understanding.

The goal of comprehension strategy instruction is to turn responsibility for using strategies over to students as soon as possible. Research has shown that students' comprehension and learning problems are not a matter of mental capacity but rather their inability to use strategies to help them learn. Expert readers use a variety of strategies to help them make sense of the text and to get the most out of what they read. Trained to use a variety of comprehension strategies, students dramatically improve their learning performance. To do this, the teacher models strategy use and gradually incorporates various kinds of prompts and possible student think-alouds as examples of the types of thinking students might do as they read to comprehend what they are reading.

Setting Reading Goals

Even before they begin reading and using comprehension strategies, good readers set reading goals and expectations. Readers who have set their own goals and have definite expectations about the text they are about to read are more engaged in their reading and notice more in what they read. Having determined a purpose for reading, they are better able to evaluate a text and to determine whether it meets their needs. Even when the reading is assigned, the reader's engagement is enhanced when he or she has determined ahead of time what information might be gathered from the selection or how the selection might interest him or her.

Comprehension Strategies

Descriptions of strategies expert readers use to comprehend the text follow.

> *Good readers continually monitor their speed and ability to understand throughout reading.*

Summarizing

Periodically it is important to summarize and check our understanding as we read. Sometimes readers reread to fill in gaps in their understanding. They use the strategy of summarizing to keep track of what they are reading and to focus their minds on important information. The process of putting the information in one's own words not only helps good readers remember what they have read but also prompts them to evaluate how well they understand the information. Sometimes the summary reveals that one's understanding is incomplete, in which case it might be appropriate to reread the previous section to fill in the gaps. The strategy of summarizing is particularly helpful when readers are reading long or complicated text. When to stop and summarize depends on the difficulty of the text as well as the type of text. Often in content area reading, it makes sense to stop and summarize the key ideas after each section. In narratives, the reader often stops to summarize after an episode has been read. Many of us will automatically summarize what has happened if we have put down a book and are about to continue reading it again. Students should think to themselves the following:

- ✦ Does this make sense? What is this selection about?
- ✦ What are the big ideas the writer is trying to get at?

- ✦ What can I delete from my summary? What is not important?
- ✦ Have I said the same thing more than once in my summary?
- ✦ How can I put what I just read into my own words?
- ✦ What is unclear? What is the meaning of the word or sentence? How can I determine this?

Clarifying

Monitoring understanding is key to reading. It allows readers to make sure they understand what they read. They note the characteristics of the text, such as whether it is difficult to read or whether some sections are more challenging or more important than others are. In addition, when readers become aware that they do not understand, they stop and take appropriate action, such as rereading, to understand the text better. As they read, good readers stay alert for problem signs such as loss of concentration, unfamiliar vocabulary, or lack of sufficient background knowledge to comprehend the text. This ability to self-monitor and identify aspects of the text that hinder comprehension is crucial to becoming a proficient reader. Clarifying may occur at the word, the sentence, the paragraph, or at the whole-text level. Students should think to themselves the following:

- ✦ What does not make sense? If it is a word, how can I figure it out? Do I use context, structure, or apposition, or do I need to ask someone or look it up in the dictionary or glossary?
- ✦ What does not make sense? The paragraph is long and full of details. What can I do? I can take some notes, I can reread it more slowly; I can discuss it with someone.
- ✦ These sentences are endless. How can I deal with long, complicated sentences?
- ✦ What is the main idea of what I just read?
- ✦ Can I summarize what I just read?

Asking Questions

Asking questions allows the reader to constantly check his or her understanding and to follow the writer's train of thought. Good readers ask questions that may prepare them for what they will learn. If their questions are not answered in the text, they may try to find answers elsewhere and thus add even more to their store of knowledge. Certain kinds of questions occur naturally to a reader, such as to clear up confusion or to wonder why something in the text is as it is. Intentional readers take this somewhat informal questioning one step further by formulating questions with the specific intent of checking their understanding. They literally test themselves by thinking of questions a teacher might ask and then by determining answers to those questions. Students should think to themselves the following:

✦ Why is this the way it is? What else is there to know about this?

✦ What question can I ask to check if I have understood what I just read?

✦ How does this connect to the unit theme? What new information will I learn?

✦ What questions do I think the author will answer as I read this selection?

✦ Do I understand the author? What is not making sense?

✦ What is interfering with my understanding?

Predicting

Predicting what will happen in the story allows the reader to summarize what has been read so far, to identify clues and events in the text, and to use prior knowledge and personal experience to make inferences about what will happen next. When reading fiction, readers make predictions about what they are reading and then confirm or revise those predictions as they go. Predictions are not wild guesses. They are made based on information provided by the author as well as the reader's background knowledge. Students should think to themselves the following: What do I already know that will help me predict? What are the clues in the text that will help me predict?

✦ Why was my prediction confirmed?

✦ Why was my prediction not confirmed?

✦ What clues did I miss that would have helped me make a better prediction?

> *The responsibility for using strategies by students should begin as soon as they understand that reading is about problem solving and making sense of text and that these strategies will help them do both.*

Making Connections

Making connections between the text and what is known from personal experience or previous reading deepens our understanding of text and expands our understanding. Comprehension is enhanced when we relate what is read to what is known. Students should think to themselves the following:

✦ What does this remind me of? What else have I read like this?

✦ What does this remind me of in my own life? In my own experiences?

✦ How does this connect with other selections I have read?

✦ How does this connect with what is going on in the world today?

Visualizing

Creating a mental image about the text involves not just the literal interpretation of the author's word but going beyond the literal to incorporating prior knowledge and experiences that deepen understanding. Readers form mental images as they read. They picture the setting, the characters, and the action in a story. Visualizing can also be helpful when reading expository text. Visualizing helps readers understand descriptions of complex activities or processes. When a complex process or an event is being described, the reader can follow the process or the event better by visualizing each step or episode. Sometimes an author or an editor helps the reader by providing illustrations, diagrams, or maps. If no visual aids have been provided, it may help the reader to create one. Creating mental images helps the reader create pictures that can be stored efficiently in his

or her long-term memory. Students should think to themselves the following:

✦ What picture does the words create in my mind? How do the words suggest feelings, actions, and settings?

✦ Would a drawing help me understand the process?

✦ How does my mental picture extend beyond the words in the text?

✦ How did this picture help me understand what I am reading?

Adjusting Reading Speed

Some texts are easy to read; others are more challenging. How difficult a text is to read depends on both author and reader variables. Good readers understand that not all text is equal. Because of this, they continuously monitor what they are reading and adjust their reading speed accordingly. Efficient readers skim parts of the text that are not important or relevant to their reading goals, and they purposely slow down when they encounter difficulty in understanding the text. Students should think to themselves the following:

✦ When I reread does this make sense?

✦ This is a long and involved sentence. Rereading may help.

Procedures

Modeling and Thinking Aloud

One of the most effective ways to help students understand and use critical comprehension is to make strategic thinking public. Modeling these behaviors and encouraging students to think aloud as they attempt to address comprehension problems and to understand text can demonstrate for everyone in a class how these behaviors are put into practice. Suggestions for think-alouds are provided throughout the *Teacher's Edition.*

The most effective models you can offer will be those that come from your own reading experiences. What kinds of questions did you ask yourself? What kinds of things surprised you the first time you read a story? What kinds of new information did you learn? What kinds of things were confusing until you reread or read further? Drawing on these questions and on your students' questions and comments as they read will make the strategic reading process more meaningful to students. Below are suggestions for modeling each of the comprehension strategies.

Before Reading

✦ **Modeling Setting Reading Goals.** To model setting reading goals, engage students in the following:

- **Activate prior knowledge.** As you approach a new text, consider aloud what you already know about the subject or what your experiences have been in reading similar material.

- **Browse the text.** To get an idea of what to expect from a text, look at the title and the illustrations. When students are reading fiction, they will browse the text to look for Clues, Problems and Wonderings. Possible clues will support comprehension— for example, genre, content, author, setting, and so on—potential problems might include things such as difficult words or dense paragraphs as well as unfamiliar concepts; and wonderings are the things students are curious to find out about from their reading— questions about the selection. Wonderings are students' purposes for reading. When students read nonfiction, they will use a KWL chart— this is what I know (K), this is what I want to find out (W), and this is what I have learned (L). Both these activities— Clues, Problems, and Wonderings and KWL—engage students in thinking before reading the selection by having them activate their own background knowledge, identify potential problems, and set purposes for reading. Have students glance quickly at the selection, looking briefly at the illustrations and the print. Have them tell what they think they might be learning about as they read the selection. Early in the year, model the thinking involved with these activities and then begin to turn the responsibility for completing them over to students.

During Reading

Modeling— or thinking aloud— about how to use strategies to solve problems is a powerful tool for teaching comprehension. While think-aloud models are included in all lessons, relate your own thinking and experiences to the lesson and the think-alouds. Early in the process you will need to model thinking about how, when, and why to use the strategies. Encourage students to stop and use them as well; engage them in thinking!

✦ **Modeling Summarizing.** Just as the strategy of summarizing the plot and then predicting what will happen next can enhance a student's reading of fiction, so too can the same procedure be used to the student's advantage in reading nonfiction. In expository text, it is particularly logical to stop and summarize at the end of a chapter or section before going on to the next. One way to model the valuable exercise of making predictions and at the same time to expand knowledge is to summarize information learned from a piece of expository writing and then to predict what the next step or category will be. Appropriate times to stop and summarize include the following:

- When a narrative text has covered a long period of time or a number of events
- When many facts have been presented
- When an especially critical scene has occurred
- When a complex process has been described
- Any time there is the potential for confusion about what has happened or what has been presented in the text
- When returning to a selection

✦ **Modeling Clarifying.** A reader may need clarification at any point in the reading. Model this strategy by stopping at points that confuse you or that may confuse your students. Indicate that you are experiencing some confusion and need to stop and make sure you understand what is being read. Difficulty may arise from a challenging or unknown word or phrase. It may also stem from the manner in which the information is presented. Perhaps the author did not supply needed information. As you model this strategy, vary the reasons for stopping to clarify so that students understand that good readers do not simply skip over difficult or confusing material—they stop and determine what they do not understand.

✦ **Modeling Asking Questions.** Learning to ask productive questions is not an easy task. Students' earliest experiences with this strategy take the form of answering teacher-generated questions. However, students should be able to move fairly quickly to asking questions like those a teacher might ask. Questions that can be answered with a simple *yes* or *no* are not typically very useful for helping them remember and understand what they have read. Many students find it helpful to ask questions beginning with *Who? What? When? Where? How?* and *Why?* As students become more accustomed to asking and answering questions, they will naturally become more adept at phrasing their questions. As their question asking becomes more sophisticated, they progress from simple questions that can be answered with explicit information in the text to questions that require making inferences based on the text.

✦ **Modeling Predicting.** Predicting can be appropriate at the beginning of a selection—on the basis of the titles and the illustrations—or at any point while reading a selection. At first, your modeling will take the form of speculation about what might happen next, but tell students from the start what clues in the text or illustrations helped you predict to make it clear that predicting is not just guessing. When a student makes a prediction—especially a far-fetched one—ask on what in the selection or in his or her own experience the prediction is based. If the student can back up the prediction, let the prediction stand; otherwise, suggest that the student make another prediction on the basis of what he or she already knows. Often it is appropriate to summarize before making a prediction. This will help students consider what has come before as they make their predictions about what will happen next. When reading aloud, stop whenever a student's prediction has been confirmed or contradicted. Have students tell whether the prediction was correct. If students seem comfortable with the idea of making predictions but rarely do so on their own, encourage them to discuss how to find clues in the text that will help them.

Modeling Making Connections. To model making connections, share with students any thoughts or memories that come to mind as you read the selection. Perhaps a character in a story reminds you of a childhood friend, allowing you to better identify with interactions between characters. Perhaps information in an article on Native American life in the Old West reminds you of an article that you have read on the importance of the bison to Native Americans. Sharing your connections will help students become aware of the dynamic nature of reading and show them another way of being intentional, active learners.

Modeling Visualizing. Model visualizing by describing the mental images that occur to you as you read. A well-described scene is relatively easy to visualize, and if no one does so voluntarily, you may want to prompt students to express their own visualizations. If the author has not provided a description of a scene, but a picture of the scene would make the story more interesting or comprehensible, you might want to model visualizing as follows: "Let's see. The author says that the street was busy, and we know that this story is set during the colonial period. From what I already know about those times, there were no cars, and the roads were different from the roads of today. The street may have been paved with cobblestones. Horses would have been pulling carriages or wagons. I can almost hear the horses' hoofs going clip-clop over the stones." Remind students that different readers may picture the same scene quite differently, which is fine. Every reader responds to a story in her or his own way.

Modeling Adjusting Reading Speed. Just as readers need to monitor for problems, they need to be aware that various texts can be approached in various ways. For example, if reading a story or novel for enjoyment, the reader will typically read at a relaxed speed that is neither so fast as to miss information nor as slow as they might read a textbook. If on the other hand, the reader is reading a textbook, he or she will probably decrease speed to assure understanding and make sure that all important information is read and understood. When modeling this strategy, be sure you indicate why you,

as the reader, have chosen to slow down or speed up. Good readers continually monitor their speed and ability to understand throughout reading.

If your students have not previously engaged in the sort of strategic thinking aloud that is promoted throughout **SRA Imagine It!,** you will have to do all or most of the modeling at first, but encourage students to participate as soon as possible. Remember, however, the goal is for students to use these strategies independently as they read both in and out of school. In addition to the think-alouds for the teachers, there are also prompts to encourage students to do the thinking. The responsibility for using strategies by students should begin as soon as they understand that reading is about problem solving and making sense of text and that these strategies will help them do both.

Reading Aloud

At the beginning of the year, students should be encouraged to read selections aloud. This practice will help you and them understand some of the challenges posed by the text and how individual students approach these challenges.

Reading aloud helps students build fluency, which in turn will aid their comprehension. Students in Grades K–3 can use **Decodables** to build fluency, while students in Grades 4–6 can use the literature from the **Student Readers. Leveled Readers** are also available for Grades 1–6. Fluent second graders read between 79 and 117 words per minute with accuracy and understanding, depending on the time of the year (fall/spring). Fluent third graders can be expected to read between 99 and 137 words per minute; fourth (119/152); fifth (139/168); sixth (123/177).

Make sure that you set aside time to hear each student read during the first few days of class—the days devoted to Getting Started are perfect for this—so that you can determine students' abilities and needs. Workshop is also a good time to listen to any students who do not get to read aloud while the class is reading the selection together.

As the year progresses, students should continue reading aloud often, especially with particularly challenging text. Model your own use of strategies, not only to help students better understand how to use strategies but also to help them understand that actively using strategies is something that good, mature readers do constantly.

Most students are unaccustomed to thinking aloud. They will typically stand mute as they try to determine an unfamiliar word or to deal with a confusing passage. When this happens, students should be encouraged to identify specifically with what they are having difficulty. A student might identify a particular word, or he or she may note that the individual words are familiar but that the meaning of the passage is unclear.

Active Response

Not only are good readers active in their reading when they encounter problems, but they respond constantly to whatever they read. In this way they make the text their own. As students read they should be encouraged to

✦ make as many connections as they can between what they are reading and what they already know.

✦ visualize passages to help clarify their meanings or simply to picture appealing descriptions.

✦ ask questions about what they are reading. The questions that go through their minds during reading will help them examine, and thus better understand, the text. Doing so may also interest them in pursuing their own investigations. The questions may also provide a direction for students' research or exploration.

✦ summarize and make predictions as a check on how well they understand what they are reading.

Tips

✦ Remember that the goal of all reading is comprehension. If a story or article does not make sense, the reader needs to choose whatever strategies will help make sense of it. If one strategy does not work, the reader should try another.

✦ Always treat problems encountered in text as interesting learning opportunities rather than something to be avoided or dreaded.

✦ Encourage students to think aloud about text challenges.

✦ Encourage students to help each other build meaning from text. Rather than telling each other what a word is or what a passage means, students should tell each other how they figured out the meanings of challenging words and passages.

✦ Assure students that these are not the only strategies that can be used while reading. Any strategy that they find helpful in understanding text is a good, useful strategy.

✦ Encourage students to freely share strategies they have devised on their own. You might want to write these on a large sheet of paper and tape them onto the board.

✦ An absence of questions does not necessarily indicate that students understand what they are reading. Be especially alert to students who never seem to ask questions. Be sure to spend tutorial time with these students occasionally, and encourage them to discuss specific selections in the context of difficulties they might have encountered and how they solved them as well as their thoughts about unit concepts.

✦ Observing students' responses to text will enable you to ascertain not only how well they understand a particular selection but also their facility in choosing and applying appropriate strategies. Use the strategy rubrics to evaluate students' understanding of and ability to use the different reading strategies. Take note of the following:

- Whether the strategies a student uses are effective in the particular situation.

- Whether the student chooses from a variety of appropriate strategies or uses the same few over and over.

- Whether the student can explain to classmates which strategies to use in a particular situation and why.

- Whether the student can identify alternative resources to pursue when the strategies she or he has tried are not effective.

- Whether students' application of a given strategy is becoming more effective over a period of time.

✦ Encourage students to use the reading strategies throughout the day in all their reading activities.

Becoming familiar and comfortable with these self-monitoring techniques gives readers the confidence to tackle material that is progressively more difficult. A good,

mature reader knows when understanding what he or she is reading is becoming a problem and can take steps to correct the situation. He or she has internalized the strategies, values them, and uses strategies automatically.

Comprehension Skills

Purpose

An important purpose of writing is to communicate thoughts from one person to another. The goal of instruction in reading comprehension skills is to make students aware of the logic behind the structure of a written piece. If the reader can discern the logic of the structure, he or she will be more able to understand the author's logic and to gain knowledge both of the facts and the intent of the selection. By keeping the organization of a piece in mind and considering the author's purpose for writing, the reader can go beyond the actual words on the page and make inferences or draw conclusions based on what was read. Strong, mature readers utilize these "between the lines" skills to get a complete picture of not only what the writer is saying but what the writer is trying to say.

Effective comprehension skills include the following:

Author's Point of View

Point of view involves identifying who is telling the story. If a character in the story is telling the story, that one character describes the action and tells what the other characters are like. This is first-person point of view. In such a story, one character will do the talking and use the pronouns *I, my,* and *me.* All other characters' thoughts, feelings, and emotions will be reported through this one character.

If the story is told in third-person point of view, someone outside the story who is aware of all of the characters' thoughts, feelings, and actions is relating them to the reader. All of the characters are referred to by their names or the pronouns *he/she, him/her,* and *it.*

If students stay aware of who is telling a story, they will know whether they are getting the full picture or the picture of events as seen through the eyes of only one character.

Sequence

The reader cannot make any decisions about relationships or events if he or she has no idea in which order the events take place. The reader needs to pay attention to how the writer is conveying the sequence. Is it simply stated that first this happened and then that happened? Does the writer present the end of the story first and then go back and let the reader know the sequence of events? Knowing what the sequence is and how it is presented helps the reader follow the writer's line of thought.

Fact and Opinion

Learning to distinguish fact from opinion is essential to critical reading and thinking. Students learn what factors need to be present for a statement to be provable. They also learn that an opinion, while not provable itself, should be based on fact. Readers use this knowledge to determine for themselves the validity of the ideas presented in their reading.

Main Idea and Details

An author always has something specific to say to his or her reader. The author may state this main idea in different ways, but the reader should always be able to tell what the writing is about.

To strengthen the main point or main idea of a piece, the author provides details to help the reader understand. For example, the author may use comparison and contrast to make a point, to provide examples, to provide facts, to give opinions, to give descriptions, to give reasons or causes, or to give definitions. The reader needs to know what kinds of details he or she is dealing with before making a judgment about the main idea.

Compare and Contrast

Using comparison and contrast is one of the most common and easiest ways a writer gets his or her reader to understand a subject. Comparing and contrasting unfamiliar thoughts, ideas, or things with familiar thoughts, ideas, and things gives the reader something within his or her own experience base to use in understanding.

Cause and Effect

What made this happen? Why did this character act the way he or she did? Knowing the causes of events helps the reader see the whole story. Using this information to identify the probable outcomes (effects) of events or actions will help the reader anticipate the story or article.

Classify and Categorize

The relationships of actions, events, characters, outcomes, and such in a selection should be clear enough for the reader to see the relationships. Putting like things or ideas together can help the reader understand the relationships set up by the writer.

Author's Purpose

Everything is written for a purpose. That purpose may be to entertain, to persuade, or to inform. Knowing why a piece is written—what purpose the author had for writing the piece—gives the reader an idea of what to expect and perhaps some prior idea of what the author is going to say.

If a writer is writing to entertain, then the reader can generally just relax and let the writer carry him or her away. If, on the other hand, the purpose is to persuade, it will help the reader understand and keep perspective if he or she knows that the purpose is to persuade. The reader can be prepared for whatever argument the writer delivers.

Drawing Conclusions

Often, writers do not directly state everything—they take for granted their audience's ability to "read between the lines." Readers draw conclusions when they take from the text small pieces of information about a character or event and use this information to make a statement about that character or event.

Reality and Fantasy

Students learn to distinguish reality from fantasy as they read different genres, including expository text, realistic fiction, fables, fairy tales, and so on. As students read, they note that a fantasy contains people, animals, and objects that do things that could not happen in the real world. Reality contains people, animals, and objects that can exist and do things in the real world.

Making Inferences

Readers make inferences about characters and events to understand the total picture in a story. When making inferences, readers use information from the text, along with personal experience or knowledge, to gain a deeper understanding of a story event and its implications.

Procedures

Read the Selection

First, have students read the selection using whatever skills they need to help them make sense of the selection. Then discuss the selection to assure that students did, indeed, understand what they read. Talk about any confusion they may have, and make any necessary clarifications.

Reread

Revisiting or rereading a selection allows the reader to note specific techniques that authors use to organize and present information in narratives and expository genres. When students have a basic understanding of the piece, have them reread the selection in whole or in part, concentrating on selected skills. Students learn to appreciate that writers use different structures, for example, cause and effect or compare/contrast, to organize their work and that recognizing these structures can help readers understand what they have read. It is these same structures that students will use in their own writing.

Limit this concentration on specific comprehension/writing skills to one or two that can be clearly identified in the piece. Trying to concentrate on too many things will just confuse students and make it harder for them to identify any of the organizational devices used by the writer. If a piece has many good examples of several different aspects, then go back to the piece several times over a span of days.

Write

Solidify the connection between how an author writes and how readers make sense of a selection by encouraging students to incorporate these organizational devices into their own writing. As they attempt to use these devices, they will get a clearer understanding of how to identify them when they are reading.

Remind students often that the purpose of any skill exercise is to give them tools to use when they are reading and writing. Unless students learn to apply the skills to their own reading—in every area of reading and study—then they are not gaining a full understanding of the purpose of the exercise.

Writing is a complicated process. A writer uses handwriting, spelling, vocabulary, grammar, usage, genre structures, and mechanics skills with ideas to create readable text. In addition, a writer must know how to generate content, or ideas, and understand genre structures to effectively present ideas in writing. Many students never progress beyond producing a written text that duplicates their everyday speech patterns. Mature writers, however, take composition beyond conversation. They understand the importance of audience and purpose for writing. They organize their thoughts, eliminating those that do not advance their main ideas, applying what they have learned in reading, and elaborating on those that do so that their readers can follow a logical progression of ideas in an essay or story. Mature writers also know and can use the conventions of grammar, usage, spelling, and mechanics. They proofread and edit for these conventions, so their readers are not distracted by errors.

Reading Big Books

Purpose

Many students come from homes where they are read to often, but a significant number of other students have not had this valuable experience. **Big Books** (Levels K and 1) offer all students crucial opportunities to confirm and expand their knowledge about print and reading, to develop vocabulary, and to enjoy literacy experiences. They are especially useful for shared reading experiences in the early grades.

The benefits of reading **Big Books** include engaging even nonreaders in

- unlocking the books' messages.
- developing print awareness.
- participating in good reading behaviors.
- observing what a good reader does: remarking on the illustrations and the title, asking questions about the content and what might happen, making predictions, and clarifying words and ideas.
- promoting the insights about print, for example, that a given word is spelled the same way every time it occurs as high-frequency words are identified.
- reinforcing the correspondence between spoken and written words and spelling patterns.
- enjoying the illustrations and connecting them to the text to help students learn to explore books for enjoyment and information.
- learning about different genre and the language of print.
- developing vocabulary and academic language.
- interpreting and responding to literature and expository text before they can read themselves.

Procedure for Reading Big Books

During the first reading of the **Big Books,** you will model reading behaviors and comprehension strategies similar to those that will later apply to their own reading. This focus on strategies encourages students to think about the ideas in the stories, to ask questions, and to learn new vocabulary. During the second reading, you will address

print awareness and teach comprehension skills such as classifying and categorizing or sequencing, which help the reader organize information and focus on the specifics in the selection. In addition, you will teach skills such as making inferences and drawing conclusions, which help the reader focus on the deeper meaning of the text. At first, teachers should expect to do all of the reading but should not prevent students from trying to read on their own or from reading words they already know.

- **Activate Prior Knowledge.** Read the title of the selection and the author's and illustrator's names. At the beginning of each **Big Book,** read the title of the book and discuss what the whole book is about before going on to reading the first selection. Initiate a brief discussion of any prior knowledge students have that might help them understand the selection.

> **Big Books** *offer all students opportunities to confirm and expand their knowledge about print and reading.*

- **Browse the Selection.** Explain to the class that browsing means to look through the pages of the story to get a general idea of what the story is about, to see what interests them, and to ask questions. Ask students to tell what they think the story might be about just from looking at the illustrations. This conversation should be brief so that students can move on to a prereading discussion of print awareness.

- **Develop Print Awareness.** The focus of browsing the **Big Books** is to develop awareness of print. Urge students to tell what words or letters they recognize rather than what they expect the selection to be about.

    To develop print awareness, have students look through the selection

page by page and to comment on whatever they notice in the text. Some students may know some of the words, while others may recognize only specific letters or sounds. The key is to get students to look at the print separately from the illustrations even before they have heard the actual text content. This process isolates print awareness so that it is not influenced by content. It also gives you a clearer idea of what your students do or do not know about print.

- **Read Aloud.** Read the selection aloud expressively, using intonation and pauses at punctuation. Not only does this enable students to hear and enjoy the text as it is read through once, it serves as an early model for fluency. Good fluency and expression support comprehension. As you read, you will stop periodically to model behaviors and comprehension strategies that all students will need to develop to become successful readers—for example, asking questions; clarifying unfamiliar words, first by using the pictures and later by using context; or predicting what might happen next.

- **Reread.** Read the selection expressively again. During the second reading of the stories, you will focus on teaching comprehension skills. Also, to develop print awareness, point to each word as it is read, thus demonstrating that text proceeds from left to right and from top to bottom and helping advance the idea that words are individual spoken and written units. Invite students to identify the rhyming words in a poem or to chime in on repetitive parts of text as you point to the words. Or students can read with you on this second reading, depending on the text. As students' knowledge of words and phonics grows, they can participate in decoding words and reading high-frequency sight words.

✦ **Discuss Print.** Return to print awareness by encouraging discussion of anything students noticed about the words. Young students should begin to realize that you are reading separate words that are separated by spaces. Later, students will begin to see that each word is made of a group of letters. Students should be encouraged to discuss anything related to the print. For example, you might ask students to point to a word or to count the number of words on a line. Or you might connect the words to the illustrations by pointing to a word and saying it and then asking students to find a picture of that word.

✦ **Responding.** Responding to a selection is a way of insuring comprehension. Invite students to tell about the story by asking them what they like about the poem or story or calling on a student to explain in his or her own words what the poem or story tells about. Call on others to add to the telling as needed. For nonfiction selections, this discussion might include asking students what they learned about the topic and what they thought was most interesting.

Tips for Using Big Books

✦ Make sure the entire group is able to see the book clearly while you are reading.

✦ If some students are able to read words, encourage them to do so during the rereading.

✦ Encourage students to use their knowledge of print.

✦ Encourage students' use of academic language as they talk about reading. Students should be comfortable using strategic reading words such as *predict* and *clarify* and book and print words such as *author* and *illustrator*.

✦ Allow students to look at the *Big Books* whenever they wish.

✦ Provide small versions of the *Big Books* for students to browse through and to try to read at their leisure.

✦ The reader of the *Big Book* should try to be part of the collaborative group of learners rather than the leader.

Strategic Reading

Purpose

Reading is a complex process that requires students not only to decode automatically and correctly what they read but also to understand and respond to it. The purpose of this section is to help you identify various reading behaviors used by good readers and to encourage those behaviors in your students.

Reading Behaviors and Comprehension Strategies

There are four basic behaviors that good readers engage in during reading: Setting Reading Goals and Expectations, Responding to Text, Checking Understanding, and Monitoring and Clarifying Unfamiliar Words and Passages. Engaging in these behaviors involves the application of certain comprehension strategies. These strategies are initially modeled while reading the **Big Books** (Level K and the first half of Level 1) and **Student Readers** (Levels 1–6). The goal of strategy instruction, however, is to ultimately turn over responsibility for using strategies to students so they set their own goals for reading, respond to text, and check their own understanding and solve problems while reading. Students need to take responsibility for doing the thinking and making sense of text.

Setting Reading Goals and Expectations

Good readers set reading goals and expectations before they begin reading. This behavior involves a variety of strategies that will help students prepare to read the text.

✦ **Activate prior knowledge.** When good readers approach a new text, they consider what they already know about the subject or what their experiences have been in reading similar material.

✦ **Browse the text.** To get an idea of what to expect from a text, good readers look at the title and the illustrations. They may look for potential problems, such as difficult words. When browsing a unit, have students glance quickly at each selection, looking briefly at the illustrations and the print. Have them tell what they think they might be learning about as they read the unit.

✦ **Decide what they expect from the text.** When reading for pleasure, good readers anticipate enjoying the story or the language. When reading to learn something, they ask themselves what they expect to find out.

Responding to Text

Good readers are active readers. They interact with text by using the following strategies:

✦ **Making connections.** Good readers make connections between what they read and what they already know. They pay attention to elements in the text that remind them of their own experiences. Readers make connections to personal experiences, to other stories they have read, and to world knowledge.

✦ **Visualizing, or picturing.** Good readers visualize what is happening in the text. They not only form mental images as they read but make inferences based on their own experiences. Visualizing goes beyond the words in text. They imagine the setting and the emotions it suggests, they picture the characters and their feelings, and they visualize the action in a story. When reading expository text, good readers picture the objects, processes, or events described. Visualizing helps readers understand descriptions of complex activities or processes.

✦ **Asking questions.** Good readers ask questions that may prepare them for what they will learn. If their questions are not answered in the text, they may try to find answers elsewhere and thus add even more to their store of knowledge.

✦ **Predicting.** Good readers predict what will happen next. When reading fiction, they make predictions about what they are reading and then confirm or revise those predictions as they go.

✦ **Thinking about how the text makes you feel.** Well-written fiction touches readers' emotions; it sparks ideas.

Checking Understanding

One of the most important behaviors good readers exhibit is the refusal to continue reading when something fails to make sense. Good readers continually assess their understanding of the text with strategies such as the following:

✦ **Interpreting.** As they read, good readers make inferences that help them understand and appreciate what they are reading.

✦ **Summarizing.** Good readers summarize to check their understanding as they read. Sometimes they reread to fill in gaps in their understanding.

✦ **Adjusting reading speed.** Good readers monitor their understanding of what they read. They slow down as they come to difficult words and passages. They speed up as they read easier passages.

Monitoring and Clarifying Unfamiliar Words and Passages

Monitoring understanding involves knowing when meaning is breaking down. The reader needs to stop and identify what the problem or source of confusion is. It might be an unfamiliar word, complex and hard-to-understand sentences or unfamiliar concepts that need clarifying. At the word level, the reader might

✦ apply decoding skills to sound out unknown words.

✦ apply context clues in text and illustrations to figure out the meanings of words.

✦ use structural elements to figure out the meaning of the word.

✦ ask someone the meaning of the word.

✦ reread the passage to make sure the passage makes sense.

✦ check a dictionary or the glossary to understand the meanings of words not clarified by clues or rereading.

Complex sentences may require the reader to look for the main idea in the sentence, to pull out clauses that may interfere with the main idea, or to ask for help. When faced with unfamiliar concepts, readers often ask for clarification from someone.

These cognitive activities engage the reader in thinking about text before, during, and after reading. Readers think about text before they read by activating background knowledge, anticipating content, setting purposes, and wondering about the text and what they will learn. During reading, the reader is constantly checking understanding—asking whether what is being read makes sense and constructing conclusions or summary statements. When the text is not making sense, the reader uses strategies to clarify words, ideas, and larger units of text or may reread more slowly for clarification. After reading, the reader reflects on what was read, connecting new information to prior knowledge, evaluating purposes, and connecting the relevance of the new information to the purpose.

Procedures

Modeling and Thinking Aloud

Modeling and encouraging students to think aloud as they attempt to understand text can demonstrate for everyone how reading behaviors are put into practice. Modeling and thinking aloud helps students learn how to process information and learn important content. It is more than asking students questions; it is letting students in on the thinking that helps readers make sense of text, solve problems while reading, and use strategies differentially and intentionally. The most effective models will be those that come from your own reading. As you model the different strategies, let students know what strategy you are using and why you are using it.

Model comprehension strategies in a natural way, and choose questions and comments that fit the text you are reading. Present a variety of ways to respond to text.

✦ Pose questions that you really do wonder about.

✦ Identify with characters by comparing them with yourself.

✦ React emotionally by showing joy, sadness, amusement, or surprise.

✦ Show empathy with or sympathy for characters.

✦ Relate the text to something that has happened to you or to something you already know.

✦ Show interest in the text ideas.

✦ Question the meaning or clarity of the author's words and ideas.

Encourage Students' Responses and Use of Strategies

Most students will typically remain silent as they try to figure out an unfamiliar word or a confusing passage. Encourage students to identify specifically with what they are having difficulty. When the problem has been identified, ask students to suggest a strategy for dealing with the problem. Remind students to

✦ treat problems encountered in text as interesting learning opportunities.

✦ think aloud about text challenges.

✦ help each other build meaning. Rather than tell what a word is, students should tell how they figured out the meanings of challenging words and passages.

✦ consider reading a selection again with a partner after reading it once alone. Partner reading provides valuable practice in reading for fluency.

✦ make as many connections as they can between what they are reading and what they already know.

✦ visualize to clarify meanings or enjoy descriptions.

✦ ask questions about what they are reading.

✦ notice how the text makes them feel.

In addition, using open-ended questions such as the following, as well as your students' questions and comments, will make both the text and the strategic reading process more meaningful to students.

✦ What kinds of things did you wonder about?

✦ What kinds of things surprised you?

✦ What new information did you learn?

✦ What was confusing until you reread or read further?

Discussion

The more students are able to discuss what they are learning, to voice their confusions, and to compare perceptions of what they are learning, the deeper and more meaningful their learning becomes.

Purpose

Through discussions, students are exposed to points of view different from their own and learn how to express their thoughts and opinions coherently. Through discussion, students add to their own knowledge that of their classmates and learn to explain themselves coherently. They also begin to ask insightful questions that help them better understand what they have read and all that they are learning through their inquiry/research and explorations. The purpose of classroom discussion is to provide a framework for learning.

Procedure

Reflecting on the Selection

After students have finished reading a selection, provide an opportunity for them to engage in discussion about the selection. Students should

✦ check to see whether the questions they asked before reading as part of Clues, Problems, and Wonderings and KWL (What I Know, What I Want to Know and What I Have Learned) have been answered. Encourage them to discuss whether any unanswered questions should still be answered. If unanswered questions are related to the theme, add those questions to the **Concept/Question Board.**

✦ discuss any new questions that have arisen because of the reading. Encourage students to decide which of these questions should go on the **Concept/Question Board.**

✦ share what they expected to learn from reading the selection and tell whether expectations were met.

✦ talk about whatever has come to mind while reading the selection. This discussion should be an informal sharing of impressions of, or opinions about, the selection; it should never take on the aspects of a question-and-answer session about the selection.

✦ give students ample opportunity to ask questions and to share their thoughts about the selection. Participate as an active member of the group, making your own observations about information in a selection or modeling your own appreciation of a story. Be especially aware of unusual and interesting insights suggested by students so that these insights can be recognized and discussed. To help students learn to keep the discussion student-centered, have each student choose the next speaker instead of handing the discussion back to you.

> *The purpose of classroom discussion is to provide a framework for learning.*

Recording Ideas

As students finish discussions about their reactions to a selection, they should be encouraged to record their thoughts, feelings, reactions, and ideas about the selection or the subject of the selection in their Writer's Notebooks. This will not only help keep the selections fresh in students' minds; it will strengthen their writing abilities and help them learn how to write about their thoughts and feelings.

Students may find that the selection gave them ideas for their own writing, or it could have reminded them of some person or incident in their own lives. Perhaps the selection answered a question that has been on their minds or raised a question they had never thought before. Good, mature writers—especially professional writers—learn the value of recording such thoughts and impressions quickly before they fade. Students should be encouraged to do this also.

Handing Off

Handing off (Levels 1–6) is a method of turning over to students the primary responsibility for controlling discussion. Often, students who are taking responsibility for controlling a discussion tend to have all "turns" go through the teacher. The teacher is the one to whom attention is transferred when a speaker finishes, and the teacher is the one who is expected to call on the next speaker—the result being that the teacher remains the pivotal figure in the discussion.

Having students "hand off" the discussion to other students instead of the teacher encourages them to retain complete control of the discussion and to become more actively involved in the learning process. When a student finishes his or her comments, that student should choose (hand off the discussion to) the next speaker. In this way, students maintain a discussion without relying on the teacher to decide who speaks.

When handing off is in place, the teacher's main roles are to occasionally remind students to hand off, to help students when they get stuck, to encourage them to persevere on a specific point, and to get them back to a discussion, and to monitor the discussion to ensure that everyone gets a chance to contribute. The teacher may say, for example, "Remember, not just boys (or girls)." or "Try to choose someone who has not had a chance to talk yet." It is not unusual early in the process for students to roam from the topic and selection. To bring the discussion back to the topic and selection, be a participant, raise your hand, and ask a question or make a statement that refocuses students' thinking and discussion.

For handing off to work effectively, a seating arrangement that allows students to see one another is essential. It is hard to hold a discussion when students have their backs to each other. A circle or a semicircle is effective. In addition, all students need to have copies of the materials being discussed.

Actively encourage this handing-off process by letting students know that they, not you, are in control of the discussion.

If students want to remember thoughts about, or reactions to, a selection, suggest that they record these in the Response Journal section of their Writer's Notebooks.

Encourage students to record the thoughts, feelings, or reactions that are elicited by any reading they do.

Exploring Concepts within the Selection

To provide an opportunity for collaborative learning and to focus on the concepts, you may want to have students form small groups and spend time discussing what they have learned about the concepts from this selection. Topics may include new information that they have acquired, new ideas that they have had, or new questions that the selection raised.

Students should always base their discussions on postings from the **Concept/ Question Board** as well as on previous discussions of the concept. The small-group discussions should be ongoing throughout the unit; during this time, students should continue to compare and contrast any new information with their previous ideas, opinions, and impressions about the concepts. How does this selection help confirm their ideas? How does it contradict their thinking? How has it changed their outlook?

As students discuss the concepts in small groups, circulate around the room to make sure that each group stays focused upon the selection and the concepts. After students have had some time to discuss the information and the ideas in the selection, encourage each group to formulate some statements about the concept that apply to the selection.

Sharing Ideas about Concepts

Have a representative from each group report and explain the group's ideas to the rest of the class. Then have the class formulate one or more general statements related to the unit concepts and write these statements on the **Concept/Question Board.** As students progress through the unit, they will gain more and more confidence in suggesting additions to the **Concept/Question Board.**

✦ **Visual Aids** During this part of the discussion, you may find it helpful to use visual aids to help students as they build the connections to the unit concepts. Not all units or concepts will lend themselves to this type of treatment; however, aids such as time lines, charts, graphs, and pictographs may help students see how each new selection adds to their growing knowledge of the concepts.

Encourage students to ask questions about the concepts that the selection may have raised. Have students list on the **Concept/Question Board** those questions that cannot be answered immediately and that they want to explore further.

> *Through discussions, students are exposed to points of view different from their own and learn how to express their thoughts and opinions coherently.*

Exploring Concepts across Selections

As each new selection is read, encourage students to discuss its connection with the other selections and with the unit concepts. Also encourage students to think about selections that they have read from other units and how they relate to the concepts for this unit.

Ultimately, this ability to make connections between past knowledge and new knowledge allows any learner to gain insights into what is being studied. The goal of the work with concepts and the discussions is to help students to start thinking in terms of connections—how is this like what I have learned before? Does this information confirm, contradict, or add

a completely different layer to that which I already know about this concept? How can the others in the class have such different ideas than I do when we just read the same selection? Why is so much written about this subject?

Learning to make connections and to delve deeper through self-generated questions and substantive discussions give students the tools they need to become effective, efficient, lifelong learners.

Tips

✦ Create an environment that facilitates discussion. Have students sit in circles or some other configuration so everyone can see each other.

✦ When students are discussing the selection, they should have their books with them, and students should feel free to refer to them throughout the discussion.

✦ Discussions offer a prime opportunity for you to introduce, or seed, new ideas about the concepts. New ideas can come from a variety of sources: Students may draw on their own experiences or on the books or videos they are studying; you may introduce new ideas into the discussion; or you may at times invite experts to speak to the class.

✦ If students do not mention an important idea that is necessary to the understanding of some larger issue, you may "drop" that idea into the conversation and, indeed, repeat it several times to make sure that it does get picked up. This seeding may be subtle ("I think that might be important here") or quite direct ("This is a big idea, one that we will definitely need to understand and one that we will return to regularly").

✦ To facilitate this process for each unit, you must be aware of the unit concepts and be able to recognize and reinforce them when they arise spontaneously in discussions. If central unit concepts do not arise naturally, then, and only then, will you seed these ideas by direct modeling. The more you turn over discussions to students, the more involved they will become, and the more responsibility they will take for their own learning. Make it your goal to become a participant in, rather than the leader of, class discussions.

✦ Help students see that they are responsible for carrying on the discussion. After a question is asked, always wait instead of jumping in with a comment or an explanation. Although this wait time may be uncomfortable at first, students will come to understand that the discussion is their responsibility and that you will not jump in every time there is a hesitation.

✦ As the year progresses, students will become more and more adept at conducting and participating in meaningful discussions about what they have read. These discussions will greatly enhance students' understanding of the concepts that they are exploring.

Discussion Starters and Questions

The following examples of discussion starters can be modeled initially, but then the responsibility for using them should be turned over to students. The starters provide the opportunity for open-ended discussions by students.

✦ I didn't know that . . . .
✦ Does anyone know . . . .
✦ I figured out that . . . .
✦ I liked the part where . . . .
✦ I'm still confused about . . . .
✦ This made me think . . . .
✦ I agree with _____ because . . . .
✦ I disagree with _____ because . . . .
✦ The reason I think _____ is . . .
✦ I found _____ interesting because. . . .
✦ I learned . . .
✦ What I learned in this selection reminds me of what we read in _____ because . . .
✦ This author's writing reminds me of . . .
✦ I had problems understanding _____ because . . .
✦ I wonder why the author chose to . . .
✦ I still do not understand . . .
✦ I was surprised to find out . . .
✦ I like the way the author developed the character by . . .
✦ The author made the story really come alive by . . .

In addition to these open-ended discussion starters, students should be encouraged to ask open-ended questions. When students ask questions, other students should respond to the question before moving on to another idea or topic. One student asking a question often helps to clarify something for the whole class and places a value on asking questions as a critical part of learning.

✦ Why did the author . . . ?
✦ What did the author mean when he or she wrote . . . ?
✦ Who can help me clarify . . . ?
✦ Who can help me figure out . . . ?
✦ How does this piece connect to the unit theme?
✦ What does this section mean?

Writing

Purpose

The writing program in **SRA Imagine It!** teaches students how to write skillfully. This is essential, as writing is a powerful tool that fosters learning, communication, creativity, and self-discovery. **SRA Imagine It!** writing teaches students how to use writing effectively for these purposes.

Writing is a complex process. It involves deftly juggling a variety of skills, strategies, and knowledge. Writers must make plans, consider the reader, draw ideas from memory, develop new ideas, organize thoughts, consider the conventions of the genre, translate ideas into words, craft sentences, evaluate decisions, make needed revisions, transcribe words into correctly spelled print, and monitor the writing process, among other things.

SRA Imagine It! writing is designed to ensure that students acquire the skills, knowledge, strategies, and dispositions they need to become skilled writers. This includes the following:

✦ Knowledge about the qualities of good writing, characteristics of different genres, intended audience, and writing topics. Skilled writers know how to obtain information about their topics, are familiar with basic features of different genres, and possess basic schemas or frameworks for accomplishing common writing tasks.

✦ The writing strategies involved in basic composing processes such as prewriting, drafting, monitoring, evaluating, revising, editing/proofreading, and publishing. Skilled writers flexibly employ these strategies to create text.

✦ Command of basic writing skills such as handwriting, spelling, sentence construction, grammar, and usage. Skilled writers execute these basic writing skills with little conscious effort.

✦ Interest and motivation to write as well as perceptions of competence as a writer. Skilled writers possess an "I can do" attitude.

Procedures

With **SRA Imagine It!** writing, evidence-based practices are used to teach students to write skillfully. These evidence-based practices are drawn from research on the effectiveness of specific writing interventions that show that the quality of students' writing can be improved by

✦ explicitly teaching strategies for prewriting, drafting, revising, editing/proofreading, and publishing.

✦ modeling effective use of writing strategies.

> *Children start school wanting to learn how to write and enjoying writing. The goal of **SRA Imagine It!** writing is for children to become lifelong writers—people who enjoy writing and use writing effectively at work as well as in their personal lives.*

✦ having students work together to prewrite, draft, revise, edit/proofread, and publish their compositions.

✦ using prewriting tools such as graphic organizers to gather information.

✦ involving students in inquiry activities designed to help them further develop their ideas for writing.

✦ making the goals for writing assignments clear and specific.

✦ teaching students how to construct more sophisticated sentences.

✦ providing students with the opportunity to read, evaluate, and emulate models of good writing.

✦ teaching students how to use word processing as a tool for composing.

The evidence-based practices in **SRA Imagine It!** are also based on the study of expert teachers who

✦ make sure their students are engaged, spending most of their writing time doing something that involves thoughtfulness, such as crafting a story or learning how to construct a complex sentence.

✦ teach basic writing skills, strategies, and knowledge balanced by ample opportunity to apply what is learned.

✦ involve students in writing for a variety of different purposes.

✦ create a writing classroom environment that is supportive, pleasant, and motivating.

✦ encourage students to accomplish as much as possible on their own (to act in a self-regulated fashion), but who are ready to offer support and instruction as needed.

✦ use reading to support writing development and vice versa.

✦ monitor students' growth in writing and encourage students to monitor their own growth.

✦ provide extra assistance to students who experience difficulty.

✦ are passionate about writing.

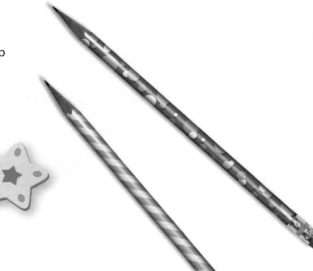

Knowledge about Writing

Purpose

Writing can be used to communicate, entertain, inform, reflect, persuade, and learn. To take full advantage of this flexible tool, students must acquire knowledge about the qualities of good writing and the various purposes and forms of writing. They must also carefully consider their audience and be knowledgeable about the topics they write about.

Procedures

Qualities of Good Writing

One way students learn about the qualities of good writing is by directly teaching them that good writing is characterized by the following seven traits:

✦ Clearly presented and fully developed ideas

✦ Writing that is easy to follow and logically organized

✦ Effective and precise word choice

✦ Varied use of sentence structure to promote fluency, rhythm, and natural speech patterns

✦ Writing that captures appropriate tone or mood to make the desired impact on the reader

✦ Correct spelling, usage, and grammar

✦ A written product that is legible, attractive, and accessible

For each writing assignment, teachers concentrate on one or more of these traits, teaching students strategies for enhancing the trait(s) in their writing. For example, students are taught to circle words that are vague in their writing and to replace them with more precise ones.

Another way that students learn about the qualities of good writing is through reading. The reading material in **SRA Imagine It!** provides concrete models that illustrate the characteristics of good writing, such as how authors

✦ present, develop, and organize ideas.

✦ use words to evoke specific images and feelings.

✦ manipulate sentences to speed up or slow down the flow of text.

✦ set and change the mood to match the action of the characters.

✦ use illustrations to reinforce and sharpen readers' understanding.

This knowledge is fostered in **SRA Imagine It!** through Reading with a Writer's Eye. Teachers and students discuss what the author of a reading selection did to achieve certain purposes. For example, after reading a mystery, the class discusses how the author planted a false lead to make the story more interesting and complex. Students are then encouraged to use the same technique in a mystery they write.

Different Purposes and Forms of Writing

Students learn the purposes and forms of a wide range of genres they need to master for success both in and out of school. This includes using writing to do the following:

✦ Communicate with others (personal letters, business letters, notes, cards, and e-mail)

✦ Create personal narratives (journal writing, autobiography, writing about a personal event, and so on)

✦ Entertain (stories, plays, poems, and so on)

✦ Learn (learning logs, reports, journal entries, summarizing, and biographies)

✦ Inform (writing lists, explaining how to do something, describing objects or places, describing events, news reports, reports, and biographies)

✦ Respond to literature (book evaluations, book reports, and book reviews)

✦ Persuade (advertisements, opinions about controversial topics)

✦ Demonstrate knowledge (for example, traditional classroom tests, high-stakes tests involving writing, high-stakes tests involving multiple-choice answers)

In **SRA Imagine It!** writing, students learn to write stories, poetry, plays, journal entries, summaries, book reviews, informative reports, descriptions, explanations, letters, critiques, and e-mail. They also use these various forms of writing to gather, think about, and report what they have learned when doing extended Inquiry projects.

One way they learn about the purposes and forms of these various genres is through the use of models of each type of writing. As students begin working on a new genre, the class analyzes an exemplary model of this type of writing to determine its characteristics and functions. They are encouraged to incorporate these features in their writing. In addition, what they write is frequently tied to what they read, so their reading material provides a model and source of information on the purpose and form of their writing.

Students are also asked to carefully consider the purpose for each of their compositions and include this determination as part of the planning process. As they plan, the form and purpose of their compositions is further emphasized through the use of graphic organizers, in which students typically generate and organize ideas for each of the basic elements included in the type of composition they are composing.

Knowledge of Writing Topics

To write well, students must have something to write about. Good writers typically know a lot about their topics or have strategies for acquiring such information. With **SRA Imagine It!** writing, students are taught effective strategies for gathering information to write about. This includes how to

✦ locate information in written and electronic sources.

✦ obtain information through interviews or surveys.

✦ summarize information in notes.

✦ reference informational sources.

Developing a Sense of Audience

While writing is often viewed as a solitary activity, it is typically meant to be read by others. Children and adults most often use writing to communicate, persuade, or inform others. Because the writer is usually not present when the composition is read, he or she must carefully consider the needs of the readers. **SRA Imagine It!** writing helps students develop a sense of audience by asking them to identify their audience when they write collaboratively or independently. Students are also encouraged to share what they write with their peers and others. The following are procedures for presenting and sharing:

✦ Before presenting, have the writer
  • decide what will be shared.
  • practice what will be shared.

✦ During presenting,
  • have the writer tell what is to be shared and why.

- have the writer read aloud his or her work or idea.
  - remind students to listen carefully.
- After presenting,
  - have students tell what they like.
  - have students offer the writer helpful suggestions.
  - take notes of students' comments to share with the writer.

Tips

- Have students keep a log of new information they have learned about the attributes of good writing.
- Develop wall charts that specify the purpose and attributes of specific writing genres.
- Ask students to evaluate their writing and the writing of others based on seven traits of good writing.
- Before students begin work on a writing assignment, hold a class discussion on the topic to share information, clarify misperceptions, and identify information students still need to locate.

Mastering the Writing Process

Purpose

To write skillfully, young writers must master the basic processes involved in writing. These processes include the strategic "know-how" involved in writing and include the following:

- **Prewriting:** Writers spend time thinking about and planning their topics. They consider their purposes, audience, and the focus of their topics. Writers make plans to guide the composing process, establishing goals for what to do and say. They gather possible ideas for their writing, drawing on memory and external sources such as books, interviews, articles, and the Internet. Writers make decisions about which information to include and how to organize it.
- **Drafting:** Writers draft or put their ideas into words, using the initial plans they developed as a guide. These plans are expanded, modified, and even reworked as writers create a first draft of their composition, often in a rough form.

- **Revising:** While some revising may occur during prewriting and drafting, writers revisit and revise their first drafts. They reread them to see whether the drafts say what the writers intended. Writers check to be sure the drafts make sense and that the meaning is clear for the audience. They consider whether their writing will have the desired impact on the audience. As they make changes in their text, they discover new things to say and new ways to present their ideas.

> Writers need feedback throughout the writing process. Feedback is one of our most powerful tools for helping developing writers.

- **Editing/Proofreading:** Writers edit/proofread their work. They recognize that spelling, grammar, and usage errors make it harder for others to understand and enjoy their published work. Writers know that readers are more likely to value their message when they correct these mistakes.
- **Publishing:** Writers share their writing by reading their entire work, or part of their work, to others. They publish their work in books, newspapers, magazines, anthologies, and so on.

Skilled writers move back and forth through these processes—from prewriting to drafting to revising and back—to create their final pieces.

Procedures

Much of what happens during writing is not visible. It occurs inside the writer's head. *SRA Imagine It!* writing makes the processes involved in writing concrete and visible in the following four ways:

- Establishing a predictable writing routine during which students are expected to prewrite, draft, revise, edit/proofread, and publish.

- Using graphic organizers and revising, editing/proofreading, and publishing checklists that help developing writers carry out basic writing processes.
- Teaching strategies for prewriting, drafting, revising, editing/proofreading, and publishing.
- Providing feedback throughout the writing process through writing conferences and students' presentation of their works in progress and completed compositions.

Establishing a Predictable Writing Routine

One way to make the basic writing processes more concrete is to create a predictable classroom writing routine, during which students plan, draft, revise, edit, proofread, and publish their work. This establishes that these processes are important and ensures that time is provided for each process. It also allows students to work with minimum teacher direction and at their own pace.

Tips

- Guide students through the steps of the writing routine. Model each step of prewriting, drafting, revising, editing/proofreading, and publishing.
- Make sure students learn that the processes of writing do not always occur in the same order but are recursive. For example, revising may occur at any stage of the composing process. You should not only model this by showing how this is done, but the predictable routine should vary at times to reflect this flexibility.

Using Graphic Organizers and Revising, Editing/Proofreading, and Publishing Checklists

Graphic organizers and revising, editing/proofreading, and publishing checklists provide students with assistance in carrying out the thinking activities involved in a writing assignment. They provide structure and information for how to carry out the process. The graphic organizer typically includes a series of prompts that ask the student to think about the purpose for writing a particular piece and the intended audience. It also provides prompts designed to help the student generate and organize possible writing ideas. This frequently involves generating possible content for each part of the target composition. The revising, editing/proofreading, and publishing checklists direct students' attention to specific features or aspects of text that would be useful to consider while writing.

Tips

It is important to be sure that students understand how to use graphic organizers and revising, editing/proofreading, and publishing checklists. Be sure to

+ explain the purpose of the graphic organizer or revising, editing/proofreading, and publishing checklist.

+ describe how students are to use the graphic organizer or revising, editing/proofreading, and publishing checklist.

+ model aloud how to carry out the basic activities on the graphic organizer or revising, editing/proofreading, and publishing checklist.

+ make sure students understand each part of the graphic organizer or revising, editing/proofreading, and publishing checklist.

Teaching Strategies for Carrying Out Basic Writing Processes

A strategy involves a series of actions a writer undertakes to achieve a desired goal. In **SRA Imagine It!** students are taught strategies to help them carry out each of the basic writing processes—prewriting, drafting, revising, editing/proofreading, and publishing. Each strategy is also designed to enhance one or more of the seven traits of good writing. These include clearly presented and fully developed ideas; writing that is easy to follow and logically organized; effective and precise word choice; varied use of sentences to promote fluency, rhythm, and natural speech patterns; writing that captures appropriate tone or mood to make maximum impact on readers; correct spelling, usage, and grammar; and a written product that is legible, attractive, and accessible.

The goal is for students to be able to use the strategy independently and to make it part of their writing tool kit. The steps for teaching writing strategies are to

+ describe the strategy.

+ tell why the strategy is important.

+ tell students when they should use the strategy.

+ model how to use the strategy when writing, making your thoughts visible by saying aloud each thing you are doing and thinking.

+ make sure students understand why the strategy is important, when to apply it, and how to use it.

+ provide students with assistance in applying the strategy until they can do it on their own.

+ remind students to use the strategy when they write.

Tips

+ Ask students to evaluate their progress and how the strategy improved their writing.

+ Be enthusiastic about learning the strategy.

+ Establish the importance of effort in learning and using the strategy.

+ Provide opportunities for students to see how the strategy improves their writing.

+ Praise and reinforce students' use of the strategy.

+ Foster students' ownership of the strategy.

Providing Feedback through Conferencing and Presentation

Writers need feedback throughout the writing process. They need reactions to ideas, drafts, and revisions. Feedback is one of our most powerful tools for helping developing writers. Writers want to know how their works-in-progress sound to someone else, whether their compositions make sense, whether they contain any incorrect or misleading information, and where and how to make changes.

Regular feedback encourages developing writers to solve problems and make meaningful changes throughout the writing process.

One way of providing feedback is through conferences. Teachers may initiate conferences, but students should also be encouraged to call conferences on an as-needed basis. Because conferences can be held at various times throughout the writing process, the focus will vary. Conferences held during the early stages of the writing process help students identify and refine a topic or identify research references. During the revision process, conferences help students

learn to elaborate and reorganize their writing. During the final stages, students learn to edit and proofread stories before they are published. Conferences offer an excellent opportunity for the teacher and student to evaluate jointly the student's progress and set goals for future growth.

The basic procedures for writing conferences are as follows:

+ Have the student read aloud his or her work.

+ Review any feedback the student has received so far.

+ Identify positive elements of the work.

+ Use one or more of these strategies to help the student improve his or her work.

  · Have the student explain how he or she got his or her ideas.

  · Have the student think aloud about how he or she will address the feedback he or she has received.

  · Ask the student to help you understand any confusion you may have about his or her writing.

  · Have the student add, delete, or rearrange something in the work, and ask how it affects the entire piece.

  · Think aloud while you do a part of what the student was asked to do. Then ask the student to compare what you did to what he or she did.

  · Have the student prescribe as if to a younger student how to revise the work.

+ Ask two or three questions to guide the student through revising (see below).

+ Conclude the conference by having the student state his or her plan for continuing work on the piece of writing.

Tips

+ Set aside a special area of the classroom for you to work with students or for students to work with each other.

+ You don't have to meet with every student every day.

+ Conferences should be brief; don't overwhelm students with too many comments or suggestions. Several short conferences are often more effective than one long one.

+ If appropriate, suggest that students take notes to help them remember where changes are to be made.

◆ Don't take ownership of the students' work. Encourage students to identify what is good and what needs to be changed, and let the students make the changes.

◆ Focus on what is good about the students' work; discuss how to solve problems rather than telling students what to do.

◆ Peer conferencing should be encouraged during Workshop.

◆ As students engage in peer conferencing, note which students are participating, the types of questions they ask, and the comments they make. Use this information to help students become more effective in peer conferencing.

◆ You may need to structure peer conferences by asking students to first explain what they liked about the composition, and then teaching them how to give constructive feedback.

Having students present or share their work provides another opportunity for them to receive feedback about their writing. Student presentations can involve

◆ presenting an initial idea or plan for a writing assignment.

◆ sharing a first draft of a paper.

◆ presenting orally part or all of a final piece of writing.

Tips

◆ Everyone must listen carefully and provide constructive feedback. Focus on what is good about a piece and ways to make it better.

◆ The student author has ownership and can decide which suggestions to use. The author does not have to incorporate all suggestions from the audience.

◆ Have a chair designated as the "Author's Chair" from which the student author can read his or her work or share ideas. This lends importance to the activity.

◆ The student author should be encouraged to give a bit of background, including where he or she is in the process, why he or she chose a particular part, or what problem he or she is having. This helps orient the audience.

◆ Short pieces of writing can be read in their entirety. As students become more proficient and write longer papers, they should be encouraged to read just a part of their writing; for example, a part they need help with, a part that has been revised, or a part they particularly like.

◆ Take notes during the presentations, and encourage older students to do the same.

◆ Be sensitive to the attention span of the class and the feedback being given. Students have a tendency to repeat the same comments to each author.

Word Processing and Other Aspects of Electronic Composing

Using a word processor to compose a piece of writing makes many aspects of the writing process easier. Text can easily be changed, deleted, or moved during drafting or revising. Software such as spell-checkers or word prediction provides assistance with basic writing skills. Information for writing can be obtained on-line or through other electronic sources, such as encyclopedias. Students can use publishing software to develop a more polished and attractive final product by adding pictures to their composition, developing a cover, changing fonts, and so on. *SRA Imagine It!* supports the use of these technologies.

Teaching Basic Writing Skills

Purpose

Young writers need to learn many basic writing skills to the point that the skills can be executed with minimal effort so they do not interfere with other writing processes. Correct handwriting, spelling, and grammar should be mastered to the point that they require little attention on the part of the writer. While sentences cannot and should not be constructed without conscious attention and effort, developing writers need to become familiar with different sentence types, and they need to become proficient at building them.

Procedures

Sentence Construction

SRA Imagine It! teaches sentence construction skills through the use of sentence frames, sentence expansion, and sentence combining.

◆ **Sentence Frames** With sentence frames, students are given part of a sentence and asked to generate the rest of it. For example, students can be taught to write a simple sentence, with a single subject and predicate, by giving them a frame containing the subject (The dog _____ _____.) and asking them to complete the sentence by telling what happened (The dog ran.).

◆ **Sentence Expansion** With sentence expansion, students are given a kernel sentence and asked to expand it by adding additional words. For example, students can be taught to make sentences more colorful by adding descriptive words to a kernel sentence: Rewrite **The cat and dog like the toy** so the sentence tells more about the cat and dog and the toy — The big dog and gray cat like the fuzzy little toy.

◆ **Sentence combining** With sentence combining, students learn how to combine two or more kernel sentences into a more complex single sentence. For example, you can lead students to produce sentences with relative clauses by combining the following two sentences:

John will win the race.

John is very fast. (who)

John, who is very fast, will win the race.

When teaching sentence construction skills, the following three steps should be followed:

◆ Describe the skill, establish why it is important, and model how to use it.

◆ Provide students with assistance until they can apply the skill correctly and independently.

◆ Ask students to apply the skill when they write.

Tips

✦ Use more than one method to teach a sentence construction skill.

✦ Ask students to monitor how often they use the sentence construction skill.

✦ Encourage students to set goals to use sentence construction skills in their writing.

Handwriting

Students need to develop both legible and fluent handwriting. An important aspect of meeting this goal is to teach them an efficient pattern for forming individual letters (both lowercase and uppercase letters). Effective teaching procedures include

✦ modeling how to form the letter.

✦ describing how the letter is similar to and different from other letters.

✦ using visual cues, such as numbered arrows, as a guide to letter formation.

✦ providing practice tracing, copying, and writing the letter from memory.

✦ keeping instructional sessions short, with frequent review and practice.

✦ asking students to identify or circle their best formed letter or letters.

✦ encouraging students to correct or rewrite poorly formed letters.

✦ monitoring students' practice to ensure that letters are formed correctly.

✦ reinforcing students' successful efforts and providing corrective feedback as needed.

In addition to learning how to write the letters of the alphabet correctly, students must be able to produce them quickly. Fluency generally develops as a consequence of writing frequently, but it can also be fostered by having students copy short passages several times, and trying to write them a little faster each time.

Tips

✦ Make sure that each student develops a comfortable and efficient pencil grip.

✦ Encourage students to sit in an upright position, leaning slightly forward, as they write.

✦ Show students how to place or position their papers when writing.

✦ Implement appropriate procedures for left-handed writers, such as how to properly place or position their papers when writing.

✦ Monitor students' handwriting, paying special attention to their instructional needs in letter formation, spacing, slant, alignment, size, and line quality.

✦ Encourage students to make all final drafts of their papers neat and legible.

Spelling

Purpose

To become good spellers, students must learn to spell correctly and easily the words they are most likely to use when writing. They need to be able to generate and check plausible spellings for words whose spellings are uncertain. They also need to learn to use external sources such as spell-checkers to ensure correct spelling during writing. In **SRA Imagine It!** students are taught how to spell words they frequently use when writing as well as spelling patterns that help them spell untaught words.

Tips

✦ Teach students an effective strategy for studying spelling words.

✦ Reinforce the correct spelling of taught words in students' writing.

✦ Have students build words from letters or letters and phonograms, for example, c - at.

✦ Teach strategies for determining and checking the spelling of unknown words.

✦ Model the use of correct spelling and how to correct spelling errors when you write in front of the class.

✦ Encourage students to correct misspelled words in all final drafts of their writing.

✦ Provide instruction and practice in proofreading.

✦ Encourage students to use spell-checkers, dictionaries, and so on to determine the correct spelling of unknown words.

Grammar and Usage

Traditional methods of teaching grammar and usage skills are not effective. With such instruction, students are initially provided with an abstract definition, such as an adjective is a word that describes a noun or pronoun. This is often followed by asking students to practice applying the skill correctly without actually generating any textual material longer than a word or a phrase. For example, students might be asked to complete the following sentence: The _____ wagon rolled through the _____ town. It is not surprising that many students do not understand the rules they are taught or how to use them in their writing, because such instruction is abstract and decontextualized.

To make grammar instruction effective, **SRA Imagine It!** applies the following five principles. To make these principles concrete, the program illustrates each as it would apply to the rule for capitalizing the first letter in a person's name.

✦ Grammar and usage skills need to be defined in a functional and concrete manner. The rule of capitalizing the first letter in a person's name can be introduced by writing a sentence with two or three familiar names on the board. With the students' help, identify each name in the sentence, and ask them what they notice about the first letter in each name—They are capital letters. Repeat this process with a second sentence, and then establish the "capitalization rule" with students' help.

✦ As soon as the skill is functionally described or defined, establish why it is important—Capitalizing the first letter in a person's name makes the name stand out and shows respect for the person named. This is an important rule for writing.

✦ Show students how to use the skill when writing. Generate a sentence using the names of students in the class, or have your students help you generate such a sentence. Write it on the board, capitalizing the first letter while simultaneously telling the class what you are doing.

◆ Provide students with guided practice in applying the skill when writing. Generate with the class another sentence that includes three of your students' names. Tell the class you will write the sentence on the board, but they will need to tell you when to capitalize a word. Next, have students work together in pairs to generate two sentences using names of their friends, capitalizing the first letter in each name. Provide support as needed. Finally, have each student generate one sentence of his or her own containing two names. Monitor to ensure that students capitalize the first letter in each name. Have them share their sentences with a peer.

◆ Ask students to apply the skill in their compositions. Have students look at one of the papers in their writing portfolio and correct any capitalization mistakes involving people's names. Remind students to capitalize people's names when writing and revising subsequent writing assignments.

Tips

◆ Ask students to correct other students' papers, focusing on specific grammar and usage rules and mistakes.

◆ Encourage students to read their papers aloud when revising. This will help them spot grammar and usage mistakes.

Fostering Motivation

Purpose

Children start school wanting to learn how to write and enjoying writing. Too quickly, however, many begin to view writing as a chore or something to be avoided. The goal of *SRA Imagine It!* writing is for children to become lifelong writers—people who enjoy writing and use writing effectively at work as well as in their personal lives.

Procedures

One way to foster an interest in writing is to have students write for real purposes and audiences. This includes having students identify why they are writing and what they hope to accomplish. Likewise, students need to share their writing with others. They are more likely to do their best writing when there is an audience. Students can share their plans, an initial draft, a portion of their composition, or the completed paper with you, their peers, or other children or adults.

Students are also likely to give their best effort when the writing environment is supportive and pleasant. This can be accomplished by the following:

◆ Establishing clear rules for student behavior during the writing period. Keep the rules simple and reasonable in number and consistently reinforce them. Students are not likely to enjoy writing, or learn well, if the classroom environment is chaotic.

◆ Creating a low-risk environment in which students feel comfortable taking risks with their writing. This means being accepting and encouraging of students' efforts and encouraging them to act in the same manner. For example, make it a rule in your class that when someone shares his or her writing, the first thing that you or other students do is say what you liked most about it.

◆ Supporting students as they begin to apply the knowledge, skills, or strategies you teach them. This can include reteaching, providing hints and reminders, giving useful feedback, and initially helping students apply what was taught.

◆ Having students help each other as they plan, draft, revise, edit/proofread, and publish their work. This is most effective when the process of working together is structured. For instance, students are more likely to give good advice for revising if they are asked to focus on specific aspects of the composition, such as identifying places where the writing is unclear or more detail is needed.

◆ Celebrating student success by displaying their work. This can be done by prominently displaying student work in the classroom or in other places in the school. Students can also be asked to publish their work in a class or school newspaper or to read their compositions aloud to younger children, in other classes, or at a special event.

◆ Fostering an "I can do" attitude among your students. Consistently emphasize that the key to good writing is effort and the use of what they have learned.

◆ Setting a positive mood during writing time. Be enthusiastic about writing and what your students write.

Tips

◆ Allow students to make their own decisions and to accomplish as much on their own as possible.

◆ Increase students' ownership of a writing topic by allowing them to develop unique interpretations of the topic.

◆ Encourage students to take ownership of their writing. This includes allowing them to arrange a suitable writing environment, construct a personal plan for accomplishing the writing task, to work at their own pace when possible, and to decide what feedback from you and their peers is most pertinent for revising their writing.

◆ Look for opportunities to give students positive feedback about their work. Let them know when they have done something well in their writing.

◆ Encourage students to monitor their progress. For example, have students select their best writing to keep in a writing portfolio, identifying why they selected each piece.

◆ Show your students that you are a writer too. Share your writing with them. Talk about the various ways you use writing each day.

◆ Connect writing to students' lives and the world in general. Have them document the types of writing they do outside school. Develop a wall chart on which the class can identify how they use writing away from school.

◆ Provide incentives for writing at home. For example, have parents document that their child writes for twenty minutes at home a set number of nights for a month. Provide a special party for these children, allowing each one to select a book to keep from an array of books donated by parents or a sponsoring business partner.

Spelling Strategies

Spelling

Many people find English difficult, because English sound/spelling patterns seem to have hundreds of exceptions. The key to becoming a good speller, however, is not just memorization. The key is recognizing and internalizing English spelling patterns. Some people do this naturally as they read and develop large vocabularies. They intuitively recognize spelling patterns and apply them appropriately. Others need explicit and direct teaching of vocabulary and spelling strategies and spelling patterns before they develop spelling consciousness.

Purpose

Spelling is a fundamental skill in written communication. Although a writer may have wonderful ideas, he or she may find it difficult to communicate those ideas without spelling skills. Learning to spell requires much exposure to text and writing. For many it requires a methodical presentation of English spelling patterns.

English Spelling Patterns

A basic understanding of English spelling patterns will help provide efficient and effective spelling instruction. Just as the goal of phonics instruction is to enable students to read fluently, the goal of spelling instruction is to enable students to write fluently so they can concentrate on ideas rather than spelling.

Sound Patterns Many words are spelled the way they sound. Most consonants and short vowels are very regular. When a student learns the sound/spelling relationships, he or she has the key to spelling many words.

Structural Patterns Structural patterns are employed when adding endings to words. Examples of structural patterns include doubling the final consonant, adding -s or -es to form plurals, and dropping the final e before adding -ing, -ed, -er, or -est. Often these structural patterns are very regular in their application. Many students have little trouble learning these patterns.

Meaning Patterns Many spelling patterns in English are morphological; in other words, the meaning relationship is maintained regardless of how a sound may change. Prefixes, suffixes, and root words that retain their spellings regardless of how they are pronounced are further examples of meaning patterns.

Foreign Language Patterns Many English words are derived from foreign words and retain those language patterns. For example, kindergarten (German), boulevard (French), and ballet (French from Italian) are foreign-language patterns at work in English.

Developmental Stages of Spelling

The most important finding in spelling research in the past thirty years is that students learn to spell in a predictable developmental sequence, much as they learn to read. It appears to take the average student three to six years to progress through the developmental stages and emerge as a fairly competent, mature speller.

Prephonemic The first stage is the prephonemic stage, characterized by random letters arranged either in continuous lines or in wordlike clusters. Only the writer can "read" it, and it may be "read" differently on different days.

Semiphonemic As emergent readers learn that letters stand for sounds, they use particular letters specifically to represent the initial consonant sound and sometimes a few other very salient sounds. This marks the discovery of phonemic awareness that letters represent speech sounds in writing.

Phonemic When students can represent most of the sounds they hear in words, they have entered the phonemic stage of spelling. They spell what they hear, using everything they know about letter sounds, letter names, and familiar words. Many remedial spellers never develop beyond this stage and spell a word the way it sounds whenever they encounter a word they cannot spell.

Transitional or Within-Word Pattern As they are exposed to more difficult words, students discover that not all words are spelled as they sound. They learn that they must include silent letters, spell past tenses with -ed, include a vowel even in unstressed syllables, and remember how words look. The transitional stage represents the transition from primarily phonemic strategies to rule-bound spelling.

Derivational The derivational stage occurs as transitional spellers accumulate a large spelling vocabulary and gain control over affixes, contractions, homophones, and other meaning patterns. They discover that related or derived forms of words share spelling features even if they do not sound the same. As spellers gain control over these subtle word features and spell most words correctly, they become conventional spellers.

Procedures

The spelling lessons are organized around different spelling patterns, beginning with phonetic spelling patterns and progressing to other types of spelling patterns in a logical sequence. Word lists including words from the literature selection focus on the particular patterns in each lesson. In general, the sound patterns occur in the first units at each grade, followed by structural patterns, meaning patterns, and foreign-language patterns in the upper grade levels.

✦ As you begin each new spelling lesson, have students identify the spelling pattern and how it is like and different from other patterns.

✦ Give the pretest to help students focus on the lesson pattern.

✦ Have students proofread their own pretests immediately after the test, crossing out any misspellings and writing the correct spelling.

✦ Have them diagnose whether the errors they made were in the lesson pattern or in another part of the word. Help students determine where they made errors and what type of pattern they should work on to correct them.

✦ As students work through the spelling pages from **Skills Practice,** encourage them to practice the different spelling strategies in the exercises.

Sound Pattern Strategies

Pronunciation Strategy As students encounter an unknown word, have them say the word carefully to hear each sound. Encourage them to check the **Sound/Spelling Cards.** Then have them spell each sound. (/s/ + /i/ + /t/: sit). This strategy builds directly on the Dication and Spelling introduced in kindergarten and taught in Levels 1–3.

Consonant Substitution Have students switch consonants. The vowel spelling usually remains the same. (bat, hat, rat, flat, splat) This is a natural extension of Phonemic Awareness activities begun in prekindergarten and kindergarten.

Vowel Substitution Have students switch vowels. The consonant spellings usually remain the same. (CVC: hit, hat, hut, hot; CVCV: mane, mine; CVVC: boat, beat, bait, beet) This is a natural extension of Phonemic Awareness activities begun in prekindergarten and kindergarten.

Rhyming Word Strategy   Have students think of rhyming words and the rhymes that spell a particular sound. Often the sound will be spelled the same way in another word. (cub, tub, rub) This is a natural extension of Phonemic Awareness activities begun in prekindergarten and kindergarten.

Structural Pattern Strategies

Conventions Strategy   Have students learn the rules and exceptions for adding endings to words (dropping *y*, dropping *e*, doubling the final consonant, and so on).

Proofreading Strategy   Many spelling errors occur because of simple mistakes. Have students check their writing carefully and specifically for spelling.

Visualization Strategy   Have students think about how a word looks. Sometimes words "look" wrong because a wrong spelling pattern has been written. Have them double-check the spelling of any word that looks wrong.

Meaning Pattern Strategies

Family Strategy   When students are not sure of a spelling, have them think of how words from the same base word family are spelled. (critic, criticize, critical; sign, signal, signature; nation, national, nationality)

Meaning Strategy   Have students determine a homophone's meaning to make sure they are using the right word. Knowing prefixes, suffixes, and base words will also help.

Compound Word Strategy   Tell students to break apart a compound and to spell each word. Compounds may not follow convention rules for adding endings. (homework, nonetheless)

Foreign-Language Strategy   Have students think of foreign-language spellings that are different from English spelling patterns. (ballet, boulevard, sauerkraut)

Dictionary Strategy   Ask students to look up the word in a dictionary to make sure their spelling is correct. If they do not know how to spell a word, have them try a few different spellings and look them up to see which one is correct. (fotograph, photograph) Have students use the ***Sound/Spelling Cards*** to help them look up words. This develops a spelling consciousness.

Use the post test to determine understanding of the lesson spelling pattern and to identify any other spelling pattern problems. Encourage student understanding of spelling patterns and use of spelling strategies in all their writing to help transfer spelling skills to writing.

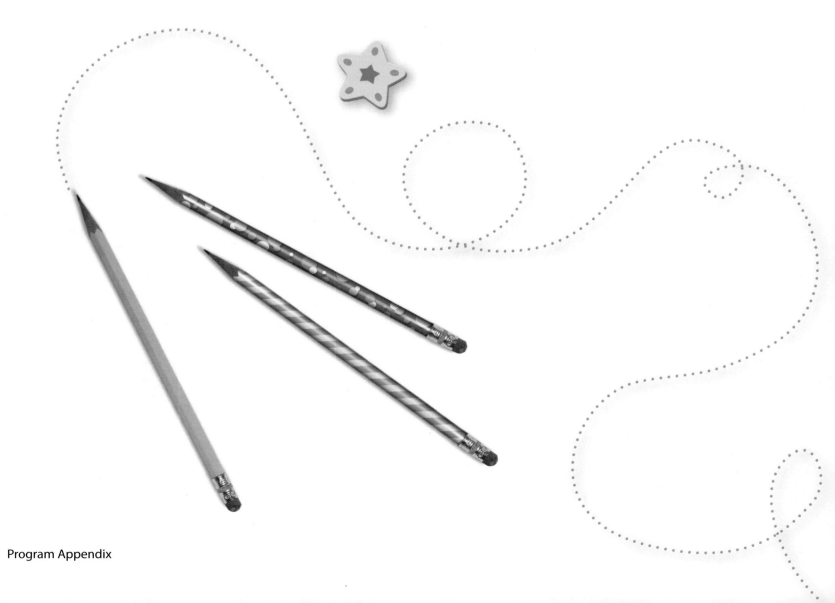

Grammar, Usage, and Mechanics

Purpose

The Study of English Conventions

Over the years the study of grammar, usage, and mechanics has gone in and out of favor. In the past century much research has been done to demonstrate the effectiveness of traditional types of instruction in the conventions of English. Experience and research have shown that learning grammatical terms and completing grammar exercises have little effect on the student's practical application of these skills in the context of speaking or writing. These skills, in and of themselves, do not play a significant role in the way students use language to generate and express their ideas—for example, during the prewriting and drafting phases of the writing process. In fact, emphasis on correct conventions has been shown to have a damaging effect when it is the sole focus of writing instruction. If students are evaluated only on the proper use of spelling, grammar, and punctuation, they tend to write fewer and less complex sentences.

Knowledge of English conventions is, however, vitally important in the editing and proofreading phases of the writing process. A paper riddled with mistakes in grammar, usage, or mechanics is quickly discounted. Many immature writers never revise or edit. They finish the last sentence and turn their papers in to the teacher. Mature writers employ their knowledge of English language conventions in the editing phase to refine and polish their ideas.

The study of grammar, usage, and mechanics is important for two reasons.

1. Educated people need to know and understand the structure of their language, which in large part defines their culture.

2. Knowledge of grammar gives teachers and students a common vocabulary for talking about language and makes discussions of writing tasks more efficient and clearer.

Procedure

The key issue in learning grammar, usage, and mechanics is how to do it. On the one hand, teaching these skills in isolation from writing has been shown to be ineffective and even detrimental if too much emphasis is placed on them. On the other hand, not teaching these skills and having students write without concern for conventions is equally ineffective. The answer is to teach the skills in a context that allows students to directly apply them to a reading or writing activity. Students should be taught proper use of punctuation or subject/verb agreement at the same time they are taught to proofread for those conventions. As they learn to apply their knowledge of conventions during the final stages of the writing process, they will begin to see that correcting errors is an editorial rather than a composition skill.

> *A paper riddled with mistakes in grammar, usage, or mechanics is quickly discounted.*

History of English

A basic understanding of the history and structure of the English language helps students understand the rich but complex resource they have for writing.

Old English

The English language began about A.D. 450 when the Angles, Jutes, and Saxons——three tribes that lived in northern Europe—— invaded the British Isles. Much of their language included words that had to do with farming (*sheep, dirt, tree, earth*). Many of their words are the most frequently used words in the English language today. Because of Latin influences, English became the first of the European languages to be written.

Middle English

In 1066 William the Conqueror invaded England and brought Norman French with him. Slowly Old English and Norman French came together, and Middle English began to appear. Today forty percent of Modern English comes from French. With the introduction of the printing press, English became more widespread.

Modern English

With the Renaissance and its rediscovery of classical Greek and Latin, many new words were created from Greek and Latin word elements. This continued intensively during the Early Modern English period. This rich language was used in the writings of Shakespeare and his contemporaries and profoundly influenced the nature and vocabulary of English. With dictionaries and spelling books, the English language became more standardized, although it continues to be influenced by other languages and new words and trends. These influences continue to make English a living, dynamic language.

Punctuation

Early writing had no punctuation or even spaces between words. English punctuation had its beginning in ancient Greece and Rome. Early punctuation reflected speaking rather than reading. By the end of the eighteenth century, after the invention of printing, most of the rules for punctuation were established, although they were not the same in all languages.

The Structure of English

Grammar is the sound, structure, and meaning system of language. People who speak the same language are able to communicate because they intuitively know the grammar system of that language, the rules to make meaning. All languages have grammar, and yet each language has its own grammar.

Traditional grammar study usually involves two areas:

✦ **Parts of speech** (nouns, verbs, adjectives, adverbs, pronouns, prepositions, conjunctions) are typically considered the content of grammar. The parts of speech involve the form of English words.

✦ **Sentence structure** (subjects, predicates, objects, clauses, phrases) is also included in grammar study. Sentence structure involves the function of English.

Mechanics involves the conventions of punctuation and capitalization. Punctuation helps readers understand writers' messages. Proper punctuation involves marking off sentences according to grammatical structure. In speech students can produce sentences as easily and unconsciously as they can walk, but in writing they must think about what is and what is not a sentence.

In English there are about fourteen punctuation marks (period, comma, quotation mark, question mark, exclamation point, colon, semicolon, apostrophe, hyphen, ellipsis, parenthesis, bracket, dash, and underscore). Most immature writers use only three: period, comma, and question mark. The experienced writer or poet with the command of punctuation adds both flexibility and meaning to his or her sentences through his or her use of punctuation.

Usage is the way in which we speak in a given community. Language varies over time, across national and geographical boundaries, by gender, across age groups, and by socioeconomic status. When the variation occurs within a given language, the different versions of the same language are called dialects. Every language has a prestige dialect associated with education and financial success. In the United States,

this dialect is known as Standard English and is the language of school and business.

Usage involves the word choices people make when speaking certain dialects. Word choices that are perfectly acceptable in conversation among friends may be unacceptable in writing. Usage is often the most obvious indicator of the difference between conversation and composition. Errors in word usage can make a writer seem ignorant and thus jeopardize his or her credibility, no matter how valid or important his or her overall message might be. Usage depends on a student's cultural and linguistic heritage. If the dialect students have learned is not the formal language of school settings or if it is not English, students must master another dialect or language in order to write Standard English.

The Grammar, Usage, and Mechanics lessons in **_SRA Imagine It!_** are structured to focus on skills presented in a logical sequence. A skill is introduced with appropriate models and then practiced in reading and writing on subsequent days to ensure that skills are not taught in isolation. Encourage students to use the focused English language convention presented in each lesson as they complete each Writing Process Strategies activity. Also encourage them to reread their writing, checking for proper use of the conventions taught. With practice, students should be able to apply their knowledge of conventions to any writing they do.

Tips

✦ Some of the errors students make in writing are the result simply of not carefully reading their final drafts. Many errors occur because the writer's train of thought was interrupted and a sentence is not complete or a word is skipped. These may look like huge errors that a simple rereading can remedy. Most

often the writer can correct these types of errors on his or her own. A major emphasis of any English composition program should be to teach the editing and proofreading phases of the writing process so students can eliminate these types of errors themselves. This involves a shift in perception—from thinking of grammar as a set of discrete skills that involve mastery of individual rules to understanding grammar as it applies to the act of communicating in writing.

✦ As students learn English language conventions, they should be expected to incorporate them into their written work.

✦ Sometimes, students write sentences that raise grammatically complex problems that require a deep understanding of English grammar. Use the Sentence Lifting strategies outlined in the Proofreading part of the Appendix to identify and discuss these more sophisticated types of errors that can include the following:

✦ **Faulty Parallelism.**   Parts of a sentence parallel in meaning are not parallel in structure.

✦ **Nonsequiturs.**   A statement does not follow logically from something said previously.

✦ **Dangling Modifiers.**   A phrase or clause does not logically modify the word next to it.

✦ **Awkwardness.**   Sentences are not written simply.

✦ **Wordiness.**   Thoughts are not written in as few words as possible. Precise words are not used.

Listening/Speaking/Viewing

Some people are naturally good listeners, and others have no trouble speaking in front of groups. Many people, however, need explicit instruction on how to tune in for important details and how to organize and make an oral presentation. While some people naturally critique what they read, hear, and see, many others need specific guidance to develop skills for analyzing what they encounter in images and the media. The abilities to listen appropriately and to speak in conversations and in groups, as well as to critically evaluate the information with which they are presented, are fundamental skills that will serve students throughout their lives.

Purpose

In addition to reading and writing, listening, speaking, and viewing complete the language arts picture. Through the development of these language arts skills, students gain flexibility in communicating orally, visually, and in writing. When speaking and listening skills are neglected, many students have difficulty speaking in front of groups, organizing a speech, or distinguishing important information they hear. A top anxiety for many adults is speaking in front of groups. Much of this anxiety would not exist if listening, speaking, and viewing skills were taught from the early years.

The Listening/Speaking/Viewing instruction focuses on the literature selection or the Writing Process Strategies to provide context, to reinforce other elements of the lesson, and to integrate the other language arts. Many of the listening, speaking, and viewing skills are very similar to reading or writing skills. For example, listening for details is the same type of skill as reading for details. Preparing an oral report employs many of the same skills as preparing a written report. Learning to use these skills effectively gives students flexibility in how they approach a task. Furthermore, listening and speaking are naturally integrated into all aspects of learning as students listen and respond to each other during discussions, writing, and Inquiry.

Procedure

Listening, speaking, and viewing skills are presented with increasing sophistication throughout every grade level of **SRA Imagine It!** in the Language Arts part of each lesson. Every unit includes at least one lesson on each of the following skills so that students encounter the skills again and again throughout a grade level:

- **Listening.** Listening skills include comprehending what one hears and listening for different purposes, such as to identify sequence or details, to summarize or draw conclusions, or to follow directions.

- **Speaking.** Speaking skills include speaking formally and conversationally, using appropriate volume, giving oral presentations, and using effective grammar. Speaking skills also include using descriptive words, figurative language, and formal and informal language.

- **Viewing.** Viewing skills include comprehending main ideas and messages in images, mass media, and other multimedia.

- **Interaction.** Interaction instruction focuses on a combination of listening and speaking skills. These include asking and responding to questions; nonverbal cues such as eye contact, facial expression, and posture; and contributing to and interacting in group settings.

- **Presenting Information.** The last Listening/Speaking/Viewing lesson in every unit usually focuses on presentation skills. These include sharing ideas, relating experiences or stories, organizing information, and preparing for speeches. These lessons often parallel the Writing Process Strategies instruction so that students can prepare their information in written or oral form. These skills are an integral part of the Inquiry process as students share their ideas, questions, conjectures, and findings.

Tips

- Identify the parallels among the language arts skills: providing written and oral directions, telling or writing a narrative, and so on. Encourage students to see that they have choices for communicating. Discuss the similarities and differences between different forms of communication, and determine whether one is preferable in a given situation.

- Ensure that all students have opportunities to speak in small groups and whole-class situations.

- Provide and teach students to allow appropriate wait time before someone answers a question.

- Encourage students (when they are able) to take notes to help them remember what they heard so they can better respond.

- Remind students to use visuals when appropriate in their presentations to support their presentations and to help keep the listeners' attention.

- Set up simple class rules to show respect for the listener and speaker. These rules should be used during Inquiry or handing off or any time of the day and should foster respect for the speaker and listeners.

  - Students should speak in a voice loud and clear enough for everyone in the class to hear.

  - Students should raise their hands and not interrupt.

  - If someone asks a question, then the person who responds should address the question before going on to another idea or topic.

  - The speaker should look at the audience, and the audience should look at the speaker.

Inquiry

Even in elementary school, students can produce works of genuine research—research that seeks answers to real questions or solutions to real problems.

Inquiry—research, investigation, and exploration—forms the heart of the *SRA Imagine It!* program. To encourage students to understand how reading and writing are tools for learning that can enhance their lives and help them become mature, educated adults, they are asked in each unit to use the content they are learning in the unit as the basis for further inquiry, exploration, and research. The unit information is simply the base for their investigations.

There are two types of units in the *SRA Imagine It!* program—units based on universal topics of interest such as friendship, heritage, and courage and content units that provide students a very solid base of information upon which they can begin their own inquiry and research. Units delving into science-related areas such as camouflage, energy, and ecology or into social studies units that address American history, geography, or money invite students to become true researchers by exploring personal areas of interest driven by problems or questions raised by students. Based upon common areas of interest, students conduct Inquiry in small collaborative groups and then present their findings to their classmates. In this way, students recognize the importance of sharing knowledge and gain much more knowledge of the unit theme than they would have simply by reading the selections in the unit.

The selections in the units are organized so that each selection will add more information or a different perspective to students' growing bodies of knowledge.

Inquiry through Reflective Activities

Purpose

The units in *SRA Imagine It!* that deal with universal topics tend to be explored through reflective activities. These units—such as Courage, Friendship, and Risks and Consequences—are organized to help students expand—perhaps even change—their perspectives of familiar concepts. As they explore and discuss the concepts that emerge from reading selections related to each unit topic, students are involved in activities that extend their experiences and offer opportunities for reflection. Such activities include writing, drama, art, interviews, debates, and panel discussions. Students will choose the activities and presentation format best suited to explore or investigate their research questions. Throughout each unit, students may be involved in a single ongoing investigative activity, or they may participate in a number of different activities. They may choose to produce a final written project or a multimedia presentation. They will share with the rest of the class the new knowledge that they have gained from their investigations. Workshop provides an ideal time for students to work individually or in collaborative groups on their investigation and/or projects.

The Inquiry activities will be those of students' own choosing, thereby allowing them to explore the unit concepts more fully. They are free, of course, to make other choices or to devise activities of their own.

Procedure

Choosing an Area to Investigate

Students may work on activities alone, in pairs, or in small groups. They have the option of writing about or using other methods for presenting their findings to the entire group. Students should decide what concept-related question or problem they wish to explore. Generally, it is better for students to generate wonderings, questions, or problems after they have engaged in some discussion at the beginning of each unit. This should be done, however, before they have had a chance to consult source materials. The goal is to have students ask questions that will drive their inquiry. This approach is more likely to bring forth ideas that students actually wonder about or wish to understand. Students may also look at the questions posted on the **Concept/Question Board** or introduce fresh ideas inspired by material they have just finished reading.

Inquiry pairs or groups are developed based upon common areas of interest or common questions that appear on the **Concept/Question Board.** Students who share a common interest for inquiry should work together to develop a common question to explore. Some of students may need your assistance in deciding upon, or narrowing down, a question or a problem so that it can be explored more easily. A good way to model this process for students is to make webs for a few of your own ideas on the board and to narrow down these ideas to a workable question or problem.

Organizing the Group

After a question or a problem has been chosen, students may choose an activity that will help them investigate that problem or question. For example, if students in Grade 3 are exploring the question "What are the common characteristics that define friendship?" they may want to develop and conduct a survey of classmates, friends, and so on. To develop the survey, group participants may want to do some additional reading about friendship, explore resources on the Internet, and so on to have a sense of the kinds of questions to include in the survey. Students' next responsibility is to decide who is going to investigate which facet of the question or the problem (when they are conducting a literature search, for example) or who is going to perform which activity related to the particular reflective activity (when they are writing and performing an original playlet or puppet show, for example). Lastly, students need to decide how, or if, they want to present their findings. For instance, after conducting a literature search, some students may want to read and discuss passages from a book with a plot or theme that relates to a unit concept. Other students may prefer performing and discussing scenes from the book.

Deciding How to Investigate

The following suggestions may help you and your students choose ways in which to pursue their investigations. For units on universal topics that are more literary in nature, students may want to do one of the following activities to pursue answers to their questions.

✦ Conduct a literature search to pursue a question or a problem. Discussion or writing may follow.

- Write and produce an original playlet or puppet show based on situations related to the concepts.
- Play a role-playing game to work out a problem related to the concepts.
- Stage a panel discussion with audience participation on a question or problem.
- Hold a debate on an issue related to the concept.
- Write an advice column dealing with problems related to the concepts.
- Write a personal-experience story related to the concepts.
- Invite experts to class. Formulate questions to ask.
- Conduct an interview with someone on a subject related to the concepts.
- Produce and carry out a survey on an issue or a question related to the concept.
- Produce a picture or photo-essay about the concept.

You may want to post this list in the classroom so that groups have access to it as they decide what they want to investigate and how they want to proceed. Encourage students to explore other possibilities as well and to add these ideas to the list.

EXAMPLE: In the Heritage unit in Grade 5 of *SRA Imagine It!,* students read "In Two Worlds: A Yup'ik Eskimo Family." This selection is about how three generations of Eskimos living in Alaska near the Arctic strive to adopt the best of modern ways without abandoning their traditional values. During the class discussion, some students may note that Alice and Billy Rivers want their students to learn both the new and the old ways of living. As the discussion continues, many students may conclude from the story that the older generations hope that future generations will continue to value their roots and their cultural traditions. Students then relate this story to their own heritage. Some students may share information about their customs or traditions.

Students choose some reflective activities that will help them learn more about family heritage and that will answer some of their questions about the unit concepts. These questions may relate to the value of maintaining traditional customs and values versus. adopting contemporary ones. Other students may ask exploring questions related to how to maintain traditional

values in the face of contemporary changes. Some students may be interested in interviewing family members or close family friends about their cultural traditions and heritages or interviewing students in their class about their cultural heritage and then looking for commonalities and differences. These students review what they know about interviewing. They should proceed by performing the following:

- Researching examples of interviews to see what they might look like and how to build in space to write answers
- Preparing a list of questions to ask
- Preparing a list of subjects to interview, deciding how to record the interview (by audiotape, videotape, or taking notes)
- Contacting in advance the person(s) they want to interview
- Deciding whether to photograph the person and, if so, getting permission to do so in advance—collecting the equipment necessary for conducting the interview
- After they conduct the interviews, students decide how they wish to present the information that they have collected.

EXAMPLE: Another group of students in the same fifth-grade class may be more interested in planning a photo-essay about one family or about a neighborhood with many families belonging to a particular culture. These students may decide to reexamine "In Two Worlds" in terms of how the text and the photographs complement each other and what information is conveyed in each photograph. They may also decide to examine some photo-essays listed in the unit bibliography. These students will need to make some advance preparations as well. They should proceed by performing the following:

- Determining which neighborhood and which family or families to photograph
- Contacting in advance the persons to be interviewed and photographed
- Touring the neighborhood in advance of the photo shoot
- Making a list of questions to ask the family or families about their heritage or about their neighborhood
- Thinking about what information to include in their essay so that they can

determine what photographs to take

- Collecting the equipment necessary for conducting interviews and photographing subjects

After students collect the information and take photographs, they may write and organize the photo-essay and present it to the class. The teacher should remind students of the phases of the writing process and encourage them to plan, draft, revise, and edit/proofread their work until they are completely satisfied with it.

Not all questions on the **Concept/ Question Board** will be explored in depth. Throughout the unit, students can continue discussing family heritage and raising and posting new questions. The teacher should remind them that as they read further, they may think of additional ways to explore the unit concepts. Students should sign or initial their questions or ideas so that they can identify classmates with similar interests and exchange ideas with them. The teacher should encourage students to feel free to write an answer or a note on someone else's question or to consult the Board for ideas for their own explorations. From time to time, the teacher should post his or her own questions on the **Concept/Question Board.**

Tips

- The *Leveled Readers* contain books related to the unit concepts. Remind students that these are good sources of information and that they should consult them regularly—especially when they are investigating concept-related ideas and questions.
- Some students work better within a specified time frame. Whenever they are beginning a new activity, discuss with students a reasonable period of time within which they will be expected to complete their investigations. Post the completion date somewhere in the classroom so that students can refer to it and pace themselves accordingly. At first, you may have to help them determine a suitable deadline, but eventually they should be able to make this judgment on their own.
- Some teachers like to do the Inquiry for the first unit with a common question decided upon by the whole class. Then students break into small groups and work on different ways to explore the question. One group may do a literature search while another might conduct a survey. The end results in students sharing new knowledge that addresses

the common research question.

Inquiry through Research

Purpose

Students come to school with a wealth of fascinating questions. Educators need to capitalize on this excitement for learning and natural curiosity. A classroom in which the teacher is the only person who asks the questions and defines the assignments, only correct answers are accepted, and students are not allowed to make errors and consider alternative possibilities to questions can quickly deaden this natural curiosity and enthusiasm. The purpose of the inquiry and research aspect of this program is to capitalize on students' questions and natural curiosity by using a framework or structure based upon the scientific method. This structure helps students ask questions and preserve the open-ended character of real research, which can lead to unexpected findings and to questions that were not originally considered.

The conventional approach to school research papers can be found, with minor variations, in countless textbooks and instructional resources. This approach consists of a series of steps such as the following: Select a topic or choose a topic from a list suggested by the teacher, narrow the topic to something of interest, collect materials, take notes, outline, and write. By following these steps, a student may produce a presentable paper, but the procedure does not constitute research in a meaningful sense. Indeed, this restrictive approach gives students a distorted notion of what research is about. We see students in universities and even in graduate schools still following this procedure when they do library research papers or literature reviews; we see their dismay when their professors regard such work as mere cutting and pasting and ask them where their original contribution is.

Elementary school students can produce works of genuine research—research that seeks answers to real questions or solutions to real problems—when they are provided the opportunity, taught how to ask good questions and develop conjectures, and work collaboratively to find information or data that will support or refute their conjecture. Being able to collect, analyze, and evaluate information are critical twenty-first century skills. In the adult world, as knowledgeable consumers, productive members of a sophisticated workforce, and lifelong learners, students will be expected to constantly identify problems, raise questions, analyze new information, and make informed decisions on the basis of this information. Preparing students for the analytic demands of adult life and teaching them how to find answers to their questions are goals of education.

Procedure

To make the research productive, the following important principles are embodied in this approach:

1. Research is focused on problems, not topics.

2. Questions and wonderings are the foundation for inquiry and research.

3. Conjectures—opinions based on less than complete evidence or proof—are derived from questions and guide the research; the research does not simply produce conjectures.

4. New information and data are gathered to test and revise conjectures.

5. Discussion, ongoing feedback, and constructive criticism are important in all phases of the research but especially in the revising of problems and conjectures.

6. The cycle of true research is essentially endless, although presentations of findings are made from time to time; new findings give rise to new problems and conjectures and thus to new cycles of research.

Following a Process

While working with the science and social studies units, students are encouraged to use this framework to keep their research activities focused and on track. Within this framework, there is flexibility. Students may begin with a question, develop a conjecture, and begin collecting information only to find that they need to redefine their conjecture. Like the writing process, there is a recursive nature to this framework. Students may go through these steps many times before they come to the end of their research. Certainly for adult researchers, this cycle of question, conjecture, research, and reevaluation can go on for years and, in some cases, lifetimes.

This cycle uses the following process:

1. Decide on a problem or question to research. Students should identify a question or problem that they truly wonder about or wish to understand and then form research groups with other students who have the same interests.
   - My problem or question is _____.

2. Formulate an idea or conjecture about the research problem. Students should think about and discuss with classmates possible answers to their research problems or questions and meet with their research groups to discuss and record their ideas or conjectures.
   - My idea/conjecture/theory about this question or problem is _____.

3. Identify needs and make plans. Students should identify knowledge needs related to their conjectures and meet with their research groups to determine which resources to consult and to make individual job assignments. Students should also meet periodically with the teacher, other classmates, and research groups to present preliminary findings and to make revisions to their problems and conjectures on the basis of these findings.
   - I need to find out _____.
   - To do this, I will need these resources: _____
   - My role in the group is _____.
   - This is what I have learned so far: _____
   - This is what happened when we presented our findings _____

4. Reevaluate the problem or question based on what we have learned so far and the feedback we have received.
   - My revised problem or question is _____.

5. Revise the idea or conjecture.
   - My new conjecture about this problem is _____.

6. Identify new needs and make new plans.
   - Based on what I found out, I still need to know _____.
   - To do this, I will need these resources: _____
   - This is what I have learned: _____
   - This is what happened when we presented our new findings: _____

Procedure for Choosing a Problem to Research

1. Discuss with students the nature of the unit. Explain to students that the

unit they are reading is a research unit and that they will produce and publish in some way the results of their explorations. They are free to decide what problems or questions they wish to explore, with whom they want to work, and how they want to present their finished products. They may publish a piece of writing, produce a poster, write and perform a play, or use any other means to present the results of their investigations and research. They may work individually, with partners, or in small groups.

2. Discuss with students the schedule you have planned for their investigations: how long the project is expected to take, how much time will be available for research, when the first presentation will be due. This schedule will partly determine the nature of the problems that students should be encouraged to work on and the depth of the inquiry students will be encouraged to pursue.

3. Have students talk about things they wonder about that are related to the unit subject. For example, in the Grade 3 unit Money, students might wonder where money in the money machine comes from or how prices are determined. Conduct a free-floating discussion of questions about the unit subject.

4. Brainstorm possible questions for students to think about. It is essential that students' own ideas and questions be the starting point of all inquiry. Helpful hint: For the first research unit, you might wish to generate a list of your own ideas, having students add to this list and having them choose from it.

5. Using their wonderings, model for students the difference between a research topic and a research problem or question by providing several examples. For example, have them consider the difference between the topic *California* and the problem *Why do so many people move to California?* Explain to them that if they choose to research the topic *California,* everything they look up under the subject heading or index entry *California* will be related in some way to their topic. Therefore, it will be quite difficult to choose which information to record. This excess of information also creates problems in organizing their research. Clearly, then, this topic is too broad and general. Choosing a specific question or problem, one that particularly interests them, helps them

narrow their exploration and advance their understanding. Some possible ideas for questions can be found in the unit introduction. Ideas can also be generated as you and your students create a web of their questions or problems related to the unit concept. For example, questions related to the topic *California* might include the following: Why do so many people move to California? How have the different groups of people living in California affected the state?

6. A good research problem or question not only requires students to consult a variety of sources but is engaging and adds to the groups' knowledge of the concepts. Furthermore, good problems generate more questions. Help students understand that the question *Why do so many people move to California?* is an easy one to research. Many sources will contribute to an answer to the question, and all information located can be easily evaluated in terms of usefulness in answering the question. Helpful hint: Students' initial responses may indeed be topics instead of problems or questions. If so, the following questions might be helpful: What aspect of the topic really interests you? Can you turn that idea into a question?

7. Remember that this initial problem or question serves only as a guide for research. As students begin collecting information and collaborating with classmates, their ideas will change, and they can revise their research problem or question. Frequently, students do not sufficiently revise their problems until after they have had time to consider their conjectures and to collect information.

8. As students begin formulating their research problems, have them elaborate on their reasons for wanting to research their stated problems. They should go beyond simple expressions of interest or liking and indicate what is puzzling, important, or potentially informative, and so forth about the problems they have chosen.

9. At this stage, students' ideas will be of a very vague and limited sort. The important thing is to start them thinking about what really interests them and what value it has to them and the class.

10. Have students present their proposed problems or questions, along with reasons for their choices, and have

an open discussion of how promising proposed problems are. As students present their proposed problems, ask them what new things they think they will be learning from their investigations and how that will add to the group's growing knowledge of the concepts. This constant emphasis on group knowledge building will help set a clear purpose for students' research.

11. Form research groups. To make it easier for students to form groups, they may record their problems on the board or on self-sticking notes. Final groups should be constituted in the way you find best for your class—by self-selection, by assignment on the basis of common interests, or by some combination of methods. Students can then meet during Workshop to agree on a precise statement of their research problem, the nature of their expected research contributions, and lists of related questions that may help later in assigning individual roles. They should also record any scheduling information that can be added to the planning calendar.

Using Technology

Students and teachers can access the Web site **www.SRAonline.com** to find information about the themes in their grade level.

What does Inquiry look like in the classroom?

Inquiry is a new concept for many students and is performed over an extended period of time. The following series of vignettes are an example of what Inquiry might look like in a third-grade classroom that is studying the third-grade unit Money.

Lesson 1

Developing questions

For the unit on money, Ms. Hernandes introduced the theme through "A New Coat for Anna" and now is focusing on having her students generate some questions. To maximize the number of resources available to her students to do their inquiry, she talked with the librarian at her local library as well as local high school teachers who are knowledgeable in the area. Both were able to provide resources for the class. Ms. Hernandes began with a discussion of money. She had prepared some basic questions to get the class started.

- Why do you think it is important to have a system of money like ours?
- What is money?
- Why do you think we have both paper money and coins?
- How have you learned about money?
- How would your life change if suddenly there were no money in the world?
- When people are using credit cards to pay for something, are they paying with real money?
- When someone writes a check, are they paying with real money?
- What is the difference between credit cards and checks and cash, or actual money?
- Why do you think people use credit cards and checks instead of cash?

The teacher felt that using open-ended questions like these would help get her students talking about what they know about money as well as give her an opportunity to informally assess students' background knowledge.

Students were able to provide some basic information such as the following:

- Money is used to buy things.
- There was not always money in the world.
- Some people used things such as animals instead of money.
- Sometimes people traded things to get something they wanted.
- Coins are made of metal.
- Some things cost more than other things.
- Sometimes you need to determine ways to get things when you do not have money.

But there were some basic misunderstandings that arose during the conversation, such as the following:

- All countries use dollars and cents.
- Everything costs the same no matter where you live.

- Money is made of paper.
- You can use credit cards whenever you want.

By discussing money in such general terms, students were able to share basic information.

To move students to the next level—asking questions—Ms. Hernandes began by thinking aloud about things related to the unit that interested her.

"I really am curious about how money is made. And another thing I've wondered about is how the government knows how much money to print." Ms. Hernandes encouraged her students to share some of their wonderings or things they are curious about. Some student wonderings included the following:

- What kind of money do people in other countries use?
- Does everyone make the same amount of money?
- What would happen if there were only credit cards and no money?
- How much money do people make?
- Does ripped money get thrown away?
- How come we cannot make our own money?

Lesson 2

Forming groups based on shared interest

Developing good research questions

Ms. Hernandes and her class have been reading about money for the past week. Many students read different trade books during Workshop to learn more about money. Every day at the end of Workshop, they shared some of their new questions. Some students even started bringing in articles from newspapers and magazines and posting them on the **Concept/Question Board.**

By now there are a number of questions on the **Concept/Question Board** and Ms. Hernandes wants to work with the class to generate more questions that will help students connect what they are learning in school to the real world. She began by modeling or thinking aloud and sharing some of her own thoughts: "I know that at the checkout stand in stores, you can buy plastic cards that have a dollar amount printed on them. I wonder how might this change our whole idea about money. Maybe instead of getting cash from the automatic

money machines, we'll get a coded card."

The focus is on asking questions. She recognized that students' questions needed to be refined to lead to functional conjectures. The class discussed what makes a good question.

- Questions or wonderings should be things that students are truly curious about.
- Questions should be generated without consulting an encyclopedia or a reference source.
- Good questions cannot be answered with a simple *yes* or *no*.
- Questions should help students deepen their understanding of the unit theme rather than focus on a character or incident in a specific story.
- A good research question often begins with *how*.

Ms. Hernandes and the class talked about their questions and how to refine them. For example, one question the class raised earlier was "Does money change?" The class decided to change the question to "How does money change over time?"

- What possible changes might we see in the future?
- Given the changes in technology today, how might our use of money change over time?

Based on the selections the class has read, students generated the following questions to add to their existing ones on the **Concept/Question Board:**

- I wonder when and how the government decided to change coins and bills.
- I wonder if the government can ever run out of money.
- What happens when people make fake money?
- How do people choose the metals they use to make coins?
- How can money be made so people cannot copy it or make counterfeits?
- What do other countries use for money?
- Where do you save money?

To help move students toward developing some good questions for inquiry, the class reviewed all the questions and grouped them together. They discussed these groups of questions and decided to think of a good representative question. The class worked over the next couple of days to think of a question they were all interested in.

Lesson 3

Forming Conjectures

Identifying Needs and Making Plans

A goal of Inquiry is to have students move from asking questions to forming conjectures. Ms. Hernandes explained to the class that they were now going to take their question and develop a conjecture. Developing a conjecture simply means thinking of what they think the best answer is, given what they know now and have read so far.

Ms. Hernandes modeled this by using one of the questions students raised in the earlier lesson. The question was "How do people choose the metals to make coins?" Ms. Hernandes thought aloud about possible answers to this question: "I think that people choose a strong metal that will last a long time but that is not too heavy for people to carry."

Then Ms. Hernandes wrote the question the class thought of last week. They discussed the question and talked about what possible answers they might find. The question the class decided to focus on was "How is money made so that people cannot copy it?"

The class conjecture was "Special paper and really detailed pictures are used so no one can copy it." However, Ms. Hernandes realized that there could be other conjectures for the same question. She arranged the class into small groups and had them think about other possible conjectures. Some additional conjectures included the following:

- Every dollar has a different number that is recorded in a computer.
- Special ink is used so colors cannot be duplicated.
- When you hold up a bill to the light, you can see a special band in it that maybe only a special government machine can make.

At the end of the lesson, Ms. Hernandes created a chart with the question and all the conjectures students developed.

During the week, Ms. Hernandes continued working with the class on Inquiry. To help the group get started on identifying needs and materials related to their conjecture, Ms. Hernandes asked the following questions:

- What information will we need to help us decide if our conjecture is accurate?
- Where can we find this information?
- Who can help us find information related to our conjecture?
- What people in our school might be able to help us?
- What family members might know something about this?
- What words could we plug in on the Internet to help us get more information?

During the rest of this week, students started collecting different resources and reading various books during Workshop. Students were encouraged to take notes and to share with their groups each day.

Lesson 4

Revising Plans as Necessary

Collecting Data and Information

Now that students have started collecting material, they need to identify individual job assignments so they are not duplicating efforts. At the beginning of this week, Ms. Hernandes took time to have students meet in their groups. During this time she met with the small groups to track their progress, discuss any problems, and help them focus their research efforts.

The group working with the conjecture "Every dollar has a different number that is recorded in a computer" was having trouble finding information to support or refute their conjecture. They had looked in books but did not really find anything. As they talked with the teacher, someone mentioned the term *mint*. As they discussed what happened in the mint, someone suggested that they write the mint with their question to see if they could get some help. This simple activity led students to the Internet to find out the address of the mint. They then spent the rest of that period composing a letter.

At the end of Inquiry that day, Ms. Hernandes made time for each group to present a summary of what it had done. If the group had any unsolved problems, it shared them with the class to get possible suggestions on how to solve the problems. When the group who wrote to the mint shared its problem and solution, several other groups realized that the Internet would be a good resource for them to use as well.

Lesson 5

Continuing Working and Planning Final Presentation

At this point students are beginning to conclude their investigations. Several of the groups realized as they collected information that they really needed to change or revise their conjectures. Ms. Hernandes asked in what ways their ideas have changed—what do they know now that they did not know before? For example, the group that had the conjecture that special ink was used so colors cannot be duplicated revised its conjecture by broadening it. After doing some research, their new conjecture was that there are many different things that the government does in addition to using special ink to protect money from being copied.

As groups presented their conjectures and progress, Ms. Hernandes modeled constructive comments such as the following: "Your points are clearly made." "Your charts and graphs help us understand each of your points." "Each one of you presented different pieces of information that all connect to your conjecture." "How was your conjecture supported?" After the lesson, Ms. Hernandes took time to reflect and realized that it was very hard for her students to give constructive feedback. She knew that this is an area they would need to work on. She would have to continue modeling but also thought about having groups exchange conjectures and provide feedback in writing to each other. This might reduce anxiety as well as give students time to reflect on the questions and conjectures and to develop some thoughtful feedback.

During this week, Ms. Hernandes took time to discuss possible ways that students could present their findings. The class brainstormed other ideas including the following:

- Writing a series of articles on their information for a magazine
- Creating a poster with diagrams of a process
- A panel discussion
- A computer presentation

Students returned to their groups to decide how they wanted to present their findings.

Final Presentation

Students have been busy working on completing their investigations and developing their presentations. While the class decided on a single research question at the beginning of the unit, different groups developed their own conjectures. Because their conjectures guided their research, each group will be presenting different information. Ms. Hernandes has created a simple web with the class's research question in the center and circles around the question. After groups present their work, the class will discuss what information was found to address the research question. As presentations are made, students will also be encouraged to make connections not only to the question but to each other's findings.

Throughout the unit, Ms. Hernandes recognized that students need more work on asking questions of each other and providing constructive feedback. She plans on modeling questions and comments as groups complete their presentations. Some examples include the following:

- How does what you presented support or refute your conjecture?
- Would you clarify . . .
- It would be helpful if . . .
- Have you thought about . . .
- Your visuals really helped me better understand your ideas.
- That was a great idea. Where can we find more information on it so we can learn more about it?
- What other questions did you think of as you were researching your conjecture?

Overall, Ms. Hernandes felt that this first attempt at Inquiry with the entire class focusing on a single question but generating multiple conjectures made Inquiry manageable for students and herself. Ms. Hernandes is now thinking about how to plan the next Inquiry unit so there are multiple questions as well as multiple conjectures. From the final presentations, she has really begun to appreciate how Inquiry incorporates all the reading and writing skills she has been teaching and how it takes students to the next level of learning—delving deeper into ideas that personally interest them, taking time and responsibility to learn about something, working collaboratively, and sharing new ideas and information.

Tips

- Inquiry takes time to develop. You may want to do the first unit as an entire class.
- Provide time throughout the unit for students to work on Inquiry. Use Workshop as well as computer and library time to support Inquiry.
- If students are careful about the problems or questions they choose to research, they should have few problems in following through with the research. If the problem is too broad or too narrow, they will have problems.

- Have students take sufficient time in assessing their needs—both knowledge needs and physical needs in relation to their research. Careful preplanning can help the research progress smoothly with great results.
- Encourage students to reevaluate their needs often so they are not wasting time finding things they already have or ignoring needs that they have not noticed.
- Interim presentations of material are every bit as important, if not more so, than final presentations. It is during interim presentations that students have the opportunity to rethink and reevaluate their work and change direction or to decide to carry on with their planned research.
- Connect Inquiry to learning in the content areas. Have students apply their Inquiry skills to learning science, social studies, and the arts.

Assessment

Assessment can be your most effective teaching tool if it is used with the purpose of informing instruction and highlighting areas that need special attention.

Purpose

The assessment components of **SRA Imagine It!** are designed to help you make informed instructional decisions, make adequate yearly progress, and help ensure you meet the needs of all your students. The variety of assessments is intended to be used continuously and formatively. That is, students should be assessed regularly as a follow-up to instructional activities, and the results of the assessment should be used to inform subsequent instruction.

You can use assessment as a tool to monitor students' progress, to diagnose students' strengths and weaknesses, to prescribe forms of intervention as necessary, and to measure student outcomes. Both formal and informal assessment can be used, though formal assessment will be your main assessment tool. Formal assessment of student learning consists of performance assessment (both reading and writing), objective tests (multiple choice, short answer, and essay), progress assessment (through students' everyday oral and written work), and assessment rubrics (used for writing, inquiry, and comprehension strategies). Informal assessment can be done by observing or listening to students as they work and jotting down notes either in the Comprehension Observation Log or in a notebook.

Procedure

Formal Assessment

Formal assessment is addressed in **SRA Imagine It!** in the form of **Benchmark Assessments** and **Lesson Assessments.** Both will help you use the results to differentiate instruction, especially for students needing some type of intervention to ensure they will not be at risk for reading failure.

Benchmark Assessments

The **Benchmark Assessments** are a form of general outcome measurement that offer an overall framework for assessment and serve as a predictor of how well students will perform at the end of the school year. Each **Benchmark Assessment** has material that students will learn over the course of the school year, and each **Benchmark Assessment** is of equivalent difficulty. Students are not expected to score high on the initial screening benchmark; instead, students are expected to show growth as they move on to each subsequent benchmark. Only at the end of the year are students expected to have mastered the materials on these assessments.

> *Observing students as they go about their regular classwork can be an effective way to learn your students' strengths and areas of need.*

One **Benchmark Assessment** will be administered at the beginning of the year for screening. This can serve as a baseline score against which you can measure students' progress throughout the year. Subsequent benchmarks will also be given at regular intervals—at the end of every other unit in grades K–1, for a total of six assessments, and at the end of each unit for students in grades 2–6, for a total of seven assessments. Since the tests are of equivalent difficulty and contain the same types of items, students' higher scores will reflect their increasing mastery of the curriculum over the course of the year. Use the data from the **Benchmark Assessments** to identify students who are at risk for reading failure, to identify strengths and weaknesses of students, and to gauge student progress toward high-stakes tests.

Depending upon the grade level, tested benchmark skills include the following:

- letter recognition,
- phonemic/phonological awareness,
- phonics,
- high-frequency word recognition,
- vocabulary,
- spelling,
- grammar, usage, and mechanics,
- comprehension,
- oral fluency, and
- maze fluency.

In addition, a writing assessment is given in the initial screening, at midyear, and also again at the end of the year for students in grades 3–6. This assessment is the type of on-demand writing performance students will encounter in high-stakes tests. Each writing assessment is of equal difficulty, and student outcomes should reflect an increased mastery of writing convention and genre expectations.

Lesson Assessments

The **Lesson Assessments** cover the most important skills featured in the lesson of a given unit—skills that are closely related to reading success and are typically in state and national standards. These assessments will help you determine how well students are grasping the skills and concepts as they are taught and will help inform you about any additional instruction they might need.

The **Lesson Assessments** are easily administered and scored. They feature the same language used in the instructional components of **SRA Imagine It!** and correspond to its sequence of instruction. The format of these weekly assessments range from multiple choice questions to short answer to an extended writing response. Depending upon the grade level, skills assessed include the following:

- letter and number recognition
- phonological and phonemic awareness
- phonics
- print and book awareness
- high frequency words

- selection vocabulary
- spelling
- grammar, usage, and mechanics skills
- comprehension skills
- oral fluency
- writing

The **Lesson Assessments** are offered in several formats so that students can demonstrate their knowledge of content in a number of developmentally appropriate ways. Wherever possible, the assessments are designed to be administered to the whole class or small groups of students. In some cases, however, individually administered assessments are included, such as the oral fluency assessments, as well as critical pre-literacy skills such as phoneme blending or segmentation as well as letter and number recognition.

The **Lesson Assessments** will allow you to monitor students' progress as they are assessed on the specific skills taught in a given lesson. The results will provide instructionally relevant information that you can use to differentiate instruction for students who may need additional learning opportunities.

Progress Assessment

Written Practice

Students work on several different skills throughout the day. Each of these assignments can provide you with valuable information about your students' progress. One very helpful resource that students will work in daily is the **Skills Practice Book** (Levels K–6). The **Skills Practice Books** include lessons that act as practice and reinforcement for the skills lessons taught before and during the reading of the lesson as well as in conjunction with the Language Arts lesson. These skills pages give you a clear picture of students' understanding of the skills taught. Use them as a daily assessment of student progress in the particular skills taught through the program.

Also included in the **Skills Practice Books** are lessons that help students with their Inquiry activities. Students can record what they know about the concepts and what they learn, they can keep a record of their research, and they can practice study and research skills that will help them in all of their schooling. You will be able to monitor their growing ability to make connections, find resources, and enhance their knowledge base as they find the answers to the research questions they have posed.

Dictation

In grades 1–3, students use dictation to practice the sound/spelling associations they are learning and/or reviewing. Collect the dictation papers and look through them to see how the students are doing with writing and with proofreading their words. Record notes on the papers and keep them in the student portfolios.

Portfolios

Portfolios are more than just a collection bin or gathering place for student projects and records. They add balance to an assessment program by providing unique benefits to teachers, students, and families.

- Portfolios help build self-confidence and increase self-esteem as students come to appreciate the value of their work. More importantly, portfolios allow students to reflect on what they know and what they need to learn. At the end of the school year, each student will be able to go through their portfolios and write about their progress.

- Portfolios provide the teacher with an authentic record of what students can do. Just as important, portfolios give students a concrete example of their own progress and development. Thus, portfolios become a valuable source of information for making instructional decisions.

- Portfolios allow families to judge student performance directly. Portfolios are an ideal starting point for discussions about a student's achievements and future goals during teacher/family conferences.

You will find that there are many opportunities to add to students' portfolios.

Fluency

- During partner reading, during Workshop, or at other times of the day, invite students, one at a time, to sit with you and read a story from an appropriate **Decodable** (grades 1–3), **Leveled Readers** (grades 1–6), **Leveled Readers for Science** or **Social Studies** (grades 1–6), or the **Student Reader.**

- As each student reads to you, follow along and make note of any recurring problems the student has while reading. Note students' ability to decode unknown words as well as any attempt—successful or not—to use strategies to clarify or otherwise make sense of what they are reading. From time to time,

check students' fluency by timing their reading and noting how well they are able to sustain the oral reading without faltering.

- If a student has trouble reading a particular **Decodable** or **Leveled Reader,** encourage the student to read the story a few times on her or his own before reading it aloud to you. If the **Decodable** has two stories, use the alternate story to reassess the student a day or two later.

- If after practicing with a particular Decodable Book or Leveled Reader and reading it on his or her own a few times, a student is still experiencing difficulty, try the following:
  - Drop back two **Decodables**. (Continue to drop back until the student is able to read a story with no trouble.) If the student can read that book without problems, move up one book. The same is true for **Leveled Readers.**
  - Continue the process until the student is able to read the current **Decodable** or **Leveled Readers.**

Assessment Rubrics

In addition to the formal assessment opportunities available in **Benchmark Assessments, Lesson Assessments,** and progress assessment, **SRA Imagine It!** provides rubrics for you to evaluate students' performance in comprehension, Inquiry, and writing. Rubrics provide criteria for different levels of performance. Rubrics established before an assignment is given are extremely helpful in evaluating the assignment. When students know what the rubrics for a particular assignment are, they can focus their energies on the key issues. Rubrics can be found in the Level Appendix.

Informal Assessment

Observation

Informal assessment is a part of the everyday classroom routine. Observing students as they go about their regular classwork can be an effective way to learn your students' strengths and areas of need. The more students become accustomed to you jotting down informal notes about their work, the more it will become just another part of classroom life that they accept and take little note of. This gives you the opportunity to assess their progress constantly without the interference and possible drawback of formal testing situations.

One tool that will help you make

informal assessment of student progress a part of your everyday classroom routine is the Comprehension Observation Log. You can record information quickly on this observation sheet and even extend your observations over several days, until you have had a chance to observe each student's performance in a particular area.

- ✦ Enter students' names in the Comprehension Observation Log, found in the **Lesson Assessment Books.**

- ✦ Before each day's lesson begins, decide which students you will observe.

- ✦ Keep the Comprehension Observation Log available so that you can easily record your observations.

- ✦ Decide what aspect of the students' learning you wish to monitor.

- ✦ During each lesson, observe this aspect in the performances of several students.

- ✦ When observing students, do not pull them aside; rather, observe students as part of the regular lesson, either with the whole class or in small groups.

- ✦ Record your observations.

- ✦ It may take four to five days to make sure you have observed and recorded the performance of each student. If you need more information about performance in a particular area for some of your students, you may want to observe them more than once.

Responding to Assessment Results

The point of assessment is to monitor progress in order to inform instruction, diagnose students' strengths and weaknesses, and differentiate instruction for students who need extra practice in certain skills or an extra challenge. **SRA Imagine It!** offers you opportunities to diagnose areas that may cause problems for students, differentiate instruction according to their abilities, monitor their progress on an ongoing basis, and measure student outcomes through **Lesson Assessments** or **Benchmark Assessments,** in addition to high-stakes state assessments. **SRA Imagine It!** also provides several ways to differentiate instruction based on the results of the various assessments. These include the following:

- ✦ Reteach lessons are available for students who are approaching level and appear to grasp a given concept but need more instruction and practice to solidify their learning. Many skills taught in the **Skills Practice Books** are available in a **Reteach** format.

- ✦ Intervention lessons provide options for you to use with students who need more intensive support and who are struggling to understand the on-level material. In addition to the support for the weekly lesson, controlled vocabulary lessons and specific skills lessons can help bring students up to grade level.

- ✦ **English Learner Support** lessons are available for students who are having difficulty with the concepts because they lack the necessary English language background. These resources will provide English Learners with the vocabulary, phonics, comprehension, grammar, and writing support they need to access the **SRA Imagine It!** lessons.

- ✦ **Challenge Activities** provide continued stimulation for those students who are doing well and working above grade level. Many skills covered in the **Skills Practice Books** are also available in **Challenge Activities.**

- ✦ **Workshop Resource Book** activities give students alternative activities to strengthen or extend their skills in areas such as letter recognition, phonics, vocabulary, comprehension, fluency, word structure, and grammar.

- ✦ **Leveled Readers** provide students at all different levels of instruction— Approaching Level, On Level, Above Level, and English Learners—with additional opportunities to practice fluency, vocabulary, and comprehension skills. Besides the general **Leveled Readers, Leveled Readers for Science** and **Leveled Readers for Social Studies** provide students cross-curricular opportunities.

These materials, along with formal and informal assessments, help ensure that assessment and instruction work together to meet every student's needs.

Workshop

Every teacher and every student needs time during the day to organize, to take stock of work that is done, to make plans for work that needs doing, and to finish up incomplete projects. In addition, teachers need time for differentiating instruction, for holding conferences with students, and for doing fluency checks.

Purpose

Workshop is the period of time each day in which students work independently or collaboratively to practice and review material taught in the lessons.

A variety of activities may occur during this time. Students may work on a specific daily assignment, complete an ongoing project, work on unit inquiry activities, focus on writing, or choose from a wide range of possibilities. With lots of guidance and encouragement, students gradually learn to make decisions about their use of time and materials and to collaborate with their peers.

A goal of Workshop is to get students to work independently and productively. This is essential because Workshop is also the time during which the teacher can work with individuals or groups of students to reinforce learning, to provide extra help for those having difficulties, to extend learning, or to assess the progress of the class or of individuals.

Procedure

Initially for many students you will need to structure Workshop carefully. Eventually students will automatically go to the appropriate areas, take up ongoing projects, and get the materials they will need. Workshop will evolve slowly from a very structured period to a time when students make choices and move freely from one activity to the next.

Setting up Workshop guidelines is key. By the time students have completed the first few weeks of school, they should feel confident during Workshop. If not, continue to structure the time and limit options. For young students, early periods of Workshop may run no more than five to eight minutes. The time can gradually increase to fifteen minutes or longer as students gain independence. Older students may be able to work longer and independently from the very beginning of the school year.

Introducing Workshop

Introduce Workshop to students by telling them that every day there will be a time when they are expected to work on activities on their own or in small groups. For younger students explain that in the beginning there may be just a couple of activities but that gradually new ones will be introduced and that students can choose what they want to do. With older students and for those who have experienced Workshop in early grades, you may want to introduce the concept of Workshop and discuss the range of Workshop options from working on fluency to completing their writing.

> *Workshop is the period of time each day in which students work independently or collaboratively to practice and review material taught in the lessons.*

Establish and discuss rules for Workshop with students. Keep them simple and straightforward. You may want to write the finalized rules on the board or on a poster. You may want to review these rules each day at the beginning of Workshop for the first few lessons or so. You may also wish to revisit and revise the rules from time to time. Suggested rules include the following:

- Share.
- Use a quiet voice.
- Take only the materials you need.
- Return materials.
- Always be working.
- When the teacher is working with a student or small group, do not interrupt.

Early in the process, review rules routinely, and discuss how Workshop is going. Is the class quiet enough for everyone to work on his or her own? Are there any rules that need changing? What problems are students having with materials?

For young students in the beginning you will assign the Workshop activities to help them learn to work on their own. Point out the shelf or area of the classroom where Workshop materials are stored. Tell students that when they finish working with the materials for one activity, they will choose something else from the Workshop shelf. New activity materials will be added to the shelf from time to time. Make sure students know that they may always look at books during Workshop.

Tell older students that they will have an opportunity each day to work on their unit inquiry activities, their writing, and other projects. Students will be working independently and collaboratively during this time.

Guidelines

- ✦ Make sure each student knows what he or she needs to do during Workshop.
- ✦ Demonstrate for the entire group any activity or game assigned for Workshop, for example, teaching students a new game, introducing new materials or projects, or explaining different areas.
- ✦ For young students, it is essential to introduce and demonstrate different activities and games before students do them on their own. With games, you may want to have several students play while the others watch. Make sure that all students know exactly what is expected of them.
- ✦ In the beginning, plan to circulate among students, providing encouragement and help as necessary.
- ✦ When students are engaged in appropriate activities and can work independently, meet with those students who need your particular attention. This may include individual students or small groups.
- ✦ Let students know that they need to ask questions and to clarify assignments during Workshop introduction so that you are free to work with small groups.
- ✦ Be sure that students know what they are to do when they have finished an activity and where to put their finished work.

Setting Up Your Classroom for Workshop

Carefully setting up your classroom to accommodate various Workshop activities will help assure that the Workshop period progresses smoothly and effectively. While setting up your classroom, keep the primary Workshop activities in mind. During Workshop, students will be doing independent and collaborative activities. In kindergarten and first grade, these activities may include letter recognition and phonemic awareness activities and writing or illustrating stories or projects. In addition, they will be working on individual or small-group projects.

Many classrooms have areas that students visit on a regular or rotating basis. Unlike traditional centers, all students do not rotate through all the areas each day.

The following are suggestions for space and materials for use during Workshop:

1. Reading Area supplied with books and magazines. The materials in the Reading Area should be dynamic—changing with students' abilities and reflecting unit themes they are reading. You may wish to add books to your classroom library.

2. Writing Area stocked with various types and sizes of lined and unlined paper, pencils, erasers, markers, crayons, small slates, and chalk. The area should also have various **Letter Cards** and other handwriting models for those students who want to practice letter formation or handwriting. Students should know that this is where they come for writing supplies. In addition to the supplies described above, the Writing Area can also have supplies to encourage students to create and write on their own:

   • Magazines and catalogs to cut up for pictures; stickers, paint, glue, glitter, and so on to decorate books and book covers; precut and stapled blank books for students to write in (Some can be plain and some cut in special shapes.)

   • Cardboard, tag board, construction paper, and so on for making book covers (Provide some samples.)

   • Tape, scissors, yarn, hole punches for binding books

   • Picture dictionaries, dictionaries, thesauruses, word lists, and other materials that may encourage independence

3. Listening Area supplied with tape recorder, CD player, optional headphones, and CDs of stories, poems, and songs for students to listen to and react to. You might also want to provide blank tapes and encourage students to retell and record their favorite stories or to make up and tell stories for their classmates to listen to on tape. You may also want to make available the Listening Library CDs that are available with the program.

4. Phonics Activities supplied with **Alphabet Flash Cards,** individual **Alphabet Sound Card** sets (Kindergarten), individual **Sound/ Spelling Cards** and **High-Frequency Flash Cards** (Grades K, 1, 2, and 3), and other materials that enhance what students are learning. Other commonly used classroom materials that enhance reading can be included, for example, plastic letters, puzzles, and games.

5. Fluency Area supplied with **Pre-Decodables and Decodables, Leveled Readers, Leveled Science Readers** and **Leveled Social Studies Readers,** and other resources for practicing fluency. Some teachers have folders for each student with materials to practice during the week. In addition, some Fluency areas have timers and tape recorders as well.

Because students will be working on their inquiry/investigations during Workshop, make sure there are adequate supplies to help them with their research. These might include dictionaries, encyclopedias, magazines, newspapers, and computers— preferably with Internet capability.

Students thrive in an environment that provides structure, repetition, and routine. Within a sound structure, students will gain confidence and independence. This setting allows you to differentiate instruction to provide opportunities for flexibility and individual choice. This will allow students to develop their strengths, abilities, and talents to the fullest.

Suggestions for English Learners

Workshop affords students who are English Learners a wealth of opportunities for gaining proficiency in English. It also encourages them to share their backgrounds with peers. Since you will be working with all students individually and in small groups regardless of their reading ability, students who need special help with language will not feel self-conscious about working with you.

In addition, working in small groups made of students with the same interests rather than the same abilities will provide them with the opportunity to learn about language from their peers during the regular course of Workshop activities.

Some suggestions for meeting the special needs of students with diverse backgrounds are as follows:

✦ Preread a selection with English Learners to help them identify words and ideas they wish to talk about. This will prepare them for discussions with the whole group.

✦ Preteach vocabulary and develop selection concepts that may be a challenge for students.

✦ Negotiate the meaning of selections by asking questions, checking for comprehension, and speaking with English Learners as much as possible.

✦ Draw English Learners into small-group discussions to give them a sense that their ideas are valid and worth attention.

✦ Pair English Learners with native English speakers to share their experiences and to provide new knowledge to other students.

✦ Have English Learners draw or dictate to you or another student a description of a new idea they may have during Workshop activities.

Book Review

Sessions can be small or large. Workshop is a good time for students to share the reading they do on their own. They can discuss a book they have all read, or one person can review a book for the others and answer questions from the group.

During Workshop, students can discuss and review a variety of books:

✦ Full-length versions of **Student Reader** selections

✦ Books that students learn about when discussing authors and illustrators

✦ Books related to the investigations of unit concepts that can be shared with others who might want to read them

✦ Interesting articles from magazines, newspapers, and other sources

When a student reviews a book others have not read, he or she can use some of the sentence starters to tell about the book. These may include "This book is about . . . ," "I chose this book because . . . ," "What I really like/don't like about this book is . . . ," and so on.

◆ When several students read the same book and discuss it during Workshop, they can use discussion starters.

Encouraging Reading

◆ Read aloud to your students regularly. You can read from your classroom library or full-length versions of **Student Reader** selections.

◆ Provide a time each day for students to read silently. This time can be as short as 10–15 minutes but should be strictly observed. You should stop what you are doing and read. Students should be allowed to choose their own reading materials during this time and record their reactions in the response journal section of their Writer's Notebooks.

◆ Establish a classroom library and reading center with books from the school or local library, or ask for donations of books from students, parents, and community members.

◆ Take your students to the school library or to the public library.

Workshop Management Tips

Use the following Workshop management tips to ensure that Workshop runs smoothly. Note that these suggestions for a weekly unit/lesson may not exactly correspond to a particular unit/lesson in a given grade level but will give you a sense of how Workshop should progress. All of the time suggestions depend upon the needs of the class and their readiness to work independently.

Kindergarten through Grade 1

Unit 1, Week 1 Introduce Workshop as whole-class workshop. Explain Workshop and its rules. Give the class an activity to do, for example, putting letters in alphabetical order (Grade 1) or copying their names (kindergarten). Tell the class that they will be doing Workshop today. As they do their activity, you will walk around, observing students and noting how well Workshop is going. The class is working quietly and independently. Workshop may last only a few minutes in kindergarten and about ten minutes in first grade.

Unit 1, Weeks 2 and 3 Depending upon your class, you can move to whole-group Workshop with two activities. Give half the class one activity and the other half the other. Explain to the class that for the next few Workshop sessions, there will be two different activities but that the class is supposed to work quietly and independently. Switch activities for the next day, and repeat this format for the next few days or so. Introduce the concept of "debriefing." Take a few minutes at the end, have several students share what they did or learned during Workshop. You may want to have students tell what they like about Workshop and if any changes need to be made.

Unit 2, Week 1 Begin introducing Workshop Areas, explaining the materials and how they can be used. Explain to students that the materials in these areas will be changing regularly so students will be able to practice and use their new reading and writing skills. Workshop activities should change routinely and reflect the changing nature of the curriculum. Often, during the early weeks of Workshop, teachers assign students to different activities and, as students become ready, turn over to students the responsibility for choosing activities.

Unit 3 Add new activities for students. Encourage them to do a couple of Workshop activities each day, perhaps working on their writing in progress and fluency practice (reading a Pre-Decodable or Decodable). Other options might include on-line phonemic awareness and phonics activities, phonics activities such as word sorts, using blended words in written sentences, practicing high-frequency sight words, and so on.

Unit 4 By this time, students should be making choices and working independently. Each Workshop session may be fifteen minutes long with the teacher working with small groups. Take time to review Workshop activities to be sure they are being used and that students are learning from the activities. If activities become stale, vary them, or change them altogether.

Grades 2–6

Unit 1, Lesson 1 Introduce Workshop to students. Make sure they know where materials are located. Post the rules on the board or other prominent place in the classroom. Keep Workshop time short (less than thirty minutes) and very directed during the first few weeks until students can work independently.

Unit 1, Lesson 2 Discuss using small groups for pre-/reteaching purposes and how you will indicate who will be in the groups. Start by forming one small group randomly and having other students do something specific such as a writing assignment. When you have finished with the small group, send them to do independent work. Call another small group of students to work with you. Continue this each day until students are accustomed to forming groups and working independently.

Unit 1, Lesson 3 Reading Roundtable is a student-formed and student-run book discussion. Encourage students participating in Reading Roundtable to choose a book that they all will read and discuss. Several different Reading Roundtable groups may form on the basis of the books students choose.

Unit 1, Lesson 4 For the first few weeks of the school year, make sure each student has a plan for using Workshop time.

Unit 1, Lesson 5 (Days 1–5) Allow time for presentation and discussion of research activities. Use an entire Workshop day, and have all groups present their findings, or split the presentations over several days, depending on the small-group needs of your class.

Unit 1, Lesson 5 (Days 6–10) Review how students have used Workshop during this unit. Have they used their time well? Do they have the materials they need? Discuss suggestions for improving their use of this time. Take a few minutes at the beginning of each Workshop to make sure students know what they will be doing.

Unit 2, Lesson 1 Form small extra-practice groups with the more advanced students from time to time, as they also need special attention.

Unit 2, Lesson 2 To keep the entire class informed about the independent research being done, every other day or so invite a research group to explain what it is doing, how the research is going, and any problems they are encountering.

Unit 2, Lesson 3 Discuss the use of Workshop time for doing Inquiry and research projects, and share **eInquiry** with different research activities.

Unit 2, Lesson 4 Make sure small extra-practice groups are formed based on your observations of students' work on the different daily lessons. Small groups should be fluid and based on demonstrated need rather than become static and unchanging.

Unit 2, Lesson 5 (Days 1–5) One purpose of Workshop is to help students learn independence and responsibility. Assign students to monitor Workshop materials. They should alert you whenever materials are running low or missing, and they can be responsible for checking on return dates of library books and making sure the books are either returned or renewed.

Unit 2, Lesson 5 (Days 6–10) Students sometimes have difficulty starting discussions in Reading Roundtable. Try some of these discussion starters with students, and print them on a poster for student use.

> I didn't know that . . .
> I liked the part where . . .
> Does anyone know . . .
> I'm still confused by . . .
> I figured out that . . .
> This made me think . . .
> I agree/disagree with because . . .

Unit 3, Lesson 1 By this time students should be accustomed to the routines, rules, expectations, and usage of Workshop time and be moving smoothly from small teacher-led groups to independent work. Monitor small groups occasionally to see that they are on task and making progress on their activities.

Unit 3, Lesson 2 Make a practice of reading aloud to students. All students enjoy being read to, no matter their age or grade. Encourage them to discuss the shared reading in groups and to bring books and read them aloud to their classmates.

Unit 3, Lesson 3 Encourage cooperation and collaboration by providing students with opportunities to engage in small groups.

Unit 3, Lesson 4 Spend a few minutes each day circulating around the room and monitoring what students are doing independently or in small groups. Students can then share with you on a timely basis any questions or problems they are having.

Unit 3, Lesson 5 (Days 1–5) Take note of various small groups. Make sure that quieter students are able to participate in the discussions. Often the stronger, more confident students dominate such discussions. Encourage them to give all participants an opportunity to share their ideas.

Unit 3, Lesson 5 (Days 6–10) If students are not productive during Workshop, keep them in the small group you are working with until they can successfully benefit from independent work. Discuss strategies they could use to become more independent.

Unit 4, Lesson 1 Individual students can monitor Workshop materials and alert you when materials or supplies are running low or missing and can check that library books are either returned or renewed.

Unit 4, Lesson 2 From time to time, join a Reading Roundtable group, and take part in their discussion. Make sure students lead the discussion.

Unit 4, Lesson 3 Encourage responsibility and independence by reminding students to show respect for each other and the materials provided.

Unit 4, Lesson 4 Be sure students discuss during Reading Roundtable what they like or dislike about a book, why they wanted to read it, and how the book either lived up to their expectations or disappointed them. Discussions should not be about basic comprehension but should help students think more deeply about the ideas presented in the book.

Unit 4, Lesson 5 (Days 1–5) Make sure students continue to use the activities provided for use with this unit at **SRAonline.com.**

Unit 4, Lesson 5 (Days 6–10) If students are not productive in Workshop, keep them in the small group you are working with until they can successfully benefit from independent work. Discuss strategies they could use to become more independent.

Unit 5, Lesson 1 Students often make great tutors for other students. They are uniquely qualified to understand problems that others might be having. Encourage students to pair up during Workshop to help each other with their daily lessons.

Unit 5, Lesson 2 Form small extra-practice groups with the more advanced students from time to time, as they also need special attention.

Unit 5, Lesson 3 To keep the entire class informed about the independent research being done, every other day or so, invite a research/investigation group to explain what it is doing, how the research is going, and any problems they are encountering.

Unit 5, Lesson 4 Most of the authors of the **Student Reader** selections are well known and have written many, many pieces of fine literature. Encourage students who enjoy the selections to find other books by the same author. Encourage them to think about and discuss what about that particular author's work attracts them.

Unit 5, Lesson 5 (Days 1–5) Share your impressions of books from your classroom library or other readings during Reading Roundtable. Note which students initiate sharing and which are reluctant to share.

Unit 5, Lesson 5 (Days 6–10) Review with students the time they have used in Workshop. Have they used their time well? Do they have the materials they need? Discuss suggestions for improving the use of this time.

Unit 6, Lesson 1 Spend a few minutes each day circulating and monitoring what students are doing independently or in small groups. Students can share with you on a timely basis any questions or problems they are having.

Unit 6, Lesson 2 Students should be accustomed to the routines, rules, expectations, and usage of Workshop time and be moving smoothly from small teacher-led groups to independent work. Make sure to monitor small groups occasionally to see that they are on task and making progress with their activities.

Unit 6, Lesson 3 Make sure students continue to use the activities provided for use with this unit at **SRAonline.com.**

Unit 6, Lesson 4 If the reading selection is an excerpt from a longer piece, encourage students to read the book from which the excerpt is taken and to discuss how the excerpt fits into the larger work.

Unit 6, Lesson 5 (Days 1–5) Students often make great tutors for other students. The fact that they, too, are just learning the materials makes them uniquely qualified to understand problems that others might be having. Encourage students to pair up during Workshop to help each other on their daily lessons.

Unit 6, Lesson 5 (Days 6–10) Allot time for presentation and discussion of research activities. You may want to use a whole Workshop day and have all groups present their findings or split the presentations over several days, depending on the urgency of the small-group instruction your class needs.

Scope and Sequence

Reading

	K	1	2	3	4	5	6
Print/Book Awareness (Recognize and understand the conventions of print and books)							
Capitalization	X	X					
Constancy of Words		X					
Differentiate between Letter and Word	X						
Differentiate between Word and Sentence	X						
End Punctuation	X	X					
Follow Left-to-Right, Top-to-Bottom	X	X					
Letter Recognition and Formation	X	X					
Page Numbering	X	X					
Parts of a Book	X	X					
Picture/Text Relationship	X	X					
Punctuation	X	X					
Quotation Marks	X	X					
Relationship Between Spoken and Printed Language	X	X					
Sentence Recognition	X	X					
Spacing Between Sentences	X	X					
Spacing Between Words	X	X					
Table of Contents	X	X					
Text Features		X					
Text Relationships		X					
Word Length	X	X					
Word Boundaries		X					
Write Left-to-Right, Top-to-Bottom	X	X					
Phonemic Awareness (Recognize Discrete Sounds in Words)							
Oral Blending: Words/Word Parts	X	X					
Oral Blending: Onset and Rime	X	X					
Oral Blending: Syllables	X	X					
Oral (Phoneme) Blending: Initial Sounds	X	X					
Oral (Phoneme) Blending: Final Sounds	X	X					
Oral Blending: Initial Vowels		X					
Oral Blending: Vowel Replacement		X					
Rhyming	X	X					
Phoneme Matching: Initial Sounds	X	X					
Phoneme Matching: Final Sounds	X	X					
Phoneme Matching: Medial Sounds	X	X					
Phoneme Manipulation: Initial Sounds	X	X					
Phoneme Manipulation: Final Sounds	X	X					
Phoneme Manipulation: Medial Sounds	X	X					
Segmentation: Final Consonants	X	X					
Segmentation: Initial Consonants/Blends		X					
Segmentation: Words/Word Parts	X	X					
Segmentation: Syllables	X	X					
Segmentation: Identifying the Number and Order of Sounds in Words	X	X					

Reading (continued)

	K	1	2	3	4	5	6
How the Alphabet Works							
Letter Knowledge (Alphabetic Knowledge)	X	X					
Letter Order (Alphabetic Order)	X	X					
Letter Sounds	X	X					
Sounds in Words	X	X					
Phonics (Associate Sounds and Spellings to Read Words)							
Blending Sounds into Words	X	X	X	X			
Consonant Clusters		X	X	X			
Consonant Digraphs		X	X	X			
Phonograms		X	X	X			
Schwa			X	X			
Silent Consonants			X	X			
Syllables		X	X	X			
Vowel Diphthongs		X	X	X			
Vowels: Long Sounds and Spellings	X	X	X	X			
Vowels: r-controlled		X	X	X			
Vowels: Short Sounds and Spellings	X	X	X	X			
Comprehension Strategies							
Adjusting Reading Speed			X	X	X	X	X
Asking Questions/Answering Questions	X	X	X	X	X	X	X
Clarifying	X	X	X	X	X	X	X
Making Connections	X	X	X	X	X	X	X
Predicting/Confirming Predictions	X	X	X	X	X	X	X
Summarizing		X	X	X	X	X	X
Visualizing	X	X	X	X	X	X	X
Comprehension Skills							
Author's Point of View			X	X	X	X	X
Author's Purpose			X	X	X	X	X
Cause and Effect	X	X	X	X	X	X	X
Classify and Categorize	X	X	X	X	X	X	X
Compare and Contrast	X	X	X	X	X	X	X
Drawing Conclusions	X	X	X	X	X	X	X
Fact and Opinion			X	X	X	X	X
Main Idea and Details	X	X	X	X	X	X	X
Making Inferences		X	X	X	X	X	X
Reality and Fantasy	X	X	X	X			
Sequence	X	X	X	X	X	X	X
Vocabulary							
Apposition		X	X	X	X	X	X
Concept Words		X	X	X	X	X	X
Context Clues		X	X	X	X	X	X
Expanding Vocabulary		X	X	X	X	X	X
High-Frequency Words	X	X	X	X			
Idioms					X	X	X	X
Multiple-Meaning Words		X	X	X	X	X	X
Selection Vocabulary	X	X	X	X	X	X	X
Time and Order Words (Creating Sequence)	X	X	X	X	X	X	X
Utility Words (Colors, Classroom Objects, etc.)	X	X					

Reading (continued)

Reading with a Writer's Eye	K	1	2	3	4	5	6
Author's Purpose	X		X	X	X	X	
Alliteration			X		X		X
Captions and Headings			X	X		X	X
Characterization	X	X	X	X	X	X	X
Choosing Good Examples					X	X	
Description			X	X	X	X	X
Diagrams							X
Dialect						X	
Dialogue		X	X	X	X	X	X
Effective Beginnings					X	X	
Effective Endings					X		
Event Sequence	X	X	X	X		X	
Expository Writing Techniques					X	X	
Fable Characteristics					X		
Figurative Language		X	X	X	X	X	X
Flashback							X
Genre Knowledge	X		X	X	X	X	X
Idiom						X	X
Irony					X		
Language Use	X		X	X	X	X	X
Mood and Tone		X	X	X			X
Onomatopoeia			X	X	X		X
Personification			X	X		X	X
Persuasive Techniques					X	X	
Plot (Problem/Solution)	X	X	X	X	X	X	X
Point of View					X	X	
Punctuation					X	X	
Quoting Sources					X		
Rhyme	X		X			X	X
Sensory Details		X		X		X	
Sentence Variety						X	
Setting	X	X	X	X	X	X	X
Sidebars							X
Similes and Metaphors					X	X	X
Stage Directions					X		
Style							X
Suspense and Surprise					X		X
Text Structure	X		X	X	X	X	X
Theme	X		X	X	X	X	X
Transitions					X		X
Using Comparisons		X	X	X		X	
Voice					X	X	X
Word Choice					X		X

Word Structure	K	1	2	3	4	5	6
Antonyms			X	X	X	X	X
Comparatives/Superlatives			X	X	X	X	
Compound Words	X	X	X	X	X	X	X
Contractions			X	X	X	X	
Connotation and Denotation							X
Content/Concept Words							X

Reading (continued)

	K	1	2	3	4	5	6
Foreign Words and Phrases						X	X
Gerunds							X
Greek and Latin Roots				X	X	X	X
Homographs			X	X	X	X	X
Homonyms/Homophones			X	X	X	X	X
Inflectional Endings			X	X	X	X	X
Irregular Plurals			X	X	X	X	
Multiple-Meaning Words					X	X	X
Multisyllabic Words			X	X	X	X	
Plurals			X	X	X	X	
Position Words	X	X					
Prefixes			X	X	X	X	X
Root or Base Words			X	X	X	X	X
Shades of Meaning/Levels of Specificity						X	X
Suffixes			X	X	X	X	X
Synonyms			X	X	X	X	X
Word Families			X	X	X	X	X
Word Origins					X	X	X

Inquiry and Study Skills

	K	1	2	3	4	5	6
Study Skills							
Comparing Information across Sources		X		X		X	
Charts, Graphs, and Diagrams/Visual Aids	X	X	X	X	X	X	X
Collaborative Inquiry	X	X	X	X	X	X	X
Communicating Research Progress Results		X	X	X	X	X	X
Compile Notes			X		X	X	X
Conducting an Interview		X	X	X	X	X	X
Finding Needed Information	X	X	X	X	X	X	X
Follow Directions	X		X	X	X		X
Formulate Questions for Inquiry and Research	X	X	X	X	X	X	X
Give Reports	X		X	X	X	X	X
Make Outlines			X	X	X	X	X
Making Conjectures	X	X	X	X	X	X	X
Maps	X	X	X	X	X	X	
Note Taking		X	X	X	X	X	X
Parts of a Book	X	X	X	X	X		
Planning Inquiry		X	X	X	X	X	X
Recognizing Information Needs		X	X	X	X	X	X
Revising Questions and Conjectures	X	X	X	X	X	X	X
Summarize and Organize Information		X	X	X	X	X	X
Time Lines			X	X	X	X	
Use Appropriate Resources (Media Sources, Reference Books, Experts, Internet)		X	X	X	X	X	X
Using a Dictionary/Glossary		X	X	X	X		
Using a Media Center/Library		X	X	X	X		
Using a Thesaurus			X	X	X	X	
Using an Encyclopedia		X	X	X	X		
Using Newspapers and Magazines		X	X		X		X
Using Technology	X	X	X	X	X	X	X

Language Arts
Writing/Composition

	K	1	2	3	4	5	6
Approaches							
Collaborative Writing	X	X	X	X	X	X	X
Individual Writing	X	X	X	X	X	X	X
Writing Process							
Brainstorming/Prewriting	X	X	X	X	X	X	X
Drafting	X	X	X	X	X	X	X
Revising	X	X	X	X	X	X	X
Editing	X	X	X	X	X	X	X
Proofreading	X	X	X	X	X	X	X
Publishing	X	X	X	X	X	X	X
Writing Genres							
Action Tale			X				
Autobiography/Biography	X	X	X	X	X	X	X
Book Review		X	X	X	X	X	
Business Letter			X	X		X	X
Describe a Process		X	X	X	X	X	X
Descriptive Writing	X	X	X	X	X	X	X
Expository/Informational Text	X	X	X	X	X	X	X
Fantasy		X	X	X			
Folklore (Folktales, Fairy Tales, Tall Tales, Legends, Myths)		X	X	X	X	X	
Friendly Letter	X	X	X	X	X	X	X
Historical Fiction					X		X
Invitation		X		X		X	
Journal Writing			X	X	X		
Magazine Article						X	X
Making a List	X	X	X	X	X	X	X
Mystery				X			
Narrative	X	X	X	X	X	X	X
News Story		X	X	X	X		
Personal Writing	X	X	X	X	X	X	X
Persuasive Writing	X	X	X	X	X	X	X
Play/Dramatization			X	X	X	X	X
Poetry	X	X	X	X	X	X	X
Realistic Fiction		X	X	X	X	X	X
Summary		X	X	X	X	X	X
Timed Writing		X	X	X	X	X	X
Writing Traits							
Audience		X	X	X	X	X	X
Conventions	X	X	X	X	X	X	X
Elaboration		X	X	X	X	X	X
Focus		X	X	X	X	X	X
Ideas/Content	X	X	X	X	X	X	X
Organization		X	X	X	X	X	X
Presentation	X	X	X	X	X	X	X
Purpose		X	X	X	X	X	X
Sentence Fluency	X	X	X	X	X	X	X
Sentence Variety		X			X	X	X
Vocabulary		X	X	X	X	X	X
Voice	X	X	X	X	X	X	X
Word Choice	X	X	X	X	X	X	X

Language Arts
Writing/Composition (continued)

Writing Strategies	K	1	2	3	4	5	6
Action and Describing Words	X	X	X	X			
Adding Details	X	X	X	X	X	X	X
Addressing Audience Needs		X	X	X	X	X	X
Brainstorming	X	X	X	X	X	X	X
Categorizing Ideas							X
Cause and Effect					X	X	X
Character Sketch					X	X	
Choosing a Topic	X	X	X	X	X	X	X
Compare and Contrast			X			X	X
Conveying a General Mood				X	X	X	
Creating Suspense				X			X
Creating Vivid Images		X		X	X	X	
Dialogue	X	X	X	X	X	X	X
Effective Beginnings					X	X	X
Elements of a Letter		X	X	X	X	X	X
Elements of Persuasion			X	X	X	X	
Eliminating Irrelevant Information		X	X	X	X	X	X
Eliminating Wordiness			X	X	X	X	X
Evaluate Personal Growth as a Writer			X	X	X	X	
Explanatory Paragraphs		X					
Figurative Language			X	X	X	X	X
Formality of Language		X	X	X	X	X	
Format		X			X	X	X
Generate Additional Ideas		X	X	X	X		
Highlight a Memorable Event		X			X		
Identifying Best Feature of Something Written			X	X			
Illustrations and Drawings	X	X	X	X			
Information from Multiple Sources				X	X	X	X
Main Idea and Details					X	X	
Making Connections							X
Organizing a Multi-Paragraph Composition					X	X	X
Planning		X			X	X	X
Plot Structure—Beginning, Middle, Climax, and End		X		X	X	X	X
Point of View						X	X
Presenting Facts and Examples Objectively				X	X	X	X
Proofreading	X	X	X	X	X	X	X
Purpose		X	X	X	X	X	X
Realism					X	X	
Referencing a Source					X	X	
Revising	X	X	X	X	X	X	X
Rhythm and Rhyme		X	X			X	
Sensory Details				X	X	X	X
Sentence Combining			X	X	X	X	X
Sequence	X	X	X	X		X	
Setting		X	X	X	X	X	X
Story Elements		X	X	X	X	X	
Style							X
Summary			X	X	X	X	X
Taking Notes		X	X	X	X	X	X

Language Arts
Writing/Composition (continued)

	K	1	2	3	4	5	6
Timed Writing		X	X	X	X	X	X
Time Line			X	X		X	
Transition Words/Devices			X	X	X	X	X
Using a Checklist		X	X	X	X	X	
Using a Graphic Organizer		X	X	X	X	X	X
Using a Model as a Guide to Writing			X	X		X	
Using Outlines to Organize Information				X	X	X	X
Using Multimedia Sources			X	X	X	X	X
Vary Sentence Beginnings			X	X	X	X	
Vary Sentence Length		X	X			X	
Vary Sentence Types	X	X	X	X	X	X	
Voice					X	X	
Voicing an Opinion		X				X	X
Word Choice		X	X	X	X	X	X
Working Collaboratively						X	X
Writing Coherent Paragraphs		X	X	X	X	X	X

Language Arts
Grammar

	K	1	2	3	4	5	6
Parts of Speech							
Adjectives (Describing Words)	X	X	X	X	X	X	X
Adverbs			X	X	X	X	X
Conjunctions			X	X	X	X	X
Nouns	X	X	X	X	X	X	X
Prepositions				X	X	X	X
Pronouns	X	X	X	X	X	X	X
Verbs	X	X	X	X	X	X	X
Sentences							
Complete and Incomplete Sentences		X	X	X	X	X	X
Fragments			X	X	X	X	X
Independent and Dependent Clauses							X
Parts (Subjects and Predicates)			X	X	X	X	X
Run-on Sentences					X		X
Sentence Combining			X	X	X	X	X
Structure (Simple, Compound, Complex, Compound-Complex)			X	X	X	X	X
Subject/Verb Agreement		X	X	X	X	X	X
Types (Declarative, Interrogative, Exclamatory, Imperative)	X	X	X	X	X	X	X
Usage							
Adjectives		X	X	X	X	X	X
Adverbs			X	X	X	X	X
Antonyms		X	X				
Articles			X	X		X	X
Contractions			X	X	X		
Nouns		X	X	X	X	X	X
Pronouns		X	X	X	X	X	X
Regular and Irregular Plurals					X	X	X
Synonyms		X	X				
Verb Tenses		X	X	X	X	X	X
Verbs (Action, Helping, Linking, Regular/Irregular)		X	X	X	X	X	X

Language Arts
Grammar (continued)

	K	1	2	3	4	5	6
Mechanics							
Capitalization (Sentence, Proper Nouns, Titles, Direct Address, Pronoun "I")	X	X	X	X	X	X	X
Punctuation (End Punctuation, Comma Use, Quotation Marks, Apostrophe, Colon, Semicolon, Hyphen, Parentheses)	X	X	X	X	X	X	X
Spelling							
Antonyms					X	X	X
Base or Root Words					X	X	
Comparatives/Superlatives				X	X	X	X
Compound Words					X	X	X
Connotation and Denotation							X
Content/Concept Words							X
Contractions				X	X		X
Foreign Words and Phrases							X
Gerunds							X
Greek and Latin Roots				X	X	X	X
Homographs				X	X	X	X
Homonyms/Homophones				X	X	X	X
Inflectional Endings		X		X	X	X	X
Irregular Plurals		X		X	X	X	
Irregular Verbs						X	
Long Vowel Patterns		X	X	X	X		
Multiple-Meaning Words					X	X	X
Multisyllabic Words		X	X	X	X		X
Phonograms		X					
Prefixes					X	X	X	X
r-Controlled Vowel Spellings		X	X				
Shades of Meaning					X		X
Short Vowel Spellings		X	X	X	X		
Silent Letters			X	X	X		
Sound/Letter Relationships	X	X	X				
Special Spellings Patterns/Rules		X	X	X	X	X	
Special Vowel Spellings		X	X	X			
Suffixes		X		X	X	X	X
Synonyms					X	X	X
Word Families		X		X		X	X

Listening/Speaking/Viewing

	K	1	2	3	4	5	6
Listening							
Analyze/Evaluate Intent and Content of Speaker's Message		X	X	X		X	X
Ask Questions		X	X	X	X	X	X
Determine Purposes for Listening		X	X	X	X	X	X
Drawing Conclusions and Making Inferences						X	
Follow Directions	X	X		X	X	X	X
Learn about Different Cultures through Discussion				X	X		
Listen for Poetic Language (Rhythm/Rhyme)	X	X			X		X
Listening for Details			X	X	X		
Listening for Information				X	X		
Participate in Group Discussions	X	X	X	X	X	X	X
Recalling What Was Heard				X			
Recognizing Fact and Opinion				X			
Respond to Speaker	X	X	X	X	X	X	X
Use Nonverbal Communication Techniques		X		X	X	X	X
Speaking							
Answer Questions	X	X	X	X	X	X	X
Asking Questions		X		X	X		
Describe Ideas and Feelings	X	X	X				X
Effective Word Choice/Voice			X	X	X	X	
Engaging the Audience					X	X	
Give Directions		X			X	X	X
Learn About Different Cultures through Discussion		X		X			X
Listen and Respond		X		X	X		
Making Announcements and Introductions		X					
Organizing Presentations				X	X	X	X
Paraphrasing			X	X			
Participate in Group Discussion	X	X	X	X	X	X	X
Present Oral Reports		X	X	X	X	X	X
Purposes of Speech			X				
Read Fluently with Expression, Phrasing, and Intonation		X	X	X	X	X	X
Read Orally	X	X	X	X	X	X	X
Share Information		X	X	X	X	X	X
Small Group Discussion			X	X	X	X	X
Speak Clearly at Appropriate Volume		X	X	X	X	X	X
Speaking Strategies					X	X	
Staying on Topic		X					
Summarize/Retell Stories	X	X	X	X	X	X	X
Understand Formal and Informal Language		X		X	X	X	X
Use Appropriate Language for Audience		X		X	X	X	X
Use Nonverbal Communication Techniques		X	X	X	X	X	X

Listening/Speaking/Viewing (continued)

	K	1	2	3	4	5	6
Viewing							
Analyze Purposes and Techniques of the Media			x	x	x	x	x
Appreciate/Interpret Artist's Techniques		x					
Compare Visual and Written Material on the Same Subject		x					x
Culture in Media		x			x	x	
Describe Pictures			x				
Gather Information from Visual Images		x	x	x	x	x	x
Interpreting Media					x	x	
Language Development							x
Literary Devices				x			x
Relating to Content				x	x		
Understanding Gestures				x	x		
Using Multimedia				x	x	x	
View Critically		x		x	x	x	x
Penmanship							
Cursive Letters			x	x			
Manuscript Letters	x	x					
Numbers	x	x					

Unit Themes

	Level K	Level 1	Level 2
Unit 1	Off to School	Back to School	Kindness
Unit 2	Patterns	Where Animals Live	Let's Explore
Unit 3	Finding Friends	I Am Responsible!	Around the Town
Unit 4	By the Sea	Our Neighborhood at Work	Look Again
Unit 5	Stick to It	What's the Weather?	Courage
Unit 6	My Shadow	North, South, East, West	America's People
Unit 7	Teamwork	I Think I Can	
Unit 8	Ready, Set, Grow!	Away We Grow!	
Unit 9	Red, White, and Blue	Home, Sweet Home	
Unit 10	Windy Days	I Am Brave	

Level 3

Friendship

Animals and Their Habitats

Money

Earth, Moon, and Sun

Communities across Time

Storytelling

Level 4

Risks and Consequences

Nature's Delicate Balance

A Changing America

Science Fair

America on the Move

Dollars and Sense

Level 5

Heritage

Energy at Work

Making a New Nation

Our Corner of the Universe

Going West

Call of Duty

Level 6

Taking a Stand

Ancient Civilizations

Ecology

Great Expectations

Earth in Action

Art and Impact

Glossary of Reading Terms

This glossary includes linguistic, grammatical, comprehension, and literary terms that may be helpful in understanding reading instruction.

acronym a word formed from the initial letter of words in a phrase, **scuba (self-contained underwater breathing apparatus).**

acrostic a kind of puzzle in which lines of a poem are arranged so that words or phrases are formed when certain letters from each line are used in a sequence.

adjective a word or group of words that modifies or describes a noun.

adventure story a narrative that features the unknown or unexpected with elements of excitement, danger, and risk.

adverb a word or group of words that modifies a verb, adjective, or other adverb. An adverb answers questions such as **how, when, where,** and **how much.**

affective domain the psychological field of emotional activities such as interests, attitudes, opinions, appreciations, values, and emotional sets

affix a word part, either a prefix or a suffix, that changes the meaning or function of a word root or stem.

affricate a speech sound that starts as a stop but ends as a fricative, the /ch/ in **catch.**

agreement the correspondence of syntactically related words; subjects and predicates are in agreement when both are singular or plural.

alliteration the repetition of the initial sounds in neighboring words or stressed syllables.

alphabet the complete set of letters representing speech sounds used in writing a language. In English there are twenty-six letters.

alphabet book a book for helping young children learn the alphabet by pairing letters with pictures whose sounds they represent.

alphabetic principle the association between sounds and the letters that represent them in alphabetic writing systems.

alveolar a consonant speech sound made when the tongue and the ridge of the upper and lower jaw stop to constrict the air flow, as /t/.

anagram a word or phrase whose letters form other words or phrases when rearranged, for example, **add** and **dad.**

analogy a likeness or similarity.

analytic phonics also deductive phonics, a whole-to-part approach to phonics in which a student is taught a number of sight words and then phonetic generalizations that can be applied to other words.

antonym a word that is opposite in meaning to another word.

appositive a word that restates or modifies a preceding noun, for example, **my daughter, Charlotte.** Appositives are also definitions of words usually set off by commas.

aspirate an unvoiced speech sound produced by a puff of air, as /h/ in **heart.**

aspirated stop a stop consonant sound released with a puff of air, as /k/, /p/, and /t/.

auditory discrimination the ability to hear phonetic likenesses and differences in phonemes and words.

author's purpose the motive or reason for which an author writes; includes to entertain, inform, persuade, and explain how.

automaticity fluent processing of information, requiring little effort or attention.

auxiliary verb a verb that precedes another verb to express time, mood, or voice; includes verbs such as **has, is,** and **will.**

ballad a narrative poem, composed of short verses to be sung or recited, usually containing elements of drama and often tragic in tone.

base word a word to which affixes may be added to create related words.

blank verse unrhymed verse, especially unrhymed iambic pentameter.

blend the joining of the sounds of two or more letters with little change in those sounds, for example, /spr/ in **spring; also consonant blend** or **consonant cluster.**

blending combining the sounds represented by letters or spellings to sound out or pronounce a word; contrast with **oral blending.**

breve the symbol placed above a vowel to indicate that it is a short vowel.

browse to skim through or look over in search of something of interest.

canon in literature, the body of major works that a culture considers important at a given time.

case a grammatical category that indicates the syntactic/semantic role of a noun phrase in a sentence.

cause-effect relationship a stated or implied association between an outcome and the conditions that brought it about; also the comprehension skill associated with recognizing this type of relationship as an organizing principle in text.

chapter book a book long enough to be divided into chapters, but not long or complex enough to be considered a novel.

characterization the way in which an author presents a character in a story, including describing words, actions, thoughts, and impressions of that character.

choral reading oral group reading to develop oral fluency by modeling.

cinquain a stanza of five lines, specifically one that has successive lines of two, four, six, eight, and two syllables.

cipher a system for writing in code.

clarifying a comprehension strategy in which the reader rereads text, uses a dictionary, uses decoding skills, or uses context clues to comprehend something that is unclear.

clause a group of words with a subject and a predicate used to form a part of or a whole sentence, a dependent clause modifies an independent clause, which can stand alone as a complete sentence.

collaborative learning learning by working together in small groups.

command a sentence that asks for action and usually ends with a period.

common noun in contrast to **proper noun,** a noun that denotes a class rather than a unique or specific thing such as **girl** versus **Susan.**

comprehension the understanding of what is written or said.

comprehension skill a skill that aids in understanding text, including identifying **author's purpose, author's point of view,** comprehending **cause-and-effect** relationships, **clarifying, comparing and contrasting** items and events, **drawing conclusions,** distinguishing **fact from opinion,** identifying **main ideas, making inferences,** distinguishing **reality from fantasy,** and understanding **sequence.**

comprehension strategy a sequence of steps for monitoring and understanding text, includes adjusting reading speed, asking questions, clarifying, making connections, predicting, summarizing, and visualizing.

conjugation the complete set of all possible inflected forms of a verb.

conjunction a part of speech used to connect words, phrases, clauses, or sentences, including the words **and, but,** and **or.**

consonant a speech sound, and the alphabet letter that represents that sound, made by partial or complete closure of part of the vocal tract, which obstructs air flow and causes audible friction.

context clue information from the immediate and surrounding text that helps identify a word.

contraction a short version of a written or spoken expression in which letters are omitted, for example, **can't.**

convention an accepted practice in spoken or written language, usually referring to spelling, mechanics, or grammar rules.

cooperative learning a classroom organization that allows students to work together to achieve their individual goals. Related term is **collaboration.**

creative writing prose and poetic forms of writing that express the writer's thoughts and feelings imaginatively.

cueing system any of the various sources of information that help identify an unrecognizable word in reading, including phonetic, semantic, and syntactical information.

cumulative tale a story, such as "The Gingerbread Man," in which details are repeated until the climax.

dangling modifier usually a participle that because of its placement in a sentence modifies the wrong object.

decodable text text materials controlled to include a majority of words whose sound/spelling relationships are known by the reader.

decode to analyze spoken or graphic symbols for meaning.

diacritical mark a mark, such as a breve or macron, added to a letter or graphic character to indicate a specific pronunciation.

dialect a regional variety of a particular language with phonological, grammatical, and lexical patterns that distinguishes it from other varieties.

dialogue a piece of writing written as conversation, usually punctuated by quotation marks.

digraph two letters that represent one speech sound, for example, /sh/ or /ch/.

diphthong a vowel sound produced when the tongue glides from one vowel sound toward another in the same syllable, for example, /oi/ or /ou/.

direct object the person or thing that receives the action of a verb in a sentence, for example, the word **cake** in this sentence: **Madeline baked a cake.**

drafting the process of writing ideas in rough form to record them.

drama a story in the form of a play, written to be performed.

edit in the writing process, to revise or correct a manuscript. Often this is part of the final step in the process with a focus on correcting grammar, spelling, and mechanics rather than content, structure, and organization.

emergent literacy the development of the association of meaning and print that continues until a child reaches the stage of conventional reading and writing.

emergent reading a child's early interaction with books and print before the ability to decode text.

encode to change a message into symbols, for example, to change speech into writing.

epic a long narrative poem, usually about a hero.

exclamatory sentence a sentence that shows strong emotion and ends with an exclamation point.

expository writing or **exposition** a composition in writing that explains an event or process.

fable a short tale that teaches a moral.

fantasy a highly imaginative story about characters, places, and events that cannot exist.

fiction imaginative narrative designed to entertain rather than to explain, persuade, or describe.

figure of speech the expressive, nonliteral use of language usually through metaphor, simile, or personification.

fluency freedom from word-identification problems that hinder comprehension in reading. Fluency involves rate, accuracy, and expression.

folktale a narrative form of genre such as an epic, myth, or fable that is well-known through repeated storytellings.

foreshadowing giving clues to upcoming events in a story.

free verse verse with irregular metrical pattern.

freewriting writing that is not limited in form, style, content, or purpose; designed to encourage students to write.

genre a classification of literary works, including tragedy, comedy, novel, essay, short story, mystery, realistic fiction, and poetry.

grammar the study of the classes of words, their inflections, and their functions and relations in sentences; includes phonological, morphological, syntactic, and semantic descriptions of a language.

grapheme a written or printed representation of a phoneme, such as **c** for /k/.

guided reading reading instruction in which the teacher provides the structure and purpose for reading and responding to the material read.

handing off a method of turning over to students the primary responsibility for controlling discussion.

indirect object in a sentence, the person or thing to or for whom an action is done, for example, the word **dog** in this sentence: **Madeline gave the dog a treat.**

inference a conclusion based on facts, data, or evidence.

infinitive the base form of a verb, usually with the infinitive marker, for example, **to go.**

inflectional ending an ending that expresses a plural or possessive form of a noun, the tense of a verb, or the comparative or superlative form of an adjective or adverb.

interrogative word a word that marks a clause or sentence as a question, including **interrogative pronouns who, what, which, where.**

intervention a strategy or program designed to supplement or substitute instruction, especially for those students who fall behind.

invented spelling the result of an attempt to spell a word based on using the sounds in the letter names to determine the sound the letter names. Gradually sounds are connected to letters, which leads to conventional spelling..

irony a figure of speech in which the literal meanings of the words is the opposite of their intended meanings.

journal a written record of daily events or responses.

juvenile book a book written for children or adolescents.

legend a traditional tale handed down from generation to generation.

leitmotif a repeated expression, event, or idea used to unify a work of art such as writing.

letter one of a set of graphic symbols that forms an alphabet and is used alone or in combination to represent a phoneme, also **grapheme.**

linguistics the study of the nature and structure of language and communication.

literary elements the elements of a story such as **setting, plot,** and **characterization** that create the structure of a narrative.

macron a diacritical mark placed above a vowel to indicate a long vowel sound.

main idea the central thought or chief topic of a passage.

making connections a reading strategy used to connect information being read to one's own experiences to other reading materials or to one's knowledge of the world. Making connections fosters engagement, while reading helps the reader make sense of the text and connect information.

mechanics the conventions of capitalization and punctuation.

metacognition awareness and knowledge of one's mental processes or thinking about what one is thinking about.

metaphor a figure of speech in which a comparison is implied but not stated; for example, **She is a jewel.**

miscue a deviation from text during oral reading in an attempt to make sense of the text.

modeling an instructional technique in which the teacher makes public the thinking needed to use critical reading and writing behaviors.

mood the literary element that conveys the emotional atmosphere of a story.

morpheme a meaningful linguistic unit that cannot be divided into smaller units, for example, **word; a bound morpheme** is a morpheme that cannot stand alone as an independent word, for example, the prefix **re-;** a **free morpheme** can stand alone, for example, **dog.**

myth a story designed to explain the mysteries of life.

narrative writing or **narration** a composition in writing that tells a story or gives an account of an event.

nonfiction prose designed to explain, argue, or describe rather than to entertain with a factual emphasis; includes biography and autobiography.

noun a part of speech that denotes persons, places, things, qualities, or acts.

novel an extended fictional prose narration.

onomatopoeia the use of a word whose sound suggests its meaning, for example, **purr.**

oral blending the ability to fuse discrete phonemes into recognizable words; oral blending puts sounds together to make a word, **see also segmentation.**

orthography correct or standardized spelling according to established usage in a language.

oxymoron a figure of speech in which contrasting or contradictory words are brought together for emphasis.

paragraph a subdivision of a written composition that consists of one or more sentences, deals with one point, or gives the words of one speaker, usually beginning with an indented line.

participle a verb form used as an adjective, for example, **the skating party.**

personification a figure of speech in which animals, ideas, or things take on human characteristics.

persuasive writing a composition intended to persuade the reader to adopt the writer's point of view.

phoneme the smallest sound unit of speech, for example, the /k/ in **book.**

phonemic awareness the ability to recognize that spoken words are made of discrete sounds and that those sounds can be manipulated.

phonetic spelling the respelling of entry words in a dictionary according to a pronunciation key.

phonetics the study of speech sounds.

phonics a way of teaching reading that addresses sound/symbol relationships, especially in beginning instruction.

phonogram a letter or symbol that represents a phonetic sound.

phonological awareness the ability to attend to the sound structure of language; includes sentence, word, syllable rhyme and phonological awareness.

plot the literary element that provides the structure of the action of a story, which may include rising action, climax, and falling action leading to a resolution or denouement.

plural a grammatical form of a word that refers to more than one in number; an irregular plural is one that does not follow normal patterns for inflectional endings.

poetic license the liberty taken by writers to ignore conventions.

poetry a metrical form of composition in which language is chosen and arranged to create a powerful response through meaning, sound, or rhythm.

possessive showing ownership either through the use of an adjective, an adjectival pronoun, or the possessive form of a noun.

predicate the part of the sentence that expresses something about the subject and includes the verb phrase; a **complete predicate** includes the principal verb in a sentence and all its modifiers or subordinate parts.

predicting a comprehension strategy in which the reader attempts to anticpate what will happen, using clues from the text and prior knowledge, and then confirms predictions as the text is read.

prefix an affix attached before a base word that changes the meaning of the word.

preposition a part of speech in the class of function words such as **of, on,** and **at** that precede noun phrases to create prepositional phrases.

prewriting the planning stage of the writing process in which the writer formulates ideas, gathers information, and considers ways to organize them.

print awareness in emergent literacy, a child's growing recognition of conventions and characteristics of written language, including reading from left to right and from top to bottom in English and that words are separated by spaces.

pronoun a part of speech used as a substitute for a noun or noun phrase.

proofreading the act of reading with the intent to correct, clarify, or improve text.

pseudonym an assumed name used by an author; a pen name or nom de plume.

publishing the process of preparing written material for presentation.

punctuation graphic marks such as commas, periods, quotation marks, and brackets used to clarify meaning and to give speech characteristics to written language.

question an interrogative sentence that asks a question and ends with a question mark.

realistic fiction a story that attempts to portray characters and events as they actually are.

rebus a picture or symbol that suggests a word or syllable.

revise in the writing process, to change or correct a manuscript to make its message more clear.

rhyme identical or very similar recurring final sounds in words, often at the ends of lines of poetry.

rime a vowel and any following consonants of a syllable.

segmentation the ability to break words into individual sounds; **see also oral blending.**

semantic mapping a graphic display of a group of words that are meaningfully related to support vocabulary instruction.

semantics the study of meaning in language, including the meanings of words, phrases, sentences, and texts.

sentence a grammatical unit that expresses a statement, question, or command; a **simple sentence** is a sentence with one subject and one predicate; a **compound sentence** is a sentence with two or more independent clauses usually separated by a comma and conjunction, but no dependent clause; a **complex sentence** is a sentence with one independent and one or more dependent clauses.

sentence combining a teaching technique in which complex sentence chunks and paragraphs are built from basic sentences.

sentence lifting the process of using sentences from children's writing to illustrate what is wrong or right to develop children's editing and proofreading skills.

sequence the order of elements or events.

setting the literary element that includes the time, place, and physical and psychological background in which a story takes place.

sight word a word that is taught to be read as a whole word, usually words that are phonetically irregular.

simile a figure of speech in which a comparison of two things that are unlike is directly stated, usually with the words **like** or **as**; for example, **She is like a jewel.**

spelling the process of representing language by means of a writing system.

statement a sentence that tells something and ends with a period.

study skills a general term for the techniques and strategies that help readers comprehend text with the intent to remember; includes following directions, organizing, locating, and using graphic aids.

style the characteristics of a work that reflect the author's particular way of writing.

subject the main topic of a sentence to which a predicate refers, including the principal noun; a **complete subject** includes the principal noun in a sentence and all its modifiers.

suffix an affix attached at the end of a base word that changes the meaning and the function of the word.

summarizing a comprehension strategy in which the reader constructs a brief statement that contains the essential ideas of a passage.

syllable a minimal unit of sequential speech sounds comprised of a vowel sound or a vowel-sound combination.

symbolism the use of one thing to represent something else to represent an idea in a concrete way.

synonym a word that means the same as another word.

syntax the grammatical pattern or structure of word order in sentences, clauses, and phrases.

tense the way in which verbs indicate past, present, and future time of action.

text structure the various patterns of ideas that are built into the organization of a written work.

theme a major idea or proposition that provides an organizing concept through which, by study, students gain depth of understanding.

topic sentence a sentence intended to express the main idea of a paragraph or passage.

tragedy a literary work, often a play, in which the main character suffers conflicts and which presents a serious theme and has an unfortunate ending.

usage the way in which a native language or dialect is used by the members of the community.

verb a word that expresses an action or state that occurs in a predicate of a sentence; an irregular verb is a verb that does not follow normal patterns of inflectional endings that reflect past, present, or future verb tense.

visualizing a comprehension strategy in which the reader constructs a mental picture of a character, setting, or process.

vowel a voiced speech sound and the alphabet letter that represents that sound, made without stoppage or friction of the air flow as it passes through the vocal tract.

vowel digraph a spelling pattern in which two or more letters represent a single vowel sound.

word calling proficiency in decoding with little or no attention to word meaning.

writing also **composition** the process or result of organizing ideas in writing to form a clear message; includes persuasive, expository, narrative, and descriptive forms.

writing process the many aspects of the complex act of producing a piece of writing, including prewriting, drafting, revising, editing/proofreading, and publishing.

Songs and Games

abcdefg
hijklmn
opq
rst
uvw
xyz

Alphabet Rap

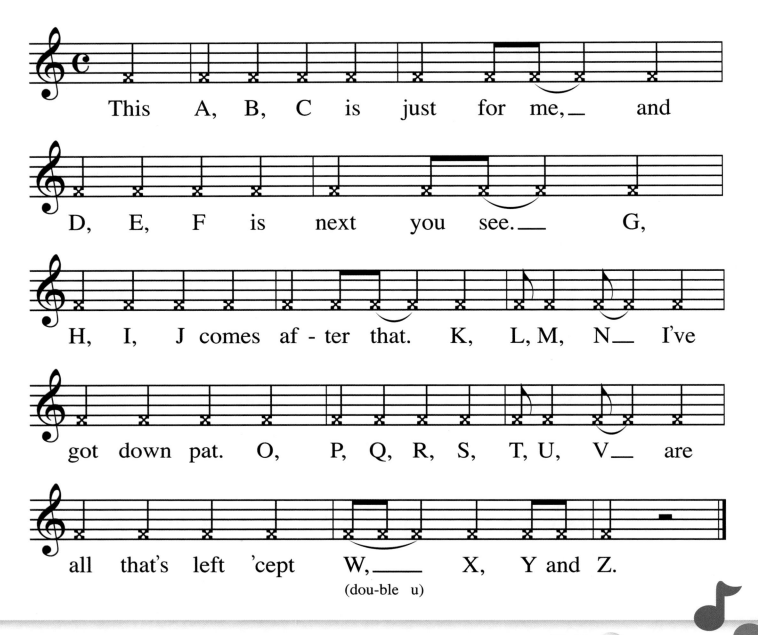

This A, B, C is just for me,— and

D, E, F is next you see.— G,

H, I, J comes af-ter that. K, L, M, N— I've

got down pat. O, P, Q, R, S, T, U, V— are

all that's left 'cept W,— X, Y and Z.
(dou-ble u)

Alphabet Cheer

We're So Glad You're Here

We're so glad you're here. We're so glad you're here. We're so glad that Jor - dan's here. We're so glad he's here.

We're so glad you're here
We're so glad you're here
We're so glad that <u>Katie</u>'s here
We're so glad <u>she</u>'s here

We're so glad you're here
We're so glad you're here
We're so glad that _____'s here
We're so glad ___'s here

If You're Happy and You Know It

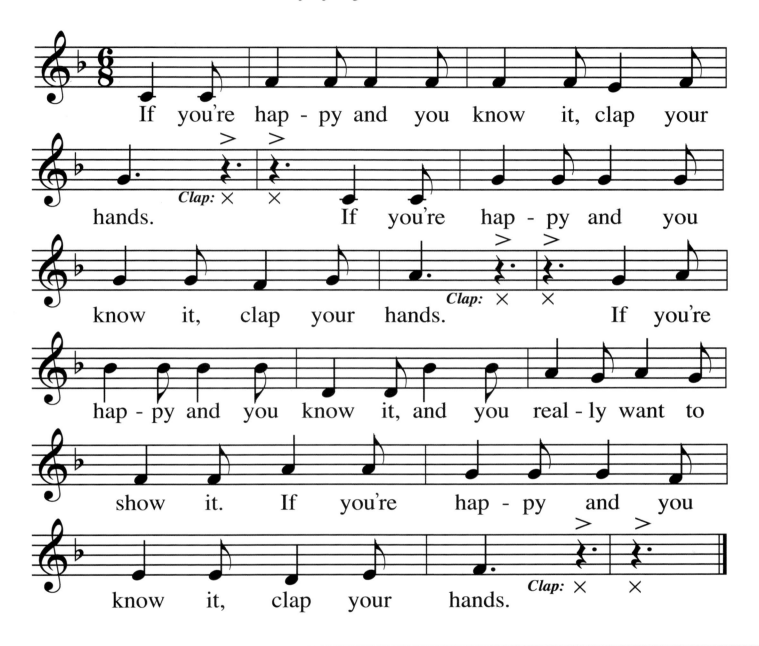

This is the Way We Come to Circle

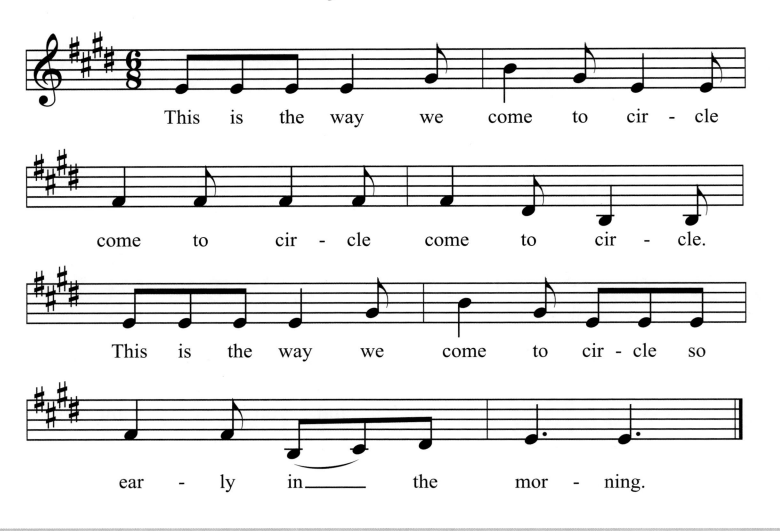

This is the way we come to circle
come to circle come to circle.
This is the way we come to circle so
early in the morning.

This is the way we sit right down,
Sit right down, sit right down.
This is the way we sit right down,
So early in the morning.

This is the way we fold our hands,
Fold our hands, fold our hands.
This is the way we fold our hands,
So early in the morning.

Hello

Hello <u>Jose</u>, hello <u>Jose</u>,
Hello <u>Jose</u>, please stand, and take a bow.

Hello _____, hello _____,
Hello _____, please stand, and take a bow.

I'm a Little Teapot

I'm a lit - tle tea - pot short and stout,

Here is my han - dle, here is my spout.

When I get all steamed up, hear me shout,

Tip me o - ver and pour me out.

Are You Sleeping?

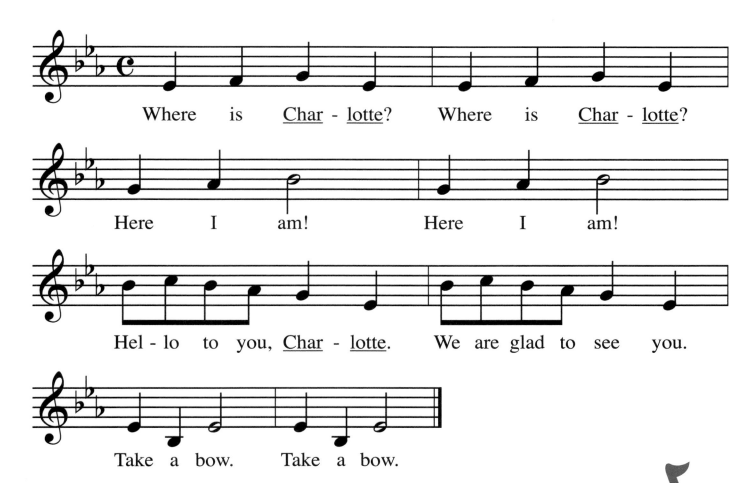

Where is Char-lotte? Where is Char-lotte?

Here I am! Here I am!

Hel-lo to you, Char-lotte. We are glad to see you.

Take a bow. Take a bow.

Where is <u>Charlotte</u>? Where is <u>Charlotte</u>?
Here I am! Here I am!
Hello to you <u>Charlotte</u>. We are glad to see you.
Take a bow. Take a bow.

Where is _____? Where is _____?
Here I am! Here I am!
Hello to you _____. We are glad to see you.
Take a bow. Take a bow.

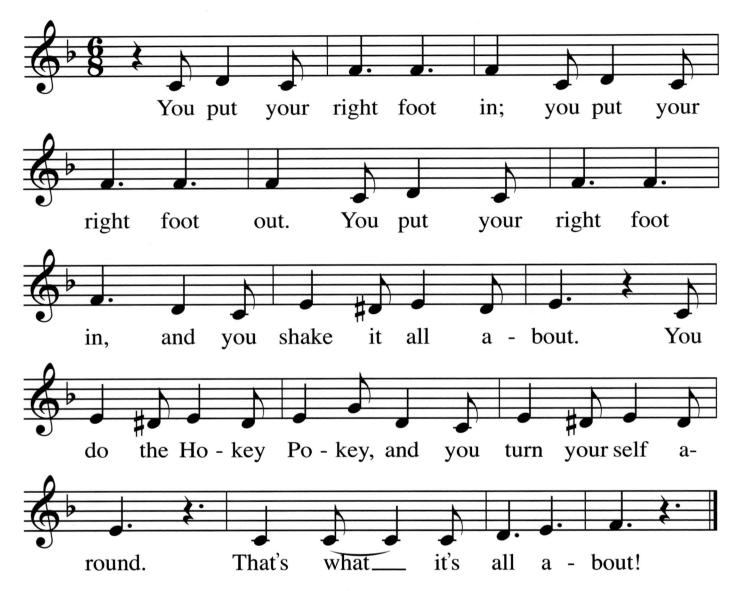

You put your right hand in; you take your right hand out.
You put your right hand in, and you shake it all about.
You do the hokey pokey, and you turn yourself around.
That's what it's all about!

You put your left foot in; you take your left foot out.
You put your left foot in, and you shake it all about.
You do the hokey pokey, and you turn yourself around.
That's what it's all about!

You put your left hand in; you take your left hand out.
You put your left hand in, and you shake it all about.
You do the hokey pokey, and you turn yourself around.
That's what it's all about!

Teddy Bear, Teddy Bear

Ted - dy Bear,   Ted - dy Bear,   turn   a - round.

Ted - dy Bear,   Ted - dy Bear,   touch   the   ground.

Ted - dy Bear,   Ted - dy Bear,   shake   your   shoe.

Ted - dy Bear,   Ted - dy Bear,   that   will   do.

Down By the Bay

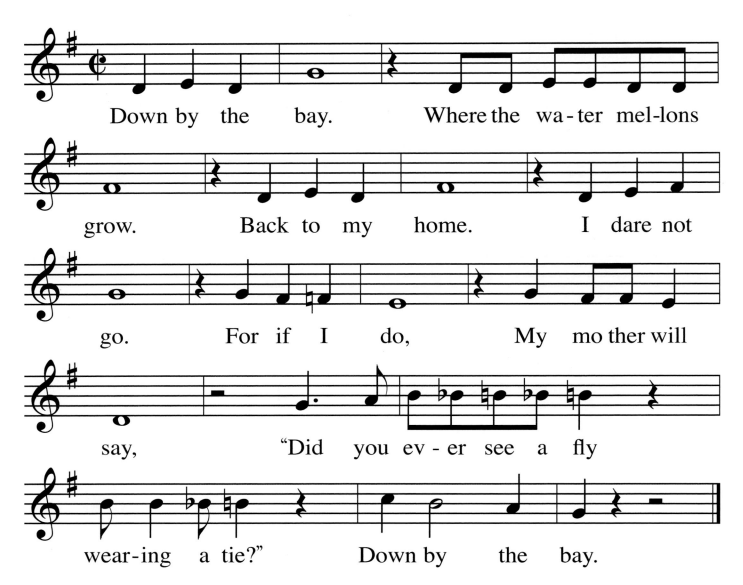

Down by the bay
Where the watermelons grow
Back to my home
I dare not go
For if I do
My mother will say
"Did you ever see a bear
Combing his hair?"
Down by the bay

Down by the bay
Where the watermelons grow
Back to my home
I dare not go
For if I do
My mother will say
"Did you ever see a moose
Kissing a goose?"
Down by the bay

Down by the bay
Where the watermelons grow
Back to my home
I dare not go
For if I do
My mother will say
"Did you ever see a whale
With a polka dot tail?"
Down by the bay

Apples and Bananas

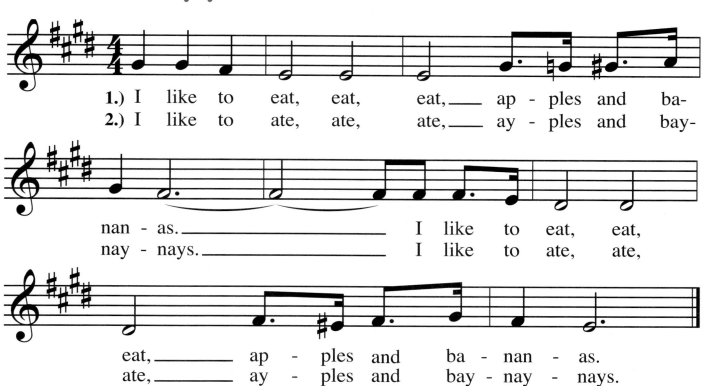

1.) I like to eat, eat, eat,___ ap - ples and ba-
2.) I like to ate, ate, ate,___ ay - ples and bay-

nan - as._____ I like to eat, eat,
nay - nays._____ I like to ate, ate,

eat,_____ ap – ples and ba - nan - as.
ate,_____ ay – ples and bay - nay - nays.

Vowel Song

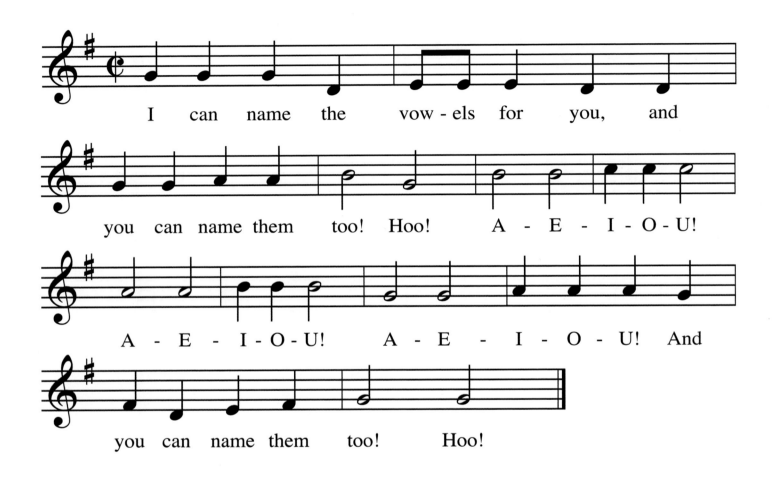

I can name the vow-els for you, and

you can name them too! Hoo! A - E - I - O - U!

A - E - I - O - U! A - E - I - O - U! And

you can name them too! Hoo!

The Ship Is Loaded With _____

Purpose

To provide students with a movement activity that will reinforce rhyming words and initial consonant sounds

Instruction

Have students sit in a circle. Explain that you are loading a ship with items that sound alike. Each student will have a chance to say a rhyming word. Use a ball or anything that can be rolled from student to student. Ask for a volunteer, and have that student say *The ship is loaded with cheese.* The student then rolls the ball to someone else who must repeat the line, substituting a rhyming word for cheese (for example, *peas, bees, keys, breeze, fleas,* or *trees).*

At this point, you might have the student roll the ball back to the first student, who will repeat *The ship is loaded with* cheese. Or have the student roll the ball to someone else for a new rhyming word.

Play the game using the following words:

The ship is loaded with *cats (mats, rats, bats, hats).*

The ship is loaded with *logs (frogs, hogs, dogs, bogs).*

The ship is loaded with *cans (fans, bans, Dans, pans).*

Play The Ship Is Loaded with _____ game, and have students choose words with the same initial sound. For example, if they choose /b/, students can say *The ship is loaded with* basketballs, begonias, baseballs, balls, *and* blankets.

Ordering Letters Game

Give each student a set of **Alphabet Letter Cards** *Aa–Nn.* (You may add letters as the student's knowledge of new letters increases). The cards in each set should be shuffled out of order and should face different ways.

Tell students they should do two things with these cards. First they should turn all the cards so they are showing either all capitals or all small letters. Then students should each show the set to a partner to check.

Next have each student work with a partner and match each capital letter with a small letter.

Simon Says

Purpose
To reinforce word concepts using a game format

Instruction
Tell students you are going to play Simon says. For those unfamiliar with the game, explain that when Simon says to do something, they must follow the instructions. Also, tell them they should not follow any directions that do not start with the words *Simon says.* Give the following instructions:

> **Simon says pat your head.**
> **(Students pat their heads.)**
>
> **Simon says rub your tummy.**
> **(Students rub their tummies.)**
>
> **Simon says hop on one foot.**
> **(Students hop on one foot.)**
>
> **Simon says hop on your left foot.**
> **(Students hop on their left feet.)**

After giving several different instructions, give another one, omitting *Simon says:*

> Jump in place.
>
> (Students should stand still.)

Students are "out" when they

- do something Simon does not say to do.
- do something other than what Simon says.
- do not do what Simon says.

When a student is "out," you can have him or her sit down. Continue the game until one student is left standing. Another alternative is to give each student an **Alphabet Letter Card** to identify if they miss an instruction. If the student correctly identifies the letter, he or she can stay in the game.

To reinforce language skills, try different and gradually more challenging instructions, such as the following:

- Students can touch their noses and then turn around.
- Add numbers *(jump three times; clap four times; pat tummy once).*
- Add prepositions and prepositional phrases designating location *(over, under, in front of, behind).*
- Add conjunctions (hop *and* skip).
- Use adjectives (take *big* steps).
- Use adjectival strings *(take three big* steps).
- Use adverbs *(clap softly).*
- Add negatives *(don't clap your hands).*
- Add conditionals *if, when, unless, until, while (rub your tummy while you pat your head).*

Mat Games

Purpose

To help students match sounds to letters

Instruction

Play each of these games on a **Game Mat,** using game markers to move around the squares. Place the mat on a table or on the floor. Have students gather around the mat, and explain to them that as they move around the squares, they will be naming letters and sounds.

Each of the **Game Mats** is generic and can be used for not only the games described here, but also for games you create with students. You and your class might enjoy creating variations of the games described here or creating entirely new games to play on the mats.

Create new rules and difficulty levels as your class needs or wants them. Challenge students to think of new games to play on the mats.

Difficulty Levels

The levels of difficulty described here are simply suggestions. Your students may need to begin with much easier tasks, or they may not be challenged enough by them. Always suit the games to the activities and levels of difficulty where you know your class will be most comfortable. The games should be difficult enough to challenge students yet easy enough for them to experience success and have fun.

Hop Along Game

The object of this game is to move the game marker from the bunny to the carrot at the end of the trail. Use a number cube to determine how many spaces a student may move the marker along the trail. If the student lands on a letter, he or she must do one of the following, depending on the level of difficulty you have chosen:

Name the letter	(Level 1)
Name the sound of the letter	(Level 2)

If the student does not name the correct letter or sound, he or she must do one of the following:

Lose a turn	(Level 1)
Go back a space until he or she is able to name the correct letter or sound	(Level 2)

If the student lands on a happy face, he or she may take an extra turn.

Ball Diamond, School Yard, A Day at the Beach, My Neighborhood, Race Track

Play all these games with the same rules. Each student rolls the number cube and moves the game marker the correct number of spaces. Use the **Alphabet Letter Cards** for Level 1 and the **Alphabet Sound Cards** for the card pack on Levels 2, 3, and 4. Have each student draw a card. Depending on the level, students will do the following:

State the name of the letter   (Level 1)

State the sound the letter makes   (Level 2)

Name a word that begins with   (Level 3)
the sound

Name the letter, the sound,   (Level 4)
and a word that begins with the sound

If students do not guess correctly, they lose the next turn.

Winning the Games

These games can be played quickly, or you can have students extend them. For a quick game, have them play until the first student reaches the goal at the end of the trail. If a student has not reached the goal when the cards run out, the student closest to the goal wins.

To extend the games, tell students to shuffle the cards when the last card has been chosen and to keep playing. The number of times the cards are shuffled will determine the length of the game. Again, the student who reaches the goal or is closest to the goal when the cards run out for the last time wins the game.

Challenges

These games are designed to be played independently by students. This means students must determine whether each given answer is correct. Encourage them to discuss any differences of opinion they may have. If they are not able to decide whether the answer is correct, tell them to raise their hands so you can help them.

Penmanship

SRA Imagine It! develops handwriting skills through Penmanship lessons three days each week. The instruction for these lessons appears in the Sounds and Letters part in this grade level. The purpose of these lessons is to develop important handwriting skills necessary for producing legible, properly spaced documents. In kindergarten, penmanship practice reinforces the sound-letter correspondence in the lesson.

The overhead projector, in addition to the board, can be an effective device for teaching penmanship. Students can move their pencils at the same time you form letters on the transparency. To further help students, you should also recite the descriptions or chants that go with each letter.

Penmanship in Grades K–1

Beginning in kindergarten, the Penmanship lessons expand on the sound/letter instruction by introducing letters students study in Sounds and Letters. Students learn that those letters are made of four basic lines: curved lines, horizontal lines, vertical lines, and slanted lines.

Next students learn letter and number formation. Students practice letter formation by writing the letter being studied and then words that contain the particular letter. This instruction continues in Level 1 and is tied to the letter formation instruction in Language Arts.

Manuscript Penmanship Models

The lessons present ball-and-stick models of manuscript handwriting, while this appendix offers an alternative method with continuous stroke models.

Hand and Paper Positioning

The **hand and paper positioning** models are for your reference and enhance the written instruction of positioning lessons. The diagrams give you a visual aid so you may better understand and demonstrate an effective technique of positioning.

A right-handed student should hold the pencil loosely about one inch above the point, between the thumb and middle finger. A left-handed student should hold the pencil the same way, but up to one half inch farther away from the point. The index fingers of both writers should rest lightly on the top of the pencil. The wrist should be level and slightly raised from the desk.

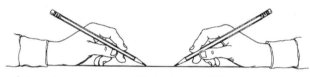

Left-handed writers   Right-handed Writers

For both kinds of writers, the paper should lie straight in front of the student with the edges parallel to the edges of the desk. A left-handed writer may find it easier to slant the paper slightly to the right and parallel to the left forearm. A right-handed writer's writing hand should be kept well below the writing. The left hand should hold down the paper.

Left-handed writers   Right-handed Writers

Ball and Stick Penmanship Models

The **ball-and-stick** models of manuscript handwriting provide you with a systematic method for teaching students to form uppercase and lowercase letters of the alphabet. The dots on the letters indicate starting points for students. The numbered arrows show students in which order and direction the line they are drawing should go to form the particular letter. You may use the chants to describe the letter step by step as students model the formation on the board. Students may also recite the chants in unison as they practice the formation, whether they are writing the letter or tracing it on the board.

Ball-and-Stick Penmanship Models

capital *A*

a Starting point, around left all the way
Starting point, straight down, touching the circle: small *a*

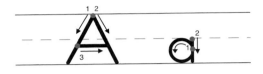

A Starting point, slanting down left
Starting point, slanting down right
Starting point, across the middle:

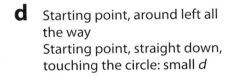

d Starting point, around left all the way
Starting point, straight down, touching the circle: small *d*

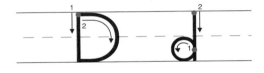

D Starting point, straight down
Starting point, around right and in at the bottom: capital *D*

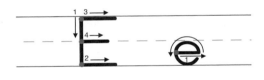

B Starting point, straight down
Starting point, around right and in at the middle, around right and in at

E Starting point, straight down
Starting point, straight out
Starting point, straight out

g Starting point, around left all the way
Starting point, straight down, touching the circle, around left to stopping place: small *g*

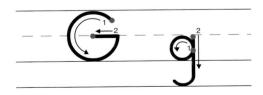

G Starting point, around left, curving up and around
Straight in: capital *G*

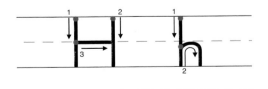

H Starting point, straight down
Starting point, straight down
Starting point, across the middle:

Ball-and-Stick Penmanship Models

j Starting point, straight down, around left to stopping place. Dot exactly above: small *j*

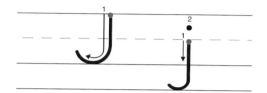

J Starting point, straight down, around left to stopping place: capital *J*

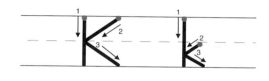

K Starting point, straight down. Starting point, slanting down left, touching the line, slanting down

n Starting point, straight down, back up, around right, straight down: small *n*

right, straight down: capital *M*

m Starting point, straight down, back up, around right, straight down, back up, around right, straight down: small *m*

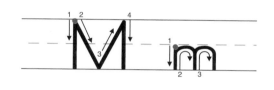

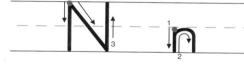

M Starting point, straight down. Starting point, slanting down right to the point, slanting back up to the

N Starting point, straight down. Starting point, slanting down right, straight back up: capital *N*

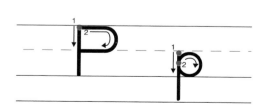

p Starting point, straight down. Starting point, around right all the way, touching the line: small *p*

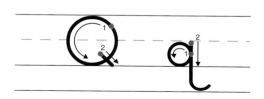

P Starting point, straight down. Starting point, around right and in at the middle: capital *P*

Q Starting point, around left all the way. Starting point, slanting down right:

Ball-and-Stick Penmanship Models

s Starting point, around left, curving right and down around right,

curving left and up to stopping place: small s

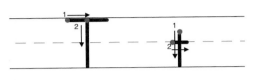

S Starting point, around left, curving right and down around right, curving left and up: capital S

T Starting point, straight across Starting point, straight down: capital T

v Starting point, slanting down right, slanting up right: small v

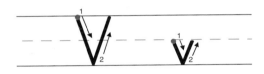

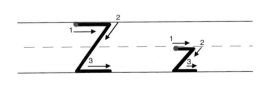

V Starting point, slanting down right, slanting up right: capital V

W Starting point, slanting down right, slanting up right, slanting down right, slanting up right: capital W

z Starting point, straight across, slanting down left, straight across: small z

Y Starting point, slanting down right, stop
Starting point, slanting down left, stop
Starting point, straight down: capital Y

y Starting point, slanting down right
Starting point, slanting down left, connecting the lines: small y

Z Starting point, straight across, slanting down left, straight across: capital Z

Continuous Stroke Penmanship Models

Continuous stroke models of manuscript handwriting provide you with an alternative to the ball-and-stick method. The purpose of these models is geared toward teaching students to write letters without lifting their pencils.

Aa Bb Cc Dd Ee

Ff Gg Hh Ii Jj

Kk Ll Mm Nn Oo

Pp Qq Rr Ss Tt

Uu Vv Ww Xx

Yy Zz

Numbers

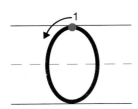

0 Starting point, curving left all the way around to starting point: *0*

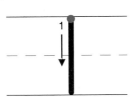

1 Starting point, straight down: *1*

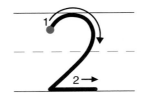

2 Starting point, around right, slanting left and straight across right: *2*

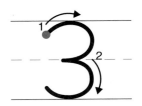

3 Starting point, around right, in at the middle, around right: *3*

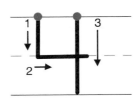

4 Starting point, straight down
Straight across right
Starting point, straight down, crossing line: *4*

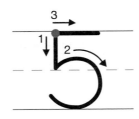

5 Starting point, straight down, curving around right and up
Starting point, straight across right: *5*

6 Starting point, slanting left, around the bottom curving up, around right and into the curve: *6*

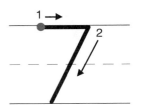

7 Starting point, straight across right, slanting down left: *7*

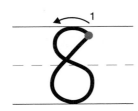

8 Starting point, curving left, curving down and around right, slanting up right to starting point: *8*

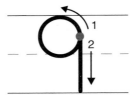

9 Starting point, curving around left all the way, straight down: *9*

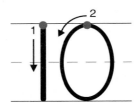

10 Starting point, straight down
Starting point, curving left all the way around to starting point: *10*

Alphabet Activities

Purpose

To provide students with activities for reinforcement of letter shapes

About the Activities

During Workshop of lessons in which you introduce letters, include activities in which students can make letters. Activities like these are included in the lessons already, while some letter-making activities you can establish in your classroom are listed below.

Most students will probably need a visual model to help them get started. Use red, blue, or green markers to print the letters on sturdy cardboard or poster board cards. Students will make yarn letters, glue letters, or other types by tracing the model.

All these activities, in addition to reinforcing letter formation, will help students' visual, perceptual, and fine-motor development.

Yarn Letters

Give each student four 4-inch pieces, four 8-inch pieces, and four 12-inch pieces of heavy yarn (such as rug yarn) to form letters. Each different length of yarn can be a different color (for example, 4-inch—red, 8-inch—blue, and 12-inch—green). When you work with students to form a particular letter, you can help them by using colors. For example, if students are making a capital *A*, they can use one blue piece and one red. Keep the yarn pieces in small plastic bags for reuse each time you introduce a new letter.

Clay Letters

Have students roll modeling clay into sticks that can be broken into different lengths and curved as necessary to form letters. When they are finished, have students roll their letters back into balls of clay. Keep these in sealed plastic bags for reuse.

Sand Letters

Provide each student with a small Styrofoam grocery tray filled halfway with sand. Have students trace with their fingers the letters they are practicing. In later lessons, have students trace words.

Pipe Cleaner Letters

Cut 12-inch pipe cleaners into 4-inch and 8-inch pieces, leaving some 12-inch pieces. Instruct students to form letters with the different lengths of pipe cleaners.

Glue Letters

Provide each student with large printed models of the letters. Tell students to trace the letters with glue and then sprinkle the glue with glitter, colored sand, confetti, salt, oatmeal, rice, or any other material that is not too bulky to stick to the glue. After the glue has begun to dry, have students shake off any excess material.

Drinking Straw Letters

Cut 8-inch drinking straws in half to make 4-inch pieces. Then cut them in fourths to make 2-inch pieces. Leave some the 8-inch length. Have students form letters using the pieces. Drinking straws are not suitable for letters that have curved lines but work well for those with straight and slanted lines.

Floor Letters

Have students form letters from various classroom materials, such as jump ropes, building blocks, beads, string, and so on.

Finger-Paint Letters

Using finger paints and finger-paint paper, have students trace letters with their fingers.

Board Letters

Encourage students to use the board or chart paper to practice their letters.

The Pocket Chart

Purpose

To provide a device that will allow students to practice word substitutions and to play with words

Developing Concepts Using the *Pocket Chart*

The **Pocket Chart** will help students understand written language. They will begin to understand the concept of words, phrases, and sentences. It is easy to substitute and play with words in the ten-line **Pocket Chart.**

Introducing Print At the beginning of the year, use the **Pocket Chart** to introduce print in another way to students. Seeing the words in the **Pickled Peppers Big Book** on the board, on chart paper, or in the **Pocket Chart** gives students several opportunities to understand print.

Words Take the **Pocket Chart Word Cards** out of the **Pocket Chart,** and allow students to handle the individual cards. Students will begin to comprehend the concept of words and learn that words vary in length.

Sequence Arrange the **Pocket Chart Word Cards** and **Pocket Chart Picture Cards** out of sequence and "read" them. Have students help you rearrange the cards in order, reinforcing their understanding of word order in phrases and sentences.

Matching Words to Pictures Show students a **Pocket Chart Picture Card.** Have them say the name of the picture, and ask them for the beginning and ending sounds of the picture name. Allow them to choose the matching **Pocket Chart Word Card** based on their answers to your questions. After students have had many experiences with written words and the **Pocket Chart,** place the **Word Cards** in the **Pocket Chart,** and have students match the **Picture Cards** with the **Word Cards.**

Matching Words to Words Use **Pickled Peppers** selections that repeat words or entire lines several times. Place portions of a selection in the **Pocket Chart,** leaving space for students to complete the excerpt by placing the appropriate repeated **Pocket Chart Word Cards** in the **Pocket Chart.**

Rhyme and Substituting Words After students have learned a **Pickled Peppers** selection, place a portion of it in the **Pocket Chart,** then substitute rhyming **Pocket Chart Word Cards** or **Picture Cards** for various words. Although the result may be a change in meaning, students will hear a new rhyme. You may want to place **Alphabet Letter Cards** over the letters that make the initial sound of key words to create rhyming words with different initial sounds. For example, you may want to place the *Mm* card over the initial consonants in "Peter Piper picked" to make "Meter Miper micked."

Position Words and Prepositional Phrases Place in the **Pocket Chart** a phrase such as "under the [picture of a bed]" and substitute the **Pocket Chart Word Cards** to make other phrases. Ask students to change the phrase by changing the position word or the **Pocket Chart Picture Card.** Position words include *after, against, at, behind, down, here, in, on, out, over, right, underneath,* and *up.*

Framing Sentences Place only the beginning of a sentence in the **Pocket Chart Pocket Chart,** such as "I hear a _____ ."

Ask students to finish the sentence by placing a **Pocket Chart Word Card** or **Picture Card** at the end. You may also choose to set incomplete lines from "Keep a Poem in Your Pocket" in the **Pocket Chart,** asking students to complete the line with an appropriate card.

Pocket Chart Card Lists

The following lists are intended to save time in gathering **Pocket Chart Word Cards** and **Picture Cards** for **Pickled Peppers** selections and other activities. **Picture Cards** are in **boldfaced type.**

Numbers

0/zero, **1**/one, **2**/two, **3**/three, **4**/four, **5**/five, **6**/six, **7**/seven, **8**/eight, **9**/nine, **10**/ten

Colors

black/black, **blue**/blue/azul, **brown**/brown, **gray, green**/green/verde, **orange**/orange/anaranjada, **pink**/pink, **purple**/purple, **red**/red, **white**/white, **yellow**/yellow/amarilla

Foods

apple, apple juice, berry/berry, **bowls of spaghetti, cherry**/cherry, **corn**/corn, **eggplants, ice, jam, juice, loaf, bread, loaves of bread, meat, noodle,** orange, **peanut butter, peppers**/peppers, **pickled pears, pie, pizza pies, potatoes, pumpkins, rice, roasted turkeys, tomatoes, vegetables, water**/water, **watermelons, yam**

Opposites

big, little; **black**/black, **white**/white; **day, night**/night; for, against; in, out; short, tall; up, down

Pickled Peppers Big Book **Selections**

I'm a Little Teapot* a, all, and, and, get, handle, hear, here, Here, I, I'm, is, is, little, me, me, me, my, my, out, over, pour, short, shout, spout, stout, **teapot/**teapot, Tip, up, When

One, Two, Buckle My Shoe* **1/**One, **2/**two, **3/**Three, **4/**four, **5/**Five, **6/**six, **7/**Seven, **8/**eight, **9/**Nine, **10/**ten, A, big, Buckle, **door/**door, fat, **hen/**hen, Lay, my, Pick, **shoe/**shoe, Shut, **sticks/**sticks, straight, the, them, up

Little Boy Blue** after, blow, **boy/**boy, **Boy Blue/**Boy Blue, Come, **corn/**corn, cow's, **horn/**horn, in, in, is, looks, meadow, **sheep/**sheep, sheep's, the, the, the, the, The, The, Where, Who, your

Jack and Jill* a, after, and, And, And, broke, came, **crown/**crown, down, fell, fetch, **hill,** hill, his, **Jack/**Jack, Jack, **Jill/**Jill, Jill, of, **pail/**pail, the, To, tumbling, up, **water/**water, Went

Humpty Dumpty* a, a, again, all, All, and, Couldn't, fall, great, had, **horses/**horses, Humpty, **Humpty Dumpty/**Humpty Dumpty, Humpty Dumpty, King's, King's, **men/**men, on, put, sat, the, the, together, **wall/**wall

Little Bo Peep* alone, and, And, behind, **Bo Peep/**Bo Peep, come, doesn't, find, has, her, know, Leave, Little, lost, **sheep/**sheep, **tails/**tails, them, them, their, them, they'll, to, Wagging, where

Peter Piper** a, A, of, of, **peck/**peck, peck, **peppers/**peppers, peppers, **Peter Piper/**Peter Piper, Peter Piper, picked, picked, pickled, pickled

One Hungry Monster** **1/**One, **2/**two, **3/**Three, **4/**four, **5/**Five, **6/**six, **7/**Seven, **8/**eight, **9/**Nine, **10/**ten, and, **apple juice,** be, **bed/**bed, begging, **bowls of spaghetti, clam, eggplants,** fed, groaning, hungry, **jam, loaves of bread,** moaning, **monster/**monster, **monsters,** my, **orange/**orange, **peanut butter, pickled pears, pizza pies, pumpkins, purple/**purple, **roasted turkeys,** to, underneath, **watermelons**

Rope Rhyme** and, and, and, Bounce, clappedy-slappedy, Get, giggle, **ground/**ground, hits, in, it, jump, kick, Listen, Listen, now, ready, right, **rope/**rope, set, sound, spin, that, the, the, to, to, when

Who Said Red?** A, A, A, **berry/**berry, **cherry/**cherry, Did, **red/**red, red, red, red, red, red, Santa, say, sign, stop, **stop sign,** very, Who, you

Rhyme*** a, A, A, and, **black/**black, blunder, Come, down, dunder, **hills/**hills, I, I, it, like, like, see, see, slow, **storm/**storm, storm, storm, stumbling, the, thunder, to, to

Tent**** A, **bone/**bone, bone, canvas, cut, for, from, I, is, It's, It's, Just, like, me, measure, My, sewn, **skin/**skin, stretched, **tent/**tent, That's, to, to, where, wonder

Little Pine* a, a, against, But, doesn't, even, feet, few, grows, have, I, I, is, it, it, it, It, just, keep, little, measuring, more, My, myself, **pine/**pine, slower, tall, the, the, **tree/**tree, trunk, watch, yet

Houses/Casitas (English)* **1/**one, A, a, a, a, an, **blue/**blue, bouquet, **bouquet of flowers,** down, **flowers/**flowers, **green/**green, **house/**house, house, house, house, is, Just, Like, look, of, **orange/**orange, ours, **street/**street, the, The, **yellow/**yellow

Houses/Casitas (Spanish)*** a, **amarilla/**amarilla, **anaranjada/**anaranjada, Asómate, **azul/**azul, **calle/**calle, **casita/**casita, casita, casita, casita, la, mira, Una, una, una, una, **verde/**verde, y

Keep a Poem in Your Pocket** a, a, and, and, at, **bed/**bed, feel, **head/**head, in, in, in, Keep, lonely, never, night, picture, **pocket/**pocket, poem, when, you'll, your, your, you're

* There are *Pocket Chart Word* or *Picture Cards* for the entire selection.

**There are *Pocket Chart Word* or *Picture Cards* for the first four lines of the selection.

***There are *Pocket Chart Word* or *Picture Cards* for the first five lines of the selection.

****There are *Pocket Chart Word* or *Picture Cards* for the first six lines of the selection.

*****There are *Pocket Chart Word* or *Picture Cards* for the first eight lines of the selection.

Introduction of Letters and Sounds

Lesson	Letters and Sounds	Pre-Decodables/Decodables	High-Frequency Words
Unit 1			
Lesson 1	A		
Lesson 2	B	*Pre-Decodable* 1: The First Day of Kindergarten	
Lesson 3	C		
Lesson 4	D	*Pre-Decodable* 2: Apple Pie	
Lesson 5	E		
Lesson 6	F		
Lesson 7	A-F	*Pre-Decodable* 3: A Farm	a
Lesson 8	G		
Lesson 9	H	*Pre-Decodable* 4: The Lunch	the
Lesson 10	I		
Lesson 11	J		
Lesson 12	K	*Pre-Decodable* 5: School	and
Lesson 13	L		
Lesson 14	M	*Pre-Decodable* 6: Go Play!	go
Lesson 15	G-M		
Unit 2			
Lesson 1	N		
Lesson 2	O	*Pre-Decodable* 7: The Zoo	had
Lesson 3	P		
Lesson 4	Q	*Pre-Decodable* 8: Colors	he
Lesson 5	R		
Lesson 6	S		
Lesson 7	N-S	*Pre-Decodable* 9: Shapes	I
Lesson 8	T		
Lesson 9	U	*Pre-Decodable* 10: Animal Tracks	see
Lesson 10	V		
Lesson 11	W		
Lesson 12	X	*Pre-Decodable* 11: The Tree	has
Lesson 13	Y		
Lesson 14	Z	*Pre-Decodable* 12: Flowers	you
Lesson 15	T-Z		

Lesson	Letters and Sounds	Pre-Decodables/Decodables	High-Frequency Words
Unit 3			
Lesson 1	initial /s/		
Lesson 2	final /s/		
Lesson 3	initial /m/		
Lesson 4	final /m/		
Lesson 5	review /s/ and /m/	*Pre-Decodable* 13: We Go	we
Lesson 6	initial /d/		
Lesson 7	final /d/		
Lesson 8	initial /p/		
Lesson 9	final /p/		
Lesson 10	review /d/ and /p/	*Pre-Decodable* 14: We Carry	of
Lesson 11	/a/		
Lesson 12	/a/		
Lesson 13	review /s/, /m/, and /a/	*Pre-Decodable* 15: In the Park	in
Lesson 14	blending		
Lesson 15	/s/, /m/, /a/, /d/ and /p/	*Decodable* 1: Sam and Pam	am
Unit 4			
Lesson 1	initial /h/		
Lesson 2	initial /h/		
Lesson 3	initial /t/		
Lesson 4	final /t/		
Lesson 5	review /h/ and /t/	*Decodable* 2: A Hat!	at, to
Lesson 6	initial /n/		
Lesson 7	final /n/		
Lesson 8	initial /l/		
Lesson 9	final /l/		
Lesson 10	review /n/ and /l/	*Decodable* 3: Nan and Lad	as, have
Lesson 11	/i/		
Lesson 12	/i/		
Lesson 13	review /h/, /t/, and /i/		
Lesson 14	review /n/, /l/, and /i/		
Lesson 15	/h/, /t/, /i/, /n/, and /l/	*Decodable* 4: Tim in Sand	is, it

Lesson	Letters and Sounds	Pre-Decodables/Decodables	High-Frequency Words
Unit 5			
Lesson 1	initial /b/		
Lesson 2	final /b/		
Lesson 3	/k/ spelled *Cc*		
Lesson 4	/k/ spelled *Cc*		
Lesson 5	/b/ and /k/	*Decodable* 5: Cal Can Bat	can, his
Lesson 6	/o/		
Lesson 7	/o/		
Lesson 8	initial /r/		
Lesson 9	final /r/		
Lesson 10	initial /g/	*Decodable* 6: Ron Hops	him, on
Lesson 11	final /g/		
Lesson 12	review /r/ and /g/		
Lesson 13	review /b/, /k/, and /o/		
Lesson 14	review /r/, /g/, and /o/		
Lesson 15	/b/, /k/, /o/, /r/, and /g/	*Decodable* 7: Glad Pam	did, girl
Unit 6			
Lesson 1	initial /j/		
Lesson 2	initial /j/		
Lesson 3	initial /f/		
Lesson 4	final /f/		
Lesson 5	review /j/ and /f/	*Decodable* 8: Jam Pot	for
Lesson 6	/u/		
Lesson 7	/u/		
Lesson 8	/ks/ (*Xx*)		
Lesson 9	/ks/ (*Xx*)		
Lesson 10	/z/	*Decodable* 9: Bud and Max	but, up
Lesson 11	/z/ spelled Ss		
Lesson 12	review /ks/ and /z/		
Lesson 13	review /j/, /f/, and /u/		
Lesson 14	review /ks/, /z/, and /u/		
Lesson 15	/j/, /f/, /u/, /ks/, and /z/	*Decodable* 10: Liz and Tad	all

Lesson	Letters and Sounds	Pre-Decodables/Decodables	High-Frequency Words
Unit 7			
Lesson 1	initial /w/		
Lesson 2	final /w/		
Lesson 3	/k/ spelled Kk		
Lesson 4	/k/ spelled Kk		
Lesson 5	review /w/ and /k/	*Decodable* 11: Kim and Sam	look, with
Lesson 6	/e/		
Lesson 7	/e/		
Lesson 8	initial /kw/ (*Qu*)		
Lesson 9	initial /kw/ (*Qu*)		
Lesson 10	initial /y/	*Decodable* 12: Quin and the Jets	her, what
Lesson 11	initial /v/		
Lesson 12	review /y/ and /v/		
Lesson 13	review /w/, /k/, and /e/		
Lesson 14	review /kw/, /y/, /v/, and /e/		
Lesson 15	/w/, /k/, /e/, /kw/, /y/, and /v/	*Decodable* 13: Vic Yelps	was, were
Unit 8			
Lesson 1	initial /ā/		
Lesson 2	initial and medial /ā/		
Lesson 3	medial /ā/		
Lesson 4	medial /ā/ and a_e		
Lesson 5	blending with /ā/	*Decodable* 14: Jake Plants Grapes	said, that
Lesson 6	initial /ī/		
Lesson 7	initial and medial /ī/		
Lesson 8	medial /ī/		
Lesson 9	medial /ī/ and i_e		
Lesson 10	blending with /ī/	*Decodable* 15: Mike and Spike	down, they
Lesson 11	review /ā/ and /ī/		
Lesson 12	review /ā/ and /ī/		
Lesson 13	review /ā/ and /ī/		
Lesson 14	review /ā/ and /ī/		
Lesson 15	blending with /ā/ and /ī/	*Decodable* 16: A Nut Pile	some, there

Lesson	Sound and Letters	Pre-Decodables/Decodables	High-Frequency Words
Unit 9			
Lesson 1	initial /ō/		
Lesson 2	initial and medial /ō/		
Lesson 3	medial /ō/		
Lesson 4	medial /ō/ and o_e		
Lesson 5	blending with /ō/	*Decodable* 17: An Old Flag	boy, out
Lesson 6	initial /ū/		
Lesson 7	initial and medial /ū/		
Lesson 8	medial /ū/		
Lesson 9	medial /ū/ and u_e		
Lesson 10	blending with /ū/	*Decodable* 18: Cute Little Mule	do, little
Lesson 11	review /ō/ and /ū/		
Lesson 12	review /ō/ and /ū/		
Lesson 13	review /ō/ and /ū/		
Lesson 14	review /ō/ and /ū/		
Lesson 15	blending with /ō/ and /ū/	*Decodable* 19: The Cutest Pet	when, then
Unit 10			
Lesson 1	initial /ē/		
Lesson 2	initial and medial /ē/		
Lesson 3	medial /ē/		
Lesson 4	medial /ē/		
Lesson 5	blending with /ē/	*Decodable* 20: We Did It!	be, she
Lesson 6	review /ā/ and /ă/		
Lesson 7	review /ī/ and /ĭ/		
Lesson 8	review /ā/, /ă/, /ī/, and /ĭ/		
Lesson 9	review /ō/ and /ŏ/		
Lesson 10	review /ū/ and /ŭ/		
Lesson 11	review /ō/, /ŏ/, /ū/, and /ŭ/		
Lesson 12	review /ē/ and /ĕ/		
Lesson 13	/ā/, /ī/, /ō/, /ă/, /ŏ/, /ĭ/		
Lesson 14	/ū/, /ē/, /ŭ/, /ĕ/		
Lesson 15	review		

Alphabet Sound Card Stories

Card 2: /b/ Ball

Bobby loves his basketball.

He bounces it all day.

The ball goes /b/ /b/ /b/ /b/ /b/

As it bounces on its way.

Card 4: /d/ Dinosaur

Dinah, the dancing dinosaur,

Had huge and clumsy feet.

They went /d/ /d/ /d/ /d/ /d/

As Dinah kept the beat.

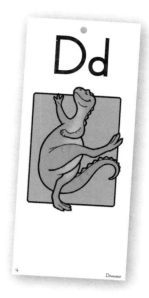

Card 3: /c/ Camera

Carlos clicks his camera

/k/ /k/ /k/ /k/ /k/ /k/ it goes.

The pictures come out crisp and clear.

So give a smile, /k/ /k/ /k/ Carlos is here.

Card 6: /f/ Fan

Franny the fan spins, oh, so fast.

Spreading fresh air with a regular blast.

When Franny the fan goes round and round

/f/ /f/ /f/ /f/ /f/ /f/ is her fast fan sound.

Card 7: /g/ Gopher

Gary is a gopher

Who gulps green grapes all day.

When he gulps and giggles,

/g/ /g/ /g/ /g/ /g/ /g/ is what he'll say.

Card 10: /j/ Jump

Jenny and Jackson like to have fun.

They play jacks, jump rope, and juggle in the sun.

Each time they jump, their feet hit the ground.

/j/ /j/ /j/ /j/ /j/ is the jumping-rope sound.

Card 8: /h/ Hound

Harry the hound dog

Hurries around.

/h/ /h/ /h/ /h/ /h/ /h/

Is his hurrying sound.

Card 11: /k/ Camera

Carlos clicks his camera

/k/ /k/ /k/ /k/ /k/ /k/ it goes.

The pictures come out crisp and clear.

So give a smile, /k/ /k/ /k/ Carlos is here.

Card 12: /l/ Lion

Look! It's Leon the Lion.

Leon loves to lap water from lakes.

This is the lapping sound Leon makes:

/l/ /l/ /l/ /l/ /l/ /l/.

Card 14: /n/ Nest

n/ /n/ /n/ /n/

What is in that noisy nest?

A nervous night owl crying?

A nosy nuthatch chatting?

A nightingale that's sighing?

No! It's a bluebird napping!

/n/ /n/ /n/ /n/

Card 13: /m/ Monkey

For Muzzy, the Monkey,

Bananas are yummy.

She munches so many,

They fill up her tummy.

She says /m/ /m/ /m/ /m/ /m/!

Card 16: /p/ Popcorn

Popcorn! Popcorn! Ping and Pong shouted,

Let's pop some in a pot, because we like it hot!

/p/ /p/ /p/ /p/ /p/ was the sound it made.

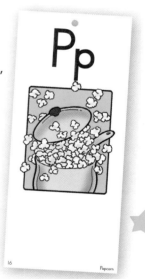

Card 17: /kw/ Quacking ducks

Quincy the duck couldn't quite quack.

He said /kw/ /kw/ /kw/.

Quincy kept trying, but all he could say was:

/kw/ /kw/ /kw/ /kw/ /kw/.

Card 19: /s/ Sausages

Sue buys sausages on Saturday.

Sam cooks sausages on Sunday.

The sausages sizzle /s/ /s/ /s/ /s/ /s/ /s/ when hot.

Sam eats sausages, but Sue does not.

Card 18: /r/ Robot

Rosie the Robot just runs and runs: /r/ /r/ /r/,

Racing around to get her chores done /r/ /r/ /r/.

Running here, running there,

Running almost everywhere: /r/ /r/ /r/.

Card 20: /t/ Timer

Tom Tuttle's timer ticks like this:

/t/ /t/ /t/ /t/ /t/.

Tonight Tom Tuttle wants tomatoes on toast.

He sets his timer. Listen carefully:

/t/ /t/ /t/ /t/ /t/.

What sound would the timer make if you set it?

/t/ /t/ /t/ /t/ /t/.

Card 22: /v/ Vacuum

Vinny the Vacuum is cleaning again.

Before visitors visit, he always begins.

This is the sound of his very loud voice:

/v/ /v/ /v/ /v/ /v/ /v/

As he vacuums and vacuums all over the place:

/v/ /v/ /v/ /v/ /v/ /v/.

Card 24: /ks/ Exit

Rex is called the Exiting X.

He runs to guard the door.

To get past Rex,

Make the sound of the x:

/ks/ /ks/ /ks/ /ks/ /ks/.

Card 23: /w/ Washer

Willie the Washer washed white clothes all week.

When he washed he went
/w/ /w/ /w/ /w/ /w/ /w/.

Willie the Washer was tired; he sprang a leak.

He washed and washed and he went:
/w/ /w/ /w/ /w/.

Card 25: /y/ Yaks

Yolanda and Yoshiko are yaks.

They don't yell.

They just yak: /y/ /y/ /y/ /y/ /y/.

Yakety-yak! Yakety-yak!

What is the sound of the curious yaks?

/y/ /y/ /y/ /y/ /y/.

Card 26: /z/ Zipper

Zack's jacket has a zipper.

Zack zips it up and it makes this sound:

/z/ /z/ /z/ /z/ /z/ /z/.

Zack zips it down and it makes this sound:

/z/ /z/ /z/ /z/ /z/ /z/.

Card 28: /e/ Hen

Jen's pet hen likes to peck, peck, peck: /e/ /e/ /e/.

She pecks at a speck on the new red deck: /e/ /e/ /e/.

This is how her pecking sounds:

/e/ /e/ /e/ /e/ /e/ /e/

When she pecks at a speck on the hen house deck.

Card 27: /a/ Lamb

I'm Pam the lamb, I am.

This is how I tell the farmer where I am:

/a/ /a/ /a/ /a/ /a/.

I'm Pam the lamb, I am.

This is how I tell my friends where I am:

/a/ /a/ /a/ /a/ /a/.

Card 29: /i/ Pig

Here sits Pickles the Pig.

Tickle Pickles, and she'll get the giggles.

This is the sound of Pickles' giggles:

/i/ /i/ /i/ /i/ /i/ /i/.

Card 30: /o/ Fox

Bob the fox did not feel well at all.

He jogged to the doctor's office.

"Say /o/, Mr. Fox. /o/ /o/ /o/."

"My head is hot, and my throat hurts a lot."

"Say /o/, Mr. Fox, /o/ /o/ /o/."

Card 31: /u/ Tug

Tubby the Tugboat can huff and puff

And push and pull to move big stuff.

/u/ /u/ /u/ /u/ /u/

That's the sound of Tubby the Tug.

He works all day from dawn till dusk.

/u/ /u/ / u/ /u/ /u/.

High-Frequency Word List

Level Pre-K High-Frequency Words

a	go	in	the
and	had	is	up
at	have	on	was
can	he	see	with
down	I	she	you

Level K High-Frequency Words

all	for	look	there
am	girl	of	they
as	has	out	to
be	her	said	we
boy	him	some	were
but	his	that	what
did	it	then	when
do	little		

Supplemental Word List

You can use the following word list in a number of ways to extend the lessons. Words are listed by beginning sounds, ending sounds, and medial vowel sounds.

Beginning Sounds

Beginning /ā/
acorn
ape
apron

Beginning /a/
acrobat
alligator
apple
apple juice
astronaut

Beginning /b/
bag
bait
ball
balloon
banana
baseball
basketball
bat
beans
bed
bee
bell
bird
boat
book
bow
bowl
bowling ball
box
bread

broom
bug
bus

Beginning /k/
cake
can
cane
cap
cat
clam
coat
cook
core
cup
cut

Beginning /d/
dad
deer
dice
dime
dish
dog
doll
dollar
donkey
door
dress
drum
duck

Beginning /ē/
eagle
ear
earphones
easel
eel

Beginning /e/
Eggplant
elephant
elk

envelope

Beginning /f/
falcon
fan
feet
fern
fir
fish
five
fly
food
football
fork
four
fox
Frisbee
frog

Beginning /g/
game
gate
glue
goat
goose
grass
green
guitar

Beginning /h/
ham
hand
hat
hawk
heaven
hen
hive
hog
hole
hook
horse
hot

house
hug

Beginning /ī/
ice
ice cream
icicles
iron
island
ivy

Beginning /i/
igloo
ill
inch
infant
insect

Beginning /j/
jam
jar
jeans
jellybean
jellyfish
judge
juice

Beginning /k/
kangaroo
kettle
keys
kitchen
kittens
koala

Beginning /l/
ladybug
lake
lamp
lion
lock
lockers

Beginning /m/
magnet

mailbox
man
map
mask
mat
meal
meat
milk
mittens
monkey
moon
moose
mop
mouse
mug

Beginning /n/
nails
necklace
needle
nest
newspaper
nickle
nine
noodle
nurse

Beginning /ō/
oak tree
oasis
oatmeal
oboe
ocean
overalls

Beginning /o/
octopus
olive
ostrich
otter
ox

Beginning /p/
pail
pan
panda
pants
pear
peas
pen
penny
pickle
pickled pears
pie
pig
pineapple
pink
pizza pies
plum bun
popcorn
post
pot
potatoes
pumpkins
purple

Beginning /kw/
quail
quart
queen
quill
quilt

Beginning /r/
raccoon
racer
radio
rake
rat
red
rice
road
robot
rock

rocket
rug
ruler

Beginning /s/
sack
sad
sail
Sam
sand
sandals
seal
seven
silk
six
skate
soccer ball
sock
spoon
star
stew
sticks
stir
store
storm
sun

Beginning /t/
table
tail
tap
tape
target
tear
telephone
television
ten
tie
toad
toast
toe
tomatoes

top
tree
turkey
turtle
two

Beginning /ū/
ukulele
unicorn
uniform
United States
utensil

Beginning /u/
umbrella
umpire
uncle
under
usher

Beginning /v/
van
vase
vegetables
veil
vine
violin
volcano

Beginning /w/
wagon
wallet
walrus
watch
well
wig
wing

Beginning /y/
yam
yard
yarn
yell
yellow

yo-yo
yolk

Beginning /z/
zebra
zero
zinnia
zither
zoo

Ending Sounds

Ending /ā/
away
bay
day
gray
hay
Jay
may
Monday
play
ray
say
today

Ending /b/
Bob
cab
cob
cub
cube
jab
job
mob
rob
robe
rub
scrub
tab
tub
web

Ending /d/
bad
bed
bread
did
feed
had
lid
mad
mud
red
rid
sad
seed
weed
yard

Ending /ē/
bee
Frisbee
he
key
knee
me
monkey
see
she
three
tree
turkey
we

Ending /f/
calf
cough
cuff
deaf
elf
half
laugh
off
rough

stiff
stuff
tough

Ending /g/
bag
big
dog
egg
hog
hug
jog
ladybug
leg
log
pig
rag
rug
tag
twig
wig

Ending /ī/
by
cry
die
dry
fly
high
my
pie
sigh
tie
why

Ending /k/
bike
black
clock
cook
dock
duck

elk
fork
hook
lake
like
lock
milk
pack
pink
poke
rack
rake
rock
sock
take

Ending /l/
basketball
bell
bill
eel
feel
football
oatmeal
pail
quail
rail
seal
snail
tail

Ending /m/
broom
dime
drum
game
hum
jam
room
seem
uniform
yam

Ending /n/
can
fern
green
hen
kitchen
lion
moon
ocean
queen
raccoon
spoon
sun
ten
unicorn
van
vine
violin
wagon
yarn

Ending /ō/
blow
bow
doe
flow
go
low
mow
no
radio
row
slow
so
toe
volcano
yellow
yo-yo
zero

Ending /p/
cap
cape
cup
deep
hip
hop
keep
lip
map
pup
skip
sleep
tap
tip
top
trap

Ending /r/
alligator
bar
car
core
deer
door
fur
four
guitar
jar
more
newspaper
otter
pour
roar
ruler
stir
usher

Ending /s/
bus
class
dress

goose
grass
horse
house
miss
moss
mouse
octopus
pass
toss
walrus
yes

Ending /t/
astronaut
bat
cat
coat
feet
gate
goat
hat
hot
infant
kite
knot
meat
pot
quilt
wallet
white

Ending /ū/
cue
few
hue
menu
nephew
preview
rescue
review
view

Ending /v/
brave
cave
dive
dove
eve
five
gave
give
glove
have
hive
live
love
save
shave
stove

Ending /ks/
ax
box
fix
flax
fox
mix
ox
relax
six
wax

Ending /z/
breeze
buzz
daze
fizz
freeze
fuzz
haze
jazz
maze
peas
quiz

size
sneeze
squeeze
trees

Medial Sounds

Medial /ā/
date
face
fade
game
gate
gave
lake
lane
late
made
make
mate
race
rake
table
wave

Medial /a/
bat
black
can
cap
hat
jam
ham
lamp
pants
sad
van
yam

Medial /ē/
beam
bean
feet

heap
keep
mean
meat
neat
seal
seed
seen
sneeze
team
weed

Medial /e/
bed
bet
head
hen
let
men
met
nest
net
pen
pet
red
set
ten

Medial /ī/
five
hide
hive
kite
life
line
mine
nice
nine
rice
ride
right

side
sight
time
vine

Medial /i/
bib
dish
fib
fin
fish
him
kittens
lip
milk
mittens
pig
pin
pink
rip
tin
tip
wig
win

Medial /ō/
boat
bowl
coal
coat
goat
hole
home
joke
mole
nose
poem
poke
post
roll
rose
toes

Medial /o/
dot
hot
knot
lock
lot
mop
not
pot
rock
sock
top

Medial /ū/
cube
cute
feud
fuel
fuse
huge
mule

Medial /u/
bug
bun
cup
cut
duck
dust
fun
hug
must
nut
rub
rug
run
sun
tub
tug

Above Level, *see* Monitor Progress

Action Words, Unit 2: T154–T155, T164, T165; **Unit 3:** T40; **Unit 8:** T120, T146, T156, T188, T220, T229; **Unit 9:** T150; **Unit 10:** T227; *see also* Grammar, Usage, and Mechanics; Verbs

Activate Prior Knowledge, Unit 1: T40, T54, T112, T124, T156, T190, T214; **Unit 2:** T40, T52, T106, T118, T150, T184, T208; **Unit 3:** T36, T96, T106, T134, T166, T188; **Unit 4:** T36, T96, T106, T142, T194; **Unit 5:** T36, T46, T100, T110, T138, T170; **Unit 6:** T36, T46, T92, T102, T130, T162, T182; **Unit 7:** T36, T96, T138, T170, T190; **Unit 8:** T36, T142, T174, T194; **Unit 9:** T36, T48, T98, T108, T136, T168, T188; **Unit 10:** T36, T46, T98, T110, T126, T142, T174, T194

Adjectives, *see* Words That Describe

Advanced Learners, *see* Challenge Activities

Alphabet, Unit 1: GS22, GS28, GS34, GS40, GS46, GS58, GS64; T26, T36, T50, T59, T61, T68, T86, T108, T120, T136, T143, T145, T152, T164, T186, T198, T210, T217, T219, T221, T228; **Unit 2:** T26, T36, T48, T64, T80, T102, T114, T121, T130, T146, T158, T180, T192, T204, T224, T244; **Unit 3:** T93, T103, T117, T131, T141, T163, T173, T183, T201, T217; **Unit 4:** T113, T199; **Unit 7:** T193, T201; **Unit 9:** T197

Alphabet Flash Cards, Unit 1: T36, T210, T212, T246; **Unit 2:** T80, T130, T180, T204; **Unit 7:** T207; **Unit 8:** T59

Alphabetic Knowledge, Unit 1: T26–T27, T36–T37, T50–T51, T59, T61, T68–T69, T86–T87, T108–T109, T120–T121, T136–T137, T143, T145, T152–T153, T164–T165, T186–T187, T198–T199, T210–T211, T217, T219, T221, T228–T229; **Unit 2:** T26–T27, T36–T37, T48–T49, T64–T65, T80–T81, T102–T103, T114–T115, T121, T130–T131, T146–T147, T158–T159, T180–T181, T192–T193, T204–T205, T224–T225, T244–T245; **Unit 6:** T49, T105, T107; **Unit 8:** T53; *see also* Capital Letters; Small Letters

Alphabetic Principle, Unit 3: T26–T27, T34–T35, T44–T45, T58–T59, T72–T73, T94–T95, T104–T105, T118–T119, T132–T133, T142–T143, T164–T165, T174–T175, T184–T185, T202–T203; **Unit 4:** T26–T27, T34–T35, T44–T45, T58–T59, T72–T73, T94–T95, T104–T105, T122–T123, T140–T141, T150–T151, T172–T173, T182–T183, T192–T193, T208–T209, T224–T225; **Unit 5:** T26–T27, T34–T35, T60–T61, T76–T77, T98–T99, T108–T109, T122–T123, T136–T137, T146–T147, T168–T169, T178–T179, T188–T189, T204–T205; **Unit 6:** T26–T27, T34–T35, T44–T45, T56–T57, T68–T69, T90–T91, T100–T101, T113–T114, T128–T129, T138–T139, T160–T161, T170–T171, T180–T181, T212–T213; **Unit 7:** T26–T27, T44–T45, T58–T59, T72–T73, T94–T95, T104–T105, T120–T121, T136–T137, T146–T147, T168–T169, T178–T179, T188–T189, T206–T207, T224–T225; **Unit 8:** T26–T27, T34–T35, T44–T45, T60–T61, T76–T77, T98–T99, T108–T109, T124–T125, T140–T141, T150–T151, T172–T173, T192–T193, T208–T209, T224–T225; **Unit 9:** T26–T27, T34–T35, T46–T47, T60–T61, T74–T75, T96–T97, T106–T107, T120–T121, T134–T135, T144–T145, T176–T177, T186–T187, T202–T203, T218–T219; **Unit 10:** T26–T27, T44–T45, T72–T73, T96–T97, T108–T109, T124–T125, T140–T141, T152–T153, T172–T173, T182–T183, T192–T193, T208–T209, T224–T225

Alphabet Sound Wall Cards, Unit 1: GS3, GS22, GS28, GS34, GS45, GS46, GS52, GS64, GS67, T26, T36, T50, T68, T86, T92, T108, T120, T121, T136, T152, T164, T166, T186, T198, T210, T228, T229, T246, T248; **Unit 2:** T26, T36, T48, T64, T80, T82, T102, T114, T115, T130, T146, T158, T160, T180, T192, T204, T205, T224, T244, T245; **Unit 3:** T26, T34, T44, T58, T72, T93, T95, T104, T118, T132, T163, T164, T165, T173, T183, T217; **Unit 4:** T26, T45, T94, T95, T104, T122, T192; **Unit 5:** T24, T26, T98, T108, T122, T188; **Unit 6:** T44, T66, T90, T114, T169, T179; **Unit 7:** T26, T44, T72, T94, T120, T121, T146, T167, T168, T177, T188; **Unit 8:** T26, T34, T98, T124, T140, T181, T191, T192, T224; **Unit 9:** T26, T46, T96, T106, T151, T185, T203; **Unit 10:** T26, T58, T96, T108, T124, T140, T152, T157, T172, T208

Antonyms, *see* Words That Mean the Opposite

Approaching Level, *see* Monitor Progress

Art Connections, *see* Fine Art

Asking Questions, Unit 1: T55, T56, T58, T60, T62, T73, T74, T76, T78, T80, T125, T191, T192, T203, T204, T215, T216, T218, T220, T222, T233, T234, T236, T238, T240; **Unit 2:** T53, T54, T56, T58, T119, T120, T122, T124, T135, T136, T138, T140; **Unit 3:** T47, T48, T50, T52, T61, T62, T64, T66; **Unit 4:** T107, T108, T110, T116, T125, T126, T128, T134; **Unit 6:** T47, T48, T50, T59, T60, T62, T103, T104, T106, T108, T117, T118, T120, T122, T163, T164, T173, T174; **Unit 7:** T47, T48, T50, T52, T61, T62, T64, T66, T171, T172, T181, T182; **Unit 8:** T47, T48, T52, T54, T63, T64, T68, T70, T195, T198, T202, T211, T212, T214, T218; **Unit 9:** T49, T50, T52, T63, T64, T66, T189, T190, T192, T194, T205, T206, T208, T210; **Unit 10:** T111, T112, T114, T116, T127, T128, T130, T132, T175, T176, T185, T186; *see also* Comprehension Strategies: Asking Questions

Assessment

Benchmark Assessment, Unit 1: T252–T253; **Unit 2:** T250–T251; **Unit 3:** T224–T225; **Unit 4:** T230, T231; **Unit 5:** T226–T227; **Unit 6:** T218, T219; **Unit 7:** T230–T231; **Unit 8:** T230, T231; **Unit 9:** T224–T225; **Unit 10:** T228, T229

Formal Assessment, *see* Monitor Progress

Lesson Assessment, Unit 1: T22, T104, T182; **Unit 2:** T22, T98, T176; **Unit 3:** T22, T90, T160; **Unit 4:** T22, T90, T168; **Unit 5:** T22, T94, T164; **Unit 6:** T22, T86, T156; **Unit 7:** T22, T90, T164; **Unit 8:** T22, T94, T168; **Unit 9:** T22, T92, T162; **Unit 10:** T22, T90, T168

Authors

Argueta, Jorge, "Shadow/Sombra," **Unit 6:** T92–T95

Asch, Frank, "Bear Shadow," **Unit 6:** T102–T109, T116–T123

Aylesworth, Jim, *Mr. McGill Goes to Town,* **Unit 7:** T36–T39

Baker, Alan, "The Ocean," **Unit 4:** T46–T53, T60–T67

Borden, Louise, *America Is . . .,* **Unit 9:** T36–T41

Brewer, Dan, "Trees," **Unit 8:** T100–T103

Brisson, Pat, *Wanda's Roses,* **Unit 5:** T190–T199, T206–T215

Bruce, Lisa, "Patterns in the Park," **Unit 2:** T52–T59, T68–T75, T111

Bulla, Clyde Robert, *What Makes a Shadow?;* "A Tree Is a Plant," **Unit 6:** T36–T39; **Unit 8:** T46–T55, T62–T71

Name Necklaces, Unit 1: T24, T26, T86, T93, T132, T148; **Unit 2:** T26, T102; **Unit 3:** T216

Naming Words, Unit 1: T46–T47, T82, T92–T93, T132–T133, T160–T161, T170–T171, T206–T207, T242–T243, T251; **Unit 3:** T40; **Unit 7:** T116; **Unit 9:** T42, T70; *see also* Grammar, Usage, and Mechanics

Nouns, *see* Words That Name

On Level, *see* Monitor Progress

Onsets and Rimes, Unit 3: T173, T183; **Unit 5:** T25, T58, T107, T166–T167; *see also* Phonemic Awareness: Onsets and rimes

Oral Blending, *see* Onsets and Rimes and Phoneme blending

Oral Language, *see* Getting Started, Phonological and Phonemic Awareness, and Warming Up

Order Words, Unit 2: T141; **Unit 7:** T68; **Unit 10:** T188; *see also* Grammar, Usage, and Mechanics

Parts of the Book, *see* Print and Book Awareness

Penmanship, Unit 1: T28, T52, T88, T110, T138, T152, T164, T166, T188, T198, T212, T248; **Unit 2:** T28, T82, T104, T132, T160, T182, T206, T246; **Unit 3:** T27, T45, T73, T95, T119, T143, T165, T185, T219; **Unit 4:** T27, T45, T73, T95, T123, T151, T193, T225; **Unit 5:** T27, T45, T77, T99, T123, T147, T169, T189, T221; **Unit 6:** T27, T45, T69, T91, T115, T139, T161, T181, T213; **Unit 7:** T27, T45, T73, T95, T121, T147, T169, T189, T225; **Unit 8:** T27, T45, T77, T99, T125, T151, T173, T193, T225; **Unit 9:** T27, T47, T75, T97, T121, T145, T167, T187, T219; **Unit 10:** T27, T45, T73, T97, T125, T153, T173, T193, T225

Periods, Unit 3: T49, T51, T111, T114, T148, T195; **Unit 4:** T68; **Unit 5:** T49, T55, T113; **Unit 6:** T191; **Unit 7:** T49, T51, T109, T195; **Unit 8:** T49, T113; **Unit 9:** T51; **Unit 10:** T51, T113, T199; *see also* End Marks

Phonemic Awareness

Listening, Unit 1: T25, T35, T49, T67, T85, T107, T119, T135, T151, T163, T185, T209, T227, T245; **Unit 2:** T25, T35; **Unit 3:** T25, T26, T33, T58, T72, T94, T102–T103, T118, T130, T133, T142, T164, T174, T184, T202; **Unit 4:** T26, T34, T44, T58, T71, T94, T104, T122, T140, T150, T182, T192, T208, T224; **Unit 5:** T26, T34, T44, T60, T76, T98, T108, T122, T136, T146, T167, T168, T178, T204, T220; **Unit 6:** T26, T34, T44, T56, T68, T90, T100, T114, T128,

T138, T160, T170, T196, T212; **Unit 7:** T26, T34, T44, T58, T72, T94, T104, T120, T136, T146, T168, T178, T188, T206; **Unit 8:** T26, T34, T44, T60, T98, T108, T124, T140, T172, T192, T224; **Unit 9:** T26, T34, T46, T60, T74, T96, T106, T120, T134, T144, T166, T176, T186, T202, T218; **Unit 10:** T26, T34, T44, T58, T72, T96, T108, T124, T140, T152, T172, T208

Onsets and rimes, Unit 3: T173, T183; **Unit 5:** T25, T58, T107, T166–T167

Oral blending, Unit 4: T56–T57, T102–T103; *see also* Phoneme blending

Phoneme blending, Unit 3: T173, T183; **Unit 4:** T25, T33, T43, T57, T71, T93, T103, T171; **Unit 5:** T25, T33, T43, T59, T75, T97; **Unit 6:** T24–T25, T33, T43, T89, T158–T159, T168; **Unit 7:** T24–T25, T33, T43, T92–T93, T166–T167; **Unit 8:** T25, T33, T42–T43, T138–T139, T206; **Unit 9:** T25, T33, T58–T59, T174; **Unit 10:** T120, T180, T206–T207

Phoneme deletion, Unit 10: T105, T121, T137, T149

Phoneme manipulation, Unit 4: T181, T191, T207, T223; **Unit 5:** T135, T145, T187, T203; **Unit 6:** T55, T99, T113, T127; **Unit 7:** T103, T119, T135, T145; **Unit 8:** T123, T139, T149, T171; **Unit 9:** T119, T133, T143, T165

Phoneme matching, Unit 3: T201, T217; **Unit 4:** T121, T139, T149; **Unit 5:** T107, T121, T135, T145, T219; **Unit 6:** T55, T67, T89, T99; **Unit 7:** T57, T71, T93, T187; **Unit 8:** T43, T59, T75, T97, T107; **Unit 9:** T45, T59, T73, T95, T105; **Unit 10:** T32, T170

Phoneme replacement, Unit 6: T210; **Unit 7:** T119, T144; **Unit 8:** T223; **Unit 9:** T94–T95; **Unit 10:** T25, T33, T43, T56, T57, T71, T92–T93

Phoneme segmentation, Unit 4: T191, T207, T223; **Unit 6:** T33, T137, T159, T169, T179, T195, T211; **Unit 7:** T167, T177, T187, T205, T223; **Unit 8:** T181, T191, T207, T223; **Unit 9:** T175, T185, T201, T217; **Unit 10:** T222

Rhyming, Unit 1: T49, T67, T85, T107, T119, T135, T151, T163, T185, T197, T209, T227, T245

Segmentation, Unit 3: T117, T131, T141, T163; **Unit 4:** T32–T33, T92, T181, T191, T207, T223; **Unit 5:** T97; **Unit 6:** T33, T137, T159, T169, T179, T195, T211; **Unit 7:** T102–T103, T167, T177, T187, T205, T223; **Unit 8:** T123, T181, T191, T207, T223; **Unit 9:** T175, T184–T185, T201, T217; **Unit 10:** T222

Syllable blending, Unit 3: T25, T33, T43, T57, T71, T93, T103, T117, T131, T141, T163; **Unit 5:** T186

Syllable segmentation, Unit 3: T103; **Unit 4:** T32–T33, T92, T181; **Unit 5:** T97; **Unit 7:** T102–T103; **Unit 8:** T123; **Unit 9:** T184–T185

Word length and meaning, Unit 3: T102–T103, T200, T216; **Unit 4:** T190; **Unit 5:** T113, T120, T195; **Unit 6:** T187

Words in spoken sentences, Unit 2: T47, T63, T79, T101, T113, T129, T145, T157

Word substitution, Unit 2: T179, T191, T203, T222, T243; **Unit 3:** T32–T33; **Unit 4:** T42

see also Phonics

S

Notes

Use this page to record lessons or elements that work well or need to be adjusted for future reference.

Lessons that work well.

Lessons that need adjustments.

Notes

Use this page to record lessons or elements that work well or need to be adjusted for future reference.

Lessons that work well.

Lessons that need adjustments.

Notes

Use this page to record lessons or elements that work well or need to be adjusted for future reference.

Lessons that work well.

Lessons that need adjustments.

Notes

Use this page to record lessons or elements that work well or need to be adjusted for future reference.

Lessons that work well.

Lessons that need adjustments.

Notes

Use this page to record lessons or elements that work well or need to be adjusted for future reference.

Lessons that work well.

Lessons that need adjustments.

Notes

Use this page to record lessons or elements that work well or need to be adjusted for future reference.

Lessons that work well.

Lessons that need adjustments.

Notes

Use this page to record lessons or elements that work well or need to be adjusted for future reference.

Lessons that work well.

Lessons that need adjustments.

Notes

Use this page to record lessons or elements that work well or need to be adjusted for future reference.

Lessons that work well.

Lessons that need adjustments.

Notes

Use this page to record lessons or elements that work well or need to be adjusted for future reference.

Lessons that work well.

Lessons that need adjustments.

Notes

Use this page to record lessons or elements that work well or need to be adjusted for future reference.

Lessons that work well.

Lessons that need adjustments.